Empire of Sentiment

In the first historical account of its kind, Joanna Lewis explores the relationship between emotion and imperialism, in Britain and Africa, from the Victorian era to the present. Focusing on the iconic figure of Dr David Livingstone, *Empire of Sentiment* moves between the metropole and central Africa to reveal how his extraordinary death and extravagant memorialisation down the generations helped to forge a number of sentimental myths about being British in Africa. An emotion culture around Livingstone married together British imperialism and Victorian humanitarianism to feed the Scramble for Africa, sustain colonial rule, assist white settlers, and provide succour to Africans whose internalisation of the myth became a crucial part of British imperialism's soft power. *Empire of Sentiment* demonstrates how the sentimentality of ordinary men and women cleaved to romantic perceptions of Britain as a liberal colonial power, even when the reality fell far short.

Joanna Lewis is an Associate Professor in the Department of International History, LSE. She holds a PhD in African Colonial History from the University of Cambridge and has won numerous student-led awards for teaching. She has also held lecturing posts at Cambridge, Durham and the School of Oriental and African Studies, and acted as Director of Studies in History at Churchill College and Corpus Christi College, Cambridge. Her research interests include the history of the colonial state in Africa, decolonisation, the British media and gender. In 2013, to mark the bicentenary of the birth of David Livingstone, she organised the only international conference to be held in Africa, bringing together scholars from all over the world, to debate the life and legacy of the man and the myth.

Empire of Sentiment

The Death of Livingstone and the Myth of Victorian Imperialism

Joanna Lewis

London School of Economics and Political Science

CAMBRIDGE
UNIVERSITY PRESS

CAMBRIDGE
UNIVERSITY PRESS

University Printing House, Cambridge CB2 8BS, United Kingdom

One Liberty Plaza, 20th Floor, New York, NY 10006, USA

477 Williamstown Road, Port Melbourne, VIC 3207, Australia

314–321, 3rd Floor, Plot 3, Splendor Forum, Jasola District Centre, New Delhi – 110025, India

79 Anson Road, #06-04/06, Singapore 079906

Cambridge University Press is part of the University of Cambridge.

It furthers the University's mission by disseminating knowledge in the pursuit of education, learning, and research at the highest international levels of excellence.

www.cambridge.org
Information on this title: www.cambridge.org/9781107198517
DOI: 10.1017/9781108182591

© Joanna Lewis 2018

First published 2018

Printed in the United Kingdom by Clays, St Ives plc

A catalogue record for this publication is available from the British Library.

ISBN 978-1-107-19851-7 Hardback

For my parents

Contents

Figures

Maps

Acknowledgements

To complete this book I had to overcome a spinal injury, a muscular-skeletal condition and RSI. I would like to thank my remedial therapist for the past five years Ms Tina Hitchens who gave me my body back. This book would not have been completed without her commitment to my recovery. I thank the doctors, consultants, occupational-health advisers, personal trainers and remedial yoga teachers who also have helped.

In Zambia, I benefited from the generosity and kindness of so many. I would like to thank and honour the historical knowledge and wisdom of Mr Flexon Mzinga, Prof. Bizek Phiri, Dr Friday Mufuzi, Dr Walima Kalusa and Mr Humphrey Mwanga. In Livingstone town I thank the Whitehead family, the late Mr Richard Chanters, Mr William Chipango, and everyone who supported the 2013 Livingstone Bicentenary conference. I am hugely grateful to the intellectual generosity of Dr Ian Manning. I warmly thank all the staff at the Zambia National Archive. I have benefited from the company and conversation of Dr Marja Hinfelaar and Prof. Jan Bart Gewald. Other Zambianists who have been extremely helpful include Prof. Robert Ross and Prof. Andrew D. Roberts, also Dr Miles Larmer and Dr David Gordon. My visits to Zambia have been enriched by the hospitality and friendship of Ms Teresa Chishimba, by Gift, also by Erico and Humphrey. I thank Mr Besa Mwaba for helping me with my questionnaires. I thank Chief Chitambo for sparing the time to speak to me.

In the UK, I am very grateful to all the archivists and librarians who have assisted me over the years especially the amazing Ms Terry Barringer, regularly furnishing me with the latest writing on Livingstone. I thank the archival staff at Rhodes House, Oxford, RGS, and at SOAS Library especially Dr Joanne Ichemura.

At LSE, I thank Prof. Janet Hartley, Prof. Matthew Jones, Prof. Nigel Ashton, Dr Antony Best, Dr Paul Mulvey and Dr Heather Jones. I warmly thank Ms Demetra Frini and Mr Matthew Betts, also Ms Nayna Bhatti, Ms Milada Formina, Ms Susana Sinfono-Carvalo and Ms

Jacquie Minter. I thank the LSE Annual Fund and Prof. Craig Calhoun for his support of the 2013 Livingstone Conference and Ms Syremmia Willoughby at the LSE Firoz Lalji Africa Centre, and Dr Shane Marotta.

I thank the many brilliant, inspiring and fun undergraduates and graduate students I've supervised at LSE over the years on their research and writing projects, some of whom I am delighted to call friends. I owe a debt of gratitude to PhD students Dr Lesley James, Dr Alicia Altorfer-Ong, Dr Ben Greening, Dr Jonas Gjerso, Dr Rosie Coffey, and currently Ms Grace Carrington, Ms Caroline Green, Ms Danielle Davenport and Ms Katherine Arnold. Thanks also to Dr Charlotte Riley and Dr Tim Livsey for teaching alongside me on Africa. I would especially like to thank Dr Ben Greening for his inspiring integrity; and Dr Jonas Gjerso for passing on Livingstone anti-slavery references and for his help organising the Livingstone conference, along with the amazing Ms Anna-Thora Mutale Varde and for their knowledge of empire and conversation, Dr Cees Heere and Mr Barnaby Crowcroft. I thank Mr Oliver Cook and his family for their interest in Livingstone and their amazing voluntary work in central Africa; Jacob Cockcroft for being so exciting to watch progress and for talking to the students. Also huge thanks to Mr Philip Rushmore for research assistance on Victorian regional newspapers; Mrs Susie Casson for proofreading an early draft of manuscript from a dyslexic; and Ms Kate Rolling at Copyman, Winchester.

Many historians have inspired me in this project. In particular I thank the world experts on Dr Livingstone, Mr Tim Jeal and Prof. John Mackenzie, and also Prof. Andrew Roberts; plus the scholarship of Profs Keith Hart, Dane Kennedy, Richard Price, John Darwin, John Illiffe, Meghan Vaughan, Catherine Hall, Stuart Ward, Nancy Jacobs, Simon Potter and Dr Ronald Hyam. I continually benefit from the friendship and intellectual inspiration of Profs Tim Harper, Philip Murphy, Jon Parry, Ato Quayson, Ian Phimister, Nonica Datta, Patricia Hayes and Saul Dubow. Also Drs Adrian Green, David Craig and Christine Whyte, plus Sybren Renema #baboonlove.

I thank Allison Pearson for her Welsh support and humour. Catherine Humphreys and Doreen Addison in Cambridge; also Antony, Evie and Thomas Lane. Thank you to Scott Crawford Triggs; and in Winchester, Karen Levi Borley, Karen Fitzsimmons, Joy Palmer, Dawn and George Kotorov, Peter Lloyd Jones, Margot and Dave Foulds plus Bertie, Catherine Rainey, Janet Hammerton, Rita 'Reetz-Petitz' Shaw, Kim and Nicky Goetlibb; Miriam Swanston and the St Cross Creative Writing Group, and Anna Tylor. I am grateful to Keith Redbourn for giving me a column on the *Hampshire Chronicle* and editor Andrew Napier. Also Karen Shook, formerly at the *Times Higher Education* for giving me the opportunity to review for her.

All my uncles and aunties in south and mid-Wales never forget my birthday, which deserves a mention. And of course warmest thanks to Mum and Dad; Sarah and Stephen; Olivia and Thomas; cousin Lisa; and for their warm shapes and hilariousness the dachshunds Mr Bibz and Delilah-Lulu, Elsa the golden retriever, all the chickens and guinea pigs, plus Beatrice the bull mastador.

My intellectual and moral compass remains, as always, Prof. John Lonsdale, who valiantly read a long draft one Christmas, above and beyond the duty of a former doctoral supervisor. I thank profusely Mr Michael Watson at CUP for not losing faith, and his brilliant team especially Mr Robert Judkins and Ms Melissa Shivers. Thanks also to the outstanding proofreaders and copy-editors – the aptly named Mr Daniel Sentance, and Ms Linda Paulus. I owe an enormous debt of gratitude to Reader B for wading through the weeds – a three-books-in-one draft – and telling me what the one that mattered was about. The most important person helping me complete this book, especially in Zambia – keeping me informed, amused and outraged in equal measure – was Dr Giacomo Macola – *un amico e Dizionario fumante meraviglioso*.

Copyright Permissions: All photographs unless otherwise stated are published with copyright permission from Getty Images.

Photograph of Matthew Wellington/Chengwimbe (1847–1935), the last survivor of the 'Nassicks' or 'Bombay Africans' who had joined the search party for Livingstone organised by Henry Morton Stanley. SOAS Archives. CWM/LMS/Home/Livingstone Pictures/Box1. File 8. Permission to publish from Council for World Mission archives & manuscripts, SOAS Archives, SOAS.

Photograph of The Livingstone Memorial built by Owen Stroud, Chitambo. Undated. SOAS Archives CWM/LMS/Home/Livingstone Pictures/Box 1. File 6. Permission to publish from Council for World Mission archives & manuscripts, SOAS Archives, SOAS.

Dylan Thomas, 'And Death Shall Have No Dominion', reproduced from THE COLLECTED POEMS OF DAVID LIVINGSTONE: CENTENARY EDITION (Weidenfeld and Nicolson). Reprinted by permission of David Higham, Literary and Film Agents, for publication the world (excluding USA).

'And Death Shall Have No Dominion' by Dylan Thomas, from THE POEMS OF DYLAN THOMAS, copyright ©1943 by New Directions Publishing Corp. Reprinted by permission of New Directions Publishing Corps for publications in USA.

The Proclaimers, 'I'm Gonna Be (500 Miles)' (Album: *Sunshine on Leith*, 1988). Lyrics written by Charlie Reid and Craig Reid. Reproduced with the permission of Warner/Chappell Music Inc.

Van Morrison, 'Moondance' (Album: *Moondance*, 1970). Lyrics by Van Morrison. Reproduced with the permission of Warner/Chappell Music Inc.

Two-line extract from John Donne, 'The Legacy', reproduced with permission by Penguin Books Ltd. (Licence No.: 6132271) from SELECTED POEMS: DONNE by John Donne, edited by Ilona Bell (Penguin Books, 2006). Editorial material Copyright © Ilona Bell, 2006.

Extract from Series 2, Episode 4 'Yes, Prime Minister', (BBC, aired 1986–1988), written by Antony Jay and Jonathan Lynn. Permission granted by Alan Brodie Representation, Paddock Suite, The Courtyard, 55 Charterhouse Street, London EC1M 6HA.

Prologue
The Pathetic Death of Bwana Ingeleshi

By the candle still burning they saw him, not in bed, but kneeling at the bedside, with his head buried in his hands upon the pillow ... he had passed away ... But he had died in the act of prayer ... commending his own spirit, with all his dear ones, as was his wont, into the hands of his Saviour; and commending AFRICA – his own dear Africa – with all her woes and sins and wrongs, to the Avenger of the oppressed and the Redeemer of the lost.

W.G. Blaikie, *The Life of David Livingstone*, 1880

In the morning, they carried the Bwana's body to a Mupundu tree ... on a large flat iron plate. They pulled out all his stomach and heart and lungs and put them in a hole in the ground near the Mupundu tree. Then they built a platform about eight feet high and put the body on that. They did not put fire under it. Then [Chief] Chitambo called all his villages to bring food and they brought a meal and goats and chickens and the Bwana's people mourned for three days. After three days, they put the body in a box that had carried guns and then they went off ... to the coast.

Headman Lupoko, son of Chief Chitambo, interviewed by district commissioner, Mapika, Northern Rhodesia, 1932

Victorians dealt in moral certainty, and Livingstone's death held all the aces. Sensational and gruesome, it was a tale of manly, masochistic endurance, a biblical parable of redemption, with a Christ-like act of self-sacrifice on behalf of all mankind. The location had been 'darkest Africa', also known as that 'savage country'. Even in the 1870s, its interior was still imagined as a land of cannibals, unicorns and men who grew tails. It was understood as the cradle, not of humanity, but of its opposite, for at its dark centre was the heart of human slavery – the 'greatest evil facing mankind'. The Serpent had seemingly slithered out of the Garden of Eden and coiled itself around Africa's plumptious middle.

Into this apparently terrible place had stumbled an aged and dying Scotsman. The accounts of Livingstone's final, agonising days in central Africa made grown men and women weep in the streets, partly because many felt they knew him, having followed his life through his

Figure P.1 David Livingstone with daughter Anna Mary, photographed during his last visit home, 1864–5, when he met her for the first time. Getty Images.

own writings plus the many publications, talks and sermons dedicated to him (see Figure P.1). But what also profoundly upset so many was the way his life – understood as one of sacrifice and suffering – had ended in agony, failure and loneliness. It turned upside down their understanding that a good life earned a good death. Here, then, was further proof – if any was needed – that central Africa was not of this world. It was hell on earth. And the rumour Livingstone had appealed to God in his final moment of suffering to 'heal Africa's "woes and sins"', by kneeling in prayer, secured his reputation *to this day* for humaneness and kindness towards Africans.

Livingstone's death produced a 'thrill' through 'the civilised world' or 'Christendom', according to observers at the time, after 'all the touching circumstances' were known. It was lauded for arousing 'a global parliament of philanthropy' which passed a resolution: 'Livingstone's work shall not die! Africa shall live!'[1] Missionaries, explorers, traders and anti-slavery activists were activated. The press was primed. Thus politicians were led to believe that public opinion would not stand for anything less than an ethical foreign policy on African slavery. Momentum gathered for intervention in Africa through an extended form of occupation. Livingstone's ghost hovered over the lofty pledges made by governments at the Berlin Conference in 1884, convened to lay down rules for Africa's partition to slow down the land grab. Colonial rule could be justified if it promoted civilisation and commerce to replace slavery (if a European power was in a position to do this, it could claim sovereignty over the interior). To millions of people across the world, Livingstone seemed to be speaking from his grave.[2] Ten years later, virtually the whole continent had been parcelled up by statesmen who would never go there.

Death became Livingstone. Well into the twentieth century, his final hours were still being described, in the influential genre of inspirational biography, as capable of wielding 'something of its ancient power that we can still hear ... as our seamen hear "Drake's Drum" ... when the great Armadas come'; and he was still lionised as 'one of "those immortal dead who live again"'.[3] The verse of the nineteenth-century American 'fireside poet', James Russell Lowell, was still being used to explain the emotional significance of Livingstone's death: it was one of the great moments in the history of individual freedom and the struggle for humanity. Lowell's 1844 poem 'The Present Crisis' compared the effect of the dying man and, by association, the establishment and nature of British colonial rule in Africa, with the campaign against slavery in the United States, and even with the very spirit that had launched the Mayflower.

When a deed is done for freedom through the broad earth's aching breast
Runs a thrill of joy prophetic trembling on from east to west ...
For mankind are one in spirit, and an instinct bears along
Round the earth's electric circle the swift flash of right or wrong ... [4]

This imperial artifice was built on a mixture of sand and sentiment. Neither of the extracts that begin this prologue are particularly accurate.

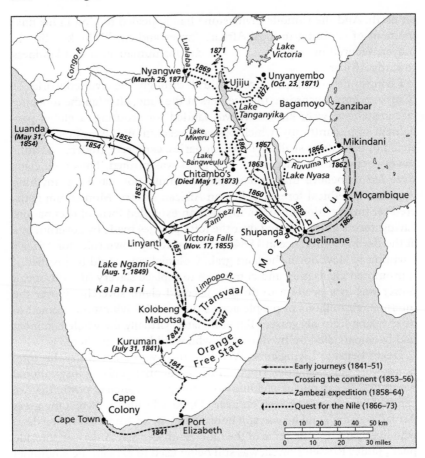

Map P.1 Livingstone's Africa expeditions

Livingstone had died in Mwela Mwape village, Ilala, seventy miles south-south-east of the southern shore of Lake Bangweulu, in present-day Zambia, not far from its border with the Democratic Republic of Congo (see Map P.1), but the death-in-prayer scenario was a lie (see Figure P.2). The account in the first extract was written by Livingstone's most influential and respected Victorian biographer, William Blaikie. This was an embellished version of an already embellished death scene. The original conceit was an imaginative fabrication, painstakingly woven together by Livingstone's devoted male admirer, the missionary Revd Horace Waller, in 1874, when 'editing' Livingstone's last field diaries for quick publication.[5]

Figure P.2 Livingstone depicted kneeling in prayer by his bedside, found dead by his servants, May 1873, Ilala District, in present-day Zambia. Original wood engraving, Paris, 1877. Engraving by Riov. Reproduced in *The Illustrated World*, 1882. Coloured. Photo by: PHAS/ UIG via Getty Images. Getty Images.

It was a stroke of duplicitous genius for, earlier, when Livingstone's servants had been interviewed after reaching the coast in early 1874, they made no mention of death in prayer.[6] Waller had incrementally imposed this arresting vision of a dying man giving his last breath to pray for Africa from the broken accounts he drew from Livingstone's two long-suffering servants, Susi and Chuma (see Figure P.3), who themselves were already carefully self-selecting what had happened in order to protect themselves.[7] Such was the urgency that the book should be on the shelves by December of the same year, they were brought to England in the summer of 1874 to help Waller to finish editing for the Scottish publisher John Murray.

An obsessive anti-slavery campaigner, Waller (and later Blaikie) transformed a sad, pathetic death into a holy martyrdom. Livingstone probably died crawling on his knees, incontinent, bleeding, delirious and in need of assistance. A young servant, 'the boy Majwara' (or Majorama) had been given the task of sitting with him during the night but had left him alone for a while, 'compelled by necessity to leave the booth for some minutes'.[8]

Figure P.3 Abdullah Susi (left) and James Chuma (right), two of Livingstone's most famous so-called servants. Date unknown. Getty Images.

He was just a boy. But Livingstone had apparently insisted that his current 'favourite' did not leave his side when he had fallen ill a fortnight earlier. When Majwara returned 'some hours later' (according to other accounts, in the early morning light), he realised that Livingstone was lying dead on the ground and ran for help.[9] Waller was able to lead, edit and fabricate the testimonies from Susi and Chuma, who were apparently first to arrive. Only a few first-hand accounts survive from Livingstone's other African servants, which aided Waller considerably.

Much later, local people reminiscing about the death, such as Headman Lupoko in 1936 (quoted in the second extract that begins this prologue) gave incomplete, conflicting versions of events they claimed to have witnessed. Inevitably factors such as the confusion of the moment, fading memories, being interviewed by missionaries or colonial officials, or adding in details perhaps to help negotiate white occupation to more advantage, naturally shaped African accounts. But key opportunities were also lost back in 1873 to fully set down the record. An official at the British consulate, Frederick Holmwood, did undertake an 'interrogation' of Susi and Chuma when they reached the coast. He mostly recorded details of time and place.[10] Following his 'careful cross-examination', Holmwood deduced that 'Kitambo the sultan', who lived at Ilala, had refused permission for the party to stay, so they had had to march three hours back to Kabende, where they built 'a rude hut and fence', with Livingstone insisting that only Majwara and Susi look after him; everyone else could only say good morning at the door.

Consequently, there is no certainty as to exactly where Livingstone died. According to Susi and Chuma, he was first placed in a temporary grass hut in a field, used by locals to watch over crops before harvesting, outside Chitambo village. Then a dwelling was made especially for him, and finished as he lay on the floor in a semi-conscious state. Locals came to pay their respects: 'in silent wonder they stood around him'.[11] Then, he was carried into the specially built house, situated across a stream for privacy. They described a bay-shaped interior, a bed standing on a pile of grass and sticks, a box at his side with his medicine chest on it, a fire burning at the door and a toilet in the corner.[12] Susi and Chuma explained there was a hole in the back wall through which his body might be carried out discreetly. Perhaps they felt compelled to disguise the fact that they were following the customary practices, for according to a missionary who visited the site two decades later, it was common to use an axe or rough tool to hack out an irregular opening to allow the spirit to fly out, symbolising and allowing for 'the new journey beyond'.[13]

Other accounts imply less elaborate preparations. One local chief later told Livingstone's daughter Agnes that Livingstone had been placed under some eaves, because he had reached his village during a rain shower, and that he had then been carried into an African hut. Other eyewitnesses felt certain that Livingstone had died in a small tent made of cloth.[14] Others still described it as a booth.

Nor is there any certainty as to exactly when Livingstone died. It is usually accepted that he died in the early hours of 1 May 1873. However, his death may have occurred several days earlier, before the party reached Chief Chitambo's village. Livingstone's last diary entry is dated 27 April.

Jacob Wainwright made a record of Livingstone's possessions after he died and recorded the date as being 28 April. Later, when interviewed, he explained that he had been mistaken and that the entry for 27 April was not the previous day, as he had assumed at the time, as a few days had lapsed.[15] Some have seized on this to argue that, by the time the party approached Chitambo village, Livingstone had already died, probably on the evening of 27 April. Since they had been in an area controlled by an aggressive chief, who would have made life difficult if he had discovered the body, they kept it hidden. There is evidence that Safene – one of Livingstone's men – had already purchased a large quantity of salt, sufficient to prepare a body, in exchange for sixteen strings of beads. Why buy salt in a place where it was expensive due to its scarcity, unless Livingstone had already died?[16]

Headman Lupoko insisted he had witnessed the scene as a boy. He was interviewed by the district commissioner for Mpika in 1936. On the one hand, he remembered that his father, the chief, had been angry with the leader of Livingstone's caravan 'because he did not want him to die in his country' and because he had 'hidden the (impending?) death of Bwana Ingelishi'.[17] Lukopo recalled that Chief Chitambo then forced the inhabitants of Mwela Mwape village to move out so that the travellers could use their huts and then 'they made a house of cloth, a tent, for the Bwana, a short distance from the village'. It has even been suggested that Chitambo might have been bribed to keep the death quiet for a while, in which case he would also have told the elders to follow suit, so although Lukopo also remembered seeing Livingstone alive, he might have simply been remembering what he was told by others. Likewise, in 1936, the incumbent chief of the area remembered how Livingstone and his men had crossed the Lulimala River in the cold season of May. Too weak to ride his donkey, 'he was supported by men on each side of him. His illness was in the stomach. He arrived at 10am and died next morning ... He was the first white man anyone had seen in our country. Livingstone was a small man and very thin. He was only bones.' (His servants claimed Livingstone could not walk by the end and had to be carried.) However, another eyewitness insisted that 'the Bwana's body was not thin or wasting'.[18]

Susi and Chuma, in 'conversation' with Waller, insisted that Livingstone's death was hidden from Chief Chitambo but that Livingstone had still been alive when they reached the village (and had died the following day). Apparently, they did not want to pay the chief a large burial fine. Their plan was scuppered because a couple of men went to buy food from the locals the next day and let slip that Livingstone had died during the night. Then the chief arrived, remonstrating with them: 'Why did you not tell me the truth?' According to their version, he then insisted that he was not angry, since he knew that the death of travellers was relatively normal. Susi took him a gift the next day, and relations were smoothed, so much so that Chitambo initiated a formal period of mourning, returning to the camp with his villagers and wives. In addition to full military honours – bows, arrows and spears were ceremoniously carried – 'two drummers joined in the wailing lamentation'. In return, the visitors fired several rounds of ammunition 'according to the Portuguese and Arab traditions', reflecting the diverse make-up of the caravan.[19] It is highly likely Susi and Chuma were holding back.

Cause of death is more certifiable. With his multiple health problems, the only mystery here is how Livingstone managed to survive as long as he did. He had been suffering from dysentery for a while, according to his own field notes, and had been self-medicating. Naturally, he was less forthcoming about a 'lingering complaint' – haemorrhoids – a condition familiar to many Victorians judging by the list of remedies advertised in many newspapers of the period. As he discreetly recorded on 10 April, 'I am pale, bloodless and weak from bleeding ever since 31st of March last; an artery gives off a copious stream and takes away my strength'.[20] Both conditions were worsened by weeks of wading through swampy water, nights camping on soggy sponges in the rain and an almost continuous 'wet seat'. Some nights, the canvas of their mouldy tents was ripped to shreds by the vicious winds. Lack of warmth and proper food further conspired against his recovery. And one evening, Livingstone was attacked by a swarm of ants, forcing him to run from his tent.

Death had already visited the party. The area was flooded, and the marshy ground could suddenly dissolve into a torrent of fast-flowing water. One tragic incident, casually recorded in Livingstone's diary, had taken place on 26 March: a child slave had drowned when the party was caught out by a hidden stream. As Livingstone wrote, 'One canoe sank into it, and we lost a slave girl of Amoda. Fished up three boxes, and two guns', lamenting most the damaged cartridges.[21] Nevertheless, the flood conditions, he admitted, were particularly hard on the 'women folk'.

Livingstone's energy was now failing due to loss of blood. Carried at first in a cot (*kitanda*) by men listed as Chowpere, Songola, Chuma, Adiamberi and Sowfere, it later fell to Chowpere or Chuma to carry him on their shoulders (see Figure P.4). He contracted malaria, which he treated with 'two scruple doses of quinine'. Now pushing sixty years old, and having been in poor general health for nearly a decade, his dire situation was compounded by a loss of vital medicaments. This brought out his sardonic humour: 'It is not all pleasure this exploration', he famously wrote, before he became too weak to hold a pencil.[22]

Figure P.4 'The Last Mile', *c*.1880. Livingstone being carried before he died. From *The Life and Explorations of David Livingstone* (London). Photo by Ann Ronan Pictures/Print Collector/Getty Images. Hulton Archive. This was reproduced as a lantern slide.

Yet Livingstone might have hung on even longer were it not for a large blood clot developing in his lower intestine. He was sick, blind, bleeding and in excruciating pain, but his diary entry for 27 April was characteristically stoic and understated. It would be his last: 'Knocked up quite and remain – recover – sent to buy milch goats'. Towards the end, according to Susi and Chuma, he was in too much pain to walk.

Apparently, he had made his final journey on a donkey (as Christ had done, of course). They told of knocking down a wall in one rest hut so that he could be carried to bed in his carry-cot. Carus Farrar, one of the Christian Nassicks among the groups – former slaves educated in a special Church Missionary Society (CMS) school in India – found it all slightly surreal: 'Yet strange to say he urged us forward though we did not know where we were hastening to'.[23]

Soon, Livingstone could no longer bear to be carried and then to move. As Farrar recalled, 'Each of us plainly saw that our Master was declining'. Now, Livingstone was reduced to writing imaginary letters to the government, formally announcing how he had pinpointed the origin of the Nile ('I have the pleasure of telling your Lordship ... I succeeded at last in reaching your remarkable four fountains'), leaving blank spaces to add in the precise details about the time, height, latitude, etc.[24] Quite telling of his preoccupations, his last question in Swahili, according to some accounts, was 'How many days is it to the Luapula?', the river where he was headed. On being informed that it was a three-day journey, he apparently sighed and whispered, 'I will never see my river again'. A few hours later, he was dead.

A confused picture also emerges of events after Livingstone died. Headman Lupoko recalled, in 1936, that Livingstone had been placed some distance from the village and that (somewhat remarkably) 'the carriers were playing football in the clearing near the village by the tent'. The night Livingstone died, 'the people with Bwana Ingeleshi were dancing and singing all night'; when the noise stopped, 'that was the time when the Bwana died and the people were too sad to dance'. According to Susi and Chuma, the only noise during the night that disturbed the Bwana in the few hours before he died was that of villagers trying to scare away a buffalo. This was not quite the tranquil scene typically remembered subsequently: 'In the silence of that hut at Ilala, he surrendered his soul'.[25]

Chengwimbe, also known as Matthew Wellington, was another of Livingstone's baptised servants, sometimes called Nassicks after the school they attended for freed slaves. The caravan was seventy-strong, according to his calculation (perhaps he included the child slaves and the slave girls, who may have been excluded from the oft-quoted figure of sixty). He implied that the locals behaved improperly – he recalled 'the most devilish and fanatical morning dance in which men, women and children promiscuously mingled'.[26] The local elders looking back, in the presence of the district commissioner, stressed that Chief Chitambo had insisted on a period of mourning. He had ordered his villagers to bring food – meal, goats and chickens – so the Bwana's people could mourn for three days. Susi and Chuma also credited Chitambo with sending a special mourner on 3 May, decked out in mourning anklets made of hollowed-out seeds filled with pebbles, to dance and perform what was described – perhaps diplomatically – as a 'low and monotonous chant'.[27]

What happened during this mourning period, and how long the mourning lasted, is also hazy. After Livingstone died, the leaders of the various groups that made up the large caravan evidently quarrelled over what to do. Tensions ran high. An Arab servant would confide much later: 'Well, as you know, he was poisoned by jealous blacks'.[28] Despite evidence that Livingstone had some intuition that his end might be imminent, he does not appear to have issued any instructions for his burial. Livingstone had once mused in his diary, while travelling relatively nearby, through Chief Kazembe's territory (in present-day DRC), about his ideal resting place.: 'This is the sort of little grave I should prefer ... in the still forest and no hand ever disturb my bones'.[29] They were now in such a place. But Livingstone had written for a metropolitan audience; there is no evidence he shared such thoughts with his African followers. Perhaps, on balance, he had not seriously anticipated his imminent end, could not bear to do so or did not trust his men. Either way, his silence on the subject placed a huge responsibility on them.

No definitive account exists of the discussion that led to the decision to carry Livingstone's body back to the coast. The surviving explanations vary. 'We wanted to prove to the white man that he had died as we said he died', sums up the general fear of being disbelieved or blamed. According to Matthew Wellington, the Christians objected to the wishes of the Muslims, who wanted an immediate burial. Chief Chitambo had told them to bury the body immediately, as carrying a corpse would be too dangerous. There would have been widespread concern that they might not be paid if they returned without him. Others knew that Livingstone was a celebrity. They had accompanied him through so much already, they might as well take his body back. Maybe for some, the sense of humanitarian mission was a shared one.

A heated debate seems to have taken place between the group leaders, and each division of the caravan eventually agreed that they would carry the body back to the coast. This decision necessitated Livingstone being embalmed. The details of this are also sketchy and conflicting. Knowledge of Western medicine was used to explain the move, since Farahla (or Farijala), who took charge, assisted by Farrar, was credited with learning the technique, having – apparently – assisted a doctor with post-mortems in Zanzibar.[30] It is more likely that the traditional technique was applied. Susi and Chuma informed Waller that the embalming was carried out in private, out of sight, with Muanasere helping them to hold up a blanket to conceal the body.

However, details later supplied by local elders suggest there was an audience for the embalming. Headman Lupoko was clear: an insertion was first made into the chest, after which the heart, lungs, stomach and other soft tissue or internal organs were removed. The contents of the stomach and intestines were squeezed out. Farahla noticed a giant blood clot in the lower intestine and signs of damage to the lungs. He then poured salt into the trunk of the body. The internal organs were placed in a tin box. Jacob Wainwright read a passage from the Bible. The box was then buried under a sacred *mpundu* tree (also known as *mvule* by its fruit, or *mpunde*), the largest one nearby. A section of bark was removed so that Jacob could carve an inscription:

LIVINGSTONE. May 4, 1873. Chzuza, Mniasere, Vchopere.

Who took charge, if anyone, remains unclear. Up to this point, these three men were the designated leaders of the separate divisions of which the caravan consisted (also known as Chuma, Uredi Manwa Seera and Chowpereh, the latter two having travelled with Henry Morton Stanley to find Livingstone in 1871–2). According to the old men of Chitambo village, interviewed in 1936, there were clear *Capitaos* (leaders) among Bwana Ingeleshi's men. The names mentioned sound familiar: 'Kasamba Milopa'; 'Juma, Munyasele and Suse'. However, Susi and Chuma informed Revd Waller, in summer 1874, that they had assumed control from this point, for it was they who summoned the whole party together to decide what should be done. The two other section leaders apparently then spoke for all of the men supplied by Stanley after he departed in 1873, by declaring, according to Susi and Chuma: 'you ... are old men in travelling and in hardships; you must act as our chiefs, and we will promise to obey whatever you order us to do'.[31]

This may have been an exaggeration of their role.[32] They certainly had been the closest to Livingstone for the longest time, and they were familiar with the route back to the coast – Chuma was the group's forward scout and controlled the intelligence gathering – but the evidence suggests that more of a collective was at work, one that relied on the various factions pulling together –the men Stanley had used as his divisional leaders; the six practising Christians/ ex-slaves educated at the Nassick school (including Jacob Wainwright and Carus Farrar); men from Portuguese Africa; and Susi, Chuma and others who were Muslim. Their loyalties were likely more to each other by this point.

The strength of African male bonds is illustrated by the circumstances surrounding the death of Amoda. He had travelled with Livingstone for many years. When 'his slave Majariwa' later drowned, he died, apparently of grief. His friends then 'carried his body about 5 miles into the wilderness'.[33] Loyalty was highly prized in these gruelling, cruel circumstances, with servants' trust and faithfulness spoken about in the same way as an army officer might speak about his adjutant, a squire his gamekeeper or a hunter his favourite hound. Explorers sought out each other's star bearers. Putting together his search party for Livingstone, for example, Stanley searched for Speke's men. He was thrilled when he scooped up men like Chowpere and Feraji, who 'out of love for Barak left Speke's service and so forfeited his pay'.[34]

Livingstone's party had been put in great danger by his death, travelling now with a corpse in a volatile region with few supplies. In this tense atmosphere, they had to wait for the mummification process to be completed. In the conventional account, Livingstone's body was placed in a hut that had had its roof removed for the purpose. Then, it was moved a little day by day, and took a fortnight to dry out. Headman Lupoko, however, recalled the corpse being laid out to dry for three days on a large flat plate. The explorer Poulett Weatherley, who found his way to the site some twenty years later, was informed that Livingstone's embalmed body had been stretched and hung up to dry in the fork of a *mulowo* tree.[35] This was the traditional method, to protect the corpse from hyenas, and appears more likely. This fact may have been concealed even from Waller out of fear of being accused of acting disrespectfully in leaving Livingstone's corpse dangling in mid-air.

Two other accounts support the body-in-the-tree account. Stanley's description of finding Livingstone contains an extract from a report written in Suez after an interview with one of Livingstone's followers who travelled with his corpse. According to this version, the body was 'disembowelled and embalmed by a native, and was put on a bush to dry'. After twelve days, it was then put inside 'two coffins'.[36] Second, when the Scottish travel writer Dugald Campbell travelled around central Africa, he researched local burial practices. He found that disembowelling and smoke-drying a corpse were much 'in vogue' in certain areas, especially if the individual had died far from home, 'on the road' – to prove that death had indeed occurred – or if the person was an important member of the tribe. Corpses, with their legs bent, might be hung for weeks over a slow, smoky fire. He told the story of a traveller who had come across a fully clothed woman sitting by a fire. After his calls to her for succour were ignored, closer inspection revealed he had been calling to an expertly mummified corpse. In other cases, mothers who had lost a child had the dead infant smoke-dried and suspended from a basket in the roof of the hut, with the head sticking out, apparently as a source of comfort. Lovale people suspended their dead high up in the forks of trees. So Livingstone's men, Campbell concluded, had been merely following 'ancient custom'.[37]

Thus for a number of days or weeks, the caravan remained in Mwela Mwape village among Ilala people. Twenty years later, Weatherley found charcoal evidence of the fires, so remote was the spot in the dense forest. Once the body had been fully mummified, according to many accounts, it was placed in the foetal position, legs folded to the chest, covered in salt and the mouth filled with brandy, which was also poured over the hair and face. According to Susi and Chuma, the corpse was tightly wrapped in calico. They stripped a *myonga* tree, hollowed out a section of its trunk and placed the body inside. Finally, they sewed it tightly into a piece of sailcloth. Ropes were made from local materials so it could be carried on a pole. (Initially, this was done by two porters for four days at a time.) They do not mention two coffins.

Before the party departed, Chief Chitambo was instructed to keep the burial site free from scrub to prevent fire spreading to the tree. They gave him a biscuit tin and newspapers so he had evidence of the events without having to exhume the remains. They even erected a wooden cross a short distance away, with two posts, and covered it in tar. Chitambo was paranoid that his enemy – Mazitu – would invade the area and that the tree above the grave would be cut down to make a canoe.[38]

What happened exactly during the return journey is lost forever, as so few accounts survive (see Figure P.5). At the end of the first day's march, even after all of the preparations, the stench from the body was so bad that it put the bearers off their food. Susi said that he then found some tar and repackaged the body. Later, to keep the corpse hidden, it was repackaged a second time and made so small that, for a while, it was carried as a single load.[39] At least twice, the whole caravan was struck down with a fever so virulent it produced temporary paralysis and in some cases was fatal. During the first episode, three days after leaving Chitambo, they were delayed a month. Susi lost the use of his legs for a while, and 'Kaniki and Bahati – two women – died'.[40] The fragmentary evidence suggests that the women suffered badly from illness throughout.

All subsequent accounts virtually obliterate the presence of women in the caravan. The contribution of women in carrying the body back was never acknowledged. Yet women such as Halima and Ntaoeka had long been present in the caravans, performing multiple roles, including some of the most personal tasks for Livingstone: they tended his weeping sores; Halima cooked for him; and they probably did much more.

Livingstone had an appreciative eye for a beautiful woman. About Ntaoeka, he wrote: 'I did not like to have a fine looking woman among

Figure P.5 Livingstone's embalmed corpse being carried back to the coast by African men and women as depicted in a Victorian lantern slide. Photo by The Print Collector/Print Collector/Getty Images.

us unattached'. But when she simply smiled at the three suitors he put forward, including Susi, he did not press her further. He considered her too good for them. They were 'too lazy ... contemptible in appearance' whereas 'she has a good presence and is buxom'.[41] Livingstone also wrote affectionately about Halima. Once she ran away after a quarrel with Ntaoeka but then returned. Livingstone gave her a gift of warm cloth for the cold, for 'she has been extremely good ever since I got her from Katombo or Moene-Mokin', implying that she was purchased. 'She is always very attentive and clever and never stolen ... She is the best spoke in the wheel'. Livingstone betrayed a fondness as well as the reality for these women: 'I shall free her, and buy her a house and a garden at Zanzibar, when we get there'.[42]

It is hugely ironic how the women present were essentially domestic slaves, which may in part explain why their presence and contribution were quickly erased or insufficiently noticed by European and African men. Of the sixty bronze medallions struck by the Royal Geographical Society (RGS) in 1875 to honour the party, none were for women.[43] In 1936, when interviewed by the local district commissioner, Chief Chitambo and Headman Lupoko insisted that no women had been present (although they may have been referring to white women). Often, the way in which women joined the caravan is described only in vague terms or even omitted. Susi and Chuma related how 'Ntaoeka and Halima, cast in their lot with the wanderers at Manyema', where Livingstone had been stuck in 1870 and been caught up in a horrific massacre of mainly African women and children. They were referred to as 'wives' and 'husbands' by Waller, but this was a fabrication.

The exact numbers of women present as slave-concubines will never be known. More invisible still are the slave girls. Their presence was virtually airbrushed out, unless they were involved in some freakish accident or catastrophe. For example, towards the end of the journey, Susi and Chuma recalled the death of one of their party from a fatal bite by a *bubu* – a poisonous snake –lying in wait at the side of the path. Its victim was 'a little girl in their train, named Losi'. She died in agony, foaming at the mouth, within ten minutes. Only through death does her contribution come to light: 'The poor child was carrying a water jug on her head in the file of people'.[44] Bought for their services, sexual and otherwise, or possibly taken by force in some cases, they were made to work hard, which explains the higher mortality rate among the women and girls in the caravan but only partly accounts for their invisibility.

Waller was keen to present the travellers as a kind of exotic Bible study group, so his version and subsequent missionary-driven accounts generally downplay the contribution of women and girls. For obvious reasons, Waller failed to chronicle Livingstone's extensive use of female slave labour. Yet – intriguingly – he mentioned in a footnote that Halima followed the doctor's remains to Zanzibar and that 'it does seem hard that his death leaves her long service entirely unrequited'.[45] They must have been very close. Even Stanley, not known for his interest in women, listed her as the fifth of the five 'faithful people' not to be forgotten: 'cook and wife of Hamoydah'.[46]

This is not to suggest that working for Livingstone was a joyful experience if you were male. The practical distinction between being free men and not free was often blurred, so great were the demands and deprivations. Livingstone displayed a particularly callous attitude towards male slaves and had a low opinion of them. They learnt to stick together, as evidenced by the slave who had feigned illness so that his fellow slaves had more time 'to negotiate for women with whom they had cohabitated'.[47] He was left behind.

The atmosphere on the return journey to the coast carrying Livingstone's corpse was clearly tense, the potential for fragmentation huge. They passed through areas populated by warring villages and chiefs. Susi and Chuma insist that they saw evidence of their fellow Africans being captured and sent into slavery. Word preceded them that they were escorting Livingstone's body. One chief – Kafooi – was adamant that the body was not to pass through his village, so he sent them a guide who took them on a long diversion. 'Petty tolls' were levied against them. They marched assertively at times, with the boy Majorama beating a drum, behind the Union Jack and the colours of Zanzibar. Sometimes they relied on local guides. The Luapula River was so wide that, when they crossed it, they were unable to make out a figure standing on the opposite bank. The river was now such 'an enormous torrent' that a single crossing took two hours. The drinking water they could obtain was often of poor quality, and they often relied on shooting game for their meals. Their successful completion of the return journey back to the coast provides clear evidence that Africans brought skills to exploratory travel and played a key role in it, gathering intelligence and 'filtering' local data, and working in roles that were far more managerial than they were given credit for.[48]

Finally, how many deaths it cost in total to return Livingstone's corpse will never be known either. As the popular children's missionary book *Livingstone of Africa* would put it, 'those faithful creatures' endured the 'most unheard of exertions' for nearly nine months.[49] The party was caught up in spates of violence and killing, which Susi and Chuma probably downplayed in their account to Waller. Incidents occurred en route, with altercations and misunderstandings leading to arguments, 'general scrimmage', guns fired and locals apparently shot by mistake. Strong intimations were made that sections of the party were involved in a killing spree and the massacre of civilians. When seeking safety in the fortified town of Chawende, the group was repulsed. So they stormed the defences and drove out the hostile local population, fearing for their lives and their cargo if they did not find safety and a place to rest out of the swamps. They then faced a counter-attack with bows and arrows. Two of the party were injured, so they went on the offensive, regretfully, according to Susi and Chuma, rounding on the two nearby villages and then attacking and burning at least six other villages on the same side of the river. They also fired on canoes, 'with disastrous results to the fugitive people'.[50]

That the caravan kept together and did not turn on each other under such pressure is impressive and intriguing, especially considering that Livingstone had not always held them in such high esteem. A couple of years before, on a previous journey, Livingstone had berated Susi and Chuma in his diary for taking up with prostitutes and using drugs. He had then clashed with Susi when the latter refused to follow orders: 'I put my hand on his arm … He seized my hand, and refused to let it go. When he did I fired a pistol at him, but missed'.[51] Livingstone had once accused Chuma of taking part in the massacre of largely women and children in the village of Nyangwe, along with other men in his service who had disappeared. Chuma, whom Livingstone had rescued from slavery, 'smoked marijuana whenever he could get it, and had sex with prostitutes or with absent men's wives'.[52] In Manyema, the former Nassicks also lived with 'the slave women whose husbands were away on trade'.[53] His opinion of them had often sunk very low: 'sneaking deception is so dear to these Nassick boys'; they are 'wretched cringing slavelings'; and their education has given then 'an extravagant idea of the value of their labour'.[54]

Moreover, neither the men nor the women would be adequately compensated for their services. After surviving a difficult five-month journey, carrying a corpse through warring districts and hostile villages, with apparently ten fatalities among the party through illness, they met an expedition of Englishmen led by Lt Verney Lovett Cameron, who had stubbornly insisted on mounting a Livingstone rescue expedition funded by the RGS when he arrived in eastern Africa.[55] It was, in his words, 'a project which [he] had so much at heart'. One member of the relief party had already succumbed to fever. Chuma found them in their camp, having gone ahead. He pleaded for help, as the party was 'nearly naked and starving'. When they all arrived with the body, another officer described the men 'as savage looking followers … who had dressed themselves fantastically in the various articles of costume, ostrich feathers, etc, picked up from the tribes whom they had wandered'.

To their relief, no doubt, Cameron accepted the party's account of Livingstone's death, but he instructed the men to bury Livingstone then and there. The son of a Dorset vicar, Cameron had a reputation for kindness towards Africans and, unlike many explorers, he shot game for food not pleasure.[56] Yet he rifled through Livingstone's possessions, confiscating his geographical instruments for his own expeditionary party. Susi tried to prevent him. Despite the pressure and this assertion of control, the men refused to submit to Cameron's bidding. They were determined to carry on to the coast with the body.

Relations deteriorated, and the situation became increasingly tense. According to another English officer, Lt Murphy, the men immediately 'converted into a drunk and riotous mob'.[57] Murphy and fellow expedition member Dr Dillon accompanied the travellers back to the coast, which was by no means an easy journey. Dillon contracted a fever. In a delirious state, he put a gun to his head and killed himself. Hostile villagers meant that they were still in danger. They had to hatch a plan to disguise the fact that they were carrying a body. Murphy claimed that it was his idea to make a false package and set off in another direction but, in an interview, Susi and Chuma did not corroborate this. Rather, they explained in detail how a duplicate corpse was created as a decoy, by gathering together 'a faggot of mapira-stalk, cutting them in lengths of six feet or so, and swathing them round with cloth to imitate a dead body'.[58] Veterans of long marches with Livingstone, Susi and Chuma found that Murphy and his men did not rise sufficiently early to avoid the heat. These tensions were never resolved. Cameron wrote: 'I place no confidence whatever in Susa [sic], in fact if rumours are true which have reached me about him he is an arrant rogue'.

This was a taste of what was to come. The party reached the coastal town of Bagamoya (in modern Tanzania) in February 1874. Chuma went to Zanzibar, where Britain's official representative was based close to the Sultanate, still passively supporting the trade in African slaves. The acting consul, Captain Prideaux, believing the corpse to be Livingstone's, sent a telegram to London in January 1874 informing them of this.[59] There was no money left in Livingstone's expeditionary fund – he was not in the employ of the Foreign Office – so Prideaux was left to pay the men a small gratuity each from his own pocket before sending them home. Livingstone's corpse was handed over to local Dutch missionaries, who transferred it to a more conventional coffin. It was taken out to sea and loaded onto a British warship, HMS *Vulture*, to be transported home.

This book is about what happened next. Like falling in love with someone you already know, it is impossible to pinpoint exactly where it began, but it would probably be somewhere in Tanzania in 1995, either in Tabora – after visiting the tiny slavery museum, hastily built in the 1950s by colonial officials with an eye on securing Britain's legacy in a postcolonial world[60] – or perhaps at Ujiji, standing next to the hideous modern obelisk that marks the spot where Stanley found Livingstone. More likely, it self-seeded during a visit to Bagamoya before leaving Dar es Salaam. There, beneath the shade of a gigantic overhanging snake-skin, the 'Professor' – resident and official guide to the ruined Arab Fort – told me that the town's other claim to fame was that it was the last place where Livingstone's body was on African soil – the spot where his African followers bade him farewell, he added, emotionally. Another museum carefully documented the slave trade, devoting considerable space to Livingstone.[61] After locating the missionary church, nestling near the coast, I sat on the nearby beach and gazed out over the Indian Ocean. The enormity of the achievement of Livingstone's followers fully sunk in. They had completed the long journey on foot carrying a corpse, a distance that takes hours by plane (the tiny aircraft that had borne us had got caught up in an electric storm, with nearly disastrous consequences). But it was the bizarreness, uniqueness and drama of the entire affair that stood out. Could there have been a greater spectacle of 'darkest Africa' juxtaposed with Christian humanitarian sacrifice and sent home to Mother England for others to tell the tale? For those who supported intervention in Africa, it was a gift that just kept on giving.

NOTES

1 William Garden Blaikie, *The Personal Life of David Livingstone* (John Murray: London, 1913), 388.

2 Jonas Fossli Gjersø, 'The Scramble for East Africa: British Motives Reconsidered, 1884–95', *The Journal of Imperial and Commonwealth History*, 43, 5 (2015): 831–60, http://dx.doi.org/10.1080/03086534.2015.1026131; Richard Huzzey, *Freedom Burning: Anti-Slavery in Victorian Britain* (Ithaca, NY: Cornell University Press, 2012); Tim Jeal, *Livingstone* (New Haven, CT: Yale University Press, 2013).

3 S. Stuart Starritt, *Livingstone the Pioneer* (The Religious Tract Society: London, undated), 151.

4 James Russell Lowell, 'The Present Crisis', 1844, www.theotherpages.org/poems/lowell02.html. Accessed 29 May 2014; Starritt, *Livingstone the Pioneer*.

5 Horace Waller (ed.), *The Last Journals of David Livingstone in Central Africa*, 2 vols. (London: John Murray, 1874; republished by Elibron Classics, 2007), ii.

6 Frederick Holmwood to Sir Bartle Frere, 12 March 1874, DL/5/1/5, RGS Collection, London.

7 This whole process was painstakingly exposed in Dorothy O. Helly, *Livingstone's Legacy: Horace Waller & Victorian Mythmaking* (Athens, OH: Ohio University Press, 1987). For Susi's previous form on being creative with the truth, see Tim Jeal, *Stanley: The Impossible Life of Africa's Greatest Explorer* (London: Faber & Faber, 2007), 103.

8 'The history of Carus Farrar of finding Dr Livingstone in Central Africa'. Signed typescript, dated 9 September 1874. CWM Africa – Odds – Livingstone Box 8. SOAS Archives.

9 John M. Gray 'Livingstone's Muganda Servant', *The Uganda Journal*, 13, 2 (1949): 124.

10 Frederick Holmwood to Sir Bartle Frere, 12 March 1874, DL/5/1/5, RGS Collection, London. His account was read out to the Society on 13 April 1874 as '"Majwara's Account of the Last Journey and Death of Dr Livingstone", by F. Holmwood, H.B.M. Consulate, Zanzibar'.

11 Waller, *The Last Journals of David Livingstone*, ii, 306.

12 Waller did not include more mundane, domestic details like the toilet in his edited version of Susi and Chuma's accounts. See Helly, *Livingstone's Legacy*, 161–92, for a forensic exposé. Not one detail survives about how clothes were laundered, for example.

13 Dan Crawford, *Back to the Long Grass: My Link with Livingstone* (New York: George H. Doran, 1922), 284.

14 A.M. Livingstone 'Recollections of David Livingstone. By his daughter', *Chambers Christian Journal* (December 1938), 967. CWM Africa. Box 8. SOAS Archives; transcript of interview, Headman Lupoko with district commissioner, Mpika, Northern Rhodesia, 30 October 1932 DL/5/6/2. RGS.

15 This was explained as an innocent mistake in Waller, *The Last Journals of David Livingstone*, ii, 312.

16 See Sybren Renema & Timmy van Zoelen, *You Took the Part That Once Was My Heart* (Glasgow, 2012), 45–6. They quote from F. Bontinck, 'La Mort De Livingstone Reexaminee' (undated), arr/RGS/375543. For an account of salt purchase, see Waller, *The Last Journals of David Livingstone*, ii, 315.

17 The question in brackets is in the original; it is not clear if this is the translator's query or the headman's words.

18 Taken from the transcript of interviews with Headman Lupoko, Chief Chitambo (II) and Headman Munamu, DL/5/6/2, RGS.

19 Waller, *The Last Journals of David Livingstone*, ii, 314–15.

20 Livingstone's diary entry for 10 April 1873, in ibid., 294.

21 Livingstone's diary entry for 26 March 1873, in ibid., 289.

22 See also the account in Jeal, *Livingstone*, 374.

23 'The history of Carus Farrar', 9 September 1874.

24 Frank Debenham, *The Way to Ilala: David Livingstone's Pilgrimage* (London: Longmans, 1955), quoted in Jeal, *Livingstone*, 373.

25 'Why Should We Celebrate This Man?', LMS pamphlet, undated. SOAS Archives.

26 Matthew Wellington, 'Account of the life of Matthew Wellington in his own words, and the death of David Livingstone and the journey to the coast'. Typescript by T.W.W. Crawford, dated 1 November 1911, *Zambia-Northern Rhodesia Journal*, 6 (1965), 99–102.

27 Susi and Chuma's version, edited and reproduced in Waller, *The Last Journals of David Livingstone*, ii, 316.

28 'Living Link with Livingstone', *Daily Chronicle*, 26 March 1924, CWM, Africa, Box 8, SOAS Archives.

29 See Livingstone's handwritten entry for 26 July 1868, in *Livingstone Journal*, vi, 191, held in Waller Papers, Rhodes House, Bodleian Library.

30 'The history of Carus Farrar', 9 September 1874.

31 Waller, *The Last Journals of David Livingstone*, ii, 313.

32 Helly argues that Waller campaigned for Susi and Chuma to be recognised for their efforts, and that as they were his major informants, he was keen for them to be at the forefront, rather than Jacob Wainwright, in the pay of the CMS. See Helly, *Livingstone's Legacy*, 113–19.

33 Donald Simpson, *Dark Companions: The African Contribution to the European Exploration of East Africa* (London: Paul Elek, 1975), 123.

34 Henry M. Stanley (Sir), *How I Found Livingstone: Travels, Adventures and Discoveries in Central Africa including Four Months Residence with Dr Livingstone* (London: William Clowes, undated), 274.

35 Diary of explorer Poulett Weatherley, Part 1, 1898–1899. Entry 14 November 1898, 47. PWE/1. RGS Archives. See Chapter Six for a full discussion of his role and observations.

36 Stanley, *How I Found Livingstone*, lviii–lix.

37 Dugald Campbell, *Wanderings in Central Africa: The Experiences & Adventures of a Lifetime of Pioneering & Exploration* (Philadelphia, PA: Lippincott, 1929), 157–65.

38 Waller, *The Last Journals of David Livingstone*, ii, 318.

39 'The history of Carus Farrar', 9 September 1874, 4.

40 Waller, *The Last Journals of David Livingstone*, ii, 320. See generally for the narrative from Susi and Chuma of the return journey, chapter XIII, 319–46.

41 Ibid., 201.

42 Waller, *The Last Journals of David Livingstone*, ii, 193.

43 F. Pridmore & D.H. Simpson, '"Faithful to the End": The Royal Geographical Society's Livingstone Medal, 1974', *The Numismatic Circular* 78 (1970), 192–6.

44 Waller, *The Last Journals of David Livingstone*, ii, 345.

45 Footnote by editor in ibid., 193.

46 Stanley, *How I Found Livingstone*, liv.

47 Waller, *The Last Journals of David Livingstone*, ii, 141.

48 B. Heintze & J. Wolfang, 'Hidden Transfers: Luso-Africans and European Explorers' Experts in Nineteenth-Century West-Central Africa', in P. Landau (ed.), *The Power of Doubt: Essays in Honour of David Henige* (Madison, WI: Parallel Press, 2011), 19–40.

49 C.T. Bedford, *Livingstone of Africa: Heroic Missionary, Intrepid Explorer & the Black Man's Friend* (London: Seeley, Service, 1925).

50 See generally chapter XIII in Waller, *The Last Journals of David Livingstone*, ii, esp. 328–38.

51 Helly, *Livingstone's Legacy*, 172.

52 Jeal, *Stanley*, 103.

53 Helly, *Livingstone's Legacy*, 173.

54 Ibid., 171. As Helly shows, these negative comments, plus the use of the word 'nigger' by Livingstone, were airbrushed from the edited versions of the

journals to present both Livingstone and his servants in as favourable as light as possible.

55 James A. Casada, 'Verney Lovett Cameron: A Centenary Appreciation', *The Geographical Journal* 141 (1975): 203–15.

56 Casada, 'Verney Lovett Cameron', 207.

57 Helly, *Livingstone's Legacy*, 119.

58 For Susi and Chuma's account, see their narrative in Waller, *The Last Journals of David Livingstone*, ii, 341–2.

59 W.F. Prideax to FO, 12 January 1874; see also Lt Cameron to Secretary of the RGS, 16 October 1873; and Capt Lindsey Brine to Rear Admiral Cummings, 15 January 1874. DL4/18/1–2. RGS Archives.

60 I am grateful to the late Dr Jan Georg Deutsch for giving me the rough date and motives of Tanzania's slavery museums.

61 On the inbound journey, we landed at Tabora, one of the main stopping-off points for the massive Swahili trade caravans of the precolonial era, which included the movement of slaves from the interior to the coast. A museum there was dedicated to commemorating the end of the slave trade. For the imperialism of slavery commemoration over the longue durée, see Jonathon Glassman, 'Racial Violence, Universal History, and Echoes of Abolition in Twentieth-Century Zanzibar', in Derek R. Peterson (ed.), *Abolitionism and Imperialism in Britain, Africa, and the Atlantic* (Athens, OH: Ohio University Press, 2010), 175–206.

Introduction

Dead men naked they shall be one
With the man in the wind and the west moon;
When their bones are picked clean and the clean bones gone,
They shall have stars at elbow and foot;
Though they go mad they shall be sane
                    Dylan Thomas, 'And Death Shall Have No Dominion' (1933)

The history of the British Empire also belongs to the history of the emotions. As the cliché goes, this was an empire of blood, sweat and tears. So far, we have been less interested in the latter. Yet surely empire was a maelstrom of radical feeling. The intensity of the lived experience of the colonial ruling class on the ground often generated strong emotions: lust, disappointment, loneliness, depression, hatred. The language of imperialism at home, so much a language of patriotism, masculinity and duty, was fundamentally a language of emotion. And life on a settler frontier – 'an island of white' – could suddenly swing between extremes, switching from the extraordinary to the mundane, from absolute power to complete vulnerability. In such a state of flux, the 'precarious hinge' of emotional control could very easily slip.[1]

Emotion is not an easy object of study. The complexity and abundance of human emotions make for challenging research. This is especially true for historians interested in a past when feelings were deliberately repressed or brushed aside, and for which records of the inner life are sparse. But it is worth trying, especially if we accept the principle that feelings are not just determined by deep psychology, genetics or biological drivers but are 'historical constructions born out of an accident of our language, relationships and material circumstances ... When we write the history of the emotions, we make available novel descriptions and associations that in turn create new ways of understanding'.[2]

This book is a history of one particular accident. It focuses on the history of the experience of British rule in Africa, at home and overseas, from the late nineteenth century. It is based on the premise that there is a powerful inner emotional life to empire and its aftermath, and that to fully understand the dominant features of the British Empire in Africa (which I would define as its profoundly ideological nature, its exceptionally polyphonic quality and its stubbornly Victorian features), it is necessary to bring in a history of emotion. As such, this book is about the emotion culture that underpinned the British Empire in Africa and the presence of sentimentality within that culture.

An empire of emotion, or 'a structure of feeling', it will be argued, helped sustain a 'human project' of an African empire, to paraphrase Professor John Darwin, paraphrasing Adam Smith.[3] Empire-on-the-cheap in Africa became possible in part because it drew on the emotions, particularly sentimentality. Britain's view of British men and women in Africa was often a sentimental one; Britain's view of how Africans viewed the British in Africa was often sentimentalised; and colonised Africans could hold a sentimental view of high British ideals. Of course, the aspiration to a human project of empire was often abandoned, mythical and rhetorical. The sentimental narrative breaks, and the emotional trail goes cold. But such a study can, I believe, provide further insight into the inner lived experience of empire – the inside pocket of colonial rule, from the politics of the personal to the hidden, private moments of the 'also-rans'. It can winkle out a little more of a culture of racial domination so carefully excised from official records. And it can better explain why empire's excesses, failures and violence failed to undermine the metropolitan view of a liberal empire.

Rationale

What people across class, gender and society really felt at a particular point about the British Empire will always be a difficult question to answer definitively. Would their answers tell us something quite different about the big picture and main drivers of change? Unlikely. But the judgement of a controversial, senior historian of the British Empire (from Cambridge University), commenting on a book written by Britain's most successful historian of empire (from Oxford University), whose impeccable story of rise and fall had focused on high politics, was this: 'There has to be something more to it'. His concern was that the men who dealt the cards or did the dirty deeds were left as one-dimensional project managers, were absent as bearers of feeling, and were at best left to project themselves as pragmatic, stoic and in control of their emotions.

Looking for answers to this question, I was inspired by Emma Rothschild's *Inner Emotional Life of Empires*. It's a history of one family's emotional entanglements over imperial issues of their day.[4] She had unearthed a rich collection of family correspondence to draw on. Although my book is not about inter-familial conversations, Rothschild's model was helpful in thinking about how imperial emotions might be created through relationships that substituted for family ones or that were created through memories of family, particularly from grandfather to father to son.

Rothschild's research was part of the 'sensory turn' in historical analysis and of a wider intellectual engagement in feelings, emotions and sensory perception as important experiences and practices.[5] Historians are now showing how the senses have shaped the past, how emotions and feelings are historically contingent experiences and performances and how feelings are produced and acted on or not.[6] Scholars have started to outline emotional arenas, communities of feeling, strategies of control, affectation, the role of tears, emotional capital. A renewed focus has been placed on the role of emotions in the exercise of power, particularly in public performances, collective behaviour, symbolic capital, political communication, populism and the role of the media. In other words, the focus is now on how those seeking power, or to influence it, and seeking to advance their own interests attempt to influence human emotions to achieve their aims – 'emotionality as a claim about a subject or collectivity' is shaped by 'relations of power'.[7] And as some imperial historians are now arguing, 'imperial relations' were shaped not just by economic and political factors but also 'by the five senses; how we understand others, and even more how we feel emotionally about them'.[8]

Empire, it seems to me, was experienced and run as a highly 'emotional regime' for three reasons. First, as hinted at already, empire generates highly emotional experiences for those living it, experiences that could swing between fabulosity and tedium, and between drama and boredom. Insecure white minorities and abused and hurt African majorities meant lives full of rules and regulations to maintain boundaries that were not irrational and that were impossible to uphold without violence or its threat. Transgression was all too easy and tempting. General unease abounded. Layered on top were fear, loneliness, sickness, death, loss and sacrifice, all putting huge pressure on the emotions. Anxiety and frustration were common. The gap between the rhetoric of moral superiority and the reality of lived experience, with the temptation to transgress racial boundaries, created emotional unease. Tempers, as well as emotions, could run high. The effects on the perpetrator and victim of violence – physical and emotional – could mean life lived on the margins of emotional control, rationality and sanity.

Second, emotion helped the British Empire in Africa – in many ways weak and superficial – function on the ground with minimal financial investment. An emotion culture – performed publicly, exercised privately, highly symbolic and creating an imperial community of feeling – was, I would argue, a natural resource of soft power, especially in the age of modern mass media. It helped mask violence and abuse. Africans, as well as Europeans, were drawn in. Moreover, the waning of emotion about empire may shed light on empire's fairly quiet, uncostly ending. An emotion culture may help better explain the empire's reach and power.

Third, emotion brought on board a multiplicity of interested parties on empire and across all classes in metropolitan Britain. Men and women could be profoundly affected by an imagined Africa, by the heroism of flawed men, by humanitarian sacrifice or by a sentimentalised image of Britain's superior race relations. Thus an imperial culture of emotion supported the ideology of empire, often enabling British intervention to be interpreted as humanitarian and as the highest stage of white morality. It also encouraged British colonial rule to be judged as benign paternalism built on liberal race relations. And it ensured that colonial civil servants were commonly understood to be virtually incapable of excessive use of force.

Thus attention to the emotions may throw new light on empire liberalism from below – especially its absence – in imperial Britain and colonial Africa, and on the Africans who invested in it, analysing it through the lens of lived experience in remote frontier regions, as well as on the 'also-rans' of exploration, bachelor colonialism, frontier thin government, sickly settlerdom and thwarted mission.

A 'Dumb Tenderness'

This book uses the history and memorialisation of Dr David Livingstone to chart a history of emotion and empire from the late nineteenth century. Uniquely, Livingstone was buried in Africa and Britain. Livingstone is an obvious choice to explore emotion around the cultural and politics of empire. First, his presence in the history of Britain and the English-speaking world's encounter with Africa is gargantuan.[9] Explorer, missionary, cartographer, medical pioneer, anti-slaver, proud Scot and a bit odd, he became the 'poster boy'[10] for imperial expansion and Christian evangelicalism. He was a living manual of Victorian self-help, inspiring Samuel Smiles and the Boy Scout movement, part Bear Grylls, part David Attenborough. It was through his popular, accessible writing on Africa that the 'continent unfolded before our gaze'; as one observer wrote in 1874, 'We now know Africa almost as well as we know our own country'. He fathered the imperial genre of inspirational biography, and at least for three generations, a book version of his life story became the most awarded prize in Sunday schools. So much was written about him that it is widely accepted he came to personify 'the ideals of empire', with their Victorian emphasis on 'morality, piety and duty'.[11]

Second is his popularity. Livingstone remained admired and loved throughout most of the twentieth century. Such affection endured the discrediting of empire as a system of rule, Britain's rapid exit from its African territories, and a sense that the failures of those new nations could be blamed on colonial rule. Livingstone's longevity is particularly impressive since he, more than any other individual, it could be argued, opened the gate that let loose into parts of sub-Saharan Africa the full force of late nineteenth-century British imperialism.

True, popular obsession and devotion were increasingly replaced by guarded affection and regret about his indirect role in the spread of racism and white settler colonialism. Nevertheless, strong, sentimental feelings stubbornly persisted in Britain and parts of postcolonial Africa, notably Malawi, Zambia and Botswana. And in juvenile literature, in the almost exclusively male-authored genre of inspirational biography and in Scottish Livingstone studies, loyal supporters have not been wanting. Only wartime national heroes such as Admiral Lord Nelson and Winston Churchill are rivals in their elicitation of a popular and sustained affection. (Nelson, of course, famously dying, in the arms of his adjutants, begging for one final kiss.)

In contrast, William Wilberforce, who actually engineered Britain's abolition of the slave trade, comes nowhere near in a popular culture of affection. Wilberforce, for example, was never included in the Ladybird Books, the English-speaking world's famous series of publications for children, which introduced millions all over the world to figures such as King Alfred and Florence Nightingale, and which published, in 1960 (the same year Harold Macmillan delivered his 'Wind of change' speech), *David Livingstone: An Adventure from History*. This fifty-page, fully illustrated homage ended with the generous credit that thanks to Livingstone's efforts, 'the movement was set on foot which abolished the slave trade in Africa'.

Moreover, as late as 1973, the well-respected scholar Professor George Shepperson began two days of academic discussion of Livingstone by comparing his fame and influence to that of Jesus. Edited collections of Livingstone's writings continued to be published, new catalogues listing documentary sources available on him appeared and still glowing biographies kept coming. In 2003, he triumphed atop the pinnacle of the 'imperial turn'. Niall Ferguson's international blockbuster on the history of the British Empire devoted twelve pages to Livingstone, not just to reacquaint a generation with his personal hero, but as a fillip to his argument that the British Empire was overall a force for good.

Naturally, the centenary, in 1973, of Livingstone's death prompted a flurry of events and publications. Not all were as reverent as Shepperson's Edinburgh proceedings. Livingstone's reputation took a major hit – equivalent to a historiographical tsunami – with a revisionist biography that shocked and dismayed many fans. Tim Jeal's book (impressively, he began it aged eighteen, completing it a few years later) drew on new letters and archives in Zambia and Zimbabwe (then still Rhodesia). He found a less than exemplary explorer-missionary whose faults and weaknesses had dramatically shaped his life and led him to his death. Basic technical blunders, stubbornness, high-handedness, emotional abuse of his wife and children and a blinding, ruthless ambition to be the first man to find the origins of the Nile were just some of the less attractive traits Jeal outlined. Jeal's work was critically acclaimed. Richard Hall in *The Observer* lauded a provocative biography in which 'Livingstone is less of a saint and more of a man'; 'a shattering exposure of the hagiographical picture' wrote Christopher Hollis in *The Tablet*; and, intriguingly, Paul Scott found that 'in cutting one hero down to size, Jeal builds up another – a hero of Conradian stamp and stature'. The figure of Livingstone, as the gatekeeper of colonialism in Africa and, by proxy, of its excesses and horrors, was now flesh and blood, and Jeal's verdict remains more or less the orthodox academic view.

Meanwhile, in Africa in 1973, a request to commemorate Livingstone's life and 'great contribution' with a series of public lectures prompted Professor William R. Ochieng, the highly respected Kenyan historian, to express the anger of Africa's liberated intelligentsia (and those still not yet liberated). Livingstone was 'a nineteenth century hippy and spy ... a very dreadful liar, a man who more than anybody else, assassinated Africa's character and image abroad by repeatedly branding her savage, primitive and heathen ... who thoroughly enjoyed the flesh pots of Central Africa'. A century had to pass after his death before his reputation as a good man in Africa was challenged.

Even so, further revelations were comparatively conservative. For example, Livingstone was never seriously charged with being a repressed homosexual or sadomasochist as he thrashed around Africa. Oliver Ransford's 1978 biography did contain a new psychoanalytical theory: Livingstone suffered from 'cyclothymia'. Apparently, he was a manic depressive who found sexual abstinence difficult. Sexual frustration due to separation from his wife, it was argued, helped explain his unpleasant, erratic behaviour. Attention focused more on his homosexual brother, Charles, and Thomas Baines, and how their pleasure in men impacted on their call to an expeditionary life in Africa.

Furthermore, Livingstone benefited from a good cop, bad cop relationship with the explorer, writer and imperialist Henry Morton Stanley. Although both men found satisfaction in relationships with young men they could dominate, Stanley seemed to tolerate sadistic and extreme violence, often explained by his rampaging homosexuality, repressed because of the conventions of the day. Moreover, Stanley pretended to be American, denying his Welshness, whereas Livingstone could not be criticised for hiding his Scottish origins. So Livingstone carried on: the oversexed heterosexual Victorian explorer, unable to stop annually impregnating Mary despite objections from her family. Even rumours from central Africa that Livingstone had arrived at Chitambo with a mysterious red-headed woman were firmly dismissed. A thirteen-year-old mixed-race son, apparently carried in a hammock, was judged wishful thinking or the result of faulty memories among the men who remembered him from sixty years before. The most a 'lustful Livingstone' was charged with was having appreciated an ample bosom, having hidden his admiration for African women behind irrational fears about miscegenation and having disapproved of old men sleeping with young women.

Yet despite the major 1973 revisionism, Livingstone's death in prayer remained untouched. Even Ochieng had been prepared to accept that he had died 'on his knees "invoking heaven's rich blessings upon anyone who would help heal the sore of the slave trade of Africa"'. This last great Livingstone myth was finally exposed in Dorothy Helly's forensic analysis, published in 1987. Helly painstakingly showed how the anti-slavery activist Reverend Horace Waller carefully crafted the myth of Livingstone. Former City investment banker turned clergyman after a moment of conversion in 1859, Waller was part of the first group of Christian men to journey with the fledgling Universities' Mission to Central Africa (UMCA) as part of his personal crusade against slavery on the continent.

Livingstone had inspired the formation of the UMCA after a lecture tour targeting undergraduates in 1857. His words were always destined to be remembered as a highly emotional and personal appeal to his male audience at Cambridge University's Senate House. But their iconic status and his reputation were set in stone when his disappearance and subsequent death confirmed what he seemed to have known would be his inevitable fate: 'I beg to attract your attention to Africa; I know that in a few years I shall be cut off again in that country ... I go back to make an open path for commerce and Christianity; do you carry out the work which I have begun. I leave it with you'. The first UMCA mission was a disaster; Livingstone had notoriously abandoned the group to its fate after playing down the dangers they would face. Yet Waller and

Livingstone had grown close, united to the death in a commitment to bring Christianity to Africans and to finally slay what they regarded as the evil serpent of slavery.

Helly painstakingly showed how Waller airbrushed Livingstone's last diaries and manipulated Susi and Chuma's accounts to advance his and Livingstone's 'shared humanitarian aims ... through the era of high imperialism in Africa', as set out in the prologue. The falsity of the death-in-prayer scene had been hinted at but never seriously pursued. But Helly cast permanent doubt on it, concluding that through Waller's manipulation, he had 'consecrated Livingstone to the everlasting image of a man beseeching his God to "break down the oppression and woe of the land", the slave trade. It is in the very image of the man at his death that the Livingstone legend was fixed'. The accepted narrative of his death had been so Christ-like and emotionally affecting, it had acted as a powerful brake on the usual pattern of scholarly revision for roughly a century. Waller's clear conscience likely stemmed from a belief that his dying version was what Livingstone would have wanted. Waller kept in his possession a strand of Livingstone's hair. He never married.

Thus the third reason to study the emotion of empire through Livingstone is because of the affecting manner of his death. As John MacKenzie, pioneering historian of the presence of empire in British culture, famously observed in 1990, so strong was the emotive power of Livingstone's death that it 'raised Livingstone to the status of a Protestant Saint'.[12] This book examines that premise, the process and its consequences in more detail. Living after the death of a loved one can be an emotional rollercoaster. The extract from Dylan Thomas's 'And Death Shall Have No Dominion', at the start of this chapter, alerts us not only to the temporary madness of grief but also to its creative possibilities to get through the pain and find meaning. As experts on grief have argued, the experience en masse of the upsetting or shocking death of a well-known, respected figure or loved celebrity 'brings to the surface the existential uncertainties and obscured grief of millions ... [in a] vast "dumb tenderness" of humanity'.[13] What exactly were the men and women crying for, who stood in the streets watching Livingstone's coffin pass? And to what extent did the tears produce a new radical feeling – a politics of affection?

An Argument

This book argues that these powerful emotions were the product of unusual circumstances and profoundly affected the project of empire in Africa. Livingstone's death created a strong emotional culture which would underpin support for empire during the mid-Victorian era and beyond. These powerful feelings drew on broader social, political and ideological trends of the time. They were re-energised, or refashioned, according to time and place. But throughout its existence and beyond, the British Empire could draw on a sentimental feeling to support colonial rule. The memory of Livingstone's death, in particular, was used by imperial and postcolonial regimes alike at key moments to create moral and political capital.

Ironically, this potent source of soft power was generated through African generosity – the responses of his African 'followers' or fellow explorers. Their actions, supporting Livingstone's last wanderings and carrying his body, facilitated an outpouring of grief in Britain, extending his posthumous emotional reach and even colonial rule itself, with a powerful ideology of intervention.[14] It is bitterly ironic that their memorialisation faded away. Yet their affectionate relationship with Livingstone helped frame the encounter between Britain and its construction of an Africa during the nineteenth century and beyond. In turn, it also helped frame Africans' understanding of colonialism and their own humanitarian impulses. They exhibited, and continue to exhibit, some of the greatest examples of a dumb tenderness, devotion and humanitarianism. Through a sentimental humanitarianism, Livingstone profoundly shaped Britain's conversation with Africa.

Livingstone's sacrificial death and the affection of his followers created a structure of feeling that helped raise support for empire and distract from its failures and cruelties. Livingstone's painful death in central Africa, the courage of Africans and their role in his two burials provided an intimate 'theatre of death'[15] that transformed intervention into a humane, peaceful mission. His funeral became a victorious campaign against the slave trade. This central African story, it is suggested, is a crucial part of the history of the British love affair with itself as a humane power overseas, even when the colonial reality fell far short. Livingstone's death, and his life retold down the generations, welded together imperialism and Victorian humanitarianism regarding intervention in Africa, creating a huge source of emotional capital for the future. Empire in Africa would have an exceptionally useable, adaptable and polyphonic emotional regime.

The book charts how subsequent memorialisations in Britain and Africa celebrated and imagined different versions of Livingstone and what he was believed to symbolise in relation to the ideals and propaganda of colonial governance, white settlerdom and African politics as they evolved according to needs across time and place. These moments, it will be argued, performed an important role in framing the past. Memorialising Livingstone extended imperial rule into Africa, pinning down the central ideologies of the British Empire. It was a process that was part of the unfolding of empire as lived and understood at home and overseas; and it was present in the representation and moderation – or not – of white settler behaviour, and was often part of the encounter between Africans and British colonial rule, especially where missionaries were present.

Livingstone's death was a humanitarian 'big bang' moment,[16] generating a large amount of emotional moral capital through its symbolic power – sacred and secular – of sacrifice to the death in a noble, national and Christian cause. It rooted the tendency whereby 'Africa is perceived as an object of compassion, calling for a charitable response at best. At worst it is viewed as a problem that needs to be contained'.[17] From the late nineteenth century, the general view of colonial rule in Africa, held by the majority of people in Britain, was of a moral duty which was philanthropic at heart, a way of alleviating suffering because it would stop African, Arab and Portuguese slavery and would put something better in its place through commerce, Christianity and civilisation.

This book traces the emotional and sentimental engagement of men, European and African, with Livingstone's memory and with each other. The experience of death, sacrifice and suffering; hero worship; the display of greatness and weakness of ordinary men; the lost and the fallen in line of duty; the tragedy of humanity. These were all felt deeply when the 'whole nation' apparently grieved for the dead Scotsman when his remains were laid to rest. It shows how and why Livingstone's particular iconicity continued to provoke strong sentimental feeling, expressed through acts of memoralisation, devotion and pilgrimage across generations. Helped by the press, and a network of suppliers who believed Africans loved him, the spectacle of his life and death inspired the Scramble for Africa, settler pioneers and Christian missionaries both black and white. This is inevitably more a history of male relationships and their heroic aspirations, and I have tried to include where possible the lives and emotions of those who left few records: the also-rans; the ordinary; the 'man-not-quite-on-the-spot'.

Death and Sorrow

This history of one emotion culture of empire draws on a number of theories. First, the close relationship between humanitarianism and the rise of the press. The presentation of Livingstone's death as a humanitarian cry and of Livingstone's life as the classic British underdog who gave himself, like the Good Samaritan, to strangers, produced a 'strongly moderating effect of empathy'.[18] Media coverage created a false sense of intimacy. The death scene response of his African servants offered an intimate portrayal of their close relations and lack of racial boundaries. Many readers already felt they knew Livingstone intimately because he had published his edited field diaries in a process an exhibition of emotional 'self-display', always exhibiting a strong 'will to self-disclosure'.[19] One of the most ubiquitous visual representations of Livingstone in action was that of a kind-faced man sitting humbly on the ground, teaching the Bible to attentive, semi-clothed African boys. Liberal paternalism immortalised the ideal of the gift-giving relationship between colonised and coloniser within a typical father–son scenario. This was a staged image of a touching encounter without boundaries and suggestive of a fatherly impulse from a natural intimacy. In this way, the idealised encounter replayed the syndrome of 'Discovery and of Abolition'[20] – the grand colonial delusion of being the giver, whether of emancipation, progress or independence.

Second, it draws on the impact theory of great deaths and celebrity funerals. Deaths have the power of transformatory intimacy, manufacturing connectivity and disinhibition, and reproducing an emotional connection; a 'site of mourning' becomes a 'site of mobilization'.[21] An emotional framework elides into 'practical consciousness', setting up (and later replaying) the possibility of what Hume termed 'the fluctuating situations' of moral evaluation, where 'internal and external' sentiment mingled[22] – what the Victorians valued as moral sentiment, in their dominant emotion culture.[23] Mourners at the funeral were strongly affected; participants at subsequent remembrance ceremonies were also often moved. The funeral became a milestone in the development a metropolitan imperial culture because it generated a well of 'emotion capital' which could be drawn on long after the death itself.[24]

Sorrow can be hugely creative, according to Jacques Rancière's theory of 'the sensible' – what is 'capable of being apprehended by the senses' from 'aesthetic acts' such as drama, poetry and art.[25] These are, he explains, 'configurations of experience that create new modes of sense perception and induce novels forms of subjectivity'.[26] Feeling thus has an important role in the crucible or very creation of micro-politics: the 'sensible politicity' is rooted in empathy and affection, and this process 'determines who have a part in the community of citizens' and determines also 'what is seen and what can be said about it ... who has the ability to see and the talent to speak ... ' – 'a system of *a priori* forms determining what presents itself to sense experience', with politics understood 'as a form of experience'.[27] This book extends this theory to public funerals and commemorations where the effect of the subject matter – a universal experience – can in certain circumstances undermine the 'regime politics' being performed: namely, those forms of power that seek to delimit or delineate the experience, or both, by retaining the power to constitute the community of grief or remembrance, design the service and write up the record. The potential intensity of the moment and the temporary creation of a visible commonality and even community, according to this view, draw on a Platonic understanding of artisanal power growing out of a shared reading of familiar signs and the rhythm of the chorus.[28] Death had to be morally instructive; it should – as William Dodd pronounced in his great work of 1763 on the subject that became a Victorian standard – 'humanize the mind'.[29]

Third, memorialisation can regenerate emotional capital and political action. Memorialisations draw on sentiments that are contingent upon individuals and circumstances thrown together by chance at commemorative anniversaries, interacting to produce 'fluctuating situations' of 'internal' and external' sentimental outbursts. The staged formality of such acts of mourning and ceremonial remembrance often centre on the display of the symbolic power and traditions of institutions of domination, including the military, producing a tendency for conservatism in such rituals. Yet potential exists for acts of protest precisely because of that. Memorialisations are a potentially rich sociopolitical historical source because such events can defy structurally determined outcomes and can circumvent and disable structured power – even if temporarily – through the generation of individual human emotion and the group collective experience of it. This becomes relevant for understanding the subsequent Scramble for Africa, in part an act of memorialisation: 'the role of political, cultural and liberal processes in compelling and justifying external intervention' should not be underplayed, as opposed to 'economic necessity' and 'the stark needs of capital'.[30]

Sentimental Feeling and the Origins of Empire in Africa

This book draws on these arguments to highlight the role of sentimentality in the human project of an African empire. Sentimentality is a philosophical theory about human behaviour (and/or its potential) and a historical trend playing out in the nineteenth century. Solomon suggests we should view sentimentality positively in relation to the development of our 'moral-emotional faculties': it is an 'appeal to tender feelings' that 'prepares and motivates ... [and] provides the precondition for ethical engagement'.[31] Just as Enlightenment philosophers David Hume and Adam Smith stressed the virtues of 'moral sentiment', so Solomon insists that an emotional response based on feeling is not necessarily negative, and need not be self-indulgent, irrational, personalised or false, or lead to inappropriate actions, unrealistic understandings or excessive feelings, or even negate an effective response.[32] It can, instead, be a motor for sympathy and for an engagement outside of the self, and can be also a source of 'innocent outrage', a precursor to love – all of which can produce an 'emotional economy' or 'human economy' that can redefine the social order but at the very least 'prepares and motives our reactions in the real world'.[33]

Close historical reading of that emotional economy created by sentimentality is important since 'every emotion has its context, its implication, its place in our personality whether or not is has objects that are real or appropriate (as opposed to fictional or merely convenient) ... [and its] overall social context'.[34] The emotional world that Livingstone lived and died in becomes significant with regard to the subsequent project of an Africa that was grounded in eighteenth-century moral philosophy. Kaplan argues that the moral economy was understood to be best built on 'natural feeling'; famous supporters included the supreme literary giants Charles Dickens and William Thackeray who, like others, were influenced by 'the grandfathers not the fathers', particularly Adam Smith and David Hume.[35] Victorian sentimentality was grounded in eighteenth-century moral philosophy, which viewed human beings as inherently good but corrupted when that natural feeling was suppressed by greed, vanity, and snobbery – 'malignant social engineering' – as well as by the 'increasingly powerful forces of philosophical and scientific realism'.[36] Thus it could be a site and mode of struggle – political and social – to defend the expression of natural feeling, since it was viewed as a way of expressing moral sentiment: 'the basis for successful human relationships' (the apotheosis to relations based on enslavement).

By the 1870s, the battle was well under way between the Victorian heart and mind. The Romantic movement after the French Revolution had elevated sentiment and passion to the status of moral superiority but was under attack.[37] The currency of natural feelings, feelings that were open to all would have strong defenders. Being able to display feeling and emotion became necessary for acceptance as fully participating, equal human beings capable of political judgement. Educated men and women were jostling for recognition as part of the functioning demos, hoping that the value of their 'natural sentiments' rather than artifice, cultivated manners and social position would be valued. Livingstone's death became caught up in this struggle.

Livingstone sometimes carried with him a copy of the most sentimental novel of the Victorian era, *Uncle Tom's Cabin*, which dramatised the abuse and horrors of black American-Caribbean slavery and was written by a woman, Harriet Beecher Stowe, who was 'the first American novel to sell a million copies' and the specific target of Immanuel Kant's attack on sentimentalism.[38] Moreover, the most powerful device in the armoury of the defenders of moral sentimentality were the lessons drawn from death: 'the epitome of Victorian sentimentalism', was the fictionalised account of the death of Little Eva in *Uncle Tom's Cabin*.

The moral platform that launched the Victorians firmly into Africa was shaped by Adam Smith's kind of moral sentimentality, which was central to his notion of the human project: 'It is by the imagination only that we can form any conception of what are [the] sensations [of our brother on the rack] ... we conceive ourselves enduring all the same torments ... the man within the breast ... a second self that we all possess ... a better self [that] serves as an internalized guide and self-corrector, a projection of our innate moral sentiments'.[39]

It seems to me the British Empire in Africa was always fundamentally a Victorian moral project that emerged out of broader political, social and ideological currents, a family affair passed from father to son, or from grandfather to grandson. The Victorian founding fathers were never that far away or out of reach. As late as the 1930s, there were still men alive who had sat with Livingstone and his generation whose sacrifices and moral mettle were understood to have made the empire. This book contributes to our understanding of the role of gender, masculinity and empire through a closer study of male heroism and the rise of empires and colonial rule.[40]

Historiograpical Positioning

This book approaches British imperial history as an important component of British history best understood through the interactions between the metropole and the regional context. It also regards the British experience of empire in Africa as distinctive from other parts of the empire. More than any other part of the empire, colonial Africa varied dramatically according to place. It was particularly ideological and racialised. And there were many British imperialisms converging in late nineteenth-century Africa – those of the missionary, the settler, the trader, the mining prospector, the explorer, the collector, the hunter, the crown agent – often with little to differentiate between them in terms of actual power on the ground. This book is in many ways is a story that stresses the importance and weight of exceptionalism, the particular and the peculiarity of regional case studies – the outliers which emerged from this variety. But, in relation to the historiography of Britain and its imperial history, it can be situated within or against a number of schools of thought or historiographical trends.[41]

First, this research belongs to the big-impact view of the late nineteenth century – a 'turbo-charged' phase in the development of an imperial state[42] that extended 'modernising' rule (and its accompanying rhetorical justifications of benevolent trusteeship) from the centre through metropolitan-sponsored military, diplomatic and governmental means. Political will, technological means, economic imperatives and ideological conviction converged. With regard to Africa, the big national Victorian selfies of the nineteenth century intertwined – antislavery, Christian duty and free trade. Critics of the abuse of contemporary versions of universal human rights combined with commercial interests, producing a policy of watered-down pragmatic idealism based on the principle that unfettered British-style commerce (and a system of governance to support it) could deliver civilisation and Christianity.[43]

Second, this analysis is driven by a view of the colonial state, as it projected itself outward, as never achieving hegemony, despite a stable government at home. Stretched to snapping point, the sinews of Victorian power could not escape a reality check. As Britain amassed territory, and as British rule fanned out from the centre, so the imperial project became more a series of 'middle grounds'. As Richard Price puts it, 'The places where power relations were negotiated' required, at the local level, 'constant work, negotiation and maintenance to remain a going concern'.[44] Although white settler enclaves might look and talk tough, frailty poked out. Messy, chaotic and backed by violence, the imperial project had to be forced through against a set of obstacles and contradictions. Racial rule was not without its critics, even if humanitarian imperialism often had limited effectiveness.[45]

Third, this book underscores the role of indigenous agency in the imperial project.[46] In this case study, African men and women were unwittingly central to the creation of one of the major myths of Victorian imperialism. They featured heavily in imperial propaganda and helped to soften the impact of colonialism, working in areas of humanitarianism, health and welfare. They also initially internalised the myths, but when the gap between rhetoric and reality widened, men and women challenged the racialised status quo. They negotiated the end of empire – anti-colonialism fired by the emotionalism of anti-racism. And, in the postcolonial context, political elites used the postcolonial state and its myths to further their own politics.

Fourth, it supports the 'new imperial history' view that empires are a cultural process and that an imperial culture emerged during the late nineteenth century in Britain, which incubated and reproduced itself well beyond the dismantling of formal rule or decolonisation. Imperial culture was a crucial component of late nineteenth-century British national culture – Christian duty, free trade, identity and patriotism were matched by literary figures, poets, writers and, of course, heroes.[47] The spread of literacy, printing presses, newspapers, journals, postcards, photographs and advertising facilitated this in a very practical sense. Male figures and masculinity might have been dominant, but it was women as well as men who invested in them and found them appealing, applying what they symbolised to their own situations and aspirations. Thus 'from the late nineteenth century to the middle of the twentieth century, to be a British citizen meant also to be an imperial citizen'.[48]

This book endorses the view that this was achieved, because events overseas intersected with domestic issues, political tensions and social change. As Richard Price has also argued, there was a 'powerful conjecture of a challenged imperial status in the world with the breakthrough to mass politics … the political subjectivity of the ordinary Briton was transitioning at this time from the deferential subject to the assertive citizen'.[49] Empire acted as both a bridge and a distraction.

Nevertheless, this book does not rely on the view that the presence of cultural representation of empire is proof of its agency or power. As Porter has argued, imperial artefacts, ballads or poems scattered here and there do not necessarily mean empire was omnipresent, or even popular, throughout British culture.[50] Nor was empire the most dynamic constitutive component of identity. However, the history of emotions can add to this debate. This study of the experience of empire through connectivity between Britain and Africa suggests there were enough cross-generational imperial figures and narratives producing an emotional sentimentality to sustain a popular understanding of an empire of Christian duty, humanitarianism and heroic sacrifice in colonial Africa. If not always present culturally, the emotional frames of imperial understanding remained full square. These frames obscured the way that empire, as understood in Britain, differed from its practice on the ground.[51] Most seriously, this meant that violence, abuse and cruelty struggled to come into the rose-tinted picture. Memoralisations, monuments and museums were important cultural reinforcers of a stable understanding of Britain and its relationship with Africans.[52] Similarly, and alongside, a new intimate history of empire down the generations is showing how imperial families exchanged and collected artefacts, photographs and memoirs, hitherto a neglected aspect of empire of sentiment.[53]

Outline

This book falls loosely into three phases. The first sets up the role of the press and popular feeling in the making of Britain's 'high imperialism' in Africa. Chapter One, 'A Parliament of Philanthropy', charts the initial response in Britain to Livingstone's death and the way Livingstone's eulogies darkened the image of Africa. As Livingstone's corpse drew closer to home, feelings were heightened, especially because of media reports of how badly Livingstone and his family were being treated by the government. Chapter Two, 'Laying to Rest a Victorian Myth', examines how the press and popular feeling triumphed with a grand reception for the remains and funeral in Westminster Abbey. Onlookers were reduced to tears; people sobbed in the street. For a variety of reasons, Livingstone now embodied the 'lost heart of the nation'. The rise of an empire of sentiment followed in the wake of an outpouring of emotion about the condition of Africa, which seemed to require British sacrifice to redeem it, feeding into the partition of the continent.

The second phase – 'Colonial futility' – explores how this was doomed to failure in central Africa as sentiment ebbed away. In the 1890s, European men were caught up in processes that increased instability. There was a scramble to find Livingstone's grave, in a region now more accessible to a range of outsiders. Chapter Three, 'Perfect Savagery', looks at the first visits to the tree of death and charts the attempts made by a series of young men to reach the *mpundu* tree in Ilala. High on youth, emotionalism and idealism, many never made it home. These men were loved, adored and admired, and their deaths elicited sorrow and anger; the inspirational heroism of wasted youth became entwined in imperial expansionism, further blurring the categories of explorer, journalist and campaigner and greatly influencing how this region was understood.

Chapter Four 'The Graveyard of Ambition', outlines how imperial rule slowly encroached on the ground and how Africa and Africans were displaced by the turn of the century, as symbolised by the erection of a concrete obelisk in place of the tree and the obliteration of the memory of an African grave at the site. Livingstone's followers were not memorialised, yet many of them devoted the rest of their lives to humanitarian work. Relationships were fractious at best, non-existent at worst. The remoteness of the site attracted lone males, its reputation for loneliness attracting the damaged or depressed. Sentimentality survived – just – and Chitambo became a pilgrimage site for white tourists and missionaries.

Chapter Five, 'White Settlers, Frontier Chic & Colonial Racism', marks the death of high imperial sentiment, the culmination of the story of a repressed sentiment within a colonial politics of forgetting from the arrival of the railway. In central Africa, a settler town was established on the frontier, bearing Livingstone's name. Death, disease and disappointment hardened people's hearts. White sentimentality was strictly rationed, reserved for the 'pioneer settler'. The romance of the Falls created dreams of a vibrant tourist destination. How ironic, then, that the town that bore Livingstone's name, and endeavoured to commemorate him on behalf of the empire, emerged as one of the most racist places in the region. Its existence as a colonial town was short-lived. As independence approached, and as racist feeling heightened, Livingstone the icon was revived as a Christian symbol of tolerance.

The third and final phase concludes with disparate (and dissolute) tales of Livingstone's partial resurrection. Chapter Six, 'The 1973 Livingstone Centenary, Apartheid & the One-Party State', looks at the 1973 Livingstone Centenary and how historical memory was used by a postcolonial political regime in Zambia in the shadow of apartheid. We follow the story of a revived colonial politics of affection and a discourse of the heart around Livingstone. Taking place at a difficult and sensitive time for Dr Kenneth Kaunda (Zambia's leader after independence) and his ruling party, the anniversary provided the perfect opportunity to strengthen his power base and position. A four-day ceremony was planned for the Chitambo grave that had been preserved – just – during colonial rule by male missionaries who had fought for the resting place of the territory's symbolic father of liberal racial paternalism, to remain a homage to his loneliness and sadness. Finally, Chapter Seven, 'Chains of Remembrance', follows the strange world of Livingstone studies, which opens up the British tradition of sentimentalising Livingstone through biography and commemoration. A means for discussing imperial intervention and the legacy of colonial rule in Africa, this conversation had been profoundly shaped by inspirational biography, dampening down critiques of the imperial project in Africa.

Britain's Conversation with a Darkest Africa

British Central Africa, the territory, did not last long, being divided into Northern Rhodesia, Southern Rhodesia and Nyasaland at the start of formal colonisation. They were reunited briefly under the administrative umbrella of the Central African Federation in the 1950s before this collapsed in the 'wind of change' moment. Independence followed for Zambia and Malawi soon after, whilst Zimbabwe had to endure a long, violent struggle. This book focuses on two sites of Livingstone's memorialisation in what was originally British Central Africa – Chitambo and the Victoria Falls. This whole region has sometimes been neglected in the story of Britain's relationship with colonial Africa, yet it was at the heart of Britain's conversation about Africa and empire and its understanding of its humanity or lack thereof. Through popular print and newspaper media, explorers, journalists, missionaries, officials and colonialists were able to shape that dialogue.

Victorian images of central Africa have endured to the present day. Although Africa's 'dark interior' could mean any part of Africa inland – east, west and south – on balance, central Africa was most boxed in for longest by the cliché of 'savage' Africa. It was the ultimate blank space on early nineteenth-century maps marked as 'uninhabited' or 'unexplored'. Livingstone was one of a number of influential Victorian missionaries, explorers, cartographers and enthnographers who were joined by hunters, arms traders, pseudo scientists, photographers and collectors in central Africa. They found a dreamscape where they could make their mark, mapping, converting, describing, collecting, racialising, shooting and stuffing. It was represented in Victorian travel writing and popular print as a mesmerising place, teeming with exotic and strange life. But it was also full of frights; a place full of disease, slavery, human disfigurement and death. Africa was the 'white man's grave', an image which began in the early nineteenth century with heroic stories of valiant British men inching up rivers into the interior and succumbing to terrible fevers. The mortality rates among early missionary settlements on the west African coast had been high and the difficulties of 'penetrating' the interior sealed central Africa in popular understanding as one of the most dangerous places on the planet for a white man.[54]

By the mid-nineteenth century, central Africa was at the heart of a masculine conversation about the challenge of going beyond 'civilisation'. The moon had been mapped; the interior of Africa had not. Adding to its notoriety was the fact that by the 1860s, it seemed to have swallowed up Livingstone, whose death had been rumoured and imagined in full horror. Central Africa was a place where men showed each other how utterly brave they were: Livingstone had 'stood on the threshold of the unexplored', according to one report (false) of his death; 'he had confronted the future and would never return'.[55] Heroic men signed up for search and rescue expeditions but were unsuccessful until Henry Morton Stanley found a 'lost' Livingstone in the interior in 1871. They celebrated with champagne. The Victorians were moved by a story of a touching father–son relationship, as they explored together, became ill together and ate meatballs and custard together; the mundane ordinariness became extraordinary and thrilling because they were in central Africa.

Livingstone and Stanley were hugely influential in shaping the popular imagination about central Africa. They achieved this through their ability to attract – and their love of – media coverage. Together in central Africa, they inadvertently laid down the prototype of the Africa correspondent in journalism, which would persist throughout the twentieth century.[56] Funded initially by the *New York Herald*, Stanley was a journalist and observed the world around him and himself observing that world in obsessive and microscopic detail. He quickly published *Travels, Adventures and Discoveries in Central Africa*. This was soon followed by *Through the Dark Continent* (two volumes), which was followed by *In Darkest Africa* (two volumes), followed by *My Dark Companions and their Strange Stories* (1893). One of his books was serialised in the *Boys Own* paper. The genre of African travel writing was being set down and that of the Africa correspondent in general.[57] Stanley took on the persona of a stereotypical upper-class English army officer and displayed a jocular disregard for violence and cruelty. He had no qualms about summing up the traits of whole group of central African people after just one encounter: 'The Wavinza', he opined, 'are worse than the Wagogo, and their greed is more insatiable'. Other popular novelists also projected central Africa using the same formats, such as Henty and Haggard.[58] Central Africa became the fantasy destination of choice for the Victorian reader.

The awesomeness of central Africa always evoked wonder, especially regarding its natural state and beauty. The sight of ten zebras 'twitching' and 'biting one another' in the sun, 'he recalled in 1872, delighted the innermost recesses' of his soul, for the scene was 'so pretty, so romantic, never did I so thoroughly realize that I was in Central Africa'. Captain Hoare organised an exhibition in Pall Mall in 1893 on Central Africa, displaying artefacts, photos and maps, on the theme of 'Brightest Africa'.[59] Livingstone's books also stressed the great potential of its resources, the industriousness of its people, the hard work of the women in their gardens and the beauty of a natural world which could be safely observed. In his last journals, he described the Makombwe men's hunting as 'the bravest thing I ever saw ... [they] are certainly a magnificent race of men, hardy and active in their habits ... '; he acknowledged historical progression on similar Western lines, seeing that iron smelting had been going on for centuries in central Africa; and he encouraged future missionaries to Africans to evangelise, writing in 1872 that it was 'indispensable that each Mission should raise its own native agency'.[60]

Central Africa also provided the more shocking, lurid and negative images for the age of hardening racial attitudes by the 1870s. And central Africa as the dark interior is an image which has persisted throughout the twentieth century, which generations of Africa correspondents have helped sustain. Livingstone's encounter with Tonga men when travelling through central Africa in 1855 was great fodder. He described them as completely naked, with not even a 'fig-leaf'; high from smoking cannabis, 'repulsive', their front teeth had been knocked out to make them 'look more like oxen and less like zebras'. Their traditional greeting involved rolling around on their backs, legs in the air, while slapping their thighs.[61] He popularised descriptions of sick Africa, its inhabitants carrying leprosy, giant abscesses, pustular eruptions and deadly fevers, describing man with 'elephantiasis scroti, descended to calves', who he met in central Africa in 1859.[62]

Central Africa supplied Britain with extreme racial stereotypes of both black and white. Negroid savagery was used to explain indigenous violence and customs. Few Africans in any of the popular exploration narratives were given an inner emotional life, a journey or a human story. They are functional and one dimensional, extras in a bigger drama, mentioned only as nameless casualties along the way. Central Africans were stereotyped as being superstitious and irrational and enjoying the taste of human flesh. Detailed, shocking accounts of such practices sprinkled through the writings of explorers. Moreover, by the end of the nineteenth century, central Africa had become the most challenging 'white man's playground', where the possession of a modern gun gave any man all power and possibility. Central Africa was where the Victorians 'manned up' and a white imperial masculinity flexed its muscles through the expression of male domination and absolute power. Stanley, gun in hand, feeling now 'proud that I owned such vast domain, inhabited with such noble beasts' – beasts which he could not resist killing: 'Hurrah!'.[63] Stanley confessed to wanting to hug Livingstone but stopped himself, both apparently able to transform their intense emotion into 'silent tears' so that 'we did not betray our stoicism of manhood and race'.[64]

Britain's conversation with 'darkest Africa' was stirred up by domestic anxiety. As Robbie McLaughlin has shown, this stubborn 'cartographic blankness' of central Africa became a handy canvas onto which metropolitan fears and visions of chaos, degeneration, barbarity, sexual depravity and motiveless violence – lurking in the unknown – were projected. The dark central African interior was also the sprawling 'modern metropolis', with its dangerous labyrinthine streets of 'migrant detritus and squalor', contaminated and reeking, the 'dark and filthy passages swarming with vermin'. William Booth began the first ever extensive research into London slum life with a reference to Stanley's accounts of his explorations in central Africa, evoking 'a darkest England' where, similar to

Africa, 'streams intersect the forest in every direction, so the gin-shop stands at every corner with its River of Water of Death'. Sigmund Freud and the genesis of modern European psychoanalytical theory were profoundly influenced by the central African *imaginaire*. Freud's development of the modern individual as prone to collapse through temptation and transgression; the pressure to repress a desire for the forbidden; and the role of projection; were shaped by stock images and beliefs in the 'horror, the horror' of the African interior.

And as is well known, central Africa became the favourite imperial measuring stick for progress and man's inhumanity. Joseph Conrad's *Heart of Darkness* was the climax of Victorian racial stereotyping of the dark interior, set in central Africa: 'A wild story of a journalist who becomes manager of a station in the (African) interior and makes himself worshipped by a tribe of savages'. First published in book form in 1902, it tightly fixed, through its literary genius, central Africa as a savage place that dragged good men down and made bad men worse than the natives.[65] It was so successful because the devices and images it used were already well known. Conrad described the river used to transport ivory by the maniacal Kurtz as 'an immense snake uncoiled, with its head in the sea, its body at rest curving afar over a vast country, and its tail lost in the depths of the land'. Britain's role in unmasking the abuses of the Congo Free State in the early 1900s, particularly through the campaigning journalists and missionaries, was another important staging post in her self-image as *the* liberal power in Africa.[66]

Warnings of the dire threats in central Africa to brave, young English men continued into the twentieth century. In the formidable Anglican cathedral in Winchester, the original capital of England, next to the commemorative stone marking the remains for its high priestess of genteel manners and female sensibility, Jane Austen, there is another plaque for pilgrims to read. It honours Captain George Gosling. He died in June 1906 'on an expedition in central Africa'. The memorial was organised and paid for by his regiment, where he was 'much loved'. An accomplished polo player (once considered Britain's best No.4), arch hunter, war hero and dog lover, Gosling died from blackwater fever in the arms of his friend and fellow explorer-officer Lieutenant Alexander Boyd. Boyd returned to central Africa three years later to complete the mission in honour of 'Goose' and his own brother, who had also died on the same expedition. Boyd then fell sick and also perished in central Africa. Such deaths, sacrifices, bonds and sentimentality are at the heart of this story of empire.

NOTES

1 I draw here from Dane Kennedy, *Islands of White: Settler Society and Culture in Kenya & Southern Rhodesia, 1890–1939* (Durham, NC: Duke University Press, 1997) and Robert Aldrich, *Colonialism and Homosexuality* (London: Routledge, 2002).

2 Dr Rhodri Hayward, contribution to Thomas Dixon, 'What is the History of Emotions, Part II', Queen Mary College blog, 22 May 2012, https://emotionsblog.history.qmul.ac.uk/2012/05/what-is-the-history-of-emotions-part-ii/. A fellow Celt in exile, Dr Hayward describes how he, too, carries around the Welsh *hiraeth*, a feeling of longing or homesickness for something which is ultimately mythical or beyond reach. There is no English translation.

3 The British Empire, wrote Adam Smith, 'has hitherto been not an empire but the project of an empire'; the inspiration for John Darwin, *The Empire Project: The Rise and Fall of the British World-System, 1830–1970* (Cambridge University Press, 2009), xii.

4 Emma Rothschild, *The Inner Life of Empires: An Eighteenth-Century History* (Princeton, NJ: Princeton University Press, 2011).

5 For example, see Sarah Pink, 'Engaging the Senses in Ethnographic Practice', *The Senses and Society*, 8, 3 (2014): 261–7; Louise Jay Lawrence, *Sense and Stigma in the Gospels: Depictions of Sensory-Disabled Characters* (Oxford: Oxford University Press, 2013); L. Seremetakis, 'The Memory of the Senses: Historical Perception, Commensal Exchange, and Modernity', in L. Taylor (ed.), *Visualizing Theory* (London: Routledge, 1994).

6 For example, see W. Reddy, *The Navigation of Feeling: A Framework for the History of Emotion* (Cambridge University Press, 2001); A. Hochschild, *The Managed Heart: Commercialization of Human Feeling* (Berkeley, CA: University of California Press, 1983); S. Thompson & P. Hoggett, *Politics and the Emotions* (New York: Continuum, 2012); Sara Ahmed, *The Cultural Politics of Emotion* (Edinburgh: Edinburgh University Press, 2004); Thomas Dixon, *Weeping Britannia: Portrait of a Nation in Tears* (Oxford: Oxford University Press, 2015).

7 A. Kantola, 'Emotional Styles of Power: Corporate Leaders in Finnish Business Media', *Media, Culture and Society*, 36, 5 (2014): 1–17, 2.

8 A. Rotter, 'Empires of the Senses: How Seeing, Hearing, Smelling, Tasting and Touching Shaped Imperial Encounters', *Diplomatic History*, 35, 1 (2011): 3–19, 4. I am grateful to Cees Heere for this reference.

9 Just some of the hundreds of popular biographies published include: Sir Harry H. Johnston, *Livingstone and the Exploration of Central Africa* (London, 1898); A.Z. Frazer, *Livingstone and Newstead* (London: John Murray, 1913); Reginald J. Campbell, *Livingstone* (New York: Dodd, Mead and Company, 1930); James I. MacNair, *Livingstone the Liberator: A Study of a Dynamic Personality* (London: Collins, 1940); Reginald Coupland, *Livingstone's Last Journey* (London: Collins, 1945); Michael Gelfand, *Livingstone, the Doctor* (Oxford: Basil Blackwell, 1957); George Seaver, *David Livingstone, His Life and Letters* (London, 1957); Timothy Holmes, *Journey to Livingstone* (Edinburgh: Canongate Press, 1993); C.S. Nicholls, *David Livingstone* (Stroud: Sutton

Publishing, 1998); Meriel Buxton, *David Livingstone* (London: Palgrave, Macmillan, 2001); Garden Blaikie, *The Life of David Livingstone (Over 40 illustrations): The Greatest Missionary That Africa Ever Had* (Kindle, 2013, Harrington, DE: Delmarva Publications).This book usesTim Jeal's biography as the standard bearer along with Andrew D. Roberts, 'David Livingstone', *Dictionary of National Biography* (Oxford: Oxford University Press, 2004).

10 Robbie MacLaughlan, *Re-imagining the 'Dark Continent' in Fin de Siècle Literature* (Edinburgh: Edinburgh University Press, 2012), 7.

11 Stephanie Barczewski, *Heroic Failure and the British* (New Haven, CT: Yale University Press, 2016), 115.

12 John M. MacKenzie, 'David Livingstone: The Construction of the Myth', in Graham Walker and Tom Gallagher (eds.), *Sermons and Battle Hymns* (Edinburgh: Edinburgh University Press, 1990), 24–42, 25.

13 John Wolffe, *Great Deaths: Grieving, Religion, and Nationhood in Victorian and Edwardian Britain* (Oxford: Oxford University Press, 2001), 274. For other examples, see Poppy Cullena, 'Funeral Planning: British Involvement in the Funeral of President Jomo Kenyatta', *Journal of Imperial and Commonwealth History*, 44, 3 (2016): 513–32, http://dx.doi.org/10.1080/03086534.2016.1175737.

14 I have put these ideas forward at a number of seminars over the years and am grateful for the positive response: 'Laying to Rest a Victorian Myth: The Death and Funeral of David Livingstone', Modern Political History Seminar, Cambridge University, November 2004, and Imperial and Commonwealth History Seminar, King's College, London, October, 2002; 'The Empire of Sentiment: David Livingstone's Funeral and Africa at the Heart of the Nation', Imperial Obsessions Conference, Zambia, April 2014, and The Life and Afterlife of David Livingstone, SOAS Conference, November 2013.

15 A concept borrowed from J. Woodward, *The Theatre of Death: The Ritual Management of Royal Funerals in Renaissance England,1570–1625* (Woodbridge, Suffolk: Boydell & Brewer, 1997).

16 M. Barnett, *Empire of Humanity: A History of Humanitarianism* (Ithaca, NY: Cornell University Press, 2011), 49–56.

17 Jean-Michel Severino & Olivier Ray, *Africa's Moment* (Cambridge: Polity, 2011), 2.

18 B. Newman, T. Hartman, P. Lown & S. Fieldman, 'Easing the Heavy Hand: Humanitarian Concern, Empathy and Opinion on Immigration', *British Journal of Political Science*, 45, 3 (2015): 583–607.

19 M. Kohl & G. Gotzenbrucker, 'Networked Technologies as Emotional Resources? Exploring Emerging Emotional Cultures on Social Network Sites such as Facebook and Hi5: A Trans-Cultural Study', *Media, Culture & Society*, 36, 4 (2014): 508–25, 516.

20 Jaques Depelchin, *Silences in African History: Between the Syndromes of Discovery and Abolition* (Dar es Salaam: Mkuki Na Nyota Publishers, 2004). I am grateful to Stephen Howe for alerting me to this in Howe, 'Macmillan's Africa in the "Long View" of Decolonization', in L.J. Butler and Sarah Stockwell (eds.), *The Wind of Change: Harold Macmillan and British Decolonization* (Cambridge: Palgrave Macmillan, 2013), 259.

21 George Mosse and Jay Winter's terms respectively, taken from P. Donaldson, 'The Commemoration of the South Africa War (1899–1902) in British Public Schools', *History & Memory*, 25, 2 (Fall/Winter 2013): 32–65.

22 Mary Chapman & Glen Hendler, *Sentimental Men: Masculinity and the Politics of Affect in American Culture* (Berkeley, CA: University of California Press, 1999), 13.

23 Kohl & Gotzenbrucker, 'Networked Technologies as Emotional Resources?', 512.

24 Ibid., 516.

25 Jaques Rancière, *The Politics of Aesthetics: The Distribution of the Sensible*, edited and translated by Gabriel Rockhill (London: Bloomsbury, 2013).

26 Ibid., 7.

27 Ibid., 7–9.

28 Ibid., 9.

29 William Dodd, LLD, Prebendary at Brecon, *Reflections on Death* (London, 1763), 5.

30 Mark Duffield & Vernon Hewitt, *Empire, Development and Colonialism: The Past in the Present* (Woodbridge, Suffolk: Boydell & Brewer, 2009), 7.

31 Robert C. Solomon, *In Defense of Sentimentality* (Oxford University Press, 2004), 4 and, more generally, 3–19 and 43–74.

32 For one example of the alternative view, see Digby Anderson & Peter Mullen (eds.), *Faking It: The Sentimentalisation of Modern Society* (London: Penguin, 1998). However, the counter position, most effectively articulated by philosophers like Immanuel Kant, attacked the trend for romance literature and writing that was charged with manipulating the emotions, blindly equating feeling with virtue. It was reason, rational thinking and control of the emotions that were the truest and best ingredients of responsible, uncorruptible and reliable citizens, according to the new scientific based way of thinking, which distinguished reason from emotion and elevated the former.

33 Solomon, *In Defense of Sentimentality*, 4.

34 Ibid., 11.

35 Fred Kaplan, *Sacred Tears: Sentimentality in Victorian Literature* (Princeton, NJ: Princeton University Press, 1987), esp. 5–7.

36 Ibid., 6.

37 See Kaplan, *Sacred Tears* for an account of how post-Enlightenment moral value was imposed on 'sentiment', esp. 17–19.

38 Solomon, *In Defense of Sentimentality*, 6–7; with reference to Harriet Beecher Stowe, *Uncle Tom's Cabin*; Immanuel Kant, *The Moral Law: Groundwork of the Metaphysics of Morals*.

39 Adam Smith, *The Theory of Moral Sentiments* (1759), quoted in Kaplan, *Sacred Tears*, 18; Chapman & Hendler, *Sentimental Men*, 3.

40 For arguments about a new approach to empire and heroism, see M. Jones, B. Sebe, J. Strachan, Bertrand Taithe & Peter Yeandle, 'Decolonising Imperial Heroes: Britain and France', *Journal of Imperial and Commonwealth History*, 45, 2 (2014): 787–825.

41 For the best historiographical essays, see Richard Price, 'One Big Thing: Britain, Its Empire, and Their Imperial Culture', *Journal of British Studies*, 45

(2006): 602–27; John Gascoigne, 'The Expanding Historiography of British Imperialism', *The Historical Journal*, 49, 2 (2006): 577–92; Tony Ballantyne, 'The Changing Shape of the Modern British Empire and Its Historiography', *The Historical Journal*, 53, 2 (2010): 429–52; Richard Drayton, 'Where Does the World Historian Write From? Objectivity, Moral Conscience and the Past and Present of Imperialism', *Journal of Contemporary History*, 46, 3 (2011): 671–85; Stephen Howe, 'British Worlds, Settler Worlds, World Systems, Killing Fields', *Journal of Imperial and Commonwealth History*, 40, 4 (2012): 691–725; Martin J. Wiener, 'The Idea of "Colonial Legacy" and the Historiography of Empire', *The Historical Society*, 13, 1 (2013): 1–32; Dane Kennedy, 'The Imperial History Wars', *Journal of British Studies*, 54, 1 (2015): 5–22.

42 For this phrase and a constructive criticism of the 'new imperialism', I am indebted to Price, 'One Big Thing', 609.

43 John Cell, 'The Imperial Conscience', in Peter Marsh (ed.), *The Conscience of the Victorian State* (Syracuse, NY: Syracuse University Press, 1979); Dean Pavlakis, *British Humanitarianism and the Congo Reform Movement, 1896–1913* (Aldershot: Palgrave, 2015); Kenneth Dike Nworah, 'The Aborigines' Protection Society, 1889–1909: A Pressure Group in Colonial Policy', *Canadian Journal of African Studies*, 5, 1 (1971): 79–91; Roderick Mitcham, *The Geographies of Global Humanitarianism: The Anti-Slavery Society and Aborigines' Protection Society, 1884–1933* (London: University of London, 2002); John Flint, 'Chartered Companies and the Transition from Informal Sway to Colonial Rule in Africa', in Stig Forster, Wolfgang Mommsen & Ronald Robinson (eds.), *Bismark, Europe and Africa: The Berlin Africa Conference, 1884–1885* (London: Oxford University Press for the German Historical Institute, 1988).

44 Lynn Lees, 'Colonial Towns as Middle Grounds: British Malaya, 1874–1920', unpublished paper, University of Pennsylvania, Philadelphia, 2005, quoted in Price, 'One Big Thing', 608.

45 James Heartfield, *The Aborigines' Protection Society: Humanitarian Imperialism in Australia, New Zealand Fiji, Canada, South Africa, and the Congo* (New York: Hurst, 2011); Alan Lester, 'Humanitarians and White Settlers in the Nineteenth Century', in Norman Etherington (ed.), *Missions and Empire* (Oxford: Oxford University Press, 2005); and Alan Lester and Fae Dussart, *Colonization and the Origins of Humanitarian Governance: Protecting Aborigines across the Nineteenth-Century British Empire* (Cambridge: Cambridge University Press, 2014).

46 Jack Thompson, *Touching the Heart: Xhosa Missionaries to Malawi, 1876–1888* (Pretoria: University of South Africa Press, 2000).

47 There is a huge literature here. For example, see John MacKenzie, *Propaganda and Empire: Manipulation of British Public Opinion, 1880–1960* (Manchester: Manchester University Press, 1988); Stuart Ward, *British Culture and the End of Empire* (Manchester: Manchester University Press, 2001); Andrew Thompson, *The Empire Strikes Back? The Impact of Imperialism on Britain from the Mid-Nineteenth Century* (Harlow: Pearson Longman, 2005); Steve

Attridge, *Nationalism, Imperialism and Identity in Late Victorian Culture: Civil and Military Worlds* (Basingstoke: Palgrave, 2003); Catherine Hall, *Civilising Subjects: Metropole and Colony in the English Imagination, 1830–1867* (Chicago, IL: University of Chicago Press, 2002).

48 Price, 'One Big Thing', 617.

49 Ibid., 616.

50 Bernard Porter, *The Absent-Minded Imperialists: Empire, Society, and Culture in Britain* (Oxford: Oxford University Press, 2006).

51 Kevin Grant, *A Civilized Savagery: Britain and the New Slaveries in Africa, 1884–1926* (New York: Routledge, 2005).

52 Annie E. Coombes, *Reinventing Africa: Museums, Material Culture and Popular Imagination* (New Haven, CT: Yale University Press, 1994).

53 Esme Cleall, Laura Ishiguro & Emily Manktelow, 'Imperial Relations: Histories of Family in the British Empire', *Journal of Colonialism and Colonial History*, 14, 1 (2013).

54 For some examples see, M. Park, *The Journal of a Mission to the Interior of Africa in the Year 1805* (London, 1815); O. M'William, *Medical History of the Expedition to the Niger during the Years 1841–2 Comprising of an Account of the Fever Which Led to Its Abrupt Termination* (London, 1843).

55 Stanley, *How I Found Livingstone*, xxxii.

56 The topic of my current research; John Simpson, *We Chose to Speak of War and Strife: The World of the Foreign Correspondent* (London: Bloomsbury, 2016).

57 B.H. Murphy, 'H M Stanley, David Livingstone, and the Staging of "Anglo-Saxon Manliness"', *Scottish Geographical Journal*, 129, 3–4 (2013): 150–63, 151.

58 See Clare Pettitt, *Dr. Livingstone, I Presume?: Missionaries, Journalists, Explorers and Empire* (London: Profile Books, 2007), 181–93; Edward Berensen, *Heroes of Empire: Five Charismatic Men and the Conquest of Africa* (Berkeley, CA: University of California Press, 2011).

59 *The Juvenile* (August 1893) quoted in MacLaughlan, *Re-imagining the 'Dark Continent'*, 47.

60 David Livingstone, *Last Journals* (London, 1874), esp. 199, 206–7, 211–12.

61 David Livingstone, *Missionary travels and researches in South Africa: including sketch of sixteen years' residence in the interior of Africa, and a journey form the Cape of Good Hope to Luanda on the West Coast; thence across the Continent, down the river Zambesi, to the eastern coast* (London, 1857), 532.

62 J.P.R. Wallis (ed.), *The Zambezi Expedition of David Livingstone, 1858–1863*, (London: Chatto & Windus, 1956), i, *Journals*, 89. See also an example of an earlier Livingstone tribute publication, Harry H. Johnson, *Livingstone and the Exploration of Central Africa* (London: G. Philip, 1891).

63 Stanley, *How I Found Livingstone*, 262.

64 Ibid., 497–8.

65 It first appeared in the thousandth special edition of *Blackwood's Magazine* in February 1899 and was then serialised in the following two monthly editions. Next, 'Heart of Darkness' was included in a book of three stories representing the ages of man: Joseph Conrad, *Youth: A Narrative, and*

Two Other Stories (London: William Blackwood, 1902). Missionary and geographical publications had steadily included accounts of exploration in the interior after Livingstone's death. For example, E.J. Southon, 'Notes of a Journey through Northern Ugogo, in East Central Africa, in July and August 1879', *Proceedings of the Royal Geographic Society* (1881): 547–53.

66 Robert M. Burroughs, *Travel Writing and Atrocities: Eyewitness Accounts of Colonialism in the Congo, Angola, and the Putumayo* (London: Routledge, 2010); Kevin Grant, 'Christian Critics of Empire: Lantern Lectures and the Congo Reform Campaigns in Britain', *Journal of Imperial and Commonwealth History*, 29, 1 (2001): 27–58.

1   'A Parliament of Philanthropy'
The Fight to Bury Livingstone

The only way to understand the Press is to remember that they pander to their reader's prejudices ... *The Guardian* is read by people who think they ought to run the country. *The Times* is read by people who actually do. *The Daily Mail* is read by the wives of the men who run the country ... and the readers of *The Sun* don't care who runs the country as long as she has big t*ts.

Yes, Prime Minister, 1987[1]

A Reuter's agent based in Aden broke the news of Livingstone's death to the British public in January 1874. The sharp-eyed stringer had intercepted a telegram from the acting British consul general in Zanzibar to the Foreign Office, and the story went viral.[2] This was symbolic of a news network more organised and tentacular by the 1870s. By the end of January, most British newspapers carried the announcement. 'Dr Livingstone is no more' ran the headline for the *Edinburgh Evening News*; it was 'delusional to hope otherwise'. The *Penny Illustrated News* ran with the marriage of Prince Albert on its front page, but further in, the news was gently broken, having been tipped off by an insider at the Eastern Telegram Company. Readers were invited to recall the memory of 'the familiar features of the illustrious explorer of central Africa whose lamentable death there is now alas no reason to doubt'.[3]

In Africa, no one had doubted the story. The previous October, Lieutenant Vernon Lovett Cameron, leader of the Livingstone Relief Expedition and Her Majesty's Political Agent, had first reported the 'melancholy news' by letter to the British authorities at the coast: Livingstone had died following an attack of dysentery 'lasting between ten days and two weeks', and he had been 'utterly destitute'.[4] The Sultan of Zanzibar had heard the news before the British, one of his soldiers having recently returned from the interior. Rumours circulated in the royal court that he had met Livingstone's servant, Chuma, who had told him they were carrying their master's body back in a box. By early January, the sultan's flag, the flags of British naval ships and all consulate flags were flown at half mast out of respect.[5] The acting British consul in Zanzibar, Captain Prideaux, sent instructions that a British naval vessel would collect the corpse when it arrived.

There were those in Britain who would have preferred that not to have happened, wishing that the body had been buried in Africa, as Lieutenant Cameron had tried to persuade Livingstone's followers to do. Had Cameron not been so 'knocked up', as he put it, he might have succeeded. As already discussed, Cameron had barely recovered from fever and was temporarily blinded from inflammation in his eyes; his close colleague would soon commit suicide in a state of delirium.

The stubborn refusal of the African cortège to give up their mission would have dramatic consequences: between January and April 1874, the 'facts' of Livingstone's death and the latest news about his body's passage home were covered by a vigorous Victorian press. London was now firmly established as the 'empire's news hub', commerce feeding 'the industrialising of the press' as telegraphic technology developed across the globe.[6] Higher literacy rates, faster networks of information exchange, cheaper print and more professional news agencies, all helped increase the power of newspapers at this time. In 1874, one Catholic bishop described the British press as 'the most powerful engine in the armoury of the devil'.[7] As A.G. Hopkins has warned, never underestimate how 'modern mythologies were being constructed and manipulated in the late nineteenth century by the rise of the popular press'.

This chapter charts a defining episode in the history of popular views about Africa and empire, constructed through the interplay of press coverage, official responses (or not), and public sentiment, both as it existed and as it was understood to exist at the time. Without the vigorous press coverage of the story of his returning body, his treatment by the governments of the day and the groundswell of popular feeling, Livingstone's funeral would never have taken place in the way it did or where it did. The months between the receipt of the news and the arrival of the body opened up a 'theatre of death'. In turn this enabled personal, regional and national issues to convert into high emotions about Britain's duty in Africa. This phase would lead to the dramatic staging of one of the most iconic and influential moments in the history of the British imperial project in Africa.

'Far from Every English Breast'

The Cosmopolitan, a London weekly, reported that Dr Livingstone had died of dysentery following a fortnight's illness but that Livingstone's death had been falsely reported many times in the press before. Such coverage was typical. Many newspapers published short factual pieces recounting the harsh conditions of the explorer's last days, choosing not to comment further at this stage. Yet one of the most influential newspapers (in terms of its powerful readership) penned extraordinarily emotional editorials oozing sentimental feeling.

'LIVINGSTONE is dead'; so began the second item in the *Daily Telegraph's* 27 January editorial; the 'unspeakably sad news sent via a telegraphic message from Aden'. The decision had been made to accept the news that the

earthly career of one of the greatest explorers ever known [was now over] ... whose name will ever be a glory to his own country, and a portion of the unwritten History of Africa. The best and truest friend whom that dark Continent ever possessed ... has perished opening up her unknown regions to light and knowledge. He has died – as he must have expected to die ... With the yearning desire to see once more the faces of his friends and the shores of his native land ... [but] he had faced the chance of 'death in harness' far too often not to be prepared for it ... Nor were there wanting ministering angels at that dark hour ... [for] we may say that no man ever better did his life work or kept a purer and kinder heart along with courage so dauntless, endurance so heroic, and purpose so resolutely fixed.[8]

Livingstone's death in Africa provided another opportunity to remind readers of the standard Manichean frame. A white male fantasy, Africa was dark and mysterious, a dangerous female presence; Livingstone had brought her light, knowledge and masculine purposefulness. Journalists and explorers, sometimes working as both at the same time, naturally enjoyed a very close working relationship with the press, shaping Britain's nineteenth-century conversations about Africa. Typical of explorers, Livingstone's exploits also simultaneously created 'opportunities, through feats of endurance and discovery, to reaffirm and strengthen the values that underpin the greatness of the motherland'.[9] Through a pro-empire newspaper like *The Telegraph*, explorers were able to make decisive contributions to the public's exposure to the romantic myth of the English hero overseas, doing battle against that 'dark continent'.

The Telegraph had been relaunched in 1855 under the slogan 'the largest, best and cheapest newspaper in the world', and was now under the editorial control of Edward Arnold, poet and Orientalist. Arnold had been very taken with Henry Morton Stanley after Stanley had found Livingstone. Stanley had written how, on arriving in Aden, he had been met with a rapturous welcome by *The Telegraph's* correspondent.[10] It is not unlikely that Stanley had a hand in the effusive Livingstone eulogies in the paper's editorials. A clue lies in Stanley's diary entry on the night he found Livingstone in Ujiji, where he describes 'the aged traveller ... cruelly belied ... [his] cordial warmth, courtesy, simple candour, modesty and meekness ... [provoking in him] such a violent reaction in his favour' that Stanley had a panic attack lest Livingstone should die during the night.[11]

Nevertheless, its coverage pinned down what was so moving about Livingstone's death. Livingstone had rejected, it seemed, a peaceful death in return for a virtuous life. Instead, he had chosen death in agony: 'Providence ways are not our ways and so it was decreed that he should die lonely, and in lingering pain, and far from every English breast'. This was a mid-Victorian nightmare. Tormented by the prospect of hell and damnation, 'all too often ... death was painful, agonizing, even foul and embarrassing'.[12] Where was the reward for a good life? Livingstone's horrific end had to be transformed for readers into an 'ideal death-chamber', with 'the familiarity of the forest', the breeze of the palms whispering 'comforting memories' and 'those friends around him with the dark faces', the most fitting mourners, considering his life's work. So 'let the full comfort be felt of the nobleness of his death'.

Sections of the religious press matched *The Telegraph* for high emotion. One of the most read and typical was the Protestant, pro-missionary *Christian World*. The paper quickly accepted the veracity of his death: 'Even in the midst of political excitement ... [a reference to a forthcoming general election which the Liberals would lose to the Conservatives] ... the heart of the nation was profoundly solemnised by the tidings that Dr Livingstone is dead. There are but few men in the world whose departure could have made the same impression at such an hour'.[13] A detailed biographical sketch on a rag-to-riches theme followed, stressing how the son of a poor man was now the envy of kings because of 'the place he had won in the hearts of his fellow-men'.

A number of themes recur in press coverage at this initial stage. Livingstone was enveloped within a discourse of the heart: he could be described as 'dwelling in the hearts of men'; his death had upset the 'nation's heart'. Second, an obsession with – and celebration of – his humble working-class origins would reach ever deeper into the emotional psyche, particularly of lower-class Victorians. A third theme was his superhuman, masculine strength, which placed him above Africans even in Africa, underscoring a view of the superiority of 'the white' man over the black man. The *Christian World* consoled itself with the verdict that only 'under the extreme physical conditions which ten of his followers could not endure ... the white man himself succumbed'.

Racism as usual reared its ugly face. *The Times* newspaper had doubted the reports of Livingstone's death because 'negro attendants' would not be capable of organising the return of his body.[14] The *Aberdeen Journal* also disbelieved the story since 'the negroes of all savages, show the least consideration for their dead comrades'. Even Livingstone's father-in-law, Robert Moffat, was quoted as cautioning against believing that Livingstone was dead because no European had confirmed this and the last account had been a hoax.[15] Livingstone's sister was kinder and showed good instinct: she could not believe it was his body, as her brother would have wanted to be buried in Africa.[16]

Others found the news boring. The *East Kent, Faversham and Sittingbourne Gazette* found the death of a pair of Siamese twins and 'Le Trembleur' (the man who beat the drum at the execution of Louis XVI) more exciting. The death of a Peninsular War veteran received equal coverage to Livingstone's, the region's strong naval and military connections shaping readers' tastes. Even further doubts, circulating in the national press by mid-February, as to whether the body steaming towards London was that of Livingstone (a meeting of the RGS had concluded that the case was still open and the remains would be examined on arrival), failed to whet the appetite. *The Gazette*'s headline for 21 February was 'Is Livingstone alive or dead?' The article expressed annoyance at 'how much the public has suffered on Livingstone's account', before ending on a weary note: 'It is a real pity that the problem cannot be left to solve itself … for the last dozen years we have been needlessly distressed and perplexed by contradictory reports'.[17]

Yet for most newspapers, it was a great story that could run and run. It was pure gothic horror: a slow death, a corpse crudely embalmed, a soldier who had blown his skull apart and the possibility of a substitute body. Many readers were not spared the gruesome facts surrounding the death as they became clearer in February, when questions were raised as to whether it was his body in the coffin. Meanwhile, differing accounts of the manner of his death were published. The *Sheffield Daily Telegraph*, under the headline: 'Alleged Suicide of Dr Livingstone',[18] reported that he had apparently shot himself.

Imperial Violence and Masculinity: The 'Anglo-Saxon Man of Peace'

Livingstone's returning corpse soon invited serious economic and political discussion, carried out in print, about empire. Banning slavery in Africa was closely linked to arguments for the commercialisation of Africa. Justifying its call for 'all reverence and pompitude' to be shown to Livingstone's corpse, a powerful editorial in *The Telegraph* called for 'the pride of the country in the deeds of pure humanity' to find expression in the ending of the slave trade. *The Telegraph*'s formula was commerce through the removal of obstacles to trade in Africa – 'the remains of our own heathenism' (i.e. slavery) – so the 'Negro family' could be introduced into the 'body corporate of nations'.[19] Livingstone and Stanley had always taken time to lecture to the industrial heartlands, making direct pleas to manufacturers and industrialists. It was all very cosy. No direct call for formal empire or colonisation was sounded at this point, though it would only take a small step.

As the conversation shifted towards the reification of imperial humanitarianism now juxtaposed to violence, Livingstone was quickly repackaged in the press as a man of peace in Africa. Significantly, *The Telegraph*'s first long eulogy, in late January, had revered a man who did not use violence but was rather the 'Columbus of Africa' – who, 'without staining his hands with any man's blood', had given his life away 'to kill slavery and to open Africa to the light making it possible for the hateful mansteiner to be replaced with free play for her marvellous products and industrious tribes'. Africa was presented in a positive light, as being capable of becoming like Europe. Yet the new emphasis on Livingstone's pacifism contrasted with the more militaristic description in 1865 of his return to Africa: 'Bible in hand, rifle on shoulder, David Livingstone strode away into the great darkness of heathenism and slavery'.[20]

A likely important driver of this new Livingstone – the man of peace – was editorial awareness of public anxiety about official policy in some areas of the British world. Press preoccupation with a hero who symbolised 'peaceful means in the bettering of humanity' needs to be read alongside negative headlines such as a devastating famine in Bengal. Likewise, the wars against the Ashanti Kingdom in west Africa unsettled some commentators, including journalists at the *Manchester Guardian*. This war was regularly depicted in newspapers through detailed reports and illustrations. It drew out two issues for public discussion: the use of proportional violence in such conflict, and the related question of what exactly was the claim to being a superior civilisation in the context of this violence. The *Christian World*'s coverage attempted to reconcile the high level of military violence inflicted on Africans, blaming it first on the Gatling gun (for inflicting head wounds that resembled 'those caused by small explosive shells when fired into small animals') and then on Africa, since bushwars meant that only the head was exposed. Alongside was generous praise for Ashanti culture and commerce: 'They may be regarded as the best native hope for the future civilization of Africa'.

Press coverage was performing an important role, sustaining the great British imperial paradox: most people, most of the time, believed in the liberalism of the empire project whilst accepting there was excessive use of force. Livingstone's death was a refuelling point, sustaining Britain's self-understanding of its positive record overseas. Clear evidence exists of a discomfort and concern about violence within some of the eulogies written for Livingstone by ordinary people. Many were sent to newspapers or organisations associated with him. One writer cynically contrasted Livingstone's past glories with those 'now from coasts where cheap are blood and gold'.[21] The issue of violence had to be carefully managed just as support for imperialism was not a given.

Stanley's intervention in this regard illustrates just how influential he was as a writer and journalist in the history of Britain's public conversation about Africa. Stanley used the press to garner support for his long-term vision of European and American commercial expansion into central Africa. The captain of the *Malwa* steamship found this out at Suez. He had taken guardianship of Livingstone's remains at Aden. He gave orders that he was not to be disturbed until 6 a.m. when they docked at Suez. But at 3 a.m., a man appeared on board demanding to see him. It was Stanley. He stayed on board until Alexandria, when one of Livingstone's sons arrived, then they both returned to England over land.[22] Stanley's purpose in being there was to prepare Jacob Wainwright, who was accompanying the body, for the huge press interest to come. Stanley was one of the first aboard the *Malwa* when it finally arrived in Britain, ensuring the press corps reported his personal interview with Wainwright. He pointedly asked him: 'Did the Doctor ever have occasion to fire his gun?' Wainwright replied 'No sir ... The Master was not fond of firing his gun'.[23]

This was not entirely accurate. When Frederick Holmwood, at Zanzibar, had interviewed Chuma and Susi, they had described Livingstone's technique for obtaining canoes from reluctant locals: he 'seized seven canoes by force, and when the natives made a show of resistance, he fired his pistol over their heads'.[24] Was Stanley's press presence here a crucial stepping stone for his career? Stanley's expedition to the Congo would be co-financed by the *Daily Telegraph*, which King Leopold II of Belgium would also bankroll. Stanley would repeatedly use both *The Telegraph* and his original employer, the *New York Herald*, to make powerful interventions in the public debate, including through his famous letters.[25]

The Christian press also used Livingstone's death to settle other scores. First, Protestant-leaning publications were keen to quash rumours about Livingstone's lapse of faith. A week after breaking the news of his death, the *Christian World*'s 'Sermons' section addressed Livingstone's religiosity. The Reverend New had addressed a large assembly at Exeter Hall to assure his audience (as Stanley had reassured him) that 'Dr Livingstone never forgot that he was a missionary', reading from the Bible and explaining Christian truths in a 'wonderfully effective and simple manner', and regarding his work as preparatory.[26] The Reverend New appealed for 'sympathy for the much wronged African race, and for more vigilant efforts to put an end to the abominations of slavery and the slave trade'.

A dead Livingstone also helped further an idealised masculinity. At the YMCA's 1874 Annual Meeting, the Reverend Donald Fraser lectured on 'Christian Manliness', branding Livingstone as the prime example of 'real manhood' which 'young men, young laides [sic] and lady-like young men ought to take heed of'.[27] If he was using Livingstone to attack homosexuality, Fraser also had other scores to settle, using him to attack 'a new kind of religion that denied the right and duty of private judgement, which diminishes the sense of personal responsibility'. Livingstone was 'no chicken-hearted Christian but a mighty man, a man of faith and holy hope, a martyr to the grand purpose of philanthropy'. Homo-worship and the cult of the masculine Livingstone were boosted by the manner of his death, from his last days of suffering. He had manned up for the grand finale of high-Victorian heroism.

Identity around being 'English' was also redefined and celebrated through Livingstone's death. Usually, any revered characteristic of Livingstone was promoted as a natural feature of Englishness, particularly by upper-class commentators. Even before Livingstone's death, Sir Bartle Frere, RGS president, had described him as 'representative of the best features of England ... an Englishman who has shown to have the best features of the Anglo-Saxon character'. Likewise, Sir Henry Rawlinson, in *The Times*, insisted that the government was 'bound not only by humanity but by duty to redeem this great Englishman, who is now suffering ... for the cause of science and humanity'.[28] Knowing Livingstone, as they did, they surely knew that he had been born outside Glasgow. Perhaps upper-class self-absorption and confidence enabled the obliteration of complexity and so they effortlessly subordinated anyone in their greater English vision of Victorian Britain and the world, a vision in which they stood atop. Even Livingstone referred to his Englishness. For example, in 1872, he wrote about his 'English stock of robust health with which to battle against the pelting rain'. The 'Scotchman', or 'Scotch', would be added during the funeral, but Englishness seems to have had more functional use when overseas.

Livingstone's identity was more of an issue for commentators when it seemed he was rather African. Livingstone was sometimes described as having 'a childlike simplicity' or 'a simple but unbending character', or as being 'simple minded'.[29] These were traits often pinned on Africans. A struggle ensued to explain why Livingstone was so committed to their cause. Anxieties about him 'going native' had already surfaced in the British press. His biting criticism of British colonialists in the Cape and their aggression towards the Xhosa in the 1850s, and his long periods spent alone with Africans, raised Victorian eyebrows. Indeed, one of Stanley's self-avowed aims in finding Livingstone was to ascertain how far he had abandoned civilised behaviour in his isolation. In this way, he constituted a living experiment for the home audience.

Livingstone's Highlander ancestry did him no favours here. Being Celtic, he was not immune to crudely racialised Victorian taxonomy. Scottish Highlanders came fairly low down the scale, even if they were often romanticised by admirers of Scottish nationalism. Scotch biographers, of course, were always keen to stress a noble, distinct lineage. But even as late as 1913, the Duke of Argyll could describe Livingstone as an example of the 'purest Celtic type', being 'rather below medium stature, broad, sturdy, and with an evident capacity for great endurance' and with a 'special feature [that] attracted notice ... his very dark hazel eye, an eye so dark as to suggest a southern origin'.[30] The Reverend Dean Stanley, in his 1874 funeral sermon in Westminster Abbey, addressing the issue of Livingstone's identity and identification, described him as 'cosmopolitan, catholic, almost African as he had become'.[31] If Livingstone was to be the poster boy for humanitarian intervention in Africa, his apparent empathy and sympathy with Africans had to be uncoupled from 'going native'. The Reverend Stanley, called on the public 'not forget that he was bone of our bone and flesh of our flesh'.[32]

Finally, press coverage of Livingstone's death illustrates the continuing process of negativising Africa. The more Africa could be represented as barbaric, the greater Livingstone's achievements became. Livingstone's death pinned down Africa. Depressing images of slavery shut down perceptions of the capabilities of its peoples, if left alone. Africans were a race to be pitied: 'the forlorn condition of the African races'. African skills, hard work and commercial aspirations were underscored in some reports, but these would soon fade from the conversation. Absent was the stress on the African expertise which Livingstone had earlier promoted: 'civilized, anxious to trade and skilful in the art of cultivation', was his verdict for one audience in 1865; and for another, 'they rather believe we are the savages'.[33]

Informed media coverage of African attitudes to death, to help explain their decision to return the body, was similarly absent. Yet even a rudimentary probing would have revealed striking theological similarities. A few years later, the Reverend Dan Crawford, a wandering missionary in central Africa, enquiring about local customs and beliefs around death, noted, in addition to burials, wakes, memorial statues and grieving, 'an imperious instinct of Immortality'. The dead were described as having 'gone to the city' or as having 'arrived'. Crawford particularly

admired how dying was called 'the awakening' in the Ilala region where
Livingstone died. He also found that in the local vernacular, the verb
'to teach' came from the root verb 'to die'. A popular saying was that
death was the 'the perfect education', that 'the dead know all things'.[34]
The Scottish explorer Dugald Campbell later confirmed this, travelling
through the remote forested regions of central Africa. Death, he found,
was also likened to crossing a river or was called 'the cold place'.[35]
He catalogued wakes, death chants, wailings, statues and embalming.
Cannibals, too, he concluded, shared similar beliefs in the afterlife. The
press found difference easier and more commercial, displaying a start-
ling lack of interest in Africa or Africans beyond their relationship to
Livingstone.

A Free Passage Home and Imperialism on the Cheap

While Livingstone's body was making its way home, emotions and sentimentality grew. Livingstone's 'pathetic death' was linked with anti-slavery.
This further resolved the government not to make a fuss when the corpse
arrived. The new Conservative government feared more public pressure
to intervene in eastern Africa, having been forced by public opinion to
ban the slave trade off the coast in 1871.[36] An elaborate funeral might
bring together disparate groups that could form, once again, a powerful
single-issue alliance. So, if government officials admired Livingstone for
his broader achievements, they kept it to themselves. Both the government
and the RGS were unwilling to organise or pay for a funeral. As late as 13
April (the funeral was scheduled for 18 April), the London Missionary
Society (LMS) were writing in bewilderment, asking about arrangements
for their involvement – questions they had first raised in early March.[37]

This lack of financial support for Livingstone after he died and for
his followers is symbolic of the ubiquitous empire-on-the-cheap attitude.
British imperialism was like the monarchy: it never seemed to carry cash.
(In Bagamoya, as already discussed, Livingstone's servants had been
paid a pittance for their efforts.[38]) Livingstone's remains were placed in
a second wooden coffin provided free by local Catholic missionaries in
Bagamoya before being picked up by the British frigate HMS *Vulture*.
Then began a series of donated free passages, first on an Austrian war-
ship; then on a British Indian Steam Navigation Company ship, the
Minora, to Aden; and finally on the Pacific & Orient ship, the *Malwa*,
to Southampton. The London and South Western Railway Company
(referred to by newspapers of the time as the South Western Railway
Company) transported the body for free from Southampton to London.[39]

This succession of free gifts created the sensational story about Livingstone's emaciated corpse (or someone else's) slowly making its way home. It was a great peg for further Livingstone press coverage, naturally creating a dramatic build-up – not what the government wanted. Significantly, it provided enough time for interventions by three religious groups, with high and low political agendas and interests. Each backed a revival of Christian mission as a humanitarian anti-slavery movement projected as the highest form of civilisation. Each acted on press information and began to expose the government's parsimony. Their combined pressure yielded an imperial burial in London.

From late January 1874, when the news broke, there was a crucial gap of a fortnight before Livingstone's body left Africa for Zanzibar in mid-February. During this time, news filtered out that Jacob Wainwright was amongst the returnees. His former headmaster contacted the CMS, who in turn telegraphed Arthur Laing, an English merchant in Zanzibar tasked with overseeing the return of the remains to Suez. The CMS informed him that they would pay for Wainwright to accompany the body home, recognising this as a great public relations opportunity[40] (see Figure 1.1).

The timing was perfect. The evangelical ascendancy was on the wane from the 1870s, 'the era of the so-called Victorian crisis of faith'.[41] Overseas missions like the CMS feared the spread of Islam in eastern and central Africa. Christian conversion was stalling and so too were their home recruitment campaigns.[42] The LMS might have fallen out with Livingstone earlier in his career but they quickly offered their condolences to his family, praising 'his integrity of Christian character; in the sight of the heathen, his indomitable energy and ecumenical activity ... preparing the way for ... British influence and commerce but also the freedom, the civilization and the spiritual regeneration of the African race'.[43]

Meanwhile, the Reverend Arthur Penrhyn Stanley, dean of Westminster Abbey, had read about the death in the first newspaper accounts in late January whilst in St Petersburg attending a royal wedding. He wrote immediately to the RGS's president, offering to 'entertain the proposal' that the body be buried in Westminster Abbey. He later became 'morally certain that the only man who could have inspired such enthusiasm ... for carrying a dead body' was Livingstone (although he still requested written proof from the surgeon who carried out the last-minute verification).[44] The dean, with his Welsh origins, was, unsurprisingly, a huge admirer of fellow Celt, Livingstone. Also, a funeral would be an opportunity to end a spate of inter-denominational Protestant fighting (which Fraser's

Figure 1.1   Jacob Wainwright, former Yao freed slave, with Livingstone's coffin, which he had accompanied all the way from Africa, here on board the steamer *Queen* after a storm at sea. This had taken the coffin from the *Malwa*, at Southampton docks so that the procession could start from the pier. 15 April 1874. Photo by London Stereoscopic Company/ Hulton Archive/Getty Images.

angry words already discussed above attest to) mentioned in several London newspapers around this time. The dean's funeral sermon would begin with St John's lesson: 'Other sheep I have, which are not of this fold ... there shall be one fold and one shepherd'. This was not just directed towards Africa.[45] Although he rejected the offer of help to conduct the service from a Nonconformist minister, he insisted that this was due to Abbey tradition and that 'every consideration ... be shown to the dissenting clergy'.[46]

This offer was controversial. One newspaper editorial argued that it would have been preferable if Livingstone had been buried in Africa, 'whose people he loved so well'.[47] The Catholic press objected to the burial on the grounds that Livingstone 'had identified himself with a sect which ... have no divinely appointed ministers or teachers ... As well we might inter the Sultan of Turkey, his Majesty of Ashantee or the King of the Cambal Islands',[48] and it created an opportunity to air more standard criticisms of the stereotypical missionary, by now almost a national sport. *Cornhill Magazine* sneered at missionaries who did nothing but 'walk about with a bible under their arm, preaching sermons to the natives'.[49] The dean's radical offer was only formally accepted in early April. The intervention of a tight-knit community of Nonconformist, commercially minded townsmen was a huge factor. Information circulating in the press brought a local dimension to the unfolding drama.

After reading that the P&O steamship, the *Malwa*, which bore Livingstone's remains from Aden, was likely to dock at Southampton in April, Southampton's mayor, Edwin Jones, went into overdrive to arrange a grand reception for the corpse. Jones was a Welsh Nonconformist from a humble background, a self-made man and philanthropist. Livingstone's story was also Jones's. The personal and the local interacted. Southampton was experiencing a commercial lull.[50] Decades of respectable growth and prosperity from trade and commerce (its being a port town surrounded by a fertile hinterland) had started to falter beginning in the mid-1860s. In 1867, incoming mail from the West Indies had been diverted to Plymouth, which now benefited from an extended railway line. There had followed a further downturn in the volume of Southampton's trade due to the effects of the Franco-German War (1870–1). More seriously, a worrying rumour had been circulating in the town early in 1874 about the possible relocation of the much-valued P&O company. The Suez Canal had opened in 1869, more cotton goods were being exported to India through it, the company had just been granted permission to send its mail through it and London was looking more attractive as the company's main base.

Sensitive to such ill winds was a group of commercial entrepreneurs in the town. Southampton had elected a new Liberal mayor, Edwin Jones, in 1874. Jones was one of Southampton's most successful and well-known businessmen. His retail stores in the town centre were thriving, plus he supplied over fifty 'branch' shops in the region (his business would become a public company in 1888, with a capital value of £200,000 at his death in 1896, and became Debenhams). A widower, he had married for a second time, in 1874, a much younger woman, and continued his tradition of lavish entertaining. In February, he had organised and paid for a ball to celebrate the marriage of the Duke of Edinburgh, to which he invited 1,600 people.[51] Although Jones does not seem to have been remembered as a high-profile supporter of the anti-slavery cause, his background and story were not dissimilar to Livingstone's, coming as he did from humble, dissenting stock. His father was a Welsh coal merchant and railway carrier, as well as an enthusiastic Congregationalist. Jones had gone from rags to riches, starting as a young apprentice before opening a small shop that sold lace and button boots. Although he owed much of his early success to his two unmarried sisters, his was the religion of manly self-improvement, his later philanthropic causes being the Young Men's Mutual Improvement Society and the Polytechnic Institute.

Jones and the council were a tight-knit community that straddled the world of business, religion and the military. A press report of a Freemason dinner held at a local hotel on 31 March 1874 to celebrate the fifteenth anniversary of Lodge Perseverance, a branch of the Order of United Britons Friendly Society, noted that Jones presided.[52] Also present – some holding office – were other members of the town council and members of the Hampshire Volunteers Regiment. The mayor was praised for being 'one of the most liberal and public spirited mayors the town had ever had. (Cheers)'. This network mobilised to ensure that Livingstone's remains would first touch English soil at Southampton.[53] A successful ceremony would be a chance to display civic prowess to an international audience, as well as court P&O and boost local trade.

In late March, on learning that the remains of 'the illustrious African traveler were expected to arrive on the 13th', the town council formed a reception committee.[54] This local initiative, involving as it did the church, council and military, exposed the lack of 'imperial ceremony' being planned for the body in London, which began to attract negative press attention. Southampton's MP, Russell Gurney, was persuaded by the council to raise the issue in the Commons, on 31 March 1874. Gurney did not need much prompting. He was a strong supporter of the anti-slavery movement and plugged into a wider network of powerful activists.[55] The big question was: who would pay for what the public wanted – a burial in Westminster Abbey? If 'an obstacle stood in the way', Gurney argued, it would be a 'great disappointment'. Cries of 'hear, hear' filled the chamber, as he went on to stress how 'disrespectful' that would be, for 'we all have reason to be proud of the glory that has been shed on this country by … one of her sons'.[56]

Scandal and Public Anger

Astonishingly, less than a week before Livingstone's body was due to arrive at Southampton, no formal agreement had been reached regarding his burial. The offer of Westminster Abbey still dangled in the air. The RGS wanted neither the responsibility nor the cost, whilst the government did not welcome the spectacle either (although one newspaper claimed preparations for the armed forces' return from the Gold Coast was an inevitable distraction).[57]

Naturally, the RGS was the first port of call for many concerning Livingstone. It was the recipient of all formal government information about his death, forwarding all letters to the family. On 12 January, a record was made of several lines written in honour of Livingstone, sent with a request from a member of the public that they be forwarded to the explorer's family. Condolences were sent there from various sister organisations, such as the French Royal Geographical Society. But he was no son. Livingstone had cost them two search expeditions already, and the payment of his servants was an ongoing issue.[58] Socially, he was not one of them. Initially, Livingstone's death was kept at arm's length. Reports of Livingstone's death were discredited at an evening meeting of the RGS on Monday, 26 January.[59] On 9 February, the council considered a request by a member that the society should strike a medal in memory of Livingstone. This request was rejected.[60] One elderly lady suggested that a piece of plate might be presented to the family.[61] No record of the response to this survives.

One contributing factor was Henry Morton Stanley. He kept popping up as Livingstone's spokesman. Stanley was held in high disdain by certain sections of the RGS elite. Just a few years before, he had beaten the RGS/Livingstone search party. To them, he published 'sensationalism geography', which was vulgar, wrong and commercially motivated.[62] 'A rank interloper' judged to be full of 'bombastic boorishness', Stanley had beaten them 'in a field that had become the society's preserve'.[63] Only after a long public campaign conducted through the press did the RGS concede to public opinion and award Stanley a medal for having found Livingstone.[64] This rivalry was also carried through into the press. Stanley was a *Telegraph* man; the RGS in close touch with *The Times*.

Nevertheless, the RGS was run by strong, independent individuals, and Livingstone was not without powerful supporters. It also had an interest in maintaining public interest in all geographical endeavours. It kept the press informed about Livingstone developments throughout February and March, particularly when relevant speakers delivered talks. It also repeatedly asked the government for help with the funeral, recognising that Livingstone's family were in no position to pay for it.

The new government repeatedly refused help. Some were sympathetic. Lord Derby, the foreign secretary, aware that Livingstone had children and maiden sisters, warned Prime Minister Disraeli: 'It is not supposed he can have left anything. He is a man whose life and work as an explorer have attracted an unusual amount of public interest'.[65] Livingstone had been titular roving consul, so their potential liability for the cost of his various expeditions alarmed them. Senior figures were concerned that foreign newspaper moguls, such as Gordon Bennett and his favoured reporter, Henry Morton Stanley, were making fools of them – Gordon Bennett had issued a detailed press release full of more 'facts' about Livingstone from letters sent to them on 30 March.[66]

However, the situation was becoming embarrassing. The RGS wrote to Disraeli after Gurney's awkward questioning, offering to help decide the matter.[67] Despite having received a letter from Livingstone's sister assuring 'there can no longer be any reasonable doubt', the prime minister still feared a hoax, insisting even by early April that certain issues required 'investigation'.[68] In desperation, the RGS formed an organising committee, which met on 7 April.[69] Having had to agree to store the approaching body in its Map Room, it now feared that this could make it look responsible for the funeral, so it engaged in a slight dalliance with the press. *The Times* published an unconfirmed report on 9 April that the government had agreed to pay for the funeral.[70] This was not the case, but the government was backed into a corner. The Chancellor of the Exchequer was forced to award £250 towards costs, still insisting that the RGS was responsible for the event.[71] This was five days before the body was scheduled to arrive in England. The press, crucial in creating the problem of Livingstone's funeral, was now playing a part in solving it.

Officially, the RGS put a gloss on events. In its record of proceedings for 13 April 1874, the government was credited with agreeing to cover the full cost of the funeral. The offer from an anonymous businessman – the self-made millionaire and philanthropist Sir George Moore – to pay for everything was deemed unnecessary. A shame perhaps. The memoirs of Dean Stanley contradict this; he recollected that the 'government hung fire' until the offer made by Sir George became known.[72]

Part of the reason for this U-turn lies with how press coverage kept the Livingstone story live through a steady trickle of news stories, letters and articles. *The Telegraph*, for example, ran with a Reuter's telegram from Aden, reporting that the body had left Zanzibar on 22 February; it also covered a discussion at an evening meeting of the RGS during which Livingstone's death was still doubted.[73] A letter from Cameron, leader of the relief expedition, who had first announced the death, was published in several papers.[74] Moreover, press coverage of the continuing official indifference increased public anger and feeling throughout April, as the body drew nearer. Rumours of slights continued to appear. Livingstone's remains had been shoved, according to one account, into the hold of the *Malwa* rather than placed in a cabin.[75] A letter to *The Times*, republished in several regional papers, including the *Western Mail*, complained bitterly that Susi and Chuma had not been given free passage.[76] Horace Waller insisted that they were 'amongst the greatest of African travellers' (not explorers, note), outraged that his informants – the 'officers' – had been passed over for a 'private'.

The government's reluctance to pay for the funeral was then matched by its poor treatment of Livingstone's family, generating further public outrage. Since Livingstone's government pension had expired on his death, his children and unmarried sisters were now left vulnerable. The *Glasgow Herald* was one of many newspapers critical of the government's 'trivial contributions'.[77] Several of Livingstone's admirers, including Waller and the heiress and philanthropist Baroness Burdett-Coutts, made a public appeal for donations to the Livingstone Testimonial Fund they had quickly set up.[78] The press gave this wide publicity in the week before the funeral.[79] 'We must no longer with-hold from this nation a trust which has fallen to it by his death', was a call publicly endorsed by Southampton's funeral committee and the RGS.

Newspapers had set the scene for the imminent arrival of the corpse of an apparently selfless, peace-loving old man, whose poor treatment contrasted unfavourably with the response of his African servants. Even Glasgow was about to erect a statue.[80] The British public were being told, as Henry Morton Stanley put it, that 'one of the noblest souls of his generation' would be remembered by 'thousands in Africa ... with far warmer feelings of affection and veneration'.[81] In an age when a vertiginous ladder of racial superiority existed, this was particularly damning. Moreover, because he had been passed over by his superiors and neglected by the government, and his family impoverished after his painful death, Livingstone was becoming, in Adam Smith's words, 'the man within the breast'. He was a symbol of the harsh reality of life for the majority, many of whom were still considered unworthy of a vote.[82]

Livingstone's Sentimental Appeal: Underdog, 'Islander' & Failure

Born in Blantyre, Scotland, on 19 March 1813, Livingstone was the second of seven children (two of whom died in infancy). The family lived in a tenement, 'Shuttle Row', which had been built in 1780 and comprised twenty-four single-kitchen rooms on three storeys. The building was close to the mill it was designed to serve. Livingstone's father descended from displaced island dwellers. These indigenous Gaels, or Celts, were part of a larger pattern of migration of people who had escaped the hardship and near famine of peasant subsistence. In the Livingstones' case, this was the Isle of Ulva (meaning 'wolf'), part of the Staffa group of islands off the Isle of Mull, off the west coast of Scotland, owned for a long while by the Macquaries. Livingstone's grandfather, arriving in Blantyre in 1792, had begun work in a local cotton mill. Blantyre was seven miles from Glasgow, situated on the banks of the River Clyde. The family's original, Celtic name was MacLeay (or MacLeigh, Maclay or Mac-an-Leigh), which had a number of translations: the son of the grey-headed' or of the physician, and the family was linked in service to the Barons of Bachuill, custodians of an ancient stone crosier, which according to local myths had belonged to Saint Moluag, the first Bishop of Argyll.[83] Livingstone's father first adopted the Saxon version. 'Livingston', dropping the 'e', before reinstating it.

Oral family history would become especially important in maintaining dignity and identity in dire and changed circumstances. Livingstone grew up with stories of a great-grandfather who had died in the Battle of Culloden (Blar Chuil Lodair, 1746) on the side of the House of Stuart against the House of Hanover;[84] one of his grandfathers could recall by name six generations of ancestors. His 'Highland blood', according to Blaikie, was the key to his character. It made him naturally cleave to and respect African chiefly authority, modifying 'the democratic influences' of urban living, and gave him 'dash and daring' that trumped 'Saxon forethought and forbearance'. It also apparently intensified his likes and dislikes and made him fiercely loyal to certain aristocratic figures in his life, such as Sir Roderick Murchinson and the Duke of Argyll, as a 'Highlander to his Chief'.[85]

Livingstone's mother, Agnes, or Nannie Hunter as she was called, was left out of many popular biographies. Her family hailed from east Lanarkshire, in the lowlands of Scotland. Her father, David Hunter, whom Livingstone was named after, had not been able to make crofting viable on the bleak moors, so moved the family to Blantyre, where Agnes was born. When interviewed, locals remembered her as a 'small and delicate' woman with a 'sweet nature'. 'Her chief physical characteristic' (which seems harsh) were her 'markedly bright eyes, a trait that her son inherited'.[86] She had a reputation for cleanliness and smoked a clay pipe, passing only the first habit onto her son. Blaikie's biography gave over two pages to her. He credited her with a motherly love, 'beaming out freely like the light of the sun', so much so that 'her son loved her, and in many ways followed her … [her] genial, gentle influences that had moved him … enabled him to move the savages of Africa'.[87] Yet despite Blaikie being the reference point of so many subsequent biographies, this theory quickly faded. T. Banks Maclachlan put his own patronising spin on her when he wrote of her appearance of delicateness, 'characteristic of so many little women who live to surprise their friends with unthought-of stories of health and vitality'.[88]

Like many families, the Livingstones lived in proximity to a brutal past that had ruptured communities. Livingstone's family history on his father's side was one of dramatic conversion from Roman Catholicism – 'the laird [ruler] coming round with a man having a yellow staff', according to some accounts. It also encompassed the 'extreme savagery' of local customs, as Livingstone once described them, such as Ulva's Kirsty's Rock, where Highlanders placed miscreants in a sack, letting the rising tide gradually drown them.[89] On his mother's side, her lowland family had a reputation for having had strong 'Covenanting' sympathies.[90] An experience of dissension, displacement and conversion went back through the generations, to be sure. But more relevant for Africa later, Livingstone was brought up bilingual, speaking Gaelic and English, which may have made it easier to converse in other languages.

In 1913, one hundred years after he was born, speculation about his ancestry and childhood loomed large in many of the centenary reflections.[91] For some, especially Scottish memorialists, naturally his childhood – Scottish and poor – was the key to the man and his future. According to one writer, weaving Livingstone into the story of the developing labour movement, 'Dave' or 'Davee' would wander along the Clyde, on both sides of the river, and on one tree he carved the inscription 'No State Church', which begat a lifelong commitment to 'My Own Order – the Honest Poor'. Further – and typical – sentimentalising of the labouring poor continued. Livingstone was praised for 'the innate simplicity of his character and bearing', for 'dying lonely, far from Blantyre Braes', and for an apparent sense of collectivism (not surprising on the eve of the First World War): 'Blood stained and black, but bright and bold, OUR rights, OUR freedom – uphold'.[92] Yet also in Blaikie's words a decade before, 'he was essentially a man of the people', with 'fellow-feeling' for 'the children of labour'; 'the burden-bearing multitude claimed his sympathies most'.[93]

A cruel childhood involving hard labour also recommended him. At the age of ten, he was sent to the local cotton mill. He clocked on at six and off at eight; temperatures could become stifling, and some children could be expected to crawl or walk up to twenty miles a day, often bent double. As a 'piecer', his job was to tie up loose threads from the spinning jennies, which included enough short breaks to allow him to read a book propped up on the cotton frames, sometimes having to doge flying bobbins from the 'mill girls' aimed at him. He was later promoted to a spinner. He attended the company evening school for two hours, returning home sometimes to study until midnight; one famous story passed down the generations was that he bought a Latin grammar guide with his first wages (though one account insisted he gave his first earnings to his mother). Livingstone later boasted he only read scientific books or travelogues as a boy; the traditional Culpeper's *Herbal* was his first medical book; and ironically, his father beat him with a stick (it would be for the last time) for refusing to read William Wilberforce's *Practical Christianity*.[94] He was the original self-help poster boy.

Many accounts heavily romanticised Livingstone in his adolescence: obsessed with missionary life in the service of others, to the death if need be, and already dreaming of dark, dusky faces. One inspirational biographical treatment, published by the Religious Tract Society, took to the present tense to evoke a boy who, at this time, 'can conceive of nothing more exhilarating than humbly serving the least of human beings ... A strange lad this ... if you like, a little queer, not quite normal, a bit of crank, something of a fanatic'.[95] Locals remembered an ordinary, unexceptional boy, 'just a sulky, quiet, feckless sort o' boy', uninterested in girls, who once made his brother hide a stolen salmon down his trousers and disguise it with a limp; and that the family was 'dour'.[96]

Like so many, Livingstone's first and great passion was for the natural world, roaming the countryside in his spare time collecting plants, flowers and fossils. Science and scientific theory brought him closer to understanding that world, but the religious teaching offered to him, endorsed by his father, wanted him to reject it. Livingstone's family were regulars at the local Scottish Calvinistic Church (the Kirk) and were exceedingly God-fearing. His father, a roving tea salesman, often distributed religious tracts along the way. Also a Sunday school teacher, he was vehemently opposed to alcohol and swearing. Creationism and a belief in the afterlife only for the chosen ones or 'the Elect' increasingly alienated Livingstone from his father and the Church. There is evidence that this caused him to break down sobbing on his own – quite heavy emotional burdens for a child. Since even a mild interest in astrology was akin to the 'devil's work', he was too frightened to keep studying it. He fell out with his father for his lack of interest in reading Christian texts; and one of his Sunday school teachers, on his deathbed implored, 'Now, lad, make religion the everyday business of your life', which, if true, implied that it was not.[97]

1832 had been a defining year for millions.[98] Anger, frustration and openness to new ideas were taking effect. Men like Livingstone's father increasingly resented the rules of the established Scottish church – the Kirk – for its hierarchical control over rural parishes, its demands for money, its imposition of ministers and its lack of interest in missionary work overseas. Neil Livingstone had listened to the preaching of a young Canadian radical minister, Henry Wilkes, at an independent church near Hamilton. Wilkes's attack on the conservative orthodoxy of the Kirk gave

Neil Livingstone the courage to leave the Kirk for this Congregational church, organised on the principles of autonomy in running its affairs, appointment of clergy and interpretations of the Bible. Jeal argues this 'new liberalism' touched father and son.[99] Neil's openness and new church brought them both into contact with more radical preachers for the times, including American preachers, who attracted huge numbers. These were confident, exciting times, reflected in the 1833 Anti-Slavery Act, a victory for humanitarian campaigners and the many supporters who were evangelical Christians or drawn from the working poor, or both.[100]

Livingstone was profoundly shaped by all these events and currents. By the age of twenty, independent reading had brought him into contact with Thomas Dick's pioneering treatise on how religious belief and scientific theory were not incompatible, as Livingstone had feared (a quarryman had once tried to reassure the disbelieving boy collecting fossils –'God had put the shells in them'). Now he underwent a personal conversion, believing it was a 'duty and inestimable privilege immediately to accept salvation by Christ' and because of such 'mercy and grace' towards such a 'depraved and deceitful heart ... it is my desire to show my attachment to the cause of Him who died for me, by devoting my life to His service'.[101] This he wrote in 1838, in support of his application to be accepted for service by the LMS, believing that focusing on the poor with the offer of medical assistance offered the best chance of getting converts.[102]

Personal and global factors are ultimately trumped by the Scottish factor, since Livingstone wanted to become a doctor and then take up missionary work, but medical training was normally still the preserve of the elite. Crucially, however, he was able to save enough money to enrol to study medicine in the University of Glasgow. One legacy of the Scottish Enlightenment was the setting up of medical schools that were deliberately not restricted to the privately educated and that kept costs to a minimum to keep open the possibility of working men entering.[103]

Thus at the end of his second year, in 1838, Livingstone applied to the LMS for consideration as a missionary in China. Initial assessment of Livingstone was not positive. His first tutor, the Reverend Richard Cecil, a tough Congregationalist minister in Essex, thought that there was a problem with 'his heaviness of manner'" and 'rusticity' but that he had 'a good temper and strength of character'.[104] Meanwhile Livingstone was going through the pains of romantic rejection, perhaps for the first time. Despite Livingstone's having sent her some copied love poetry, Catherine Ridley had preferred – and later married – the more genteel and polished Thomas Prentice.[105] Livingstone buried the hurt, insisting he had finished it, but this and subsequent remarks suggest he was bitter and the wounded party.

Livingstone was not blessed with good looks, and had been jilted. As one contemporary described him, 'he was "no bonny"'. He never relaxed, nor did he ever betray a sense of humour. Work brought little solace. He was unable to perform extempore prayer. When he did speak, many people found it difficult to understand what he said: he had an abnormally large uvula at the back of his throat (which he later had surgically removed) and a heavy west-Scottish accent. He could neither sing a note in tune nor play any musical instrument. When asked to give his first sermon, he committed it to memory but in the pulpit was so nervous forgot it and just walked off. 'Ungainly in movement, slow and indistinct of speech', was one verdict, yet the same colleague also waxed lyrical about him after he became famous: 'I grew daily more attached to him. If I were asked why, I should be rather at a loss to reply. There was truly an indescribable charm about him which with all his ungainly ways, and by no means winning face, attracted almost everyone ... a kind of spell'.[106] 'Simple and resolute', was how another remembered him. One adoring biographer compared his powerful personality with that of Napoleon.[107]

It does seem Livingstone could always affect a few men strongly. They responded positively to his bold actions, which perhaps were acts of compensation, a lesson he would put into practice for the rest of his life. For example, he astonished his fellow probationers by walking twenty-seven miles to visit a friend of his father's who had come down to London, then making the return journey in the same day, climbing up a road sign to read the stars when he got lost in the dark. But his dismal praying and preaching all but got him thrown off the programme. One man did speak strongly on his behalf. That intervention, along with his medical skills, seem to have saved him, because when he came before the board a second time he passed, and was instructed to finish his medical training in London. As the fees charged by the Royal London College of Physicians and Surgeons were too high for the LMS, he was told to qualify as a doctor at home. He became a Licentiate of the Faculty of Physicians and Surgeons at Glasgow University in November, 1840, nearly failing after arguing with his examiners over how to use the stethoscope.[108]

Livingstone's suffering from ill health also increased his appeal. He had nearly died from bronchitis and liver disease, having to return home to be nursed. Many in London thought they would never see him again. The LMS then decided he was suitable material for the West Indies, but he had no interest in a region with a white community that had medical doctors already, so he suggested South Africa. From here on, events moved quickly. On 17 November 1840, he said goodbye to his father for the final time. On 20 November, he was ordained as a missionary in Albion Chapel, London, and on 8 December, he boarded the *George*. Three months later, in March 1841, after a voyage that had taken him to Rio de Janeiro (because of a damaged mast), he landed at the Cape, before heading to Algoa Bay and then journeying inland to Kuruman, a mission station amongst the Tswana people, roughly six hundred miles into the interior (in today's Botswana) north-east of Cape Town. He was twenty-eight years old.

Livingstone would embody the British anti-slavery tradition. In June 1840, he had attended an open meeting of the Society for the Extinction of the Slave Trade and the Civilisation of Africa. In a crowded Exeter Hall, he had heard William Wilberforce's successor, the charismatic Thomas Buxton, argue passionately that only normal trade and Christian conversion could stop the evil. The anti-slavery campaign, cutting-edge and radical, appealed to lower-class men and women in very emotional ways. For many Victorians, the slave trade was the supreme evil of their times. The 1833 Parliamentary Bill had freed slaves in the British Empire, but the slave trade continued. In the age of atonement, many Victorians felt guilty and that they still owed Africa for their contribution to the spread of the trade.[109] Buxton put forward a practical formula in a book and organised an anti-slavery expedition on the west coast of Africa in 1841. Buxton's model would be Livingstone's second bible. Because Livingstone was living in London, a visitor had called in at his lodgings. Dr Robert Moffat had been in the employ of the LMS since 1816 and was a celebrity missionary. 'Would I do for Africa?', Livingstone is reputed to have asked him. 'Yes, if you are prepared to leave occupied ground and push on to the North'.[110]

Added to Livingstone's humble origins and personal commitment to anti-slavery and evangelicalism, it also helped his persona that he was a married man, then widowed. First, he sensibly married into missionary royalty. Mary Moffat, daughter of Robert, aged twenty-three, and fluent in Setswana. As Julie Davidson writes of her, 'She knew how to butcher and dry meat, preserve fruit and vegetables, bake bread, make candles, soap and clothes, improvise remedies, manage servants and barter with the Tswana ... she knew her worth, and knew it was valued by her parents and other mission families ... At this stage in her life Mary was not the victim she later became'.

Without this extremely strong, kind and generous woman, who gave him not only respectability and support but also a family name that carried weight among many chiefs in the interior, Livingstone would not have escaped the mediocrity of his own circumstances and abilities in Africa, going from 'worthy but remote from brilliant' to international celebrity. Mary's reputation and family name opened up the interior to him, enabling him to travel further and further afield. She was also willing to make sacrifices for him: once, because she and their young children were threatening to hold him back, she agreed to be sent back to Scotland with them (a much greater sacrifice than she could ever have imagined because her rupture from her home and all that was familiar to her, and poor treatment, all but destroyed her health, sanity and religious belief).

Livingstone received an enthusiastic welcome when he returned to Britain after successfully crossing the African continent from west to east – the first white man to do so (see Map P.1). This included an audience with Queen Victoria, honorary degrees from two universities, the freedom of six major cities and, probably most prized of all, an RGS Gold Medal. His geographical achievement had been immense and set off a Victorian feel-good factor: now, 'literally, the whole world is full of our labours', the *Daily News* reported. The propaganda and myth-making were already in full swing in the press; the attack by the lion,[111] for example, was now presented as a consequence of Livingstone having taunted local natives for their 'cowardice', which then inspired them to take action; and 'he was received with open arms by every man in Great Britain' interested in Africa or in 'physical endurance and matchless perseverance'. He was wined and dined at the tables of the rich and famous, and he certainly was not following in his father's footsteps as an abstainer. The time he spent with his family was limited, not least because he considered Mary something of an embarrassment in polite society.

Thousands remembered an ordinary, awkward man from one of his many public talks. He still wore the same naval-type working man's cap he had on his travels. His face was so sunburnt he was often described as 'a foreign-looking person ... when he speaks you think him first to be a Frenchman'. His arm hung limply to one side, disabled from the lion incident. And his accent was difficult to understand having not spoken much English for sixteen years, as he would explain, on top of a Scottish lilt. He was considered 'plain' with 'an expression of severity'; his style often 'unanimated', his manner 'awkward'.

These factors only increased his popularity. His effect on university students became the stuff of legends, from deafening clapping and stamping in Cambridge to the subduing of usually unruly students sitting at the back of the lecture hall at Glasgow University. Their 'peashooters, sticks and other instruments' were put down at the sight of the 'gaunt and wrinkled [man] ... dark by the sun and with one arm hanging useless'. Significantly, what newspapers often commented on, reflecting a general dissatisfaction and cynicism towards public figures, was his honesty and lack of pretence or affectation, being as he was, or so it was said, without ego or motivation of financial reward. The *Daily News* once described him as 'one of the few men whose words are realities'. His view of Africa was positive and dynamic for the times, full of commerce and Christianity, as illustrated by the huge stress he put on the financial rewards to be had from opening up the continent, especially when he gave talks at the cities honouring him, and to organisations such as the Chamber of Commerce and the Cotton Supply Association, although he did mention mutual advantages and anti-slavery. The rise of the Victorian press made him an international celebrity.

Livingstone's *Missionary Travels and Researches in South Africa*, published in 1857, became a best-seller. Among his literary admirers, for his natural style, was Charles Dickens. 'The effect of it upon me', Dickens wrote, 'has been to lower my opinion of my own character ... I used to think I possessed the moral virtues of courage, patience, resolution and self-control', but they were 'nothing but plated gold'. Dickens's review in *Household Words* set Victorian pulses racing with the 'manly truthfulness', 'unaffected modesty' and 'unflinching honesty' he found in the account. He also praised the book for lacking 'sectarian influences', even though it was the work of a religious man preaching the gospel. Also worthy of praise was the absence of the kinds of 'flipant mockery' and 'wearisome self-conceit' usually found in travel narratives. *The Telegraph* described the book as 'a national monument, rare, noble and enduring'. *The Times* published extracts, the second in its Christmas Day edition, 1857. It sold 70,000 copies in its first edition, netting Livingstone a much-needed £9,000. Livingstone was lucky to be living through a print revolution and he had been aware of his fame spreading. However, it was not just the new technology. As Professor Andrew Roberts writes, 'Livingstone the loner talks much to himself', but also with others, whose thoughts interact with his own experiences. And this 'internal debate, leavened with a pawky, sardonic Scots humour is what gives enduring life to Livingstone's narratives. Among 19th-century travellers in Africa, Livingstone remains the best of company'.[112]

Attitudes to the book were also affected by the wider context of the times. The public had been reading the blood-chilling accounts of the Indian Mutiny and the Crimean War not so long before. A good news story about Britain overseas was appealing. Also, the book had been published in the knowledge that Livingstone was leaving again soon to continue his 'great work' despite the dangerous conditions. The public had willingly set up testimonials to help Livingstone's work in Africa civilising heathen. Although Livingstone returned to Britain a failure after his second African exploration, this personal setback, which he put to one side, merely added to his reputation after he died. He was the people's hero, a good man who had lived a flawed and fabulous life.

As Professor Roberts observes, this adoration was not accidental. Livingstone wrote with a strong sense of his own place in history and of the place of the nineteenth century in the history of the Christian cause. He was a missionary first and 'quite self-consciously ... constructed his career in order to make the most of the common ground between the secular and the sacred – and much of this common ground, in the middle of the 19th century was in tropical Africa'. He was 'a "moral steam engine – or giant with one idea" – the phrase bestowed on Thomas Clarkson, the abolitionist, by his friend Coleridge'.[113]

Poetry in Motion: Last Letters, Intimacy & Loneliness

So, as Livingstone's body drew near in April 1874, a public drilled in his life story once more felt an intimate connection with him: they heard him speak directly to them when unposted letters written by Livingstone reached the Foreign Office and were published. These included letters to Gordon Bennett and Henry Morton Stanley. Bennett sent a copy of his letter to the London office of his *New York Herald*. Subsequently, emotive headlines appeared in other newspapers: 'A last letter from Livingstone'; the 'Last Days of Livingstone'. In the *Christian World*, 'How he died', was introduced as 'a profoundly pathetic tale' which would 'move many a reader to tears'. The news that Jacob Wainwright, 'a noble lad', was bearing the body home was comforting because it would 'do much to stir the missionary impulse in English hearts'.[114]

Several newspapers chose to reproduce long extracts of Livingstone's own words. The *News of the World* and the *Glasgow Herald*, like many newspapers, offered Livingstone a powerful posthumous platform from which to decry slavery.[115] His targeted letters had the desired effect of underscoring his liberal (rather than imperial) impulses. One illustration of this was Livingstone the feminist: the coverage to his apparent promotion of the equal rights of women. 'Dr Livingstone's visit to a harem' was a thinly veiled attack on Arab barbarity. Livingstone recorded how 'a half-caste Arab prince' believed that all women were 'utterly and irretrievably bad', contrasting this with his own belief in women's right to liberty and his distaste for a chief's polygamy, detailing how the first wife, aged and deferential, always knelt 'until he had gone passed' (in contrast to the younger ones, with 'fine shapes').[116] In an age when the struggle for women to be enfranchised was beginning to take shape, this sympathy would have greatly increased Livingstone's appeal to women.

The press also circulated the growing myths about Livingstone's death. The two great rivals for Livingstone's affections and close associations, H.M. Stanley and the Reverend Waller, had much to do with this. *The Graphic* (for which Stanley wrote) informed its readers that there was 'something very touching in the details just received of the great traveller's death'.[117] 'Build me a hut to die in', encouraged a view of an agonised last few days; now, his last words were 'I am going home'. This kind of detail was typical of Livingstone's printed self in his published journals: the self-display of his inner emotional life and his recording of the everyday, banal details of the life of an ordinary person. Now, it extended to the moments leading up to his death. His audience thus lived and died with him.

In the build-up to the funeral, all over the country, ordinary men and women wrote eulogies, some of which were sent to the RGS or published in the press. These letters evidence a groundswell of popular emotion about to climax. One eulogy, typed on mourning paper, began: 'Who shall write the epitaph to the sainted dead?'[118] All classes, it appears from the evidence. One writer described 'a surging wave of feeling rolls across the land'; another described a nation 'sadly mourning for the ending, of a brave and loving heart'. Others imagined the funeral, when 'hearts of love, with tearful eyes, gaze upon the sleeping shrine'; or 'Open the Abbey doors and bear him in, To sleep with King and Statesmen ... The missionary come of weaver-kin'. One handwritten eulogy from a self-described 'unknown person' read: 'Calm lies the pilgrim old, still rests the martyr bold, Dead – his brave heart cold, oh how we loved him'.

Many focused on Livingstone's physical suffering. A poem published in *Punch* described a 'worn frame', the 'agony of fever, brain and boil'; another, 'his shrivell'd brow'.[119] Yet many also brought him back to life: 'He being dead, yet speaketh'; another, 'Speaks he yet, although now dead'. The large quantity of poetic verse, often written anonymously on mourning paper, points to the build-up of a well of emotional capital, of what has been termed an 'emotional regime', potentially volatile and malleable.

Africa became a sensational backdrop for Livingstone's life and death, where a palm tree like a hand came down at his deathbed. It was a place where he was lauded for ceaselessly toiling 'To raise as Man, the slave-doomed Africa' and where he struck 'the chains from the Slaves fettered hands'. Africans were synonymous with slaves in popular discourse. For an anonymous poet in Cardiff, Westminster Abbey was the correct resting place for Livingstone's body because Livingstone was being buried with men who 'fought for truth and right in evil days ... struck off the gyres which manacled the slave ... a brother and a man'. In a revealing and rare working-class evocation of empire, these were men 'who spread her empire o'er the earth'.[120]

As the intimate connection with Livingstone was renewed through newspaper coverage of the slights and his letters, so an emotional framework of sentimentalised feeling elided into political consciousness. Hume's model of the fluctuating situations of moral evaluation is useful here: the creation of a moment when 'internal and external sentiment' merged. Livingstone's death as a cry of humanity, a cry from God himself, it seemed, revived the politics of Britain as an anti-slaving power for the next generation.

Not everyone was in an inner state of emotional turmoil. The *Catholic Opinion* had earlier extolled Livingstone's virtues.[121] Yet three days before his funeral, readers were informed that he had died with 'Catholic sympathies in his heart'.[122] He had apparently bestowed huge praise on the Catholic missions and written sarcastically about the failures of 'the so called Anglican "Central African Mission"'. This was taken up by other members of the clergy, too. The *Western Mail* reprinted a sermon on Livingstone delivered by the rector of Merthyr. He used the death to reiterate criticism of Livingstone, demanding why, over the last twenty-five years since bishops had been appointed in colonies, precious little evidence existed that much work had been carried out in the diocese of Central Africa. There was no point in 'days of humiliation', he thundered, until the money collected went beyond these 'telescope' bishops.[123]

Nevertheless, the prospect of a funeral in London was now gathering momentum. The *Christian World* hoped for a funeral that would be 'the most impressive spectacle which the present generation of Englishmen has ever witnessed', because the moral effect would 'surpass that which is produced by the burial of any mere King or woman, when he ... began life as a factory boy'.[124] Being 'the first of his class' to be buried in Westminster Abbey was a particularly popular theme within the Welsh and Scottish press coverage.[125] For some, this was a welcome reverse of the 'cheapening' of a burial in the 'Valhalla of the nation' or a peerage; rewards less for noble deeds than for 'meeting with a volley a hoard of barbarians rushing down a hill, or else giving a vote to prop up a falling minister'.[126] Sometimes, intertwined with distaste for violence, press coverage of the treatment of Livingstone expressed mid-Victorian concerns about the moral decline of their institutions and a lack of heart in the attitude of their so-called betters.

Conclusion: 'Hearts of Love' for the 'Slave-Doomed Africa'

Livingstone would be interred in Westminster Abbey, but only just. A funeral took place despite the misgivings, and in spite of the meagre resources typical of 'empire on the cheap' in British Africa. Pushing for a big imperial ceremony had been a powerful network of mutual interests: commercial entrepreneurs and Christian evangelicals. In the middle of these was the journalism of Stanley. Newspapers had played a decisive role in the staging of Livingstone's funeral. Press coverage increased the support for Livingstone among ordinary Victorians and sentimentalised him (and them, in their grief). Popular feeling had been aroused not just for a peaceful martyr to anti-slavery who was loved by Africans: a perception that Livingstone was being badly treated was a significant factor in the growing public sentimentality towards him, as his body travelled ever closer to Britain – to such an extent that supporting his mission also constituted a gesture against the ruling classes, the high public offices and the high church.

Calls to honour Livingstone, and to thereby continue a very British, peaceful fight against slavery, were not just an expression of powerful financial interests that found an eloquent spokesperson in Stanley, successfully uniting imperialism and humanitarianism. Such sentiments were also deeply felt by many ordinary people and played an important role in the 1870s, partly as a device for displaying moral sensibility in an age of disenfranchisement. These dynamics helped to produce an image of Livingstone as a wronged saint who had, by peaceful means, devoted his life to saving Africa from slavery. Africa became homogenised, a continent that needed saving. Livingstone became whiter; Africa, blackened.

To achieve its long-term aims, the imperial policy of intervention in Africa needed to manipulate human emotion. It did so by using the rhetoric of peaceful humanitarianism. What we see evolving is an important moment in that process: the construction of a powerful emotional arena that would receive Livingstone's body and endow it with a large amount of symbolic capital for generations. The vibrant Victorian press was at the centre of a community of grief, and the emotion regime would have its way.

NOTES

1 Part of an exchange between Sir Humphrey Appleby, PM James Hacker and Civil Servant Sir Bernard Woolley, in Series 2, Episode 4 'A Conflict of

Interests', *Yes, Prime Minister* (1987). www.youtube.com/watch?v=
DGscoaUWW2M. Accessed 16 June 2014.

2 Telegram from Capt Prideaux to FO, 12 January 1874 and from Capt Lindsey
   Brine to Rear Admiral Cummings, 15 January 1874, DL 4.18.1-2, RGS
   Archives.

3 *Penny Illustrated News*, 31 January 1874.

4 Letter from Lt Cameron, Unyamyembe, 16 October 1873, DL 4/11–4/19,
   RGS Archive.

5 Capt Lindsey Brine, HMS Briton, Zanzibar, to Rear Admiral Cummings, ibid.

6 Aled Jones, *Powers of the Press: Newspapers, Power and the Public in Nineteenth-
   Century England (The Nineteenth Century Series)*, (Routledge, 1996); Simon
   Potter, *News and the British World. The Emergence of an Imperial Press System*,
   (Oxford: Clarendon Press, 2003).

7 *Christian World*, 24 April 1874.

8 *Daily Telegraph*, 27 January 1874.

9 Hopkins, 'Explorers' Tales', 671. See Beau Riffenburgh, *The Myth of the
   Explorer: The Press, Sensationalism and Geographical Discovery* (Oxford: Oxford
   University Press, 1994).

10 Stanley, *How I Found Livingstone*, 533. A Dr Hosmer.

11 Ibid., 238.

12 D. Cannadine, 'War and Death, Grief and Mourning in Modern Britain',
   in J. Whaley (ed.), *Mirrors of Mortality: Studies in the Social History of Death*
   (London: Routledge, 1981), 190. According to Hopkins, fear of the afterlife
   because of his illegitimacy unlocks much of Stanley's life since he 'set himself
   a series of abnormal tests that would enable him to achieve fame, respect and
   redemption from a sin he had not committed'. Hopkins, 'Explorers' Tales',
   669–84.

13 *Christian World*, 30 January 1874.

14 *Times*, 3 February 1874.

15 *Aberdeen Journal*, 11 February 1874, and *Glasgow Herald*, 19 February 1874.

16 Janet Livingstone to John Murray, 13 February 1874, quoted in Wolffe, *Great
   Deaths*, 139, fn 8.

17 *East Kent, Faversham and Sittingbourne Gazette*, 21 February 1874.

18 *Manchester Guardian*, 19 February 1874; *Sheffield Daily Telegraph*, 24
   February 1874.

19 *Daily Telegraph*, 28 January 1874.

20 *Daily Telegraph*, 7 January 1865, quoted in O. Cook, 'The immortalisation of
   David Livingstone', unpublished BA dissertation, Department of History,
   London School of Economics, 2011, 19.

21 Poem by C.H.B., 'David Livingstone', reprinted in *Hampshire Chronicle*, 18
   April 1874.

22 Reader responses to 'Do You Know … ', *Southampton Evening Echo, c.*19–22
   March 1930, David Livingstone Collection, Southampton County Council
   Library.

23 *Southampton Observer and Winchester News*, 18 April 1874, Hampshire County
   Archives, Winchester Library.

24 Typescript of letter from Holmwood, DL/4/18/1, RGS Archives.

25 For example see Jeal, *Stanley*, 173, 178, 192.

26 *Christian World*, 27 February 1874, 822.

27 Ibid.

28 See Oliver Cook generally.

29 *Catholic Opinion*, 18 April 1874; *London Illustrated News*, 18 April 1874; Sir William Ferguson, writing of him in *The Lancet*, published in *The Times* and republished in the *Western Mail*, 18 April 1874.

30 Duke of Argyll, Reflections in 1913, Livingstone Collection, Box 3, Jacket A, SOAS Archives.

31 Dean Stanley, 'The Mission of the Traveller', funeral sermon, 19 April 1874, Westminster Abbey, 176. Westminster Abbey Collection.

32 Ibid.

33 *Daily Telegraph*, 6 January 1865, and *Daily News*, 7 November 1864, both quoted in Cook, 'The immortalisation of David Livingstone', 21–2.

34 Crawford, *Back to the Long Grass*, 289–90.

35 Campbell, *Wanderings in Central Africa*, 157–64.

36 See Suzanne Miers, *Britain and the Ending of the Slave Trade* (London: Longman, 1975).

37 LMS Board Minutes, 13 April 1874, Item 2k, 551–2, Box 38 LMS Collection, SOAS Archives.

38 Many died in poverty. See generally Simpson, *Dark Companions* and Chapter Four.

39 Compiled from a range of British newspapers that published detailed accounts of the funeral in April 1874.

40 Simpson, *Dark Companions*, 101; account by Mr Hutchinson, secretary of the CMS given to the RGS at a meeting on 23 February 1874, reported in the *Daily Telegraph*, 24 April 1874, 5.

41 D.W. Bebbington, *Evangelicalism in Modern Britain: A History from the 1730s to the 1980s* (London: Routledge, 1989), esp. 141.

42 For the long duration of this British social and religious movement, see Seymour Drescher, 'Emperors of the World: British Abolitionism and Imperialism', in Peterson (ed.), *Abolitionism and Imperialism*, 129–49.

43 LMS Board Minutes, 30 March 1874, 539–41, Box 38 LMS Collection, SOAS Archives.

44 Dean Arthur Penrhyn Stanley, Book of Recollections, ms, fos 36–7, Westminster Abbey Library; Certification Note from Sir William Ferguson, 17 April 1874, RCO Box 5, Westminster Abbey Library.

45 John, Chapter X, 16, 'The Mission of the Traveller', Dean Stanley's funeral sermon, 19 April 1874, Westminster Abbey, reprinted in his edited collection of sermons and in many newspapers as 'Dean Stanley on Livingstone', Westminster Abbey Library.

46 Stanley, Recollections, fos 36–7, Westminster Abbey Library.

47 Editorial, 18 April 1874, *Southampton Observer and Winchester News*, Hampshire County Records Office.

48 *Christian World*, 17 April 1874, 242.

49 Ibid.

50 A. Temple Paterson, *A History of Southampton, 1700–1914*, 3 vols. (Southampton: Southampton University Press, 1966), iii, *Setbacks and Recoveries, 1868–1914*.

51 He is also credited with having hosted, later in his career, a large meeting of the High Court of the Ancient Order of Forresters.

52 *Hampshire Advertiser*, 1 April 1874, 2.

53 According to local historian Genevieve Bailey, most of the council were Freemasons at this time. Notes from a telephone conversation, April 2002.

54 Record of Council Meeting, 1 April 1874, Council Minute Book, 1874, 602, Southampton City Council Archives.

55 See Huzzey, *Freedom Burning*.

56 Disraeli Papers, BodL, Dep.Hughenden, 1 April 1874, fos 65–6, Oxford University Library.

57 *Hampshire Advertiser*, editorial, 4 April 1874.

58 For example, Captain Prideaux wrote to inform the council that he had received payment for Halima, Livingstone's cook; previously, in July, he had written to say that awarding the men medals was 'undesirable' but that Chuma might have a 'silver watch'; Council Minute Book, entries for 10 November 1874 and 13 July 1874 respectively, RGS Archive.

59 Council Minute Book, 12 January 1874; Committee Minute Book, 23 January 1874, RGS Archives; Simpson, *Dark Companions*, 100.

60 Committee Minute Book, 23 February 1874 and 9 March 1874, RGS Archives.

61 Council Minute Book, 23 March 1874, RGS Archives.

62 And he was Welsh. See Felix Driver, *Geography Militant: Cultures of Exploration and Empire* (Oxford, UK: Blackwell), esp. 127–31, and generally Riffenburgh, *The Myth of the Explorer*.

63 Casada, 'Verney Lovett Cameron', 206.

64 See Jeal, *Stanley*.

65 Derby to Disraeli, 2 March 1874, Disraeli Papers, BodL, Dep.Hughenden, 55/3, fos 71–82, Bodleian Library, Oxford.

66 Ibid., and fos 63–4; Northcote to Derby, 10 April 1974, quoted in Wolffe, *Great Deaths*, 140, fn 23.

67 Bartle Frere to Disraeli, 1 April 1874, Disraeli Papers, BodL, Dep. Hughenden, 55/3, fos 61–2, Bodleian Library, Oxford.

68 Reply to Gurney, Disraeli Papers, BodL, Dep.Hughenden, 55/3, fos 65–6, Bodleian Library, Oxford.

69 This was chaired by Sir Bartle Frere and consisted of four other persons: Committees Record Book; Special Committees, 103–4, RGS Archives.

70 *Times*, 9 April 1874, quoted in Wolffe, *Great Deaths*, 139–40.

71 This figure was retrospectively increased some months later. See Wolffe, ibid.

72 Proceedings of the RGS, 13 April 1873, 243; 'David Livingstone's Funeral, 1874', in 'Recollections', Dean Stanley, Westminster Abbey Manuscripts.

73 *Telegraph*, 24 February 1874.

74 For example, *Aberdeen Journal*, 18 February 1874.

75 *Southampton Observer*, 1 April 1874.

76 *Western Mail*, 1 April 1874.

77 *Glasgow Herald*, 14 April 1874.

78 *Cosmopolitan*, 16 April 1874.

79 *Cosmopolitan*, the *Leeds Mercury* and the *London Illustrated News* illustrate the wide publicity that this received.

80 Notice in *Pall Mall Gazette*, 17 April 1874.

81 *The Graphic*, 4 April 1874, 310.

82 Voters had to be male, over twenty-one and subject to a property qualification as to eligibility. In 1867, the Conservative government introduced the Parliamentary Reform Act. This increased the electorate to almost 2.5 million. The most important change was the granting of the vote to occupiers in the boroughs (people who rented properties rather than owning them) and as a result the electorate in some of the newer towns in England and Scotland increased dramatically. www.bbc.co.uk/education/guides/z9hnn39/revision/2.

83 MacNair, *Livingstone the Liberator*, 26.

84 This was the last battle on British soil and was the final attempt of the Stuart monarchy to challenge the Hanoverians. One army made up of Scots, French and Irish was defeated in an hour, with large casualties by the Hanoverian forces, made up of English, Ulster, German, Austrian and Scottish forces.

85 Blaikie, *The Personal Life of David Livingstone*, 4.

86 MacNair, *Livingstone the Liberator*, 28–32.

87 Blaikie, *The Personal Life of David Livingstone*, 6–7.

88 T. Banks Maclachlan, *David Livingstone* (Edinburgh: Oliphant Anderson & Ferrier, 1901), 10.

89 Ibid., 2–3.

90 A National Covenant had been signed in 1638 binding those in opposition to the Stuart monarchy's insistence it was God's representative on earth. The Presbyterian Church opposed such a notion of divine monarchy. Many lowlanders were persecuted and tortured and in 1678 a force of Highlander troops attacked and pillaged the area. www.covenanter.org.uk.

91 For example, 'New story of David Livingstone's youth' by Flora Eglinton, Box 3, Jacket A, Folder 1, SOAS Archives.

92 W Jolly. 'Dr David Livingstone', Box 3, Jacket A, Folder 1, SOAS Archives.

93 Blaikie, *The Personal Life of David Livingstone*, 13.

94 Starritt, *Livingstone the Pioneer*, 20–1.

95 Ibid., 12.

96 MacNair, *Livingstone the Liberator*, 35.

97 Starritt, *Livingstone the Pioneer*, 20.

98 1832 had been an important year in the slow history of the extension of the franchise to all adult men and women. Bowing to public pressure, the Act of 1832 tackled corruption and increased the electorate from around 366,000 to 650,000, about 18 per cent of the total adult male population in England and Wales (one in five), but eligibility was tied to economic wealth. The vast majority of working-class men, and all women, were still excluded from voting. www.bl.uk/learning/histcitizen/21cc/struggle/chartists1/historicalsources/source2/reformact.html.

99 Jeal, *Livingstone*, 12–14.

100 For a fuller discussion, see Chapter Three.

101 Blaikie, *The Personal Life of David Livingstone*, 11–12.

102 MacNair, *Livingstone the Liberator*, 41.

103 Brian Stanley, 'The Missionary and the Rainmaker: David Livingstone, the Bakwena, and the Nature of Medicine', *Social Sciences and Missions* 27, 2–3 (2014): 1–18, doi: http://dx.doi.org/10.1163/18748945-02702003.

104 MacNair, *Livingstone the Liberator*, 46.

105 Jeal, *Livingstone*, 20.

106 Blaikie, *The Personal Life of David Livingstone*, quoting recollections from Livingstone's friend and lodging companion, the Reverend Joseph Moore, 20–1.

107 Starritt, *Livingstone the Pioneer*, 27.

108 Blaikie, *The Personal Life of David Livingstone*, 29.

109 For a fuller discussion of the slave trade and the anti-slavery movement, see Chapter Three.

110 MacNair, *Livingstone the Liberator*, 51.

111 Travelling through what is now Botswana, Livingstone fought with a lion and became famous for trying to defend the livestock belonging to the village he was staying in, resulting in an encounter that seriously wounded his left arm. He reset the broken bone himself which healed enough for him to shoot a gun and lift heavy items. However, he was unable lift the arm again higher than his shoulder.

112 A.D. Roberts, 'David Livingstone: The Man and His Work', lecture given at the National Portrait Gallery, 16 May 1996, 19. Unpublished draft kindly given to me by Professor A.D. Roberts.

113 Ibid., 3.

114 *Christian World*, 3 April 1874.

115 For example, this letter to Gordon Bennett containing the material was published over two days in the *Glasgow Herald*, 10–11 April 1874, and in the *News of the World*, 20 April 1874.

116 *News of the World*, 20 April 1874.

117 *Graphic*, 4 April 1874.

118 These extracts are from a collection of handwritten and typed eulogies, mostly anonymous, sent to the RGS, DL/5/4, RGS Archive; and poems printed in newspapers before and immediately after the funeral.

119 This was republished; for example, see the *Glasgow Herald*, 4 February 1874.

120 *Western Mail*, 18 April 1874. For the popular view of the appropriateness of the Abbey, see also the *Dundee Courier and Argus*, 13 April 1874.

121 *Catholic Opinion*, 4 February 1874, 167.

122 Ibid., 15 April 1874, 319.

123 *Western Mail*, 22 April 1874.

124 *Christian World*, 10 April 1874.

125 *Wrexham Advertiser*, 11 April 1874.

126 *Western Mail*, 22 April 1874.

2 Laying to Rest a Victorian Myth

The 'Lost Heart of the Nation', Victorian
Sentimentality & the Rebirth of Moral Imperialism

He will be home, amongst his people, once again, forever.

John Irvine, ITV correspondent, reporting the funeral of
Nelson Mandela, 8 December 2013

If there is love between us, inconceivably delicious, and profitable will
our intercourse be; if not your time is lost and you will only annoy me.
I shall seem to you stupid, and the reputation I have false. All my good
is magnetic, and I educate not by my lessons, but by going about my
business.

Ralph Waldo Emerson, *Representative Men*[1]

This chapter tells the story of the four most influential days in the history of imperial propaganda. The climax of a combination of press
coverage, popular sentiment and public mobilisation would transform
Livingstone's death into a rich emotional resource for the project of
an empire in Africa. Livingstone's chaotic and bodged funeral wavered
between a wake, a celebration of Britain's anti-slavery tradition and a
comic operetta. But a clear path towards national redemption came out
of it. Thousands, primed by press coverage, flocked to see the cortège and
attend the ceremonials. A spontaneous outbreak of weeping at the sight
of his coffin took many onlookers by surprise. It was not just the affecting nature of his death which produced a powerful surge of feeling. What
gathered in strength was a highly sentimental image of Livingstone's love
for his African 'boys', their corresponding love of him and the suffering
of Africa.

As such, this event brings the history of empire closer to the history
of emotions. Spontaneous and manipulated feeling merged to become a
powerful force shaping Britain's conversation about Africa and its subsequent will to empire. Nevertheless, it was a case of the local intersecting
with the global, of the inner life marrying with the external circumstances.
Through feeling and emotion, many men and women in 1874 were staking a claim to political respectability. Soft sensibility was hard currency.
Press coverage once again played a crucial role in shaping this emotional

conversation between empire and Africa. Yet the press was polyphonic; the interest groups in Britain wanting to direct that conversation and use the press were particularly diverse and multiple at this point. Out of this emerged an imperial project in Africa more widely shared, but it nearly did not happen this way.

Saved from the Jaws of Disaster

'Let England Mourn'. This was the title of one of a number of special anthems written to mark the return of Livingstone. Oswald Allen's 'LIVINGSTONE: The Great National Song' was advertised in the press as 'suitable for lady and gentleman', priced at a tempting three pence including postage.[2] But would England be denied the chance? The *Malwa* was scheduled to dock at Southampton on Monday, 13 April 1874. Up until the week before, the dean's offer of Westminster Abbey had still been open, somewhere between the Houses of Parliament and the RGS's headquarters in Savile Row.

Livingstone's corpse was a hot topic. National and regional newspapers were reporting events and stirring up speculation. Southampton's organising committee was micromanaging a major three-day event. The American Geographical Society had contacted the Southampton council asking for details so it could be observed on both sides of the Atlantic simultaneously. Suddenly they were hit with the news that the *Malwa*, at the request of the family, would head straight to London. Rumours of the remains being stored deep in the bowels of the ship had added credibility. Immediately, Southampton's mayor and town clerk sped up to London and called on the Foreign Office, demanding the coffin be dropped off at Southampton. Two days later, on Friday, Lord Teuterdon confirmed Lord Derby's reassurances.[3] Local journalists praised their officials for ensuring that 'we shall have the melancholy satisfaction of receiving on behalf of our age and our nation, one who belongs, not to our age and nation only, but to the world'.[4]

No expense was spared; no detail overlooked. The weekend before, an official welcoming party was put up at a local hotel: Livingstone's blood relatives, Dr Moffat (his father-in-law), Henry Morton Stanley, the hunter-traveller William Webb, the Reverend Horace Waller, Admiral Sir William Hall and Arthur Laing, the Zanzibar merchant who had looked after Livingstone's body after it left HMS *Vulture*. On the Saturday, the mayor hosted an impromptu dinner. On the Sunday, churches and chapels preached special sermons commemorating Livingstone, some of which were delivered by the ordained visitors, Waller included. All flags were flown at half mast.

Not everyone was pleased. The *Southampton Times* fretted as to how 'information could be conveyed to those African tribes' by whom 'the wonderful white man has been for 5 and 20 years known and respected, whether by beating of drums or firing of guns, in some rude way or other'. And, when the town council published an official programme detailing the arrangements, it was criticised for being 'an all official affair'. Relevant societies and individuals had to apply to the committee for permission to join the procession. Ominously, concerns were raised about an absence of information regarding the funeral arrangements in London.

Villagers started to arrive on the Sunday evening. When the *Malwa* came into view early the next morning, all local railway stations would be telegraphed so that more people could be brought in. However, on Monday morning 'hundreds of persons of all classes and conditions' were left standing around, having assembled in pouring rain. A storm had blown up in the night out at sea. Two emergency meetings later, at 4 p.m., it was decided that, even if Livingstone arrived that day, he must not be brought ashore. Leaflets announcing that the body would now arrive the next day were circulated.

Tuesday proved to be 'another day of watching and waiting; ... of disappointment'. A storm had blown in out at sea during the night. We will never know how close the steamship came to sinking in the violent storm, with the loss of Livingstone's remains, but the conditions were so bad that a woman gave birth prematurely to twins and – unconnected – the *Malwa*'s engines flooded.

Finally, at 6 a.m. on Wednesday, 15 April, the *Malwa* appeared, despite a heavy gale during Tuesday night. Onlookers, including young apprentices from the town, gathered. But the *Malwa*, having been stuck out at sea, had now run out of coal, so had to make for the docks to refuel. Since the docks were close to the railway station, it was suggested that Livingstone's body would leave for London from there. But the council, having invested so much effort into its arrangements, refused. The reception committee had chartered a special boat, the *Queen*, to transport Livingstone's body to the Royal Pier, from where a grand procession would wind its way through the town. At another meeting, the council got its way. A steam tender took a small party of close family, friends and journalists out to meet the badly damaged ship. As they arrived, the ship's funnel let out a belch of thick black smoke. The *Southampton Times* reported this as 'a remarkable incident' since 'it covered the ship like an enormous pall'. The coffin had been placed in the ship's mailroom. The dark room was lit by sailors holding lanterns, described in some accounts as 'a couple of Manilla men and Lascars'. According to one report, 'this was a scene likely to be long remembered'.

Figure 2.1 Southampton's funeral procession for Livingstone, 15 April 1874, as depicted in many newspapers at the time. Photo by DeAgostini/Getty Images.

From then on, events went to plan. The coffin was hoisted onto the small steamship. The P&O company flag over the coffin was replaced with a Union Jack and 'a magnificent wreath of immortelles'. By this time, all ships, public buildings and foreign consulates were flying their flags at half mast. The boat proceeded to the Royal Pier, where those involved in the procession disembarked and made their way to Audit House, from where the ceremonial procession would begin. Livingstone was being received like royalty. This was the closest he would get to a state reception with full honours (see Figure 2.1).

Livingstone's Grand Victorian Wake

The arrival of Livingstone's body on English soil was a huge media event. Jacob Wainwright became the focus of press attention. Detailed descriptions of his appearance featured in newspapers across the country. According to *The Times*, Wainwright was not more than 5 feet in height and wears close woolly hair, his nose is almost flat ... whilst his lips were thicker than usual having being struck on the mouth the previous day by a rope.

Wainwright was an adult but naturally short, which fed the racialising impulse to call him a boy. Such scrutiny must have been extremely stressful, and when the *Malwa* docked, Wainwright was humiliated by being made to take off his clothes and change into something considered more suitable. He had been wearing 'a pea-green jacket and a pair of fieldglasses slung over his shoulder'. Nothing was going to get in the way of the council's determination to put on a respectable show.

Livingstone's remains drew massive crowds despite the false starts. From Audit House, the mayor and Livingstone's family led the way down to the Royal Pier, preceded by policemen and the band of the 1st Hants Volunteer Engineers, as yet silent in black frock coats and top hats. They were followed by every municipal and county office holder, town councillors, harbour officials, magistrates, aldermen and Sir Fred Perkins MP. Then came the local clergy; representatives from the RGS, the Medical Society and the medical profession; American and German consular officials; Colonel Lacy (staff officer of the Pensioners); members of the press; and Guardians of the Southampton Incorporation. Behind these came members of the Council of the Hartley Institute, the members of the Southampton School Board, the committee of every literary and philosophical society in the town, the executive council of the Ancient Order of Forresters, the Royal Navy Reserve and 'representatives of other bodies', including fifty Nonconformist school teachers. Nothing on this scale would materialise in London.

At 11 a.m., the procession reached the Royal Pier and prepared to receive the coffin. From here, the council changed the order, putting themselves in front of the coffin, which was mounted on a gun carriage, as in a state funeral. Following directly behind were family and friends. Front of the queue 'strode the tall thin figure of Henry Stanley'. 'It was a great sight', recalled one onlooker in 1930, 'and has remained vividly in my memory ever since'. The procession formed a 'long black line'. The numbers swelled with naval reserve men marching under their own flag and schoolchildren, sponsored by P&O, under theirs.

No detail had been overlooked by Jones and his committee, nor any expense spared. Items billed to the mayor included the loan of the best hearse and horses with plumes, the best pall, thirty-one yards of silk and two pairs of kid gloves, plus nine mourning coats. Due to the storm, the driver, undertakers and horses had to be paid for three days. All officials wore black crêpe on their arm and were decked in their municipal robes.

All maces and corporate regalia were encased in black. As the procession moved slowly through the town, the band of the 1st Battalion of the Hampshire Artillery Volunteers, based in Southampton, played 'Dead March in Saul' (the funeral march from Handel's oratorio Saul, 1739, used on stated occasions such as the funeral of a sovereign). Minute guns from the platform battery were fired by the 1st Hampshire Artillery Volunteers. Meanwhile, the muffled bells from the Holy Rood rang out. Slowly and solemnly, the cortège made its way along the town quay then through the town, ending up at the station at 12.30 p.m. – a mile-long journey.

Reports suggested a massive turn out: along the route 'every balcony crowed, every window occupied, save where the blinds were drawn down, not a shop could be seen without closed shutters'. As the procession moved along, at the corner of Bridge Street, there was a rush of people; the crowd at the railway station also swelled towards the hearse. The police had to hold people back while the horses were detached. The hearse was then placed on a truck and attached to a special train courtesy of the London and South Western Railway Company. It left the station at 1 p.m., arriving at Waterloo around 3 p.m. The *Southampton Observer* reported that 'people came in their 1000s ... to do such honour as they might to the poor remains of the noble-minded man who died like a true soldier of humanity'. *The Times* judged the event 'magnificent' and unique because of the absence of crowd violence, 'rarely seen in any English town great or small'. Reports recorded that the great majority showed some sign of mourning; apparently, no discordant remarks were heard.

Journalists also reported something unexpected: the moment onlookers saw Livingstone's coffin, many started sobbing. Others became stricken with repressed emotion. The scene was described as 'imposing'; 'a repressed murmur' could be heard alongside the Dead March and muffled bells; and all of this 'affected the spectator strangely'.[5]

One distraction was the 'other negro in the ceremony'. This was John Thomas, whom the *Southampton Observer* described as 'a black and well known in the town as one that can speak seven languages'. Apparently, a local man had paid for a horse-drawn cab to join the procession. Thomas, mounted on the box, held a large white banner, edged with a black fringe and crêpe, on which was written, in large black letters: 'In memory of Dr Livingstone, the friend of the African'. According to the *Faversham Gazette*, the banner read 'Livingstone, friend of the slave', suggesting that these two terms may have meant the same to many British people.

The corporation's efforts won them much admiration and a place of honour in the funeral procession in Westminster Abbey.[6] Forty years

later, the event was written into local history as having been one of
Southampton's 'best conducted receptions'.[7] At the time, the local
papers praised everyone for the way in which 'everything was carried out
in a liberal and satisfactory manner'; the editorial of the *Southampton
Times* similarly reported how 'the multitude respectfully raised their
hats'; even the train displayed the correct degree of solemnity, 'quietly'
leaving the station. Yet not everyone was impressed. An editorial ended
on a stern note of mid-Victorian political correctness: surely 'it would
have been more appropriate to the life and works of the man, had his
body been interred on the shores of one of the mighty rivers or in the
depths of some interminable forest in the country of that Africa whose
people he loved so well'.[8] For others, 'the ceremony was as perplex-
ing as his Africa (and a love of that "country") was so incomprehen-
sible'. Meanwhile, a local fisherman was left fuming: his boat had taken
a direct hit from one of the minute guns. By the end of the day, journalists were airing serious concerns that London was not showing the same
kind of respect and reverence as Southampton had. 'The contrast was
striking', noted the *Hampshire Chronicle* disapprovingly. Only five or six
people were standing on the platform at Waterloo when the train pulled
in, two of whom were railway employees. Only six policemen were put
on duty outside the station. Just three mourning carriages followed the
hearse, plus two 'with no signs of mourning at all'.[9] The grand ceremonial was over.

The Bodily Suffering of Working Men

Livingstone's remains were taken to the RGS. Confirmation was still
required that this was actually Livingstone's body, a fact which had not
bothered Southampton's organisers. A formal examination had to take
place, adding to the suspense and sensationalism. A senior London
surgeon, Sir William Ferguson, certified it was indeed the body of
Livingstone on 17 April 1874, and he wrote a note to that effect one day
before the funeral.[10] Details of the gruesome examination of the body
were published, in some cases alongside accounts of funeral. Ferguson
had noticed that Livingstone's facial features had decayed and that his
moustache had gone but not his whiskers.[11] Such macabre details drew
audiences in closer, all the more sobering since 'one of the greatest men
of the human race', as Ferguson described him, had been reduced, after
a life of toil and illness, to a small box of bones and mummified flesh.
Verification from evidence of the wound he had sustained fighting a lion
was a reminder of his heroism, and the return of the corpse drew attention to the honesty and courage of his African followers.[12]

Nevertheless, the press contained no appreciation of African skill in making such an excellent job of mummification, even though a rudimentary investigation could have revealed the expertise that many Africans possessed in undertaking complex procedures of this nature on animals and humans. Moving around the Ilala region, explorer-travellers found evidence of full human mummification, with corpses smoke-dried, body bent, and then anointed in oils. They might then be encased in bark cylinders.[13] It was a skill employed to deal with the problem of people dying away from home. If they were poor, a lone finger might be preserved; but a rich person's whole body would be prepared.

Some sections of the public would have felt victorious because of the recent controversy over the 'Titchborne claimant'.[14] A man had attempted to claim an inheritance but had been rejected in the courts as a hoax. But many ordinary Victorians believed that he was being denied authentication and defrauded by the greedy, ruling classes. The continual insinuation that the body was not Livingstone's may well have been interpreted as another example of the disrespect shown to working people. In contrast, the government was possibly disappointed since verification denied a sweet victory over the press: if the body had been a fake, it would have thrown into question the reputation not just of the British press but also of the American press, especially Henry Morton Stanley and Gordon Bennett. When Stanley had returned to London in 1872 with Livingstone's letters, rumours had circulated that 'Stanley had not been within a thousand miles of Livingstone but had simply acquired his diary and letters by robbing an African messenger'.[15]

To make matters worse for the government, the press was now reporting the mistreatment of Livingstone's remaining family members. (With Livingstone's government pension having expired on his death, his children and unmarried sisters were left financially vulnerable.) A group of his ardent supporters, most notably the Reverend Waller and Baroness Burdett-Coutts, made a public appeal for donations to the Livingstone Testimonial Fund that they had helped to establish.[16] The national press widely publicised this in the week before the funeral.[17] 'We must no longer with-hold from this nation a trust which has fallen to it by his death', was a call publicly endorsed by Southampton's funeral committee and the RGS.

Again, the government had to back down, announcing that, in view of the fact that the £300 pension granted by the Gladstone government had expired on Livingstone's death, his family would henceforth receive a pension of £200.[18] A deputation had visited the foreign secretary, presenting a signed plea for a pension for Livingstone's relatives in view of his services to humanity. Although he agreed that Livingstone's scientific contributions were immense, he refused.[19] Yet even after the subsequent U-turn, the 'niggardly' attitude of the state regarding such a 'circumscribed fund' was still criticised. Even in late April, when it was announced that the organisation raising a public subscription was now in abeyance, pending the government's decision, sections of the press remained unimpressed: 'We confess we do not see the necessity for this suspension', until the amount raised was deemed to be adequate for the structure in mind.[20] Henry Morton Stanley of course added his support. Livingstone had never wanted any reward, Stanley wrote, other than the government stopping slavers, whether Arab or Portuguese. Such 'self-abnegation' was so rare in this age, Stanley pronounced, and his family should be provided for.[21]

Livingstone's family were often relegated to bystanders. They had chosen a representative to deal with the funeral arrangements, William Webb, Livingstone's 'tried and trusted companion' in southern Africa, who stood by to let Livingstone take the credit for their joint expeditions.[22] (Webb had famously outbid Queen Victoria to buy Newstead Abbey, the home of Lord Byron, arch-hero of the British Romantic Movement, respected poet and sex symbol. Newstead Abbey had opened its doors to Livingstone and his family and would later house Waller, Susi and Chuma while they prepared Livingstone's last journals.) The Special Livingstone Funeral Committee of the RGS failed to keep to its plan of allowing more time for Scottish relatives to gather for a funeral. It only met once formally, on 7 April 1874. Dean Stanley had offered Saturday, 18 April, as a good date, so they went ahead, without discussion, and the committee seems to have consisted of the RGS president, two of its council members, the Reverend Horace Waller and the LMS director. Some of Livingstone's artefacts at least were made into a small display, and Jacob Wainwright was photographed with them. A committee meeting on 13 April agreed that all of Livingstone's letters and journals should be handed over to them, so that they could be made available to the public, a clear signal that it did not want the likes of Stanley and Gordon Bennett to take over.

The Stanley/RGS rivalry ensured the Westminster Abbey funeral was low key. Stanley was kept at arm's length because he might have insisted on a more elaborate affair if he had had control, which would have been possible had an alternative offer of financial assistance been accepted. Through the offices of MP Russell Gurney, a wealthy London businessman had offered to bear the whole cost of the funeral, 'whatever it might be'. The RGS had declined, using the excuse of the government's willingness to foot the bill.

Nevertheless, the press prepared well in advance for a big send-off. Many weekly publications, such as the *Penny Illustrated News* and *The*

Graphic, had printed bulky souvenir editions, ready for the funeral, containing several pages of illustrations covering the whole of Livingstone's life. These often depicted him exploring, fighting with a lion, speaking with chiefs, reading the Bible to children, joyfully meeting Stanley and battling on foot through pouring rain. They included accounts of Livingstone's life, a commentary and, if published after 18 April, illustrations and details of the funeral. The RGS used the London press quickly to advertise the funeral, and tickets were printed. The dean organised the hymn sheet and order of service. Despite the last-minute preparations and minimal funding, something ressembling a grand imperial funeral now appeared to be within their grasp.

Westminster Abbey for the 'Weaver Boy'

Early on the Saturday morning, a private ceremony was held for the family in the RGS's Map Room, led by the Scottish minister of their choice, the Reverend H.W. Hamilton, from the Church of Scotland and the village of Hamilton. The *Pall Mall Gazette* covered the ceremony at Savile Row in detail – unlike most other papers – and the funeral itself, suggesting that its editor and chief reporter, Frederick Greenwood (a Conservative who encouraged the government to purchase the Suez Canal), attended. The room was hung with black, and a black velvet pall covered the stand on which the coffin rested. White flowers had been placed on the pall, and a single white wreath on the coffin. Significantly, the point was made how this contrasted with the 'simplest' preparations at the Abbey. After readings from the Bible, 'Hamilton delivered an extemporised prayer offering thanks to God, including:

We bless Thee for his uprightness, his faithfulness, his believing and loving spirit, his patience and perseverance in the midst of difficulty and danger. We praise Thee for that Thou didst enable him to use all his great gifts for the good of his country and of that far distant land, where he was the means of affording to the oppressed and enslaved, and to bring the light of the Gospel of peace to those who were sitting in darkness and the shadow death ... and we rejoice to believe that Thou has taken him to the eternal rest.[23]

Thoughtlessly, the family had been told to be at Westminster Abbey by 9.30 a.m., so were asked to leave immediately. They waited until 1 p.m. – 'a long and wearisome time for us all', Livingstone's daughter Agnes later recalled.[24]

Despite the rushed arrangements, the demand for tickets far outstripped supply. On the morning of the funeral, large crowds gathered outside the Abbey and along the route of the procession from Pall Mall and Whitehall. Most newspapers carried extremely detailed accounts of the funeral, plus editorials in the week following the funeral (printing took longer then). Some of London's newspaper accounts were reprinted elsewhere. Regional papers also reported on local events marking the occasion.

According to most press accounts, the funeral ceremony in Westminster Abbey on 18 April 1874 was impressive: a 'solemn and beautiful Church of England ceremony', the pall

remarkable for the beautiful wreaths of azaleas, white camellias, geraniums and spring flowers with a fern and African palm leaves contributed by Her Majesty and Baroness Burdett Coutts ... the body ... placed in a hearse with plumes but no other decoration, and a portion of the large numbers of Livingstone's friends and admirers who attended the funeral were conveyed in 12 mourning coaches.[25]

A detailed list of high society attendants was printed, and it was stressed that the Queen had sent mourning carriages. Journalists seemed generally impressed also at the range of people at the Abbey. *The Times* pronounced that 'all ranks from the highest and humblest in the land vied to pay him honour'.

However, the London press was painting an overly positive image. Dean Stanley had been disappointed at the lack of senior representatives present from the Church, detecting 'a complete gulf between the highest and middle classes of society'. Lord Shaftesbury and Lord Houghton were the only peers present, plus a representative of Queen Victoria, he recalled. Snobbery must have been at work, putting off many who feared that the Abbey would be full of common people. The high number of Nonconformist ministers present might have offended others. The RGS, more upper class in its origins and tastes, had neither the means nor the inclination to make the funeral that inclusive or extensive. Just a handful of peers turned up, in addition to the Mayor of London and a few representatives of foreign embassies.[26]

Ordinary people put on a better show. At St James' Street, according to the *Penny Illustrated News*, 'a deputation of working men obtained permission to add the name of their order – a laurel wreath, with an appropriate description'.[27] And, as in Southampton, a high degree of mourning etiquette was observed among the 'large concourse which had gathered in the streets', according to the *London Illustrated News*, 'reverently uncovering here and there'.[28] Virtually everyone wore mourning (printed as a requirement on the tickets), thereby creating a scene of 'sombre garb', reported *The Times*, that was only relieved 'by the white gowns of the clergy ... and the oriental costume of the Rev Navayan Sheshadir, an Indian Missionary of the Free Church of Scotland'.[29] The

Figure 2.2 Livingstone's coffin being interred in Westminster Abbey by Dean Stanley, 18 April 1874. Photo by DeAgostini/Getty Images.

Penny Illustrated News particularly liked the way in which the coffin bearers represented the three stages of Livingstone's life: as explorer (William Oswell, William Webb); his activities in central Africa (Horace Waller, Dr Kirk); and then his elusive phase (Stanley), as they diplomatically put it. The *Glasgow Herald* saw this as reflecting Livingstone's life as the 'marriage of science and religion'.[30] The *Christian World* seemed happy too: 'The famous church has never opened its doors to receive ... more precious remains', with a procession first dominated by 'half-civilised men' then by 'the most honoured men on earth'[31] (see Figure 2.2).

The religious service received widespread praise. Some journalists got carried away by the moment, believing that they were witnessing divine intervention. When the bands were removed from the lowered coffin, 'the sun suddenly burst through the clerestory window ... and played upon the heads of the mourners and the faces of the people. Before Croft's and Purcell's music was finished the shadows had again appeared'.[32] Accounts of the final graveside scene varied. Some described how Jacob Wainwright had thrown down an African palm leaf; others, that it had been Livingstone's granddaughter. It took two hours for the mourners to leave the Abbey. Hundreds chose to file slowly past the grave. The main draws were Stanley and his young African servant boy, Kalulu; Jacob Wainwright; and the old, bearded Dr Moffat.[33] Agnes Livingstone did not recognise Stanley at first, as he had tried to dye his hair and it had gone a green colour.

That the event could be passed off as a success despite the meagre resources, lack of will, and last-minute planning was due to Dean Stanley. He kept costs to a minimum, charging for the basics, including eighteen choir-singers, twenty-two choir boys and three organ blowers, and cancelling the ten shilling fee for the gravediggers.[34] The final bill was £37 4s 6d. His inclusion of the favourite Nonconformist hymn, Dodderidge's 'O God of Bethel, by whose hand/Thy people are still fed ... Be the God of/Each succeeding race', was, for some commentators, the highlight of the service.[35] It was a radical move, greatly anticipated. His politics of inclusion carried through into his sermon on the Sunday after the funeral, which many newspapers reported in detail. In a packed Abbey, the congregation included the Archbishop of Canterbury and every senior figure of the Nonconformist churches. The dean's sermon focused on the great achievements of travellers from biblical times to the present Alpine climber, placing Livingstone within the nation's pantheon of great heroes. As the *Kensington Advertiser* concluded, people watched the return of the mortal remains of a man whose life had been 'devoted to the cause of humanity' and who had never lost 'a buoyancy of feeling ... vivacity of mind ... [a] cheerful, helpful, indomitable spirit ... of which true heroes are made'.[36]

An 'Incongruous Procession' and an Unqualified 'Mob'

Not everyone was that impressed or interested. A Catholic newspaper, in a disparaging announcement that Livingstone's burial had taken place, commented that he had earned his title to be buried in the Abbey 'according to modern ideas'.[37] An etching portraying a sombre graveside scene with weeping mourners was included, but mischievously this portrayed a pilgrimage to the tomb of St Francis Xavier – a real saint. Newspapers like *Cosmopolitan* registered only mild interest, a week later printing a eulogy delivered by Lord Houghton entitled 'Ilala – May 1873'. Under 'Spirit of the Press', a piece from the *Daily Telegraph* was reprinted (a common practice) that detailed how the plot had eventually been chosen in the Abbey. Finally, Dean Stanley's funeral sermon was noted – sardonically – under 'Weary at Rest'. 'The scene and the services were profoundly impressive', the paper judged, 'only a little too long'.[38]

The behind-the-scenes chaos and rush had, however, left their mark. *The Times* printed a correction on the Tuesday after the funeral stating that the wreath of azaleas adorning the bier had not been sent by the Queen, whose wreath had arrived only after the coffin had been placed in the Abbey and which had been laid shortly before the grave was sealed.

Shortly after the funeral, a long letter of complaint was published in the *Pall Mall Gazette*, written by a veteran of similar public ceremonies (possibly its own editor in disguise). The anonymous letter, published on 20 April 1874, was from a man who had returned from Westminster Abbey incandescent, possessed of feelings which he felt 'many readers would share'. He conceded that the funeral had contained all the elements of a great ceremonial but that it had been 'badly handled' and had left onlookers 'puzzled and wearied'. Livingstone's daughter might certainly have agreed, given the long wait that the family had been forced to endure:

> It is difficult to conceive a more incongruous procession than that which followed Livingstone's coffin. Scotch municipal authorities, African travellers, medical men, missionaries, some men of other appropriate qualifications, and very many who appeared to have little or none, walked in a mob.[39]

The occasion lacked the formality and planning of the Southampton procession; at least one newspaper account corroborates a scene of chaos. The 'Westminster Review' of the *Chelsea Times* included a description of what happened after the first hymn had been sung: as the chief mourners approached the grave, in the same order in which they had arrived, large numbers of the congregation rose from their seats and made for the grave, blocking the way for many who should have assembled around it.[40]

The absence of any of Livingstone's personal relics on the coffin was also judged to have been a huge omission. Military officers threw down their boots, the anonymous *Pall Mall* complainer explained, which formed the most touching part of military burials, so why were 'one of Livingstone's well-known blue caps with its gold band, and a few other relics' not laid on the coffin? Everything had evidently been so rushed that there had been little time for similar touches. The minimal effort may also reflect the lack of affection in which the RGS held Livingstone. The author also felt that Africa was being neglected: 'I should also have liked to see', he continued, 'a rough but clear diagram of Africa, arranged as a square-scraped banner, carried in front of his coffin on which his great lines of discovery should have been broadly marked'. And the original coffin, made in Africa, had been replaced by the 'gratuitous exertion of the British undertaker', in everyday oak.

Nor was it just the RGS who were judged to have been lacking; the Abbey had not quite risen to the occasion either, in his view. In addition, the 'music might be mended and the choristers should have a hint to wash their surplices'. Finally, the complainant criticised the lack of sentiment surrounding the final funeral rite, insisting the full meaning of the final 'dust to dust' could have been conveyed with far more realism through the use of earth. Now they had 'lost their heart'.

Tears and Tenderness for the Lost 'Heart of the Nation'

Nevertheless, such a poorly organised, rushed funeral did nothing to mute the general public's emotional response to Livingstone's corpse. Indeed, the shambles may even have increased it. Journalists repeatedly described mourners in London as having been overcome with grief at the sight of the coffin. According to *The Times*, the onlooker 'could not but help insensibly reverting to the place where he died', and to him 'whose fate they pitied';[41] the *Chelsea Times* judged the funeral to have been so dramatic in effect because of 'the pathetic circumstances under which the eminent traveller died far away from home and friends';[42] Lord Houghton wrote of a dying man imagining his homeland as he lay in an African hut; and Agnes Livingstone never forgot how, at the sight of the coffin at the deanery door, a 'strange thrill ... seemed to sweep up the entire concourse'.[43]

The *Christian World* had initially assumed that time 'would have sealed up the fountain of tears ... [but] a 1000 eyes were wet with tears; a 1000 heads were bowed in reverent sympathy and sorrow'. Readers were comforted by the notion: 'We left him securely resting beyond the roar of the wild beast ... he had come home in peace and [now] ... sleeps, the sleep of the just'.[44] H.M. Stanley's description bore a strong resemblance to evangelical accounts. Just as 'pathetic' as his last days, he wrote, was 'the sight of weeping of sorrowing multitudes lamenting his loss', and he ended his long essay in *The Graphic* with a dose of soothing sentimentality: 'Sleep, then O Livingstone, in thy dreamless bed'.[45]

Reasons for such weeping – that 'dumb tenderness' – are impossible to pinpoint. Exactly where the lines are between natural empathy, 'innocent outrage' and media manipulation of the 'tender feelings' can never be clearly demarcated. Certainly, this sentimental response was in part the culmination of press coverage of a national story: 'the romance of Livingstone', according to the *Edinburgh Evening News*, was now greater than that of Nelson or Wellington. The sight of the 'great explorer' reduced to a lightweight coffin was a pathetic sight; the painful death, sad. The press had also played a central role in staging an emotional, sentimental reading of Livingstone by exposing his poor treatment by the government, and a powerful force field was emerging, but death, for the Victorians, was always best served as a set of moral instructions.

In the 'annals of blubbering', using the words of Chapman and Hendler, tears and their significance have their own biographical history.[46] Victorian sentimentalists believed in their healing and moral power; that it was wrong 'to separate human beings from their natural sentiments'; drawing on a poetic notion, promoted by such national favourites as Keats, of the 'healing nature of the heart ... the holiness of the heart's affection'.[47] With his tragic, drawn-out death scenes, Dickens reveals the powerful cultural context for the tragic romance of Livingstone's fabricated 'chamber of death'. His famous tear-jerking ending of Little Nell or Clarissa reflected the view that 'it was impossible to be excessively feeling or "sentimental" in any pejorative way about such losses'.[48] Death was regarded by the Victorians as a process that humanised the mind; grief was a means whereby people could reconnect to their heart, so the expression of grief was also performative: the display of moral feeling unfettered, and thus of natural feeling. It was an assertion of the Romantic tradition; tears expressed the sacred and were an assertion of freedom of expression.[49] If the freedom of the heart was not allowed, then moral development was curtailed. Livingstone tried to convey this sentimental view of freedom when he wrote of broken-hearted African slaves willing themselves to die. The essence of being free was a free heart.

Significantly, a growing sentimentality towards the dead figure of Livingstone flourished around the notion of the 'heart of the nation' and became the motif for the emerging emotion of the moment. The image of the heart continued to feature strongly in the many reflections on the funeral and the meaning of Livingstone's death. The recurring theme of Livingstone embodying the heart of the nation reflected the way many Victorians melodramatically feared that they had lost theirs. The toleration of slavery was often a key litmus test. As Parry has argued, by the 1870s, many Victorians felt guilty about their aggressive materialism.[50] Newspapers covered the violent Ashanti wars alongside the funeral, many critical of its cost, as the last chapter showed. The latest reports on the Bengal famine also appeared alongside. The Gladstone government had been forced to ban the slave trade off the east coast of Africa in 1871 only after extensive lobbying by abolitionists, who had used evidence (unwittingly) supplied by Livingstone.[51] A decade earlier, a similar reluctance was shown towards slavery on Africa's west coast. Now, Livingstone had

died a horrible death. Fear of retribution – of God's wrath – for not acting with a heart may have been bubbling below the surface.[52] Thus the
use of the term 'loss of heart' had a deep resonance with the cultural
politics of the 1870s.

Moreover, the display of emotion and 'sacred tears' from the heart was
also performing a function: the display of feeling was a measure of political worth. Anxiety floated around about the extension of the franchise
in 1867 and its effect on the election results. Many newspaper owners,
particularly those of urban-regional publications, had liberal sympathies
and were still reeling from the 'downfall of the English Liberal Party'
just weeks before. The English elite were nervous. A page-long editorial in the *Pall Mall Gazette* warned that the extension of the franchise
in 1867 had given gave a vote to ordinary men, who usually acted out
of 'abject fear of the Pope or the Devil'. Men with the vote, the paper
warned, did not become 'less ignorant, less superstitious, less envious,
less greedy'. Thus Livingstone's admirable, noble character, together
with his capacity for hardship and pursuit of non-monetary rewards, was
a timely way of holding up a template to the ordinary working man,
whom Livingstone embodied. *Cornhill Magazine* was quoted as praising
Livingstone as having been rare amongst the poor, in that he had not
sought fame or fortune.[53]

As Joyce argued, the cult of the heart was, by the 1870s, an established
device for presenting the worth and capability of ordinary labouring
men, men like Livingstone, who were showing themselves to be capable of speaking 'from the heart', a heart that was honest and pure – no
'counterfeit humanity' here.[54] Thus 'the heart was the centre of humanity',[55] the implication being that all humanity – from serf to labouring
man to slave – was capable of enjoying an inner emotional life. Moreover,
according to the cult of the heart, 'God is realized in the heart', so the
heart was a means of asserting a 'religion of humanity' to defeat evil, suffering and, of course, slavery.[56]

Self-made men had only recently been enfranchised, but others were
not, suggesting that the experience of exclusion encouraged the quest
for recognition and respect. Identifying with the heart of the nation –
Livingstone – meant being capable of recognising and valuing character,
religious duty, 'the romance of improvement' and self-help; it was an
acceptance of the rationale of science and the rule of the law.

What was also unfolding was a tussle over 'the heart of the
nation': whose heart, and how should it behave? By the late 1870s,
William Gladstone referred to the 'great human heart of this country'
which beat outside parliament and should not be ignored.[57] This politics of an English heart was extended and debated in 1874 in relation

to what Livingstone symbolised regarding an ethical foreign policy. It became lodged in the collective consciousness and remained a feature of Britain's engagement in Africa. In an important moment of national self-understanding, Livingstone became the heart of the nation, through the celebration of shared sorrow and the British tradition of anti-slavery. A new romance and sentimentality was injected into the pursuit of British control in Africa by linking it to the display of the 'hidden hearts of men'. Subsequent violence, inequality and unfairness because of the encounter would be shrouded in this romantic, sentimentalised ideal.

Stanley's brilliance as a journalist found expression through a souvenir edition for *The Graphic* (also reproduced by other newspapers). In a long essay he gave full expression to the Romantic notion of a loss of heart while interpreting Livingstone's life and death as the triumph of the right kind of (masculine) heart. The sight of weeping, he claimed, had surprised him initially, since the younger generation knew little of Livingstone's exploits. However, all ages, he decided, had become united in grief for a man who had lived by 'meekness, self-abnegation, purest philanthropy', qualities that were 'rare in an age like this', when there existed 'an all-absorbing desire for the acquisition of wealth and luxury'. Stanley, performing the role of grieving son, was also giving expression to a related cross-class generational anxiety, particularly strong on the Right and within religious opinion, about what the English had become morally compared to what they had been in the past. Livingstone's pathetic death, apparently in pursuit of humanitarian goals, was interpreted as a Christ-like act of sacrifice through which they now had another chance to redeem themselves by resuming a very English pursuit – the abolition of slavery. As Stanley concluded, Westminster Abbey had been impressive, but no more so than the burial in Africa a year before, 'when the heart of Livingstone was committed to the soil', which had beaten 'for the enslaved children so long in sorrow over their sufferings'.

Sentimental Paternalism for the 'Lost Boys' of Africa

Africans were brought into the Victorian home and into the heart of the empire through Livingstone's funeral. One poem sent to the RGS included the lines: 'But Africa's sons with loving hearts, Helped the man they held so dear'. Dean Stanley's Sunday sermon spoke of Livingstone's followers, 'by whose faithful affection they were subdued'. It asked, 'those African boys have done their duty. What is ours?' An anonymous eulogy in the *Western Mail* included the lines, 'Thou has shown, that pity, gratitude and love still dwell within the harried bosom, of thy race'.[58] Wainwright was rhetorically asked to look 'statesmen in the face' and state that all of 'Africa's children', like himself, if given 'gentle treatment, culture ... liberty and freedom', could become like him. As Joyce has shown, it was the realm of the family that was the medium through which the correct level and type of emotions were expressed – typically kindness, fairness and tenderness – the device through which the self-made man made a bid for recognition and respect in wider society.

A sentimentalised reading of the bonds of affection between the Englishman and Africans fuelled Victorian feeling. Jacob Wainwright, at the side of the coffin and usually always described as a 'former or freed slave', was the object of childish, microscopic scrutiny from the moment he arrived at Southampton.[59] At the funeral, the way he held 'the printed page in his hand, intently following the words as they were slowly uttered', was deemed worth noting. He was lauded for being 'a good type of African', and it was said that all the 'good boys' with him should be rewarded.[60]

Again, the lack of any deeper enquiry or attempt to give him a social and cultural context outside the Livingstone relationship is striking. Victorians' self-absorption and self-congratulation, plus their sense of exceptionalism, which Livingstone indulged, could not surrender any space. Had any investigation taken place regarding indigenous beliefs and funeral rites, then it would have been quickly ascertained that non-Christian men and women with a similar background and from a similar region to Wainwright shared similar beliefs and practices to Victorian Christians. 'He has gone to God' or 'God took him' were phrases that were repeated to European travellers moving through central Africa, where Livingstone died, as an explanation of death. Immortality was a universal concept; the Ilala people in the area around the grave referred to Livingstone as 'he sleepeth'; death was 'the awakening', offering a similar opportunity for moral instruction.[61]

What dominated the coverage instead was the relationship that Africans had formed with Livingstone because of his apparent 'unique and rare' character and example; he had 'subdued' them; and 'he had a special gift of making people love him'.[62] Accompanying the account of the arrival of the body, the *Leicester Chronicle* published an intimate portrayal of Livingstone's relationships, suggesting that his behaviour towards his 'good boys', which included stopping if one of his men was ill but carrying on if he himself was ill, produced the African goodwill that carried his corpse home; the man they called 'Father' apparently greeted them every morning, after his 'pet boy' had brought the tea![63] One journalist remarked how Wainwright's devotion to Livingstone appeared 'almost romantic'; and, when commended for his loyalty, 'his shining dusky flat face was lit up with a pleasant smile'.[64] Newspapers also carried images of Livingstone

reading from the Bible to African children; he was described as leading Africans like their father; the Makololo, 'the guileless children of the
African interior', were quoted as describing how they had 'marched along
with our Father'.[65]

And so, sorrow blended with shame, as a public was chided into
accepting that their own indifference to humanity had led Livingstone
to his death, and the children of 'the slave-doomed Africa' had lost their
father.[66] Victorians may have shed tears of shame for their lost heart,
symbolised by their indifference to Livingstone's cause. Dean Stanley's
influential funeral sermon, in 'the heart of England', as he referred to
Westminster Abbey, invoked Wilberforce, pitting him against his audience and placing Wilberforce and Livingstone together in the same
national heroic narrative (the struggle against 'that monster evil … a
deadly serpent').[67] It was reprinted in many newspapers and inspired
other sermons. Livingstone's message from his grave, the dean informed
his audience, was that 'individuals, the nation and nations of the civilized
world must redeem … a whole continent and race of mankind from the
curse of barbarism and heathenism, and from the curse of the wicked-
ness of civilised men'. He ended with a call to 'the rising generation', to
'English lads', 'to statesmen and merchants, explorers and missionaries'
to continue the work that Wilberforce and Livingstone had begun.

Dean Stanley did not indulge in the emotionalism of Livingstone dev-
otees like Waller who, when preaching at Southampton just before the
body had arrived, had described how Livingstone had felt forgotten at the
end. Evidence suggests that other churches, across denominations, also
chose to focus on Livingstone during post-funeral sermons, often contrasting his own sense of failure and sad ending with his having achieved
greatness without 'blood stained banners', ending with rallying calls to
stop the disparaging of missionary work and to instead deal a final death
blow to African slavery.[68] Likewise, the day after Livingstone's funeral at
Westminster Abbey, the emotional and grieving Reverend Edmund Lane
of St George the Martyr, Southwark, preached that Livingstone had sac-
rificed his life to end slavery and had died in full knowledge of his failure
to do so. Lane believed that, through the work of 'Christian patriots and
philanthropists', his 'grand design' would be realised and that, soon, all
of Africa would speak English and live by English laws and institutions.
He saw an angel flying over the continent, spreading the gospel.[69]

No arguments about the cost of the permanent gravestone survive in
the wake of such an emotional event. Money was no object, because it was
paid for by Sir George Moore, who had offered to cover all funeral costs.
The expensive stone was covered in gold-lettered epitaphs. 'Brought by
faithful hands' was a vague, patronising reference to the African men and

women who had made it possible. The last words and main thrust of the tombstone was Livingstone, the anti-slaver. This was due to the Reverend Horace Waller's intervention. For the epitaph, he gave the dean what he termed Livingstone's last written words: his blessing upon all those who came after him, whether 'American, English or Turk/Who will help heal this sore of the world'. These were not 'with his last words he wrote', as Waller advised and as appear on the stone, but they were apparently contained in a letter, one of the last Livingstone wrote, to the editor of the *New York Herald*.[70] Dean Stanley had the title of his post-funeral sermon squeezed in ('Other Sheep I Have') and, finally, he agreed to have a Latin inscription down one side, apparently suggested by a high society diplomat, Robert Morier, who had attended the funeral and was a member of the RGS. Morier, a Balliol man, had suggested a few lines from the classical poet Lucan's poem 'Pharsalia', in which Julius Caesar explains to Cleopatra that his greatest passion is the love of truth, for there was 'nothing he would rather know more than the true source of the Nile'. The stone was as polyphonic a mishmash as the African empire to come.

Conclusion: 'Take Up the Old Man's Burden'

Livingstone's funeral was a transformational moment in the history of the imperial project in Africa because of the manner of his death. Sustained press coverage and a tender, human response illustrate a complex interplay of manipulated and organic feeling, as well as the potency of feelings when external circumstances and inner lives collide. Powerful emotions thus elided into political consciousness, the process Hume observed – or, as Rancière argued, a moment – of theatre, when the sensory experience becomes understood as political. As the *Aberdeen Journal*'s coverage reassured its readers, once more, at Livingstone's funeral, 'the heart of the nation was with him'.[71]

On 14 December 1874, the charismatic preacher and diarist the Reverend Francis Kilvert described how he had taken 'twenty one of our school children into Chippenham to the Temperance Hall to see a Panorama of the African travels of Dr Livingstone' and how 'one of the most favourite pictures with the children [had been] the Funeral of Dr Livingstone in Westminster Abbey'.[72] Just a few pennies, he wrote, had brought such 'pleasure' to these 'young hearts'. Kilvert had chosen to deliver a lecture on Livingstone's funeral, and the response he received must have led to this visit. No doubt Kilvert was not alone in being so moved by the event as to include it in sermons and mini-pilgrimages.

The extraordinary phenomenon of the 'profound appeal', as Larner puts it, of Livingstone among the mid-Victorians was amplified by his death.[73] In a lecture delivered on 23 January 1913, the centenary of Livingstone's birth, the Reverend Dan Crawford played on the emotional appeal of death: when Livingstone had known he was going to die, he had 'resolved to die on his knees'. Crawford offered highly intimate and personal details: he claimed to have seen the three pot-stones on which Livingstone had boiled his last cup of tea or coffee. He insisted locals remembered him as 'Mr He-hath no toes' and 'Mr He Sleeps on the Waves'; and that 'Arabs' called him 'Daveed' and remembered his hearty laugh and red beard.[74]

Livingstone's death opened up the experience of ordinary pain. He offered a means to share the intimate, often hidden experience of death, suffering and pain on the imperial frontier, shared between Britain, the United States and the colonies of white settlement. Laura Ingalls Wilder, the American author of the sentimental *Little House on the Prairie* books, recalled how her family had lived through the dark blizzards of the harsh winter of 1880–1 by sitting round the fire reading extracts from Livingstone's lonely travels in Africa.[75] Livingstone was often, it seems, a good read when sick or bedridden, and not just among the English-speaking global reading public: his writing was not demanding, noted the French writer Alphonse Daudet in his journals (published posthumously as *Land of Pain*). Livingstone, Daudet explained, 'provided a framework within which the mind could wander'. This seems to have reflected the symptoms of his illness – locomotor ataxia as a result of neurosyphilis – in the 1880s and 1890s, for he mischievously wrote that 'the monotony of his endless and virtually pointless journey, the constant obsession with barometric pressure and meals that rarely arrive, and the silent, calm unfolding of vast landscapes' made for a wonderful read.[76]

Newspaper coverage of a litany of slights towards the dead man and his family, juxtaposed with accounts of his slow, painful death, and the rise in popular sentimentality towards the old man, would not have been so strong. The press covered in detail the funeral as well as funeral sermons from Westminster Abbey to local churches. These accounts, editorials and popular eulogies helped to transform a disorganised, penny-pinching funeral into a climactic event, heavy with emotion and grief. There was now a desire to make Livingstone live in death; to vanquish death; to produce a 'deathless memory' and a 'living' legacy.[77]

Yet an analysis of the press coverage also cautions against the notion of the blanket manipulation of a universally popular figure. To be sure, the sentimental and emotional press coverage helped to produce a pivotal moment in mythologising Livingstone, a process started by Livingstone himself with his self-censorship and cause-motivated writing, and promulgated by the sensational double burials and his African servants' boldness. But popular poetry, hymns and press coverage also open up the neglected context of the mid-Victorian era, showing exactly what was so emblematic, troubling and celebrated by this death. The domestic context did much to stir feelings, including reluctance among the elite to make a fuss. More generally, the shared Victorian guilt, anxiety and self-doubt (rather than issues related to identity or race) shaped the responses. Remaining fundamentally insular and religious in outlook, many identified with Livingstone's poor treatment, lower-class origins, illness and disappointments. A nostalgia for a lost past surfaced among a generation who had read about Livingstone's exploits in their youth. Reminders of his child slave labour were shameful. The defeat of the Liberals; the enfranchisement of the lower classes; excessive materialism and violence overseas; the cost of imperial wars; and a decline in evangelicalism were some of the major anxieties of the generation who remembered more confident selves: a Victorian mid-life crisis. They feared they had lost their heart and what might be their divine punishment in a cycle of sin and atonement. As the first abolitionists understood: 'Individuals might be judged at the Last Day, but states and societies risked judgement and punishment here and now'.[78]

From his dead, emaciated frame, Livingstone was reborn. Multiple, conflicting and lesser Livingstones were honed into a more idealised, homogeneous, singular figure who had died in peaceful pursuit of humanitarian goals. His heroic death was thus easily interpreted by a worried generation as a sacrifice so that they might see what they had become or lost. Likewise, Africa was now less a continent of potential, variety and the unknown, but was more understood, doomed and slave-ridden, since Livingstone's authority on Africa was deemed unbounded. As one minister commented, his exploration 'unfolded the whole continent to our gaze ... we now know Africa almost as well as we know our own country'.[79]

The funeral of David Livingstone, whom people felt they knew through his personalised writing, shows how his powerful legacy evolved from melting compassion to a new imperial humanitarian politics of intervention. A masculine sentimentality towards the heroic self-made man and female tenderness towards a good father, husband and supporter of women's rights became inseparable in the new imperial politics of the heart. A new community of grief reorganised and morally rearmed itself around a notion of acting from the heart to defeat slavery, finally, in Africa. Commercial interests had played a huge role in shaping the press coverage but so had the government, by treating Livingstone badly. The presentation of Livingstone as a man of peace gave a new generation the green light for its humanitarian mission. Emotional press coverage of Livingstone's funeral helped to nudge British liberalism and anti-slavery to drive forwards the formal colonial rule in eastern and central/south Africa as a national duty. Enticed away from a typical 'ambivalence' towards empire, a younger generation came to accept their role as the new representatives of the civilised world and to 'go back to Africa' for humanitarian purposes, as Livingstone had done. Those who took an active interest in intervention in Africa as moral humanitarianism had a memory either of him or of his death – a personal connection or a craved one.

Livingstone's funeral heartened high Victorian imperialism for one last conquest. An imperial politics of affection in Africa had been constructed out of the myth of Livingstone's special love for his followers and theirs for him, embodied by the presence of Jacob Wainwright at the side of the coffin right to the end. This symbolised for a new generation the 'Am I not a man and brother' anti-slavery discourse, the terms through which large swathes of an unsuspecting British public generally understood their African empire, remaining passive supporters throughout its existence and despite its excesses. Press coverage of the funeral popularised the generic and naturally good white man in Africa, who was loved by Africans and who loved them in return. During the twentieth century, the rhetoric of the high standard of British race relations would become a constant, replenished by the retelling of the sentimental story of Livingstone's followers. The contribution of this to Britain's imperial soft power has been phenomenal.

Through the looming Scramble for Africa, the British Empire in Africa become one of the most ideological of empires. An anti-slavery rationale for formal rule in Africa was invoked by many crucial actors on the ground in the last quarter of the nineteenth century, as recent research has shown.[80] Public opinion could easily be ignited in their cause if there was evidence that Britain's duty in Africa – humanitarianism – was being neglected.

Queen Victoria took much more of an interest in Africa after Livingstone's death. As is well known, on hearing that Livingstone had died in his futile quest, Stanley resolved to 'take up the old man's burden', return to explore central Africa and 'succeed him in opening up Africa to the shining light of Christianity'.[81] In doing so, he came to the attention of King Leopold II of Belgium, who used him to achieve his ambition to create an empire in Africa, the Congo Free State.

Less acknowledged, yet crucial to the British annexation and occupation of east and central Africa, were political agents, consular officials and naval officers. For example, junior consular official Frederick Holmwood Esq, who had interviewed Livingstone's servants in 1873, was aware of the persistent slave trade, linked with the interior. Well-connected in various circles in London, he made an impassioned appeal to the businessmen of Manchester, preaching in 1885, for example, the dual benefits of spreading legitimate commerce and thereby extirpating the evils of the slave trade.[82] He insisted that a 'Central Africa Railway' could transport Manchester textiles in exchange for ivory, rubber, cattle and other goods. The Imperial British East Africa Company, established in 1888 and financed by Scottish businessman and philanthropist Sir William Mackinnon, agreed.[83] The same argument was made – ending the slave trade would benefit commerce and uphold British prestige and a moral commitment which went back to Livingstone. Holmwood and others illustrate the continuity of British Africa policy: their involvement with powerful networks of shared interests able to mobilise public opinion into carrying a huge amount of emotion capital towards an idealised, noble anti-slavery African humanitarian foreign policy in Africa. In 1892, the Foreign Office's arch African expert, Sir Percy Anderson, submitted a crucial report, arguing for the retention of Uganda, stressing, as Jonas Gjersø has shown, the problem of the slave trade and missionary presence as interests that needed protecting. He was aware of the 'truly remarkable movement in public opinion' again in 1892, whereby Victorian sensibility and sensitivity regarding its prestige as the foremost anti-slaving power in Africa had been activated by an impressive propaganda campaign largely organised by the CMS and the British and Foreign Anti-Slavery Society.[84] As Huzzey has also shown, these interests and networks of opinion were powerful and overlapping. With Uganda reoccupied, British eastern Africa was a fait accompli.

Moving southwards, the government's 'men on the spot' included Harry Johnston, also close to Rhodes and sympathetic to the Livingstone legacy of the Scottish missionaries around Lake Nyasa. He, too, was moved by arguments about a strong missionary presence in the region that had the backing of public opinion in Britain, keeping Lord Salisbury focused on a vision of a partitioned Africa and pressuring him to engage in more formal involvement.[85] Despite the lack of strategic value, the Shire Highlands were annexed, morphing into Nyasaland, requiring a strong ultimatum to the Portuguese (in the form of naval vessels moving into their African waters).

The first contemporary account of what was called the 'Scramble for Africa' in the 1880s, by the president of the RGS, Sir John Keltie, credited it to the death of Livingstone. He had turned it into 'a kind of holy crusade'.[86] But the scramble in the 1890s to find his African grave, the subject of the next chapter, would mark the end of the Livingstone age of high moral imperialism.

NOTES

1 Stanley chose this quote to begin his chapter on meeting Livingstone. Ralph Waldo Emerson was a key figure in the American Romantic movement of the mid-nineteenth century who had moved slowly to support the abolition of slavery and revolutionary politics. Although twice married, he was prone to homo-erotic love and passion and once described his central philosophy as being 'the infinitude of the private man'.

2 *Leeds Mercury*, 24 April 1874.

3 *Hampshire Advertiser*, 18 April 1874, 3.

4 Editorial, *Southampton Times*, 11 April 1874, 4. This was only the second item in the editorial, however.

5 *Times*, reprinted in papers such as the *East Kent, Faversham & Sittingbourne Gazette*.

6 *Hampshire Chronicle*, 18 April 1874, 3.

7 Sir James Lemon, *Reminiscences of Public Life in Southampton, 1866–1900* (Southampton, 1911), i. Minutes of RGS Council, 11 May 1874, RGS Archives.

8 *Southampton Observer & Winchester News*, 18 April 1874, editorial, 4.

9 'Arrival of David Livingstone's remains', *Hampshire Chronicle, Southampton and Isle of Wight*, 18 April 1874, 3.

10 Handwritten note Ferguson to Dean Stanley, 17 April 1874, RCO Box 5 WAM.

11 Letter of verification by Sir William Ferguson, reproduced in the *Pall Mall Gazette*, 17 April 1874, 9.

12 The main argument put forward in Justin Livingstone, 'A "Body" of Evidence: The Posthumous Presentation of David Livingstone', *Victorian Literature and Culture* 40, 1 (2012): 1–24.

13 Campbell, *Wanderings in Central Africa*, 157–60; Crawford, *Back to the Long Grass*, 290.

14 See discussion in Chapter Three.

15 Jeal, *Stanley*, 138.

16 *Cosmopolitan*, 16 April 1874.

17 *The Cosmopolitan, Leeds Mercury* and *London Illustrated News* illustrate the wide publicity this was given.

18 For examples, see *The Cosmopolitan, Leeds Mercury* and *London Illustrated News*.

19 *Leeds Mercury*, 24 April 1874.

20 *Hampshire Advertiser*, 25 April 1874.

21 *Graphic*, Supplement: 'The Life and Labours of David Livingstone by H M Stanley', 25 April 1874.

22 'Arrangements for the funeral of Dr Livingstone', RGS Council Minutes, 13 April 1873, 243.

23 *Pall Mall Gazette*, 18 April 1874.

24 A.M. Livingstone, 'Recollections of David Livingstone, by his daughter', *Chambers Christian Journal* (December 1938), 966. Livingstone. Box 3 Jacket A, Folder 1, SOAS Archives.

25 *Chelsea Times/ Kensington, Brompton and Fulham Advertiser*, 25 April 1874.

26 Wolffe, *Great Deaths*, 141, quoting *The Times*.

27 *London Illustrated News*, 25 April 1874, 261. This account was similar in detail to many others, publishing on the day of the funeral the account of the arrival of the remains and then, on the following Saturday, detailed accounts of the funeral.

28 *London Illustrated News*, 25 April 1874, 261

29 *Times*, 25 April 1874. This account was reprinted in regional papers such as the *Faversham Gazette*.

30 *Glasgow Herald*, 21 April 1874.

31 *Christian World*, 24 April 1874, 262.

32 *Kensington Advertiser*, 25 April 1874.

33 *Chelsea Times, Kensington, Brompton and Fulham Advertiser*, 25 April 1874.

34 'Fees in lieu of fittings at Westminster Abbey 1874'. WAM 60086.

35 'Hymn sheet', Livingstone Funeral, RGS Archives.

36 *Kensington Advertiser*, 25 April 1874.

37 *Catholic Opinion*, 22 April 1874, 335.

38 *Cosmopolitan*, 23 April 1874, 469–71.

39 'A public funeral'. Unsigned letter to the editor published under 'Correspondence' section, *Pall Mall Gazette*, 20 April 1874, 3.

40 *Chelsea Times, Kensington, Brompton & Fulham Advertiser*, 25 April 1874.

41 *Times*, reprinted in papers such as the *East Kent, Faversham & Sittingbourne Gazette*.

42 *Chelsea Times, Kensington, Brompton & Fulham Advertiser*, 25 April 1874.

43 'Recollections of David Livingstone, by his daughter', *Chambers Christian Journal* (December 1938), 966, SOAS Archive.

44 *Christian World*, 24 April 1874, 263.

45 Stanley, Souvenir Edition, *The Graphic*, 25 April 1874, 399.

46 Chapman & Hendler, *Sentimental Men*, 1; Dixon, *Weeping Britannia*.

47 Kaplan, *Sacred Tears*, 40–2.

48 Ibid., 52.

49 Ibid.; Solomon, *In Defense of Sentimentality*.

50 See generally for 1870s, J. Parry, *The Politics of Patriotism: English Liberalism, National Identity and Europe, 1830–1886* (Cambridge: Cambridge University Press, 2006). For the ménage à trois between Victorian politics, religion and culture, see Boyd Hilton, *The Age of Atonement: The Influence of Evangelicalism on Social and Economic Thought circa 1795–1865* (Cambridge: Cambridge University Press, 1988).

51 Jeal, Livingstone, 351–3.

52 See Drescher, 'Emperors of the World' and Boyd Hilton, '1807 and All That: Why Britain Outlawed Her Slave Trade', in Derek R. Peterson (ed.), *Abolitionism and Imperialism*, 63–83.

53 *Cornhill Magazine*, quoted in *The Graphic*, 18 April 1874.

54 Ibid., 59.
55 Ibid., 60–1.
56 Ibid., 'The struggle for the moral life', 41–8.
57 Ibid., 205.
58 *Western Mail*, anonymous poem, 22 April 1874.
59 *Southampton Observer & Winchester News*, 18 April 1874, 'The arrival of the Malwa', 5.
60 *Dundee Courier and Argus*, 20 April 1874, and *Edinburgh Evening News*, 24 April 1874.
61 Campbell, Wanderings in Central Africa, 157–63; Crawford, *Back to the Long Grass*, 290.
62 *News of the World*, 18 April 1874.
63 *Leicester Chronicle and Leicestershire Mercury*, 18 April 1874.
64 *East Faversham Gazette*, 18 April 1874.
65 Stanley, Souvenir Edition, *The Graphic*, 25 April 1874, 399.
66 Anonymous poem written to mark the funeral of Livingstone, April 1874, Livingstone Collection, RGS Archive.
67 Stanley, 'The Mission of the Traveller', chapter in his Collection of Sermons, 181. WAM.
68 For example, quoting Isaiah, 'I have laboured in vain'.
69 E. Lane, *Hope for Africa; or a memorial to Dr Livingstone* (1874), quoted in Wolffe, *Great Deaths*, 144.
70 Blaikie, *The Personal Life of David Livingstone*, 366.
71 *Aberdeen Journal*, 22 April 1874.
72 William Plomer (ed.), *Kilvert's Diary*, iii, *14 May 1874–13 March 1879* (London: Jonathan Cape, 1940), 121–2, quoted in A.J. Larner, 'Reading Livingstone – Editorial', *Journal of Medical Biography*, 17, 63 (2009): 1.
73 Larner, 'Reading Livingstone', 1.
74 Lecture by Daniel Crawford, *The Christian*, 23 January 1913. Livingstone. Box 3 Jacket A, Folder 1, SOAS Archives.
75 L.I. Wilder, *The Long Winter* (London, 1968), 178–9, quoted in Larner, 'Reading Livingstone', 1.
76 J. Barnes (ed/trans), *Alphonse Daudet: In the Land of Pain* (London: Jonathan Cape, 2008), 2, quoted in Larner, 'Reading Livingstone', 1.
77 Crawford, *Back to the Long Grass*.
78 Ronald Hyam, *Understanding the British Empire* (Cambridge: Cambridge University Press, 2010), 165.
79 *Western Mail*, 22 April 1874.
80 Gjersø, 'The Scramble for East Africa'.
81 Dorothy Stanley (ed.), *The Autobiography of Henry Morton Stanley* (London, 1909), quoted in J.M. MacKenzie, 'David Livingstone and the Worldly After-Life: Imperialism and Nationalism in Africa', in *David Livingtone and the Victorian Encounter with Africa*, ed. John M. MacKenzie (London: National Portrait Gallery, 1996), 203–16, 208.
82 Jonas Fossli Gjersø, 'Continuity of Moral Policy: A Reconsideration of British Motives for the Partition of East Africa in light of Anti-Slave Trade

Policy and Imperial Agency, 1878–96', unpublished PhD thesis, Department of International History, London School of Economics, 2015.

83 H. Gunston, 'Planning and Construction of the Uganda Railway', *Transactions of the Newcomen Society*, 74 (2004): 45–71.

84 Quotation from D.A. Low, *Buganda in Modern History* (London, 1971), 61, taken from Gjersø, 'Continuity of Moral Policy'.

85 D.A. Low, 'Review of R Oliver, Sir Harry Johnston and the Scramble for Africa (London: Chatto & Windus, 1957)', *Africa: Journal of the International African Institute*, 28, 4 (1958): 377–9.

86 J.S. Keltie, *The Partition of Africa* (London, 1893), 114, quoted in J.M. MacKenzie, *David Livingstone and the Worldy After-Life'*, (1996), 208.

3   A Perfect Savagery

The Livingstone Martyrs & the Tree of Death on
Africa's 'Highway to Hell'[1]

> I am in blood
> Stepp'd in so far that, should I wade no more,
> Returning were as tedious as go o'er
>
> William Shakespeare, *Macbeth*

Livingstone's African grave lay undisturbed for nearly twenty years. The
remoteness, violence and harsh climate of the region meant that the
quest to find the Livingstone grave became one of the last nineteenth-
century grand European expeditionary competitions in Africa. Tragedy
would run through these attempts, ensuring that this final stage of establishing colonial rule was cloaked in the sentimentality of lost loved ones
and doomed youth.

After Chief Chitambo's death in 1874, the local population had to sub-
divide into two villages.[2] A long-standing feud between the peoples on either
side of the Luapula River had often turned ugly, but now raiding parties
from the east by armed Bemba intent on capturing slaves caused the villages
to be abandoned ten years later. Leaving behind their own sacred sites, the
villagers moved closer to the Luapula, building first a small stockade. A new
village grew up ten miles away.[3] Chitambo had requested that he be placed
alongside Livingstone. Apparently, he was buried on the south side of the
mpundu tree; Livingstone to the north (see Figure 3.1). But his descendants
who told this story may have decided to invent it in order to seek protection
through such a bond in death. (The current Chief Chitambo insists that his
predecessor lays buried in a private chiefs' graveyard.)

One of the first Europeans to reach Livingstone's grave, in 1894, was
Edward J. Glave, journalist, explorer and Victorian heart-throb. He published an illustrated account of his journey through central Africa to find
'the heart' of Livingstone, in the Victorian epic tradition. But his words
would carry an extra emotional appeal. By the time readers followed his
pilgrimage, he too had perished, another martyr to the 'great' Livingstone
cause. Leaving no doubt about his mission, Glave described how 'the
sacred tree has often heard the fierce yell of the man-hunters, and the

Figure 3.1 Photograph of the Livingstone Tree from the early 1890s with the inscription carved into the *mpundu* tree by the leaders of each section of Livingstone's caravan after the body was successfully embalmed and then buried beneath the majestic tree. Hulton Archive. Getty Images.

screams of women and children and wounded men. Livingstone's long prayers for Africa's deliverance have not yet received fair response'. He also observed how the 'Livingstone tree looks sturdy and healthy' and appeared 'likely to last many years'. Yet five years later, the tree had been chopped down, its trunk sliced into bricks and a telegraph pole shoved in the stump. The site was cleared of trees and a fence built. No record was made of any chief's grave.

This chapter charts the series of 'heroic' attempts made, between 1890 and 1899, to find the 'Livingstone' tree and to claim the Livingstone mantle of humanitarian imperialism. These epic tales – as they would be laid down in the press – of bravery, sentimentality and anti-slavery accompanied the violent establishment of Belgian and British rule in this part of central Africa. The first attempts failed, but the grave became the object of growing European interest from the 1890s onwards, in a competition that blurred the lines between male rivalry, national pride and a battle to control the resources of central Africa. Quick and cheap methods used to annex Africa often meant brute force (the unedifying example of the British in Sudan was in the public's mind). So an added incentive existed to find the 'lost heart' of imperialism: it was a way to reassure home audiences that the world's conscience regarding Africa was still alive, and still British.

This episode highlights how 'the humanitarian and abolitionist belief in the transformative power of the Bible and the plough ... the role of personal conversion and individual initiative in spreading Christianity and promoting development'[4] converged with the more assertive, formal and exploitative imperialism in the last decades of the nineteenth century. A new generation of men formed a small but tight network, inspired by notions of heroic mission. They were often caught up in their own type of 'father-and-son' relationship. The more minor figures of Victorian exploration quietly influenced events, often through the press and popular writing. Lieutenant Verney Lovett Cameron was one such 'also-ran'. In the 1870s, he had witnessed 'the barbarism and atrocity' of slavery on the dhows he helped capture. This resolved him 'in his heart' to search for Livingstone and 'instilled a strong desire to take some further part in the suppression of the trade in human traffic'.[5] Until his death from a riding accident in 1894, he 'enthusiastically propagandized' for British intervention in Africa as a duty 'to terminate the great wrong we once did to that continent' through legitimate commerce. It was also a continent, he believed, where the educated sons of gentlemen could find their way in the world, India being too crowded. Cameron published hero-explorer books and journal articles over three decades. Yet his was a humanitarianism that was often flawed, like others' we see below, weakened by his imperial vision and 'a sense of wonderlust'.

In the Stanley and Cameron traditions, their self-styled sons were willing martyrs to the great cause, journeying to central Africa in search of Livingstone's heart, risking death. They blurred the categories of journalist, explorer and humanitarian activist. The prosopography of the journey within their articles, books and eulogies (a journey that took its mortal toll on more than a few) offers rich sources on the emotionality surrounding the dying gasps of nineteenth-century high imperialism. These pilgrimages to the grave provided romantic, masculinised narratives of death, sorrow and sentimentality, which accompanied the establishment of a feeble, shadowy colonial state in this region. And the tragedy of their lives helped erase from metropolitan narratives the European violence against Africans.

The Destabilisation of Central Africa

When Glave, disguised as a hunter to outwit the Belgians, found the Livingstone tree in 1894, he depicted a veritable Garden of Eden. Turtle doves cooed overhead; a litter of young hyenas played in the sun; and roan buck and eland roamed around in safety. A year later, maverick explorer and hunter Poulett Weatherley reached the grave. He found its solitude 'rather depressing' and was 'glad to get away'.[6]

These images of tranquillity contrast with the reality of those who lived in this awesome landscape, with its massive lakes, as big as seas, and meandering rivers up to two miles wide. This area can be roughly delineated as the area of land from the upper Zambezi River to the lower region of Lake Mweru on the northern and western shores of Lake Nyasa. It was still free of formal colonial occupation but not of creeping imperial frontiers and violent incursions. To the south-west lay Portuguese Angola and the Congo Free State. To the north, the British were moving downwards from Lake Victoria through the British East Africa Company. Further south were the growing power bases of Cecil Rhodes, competing with the older Portuguese presence in Mozambique; to the east, new and old groups – German traders, Scottish missionaries and Swahili-Arab dealers in ivory and slaves – vied for control.

From the 1890s, the area in which Livingstone died had become snared in a set of local, regional and global imperialisms, each interacting with and bringing out the worst features in the other. This complex picture was not understood in the outside world. Many European travellers focused on Arab slavery. A thin missionary presence often focused on itself, building up its power base and alliances with the prevailing power. Meanwhile, the concession companies were desperate to make money, despite the huge 'opportunity costs' associated with such an unstable environment. Four sources of instability in particular interacted and impacted on Africans.

i. African Kingdoms and Polities under Pressure in the Mweru-Luapula

Oral tradition described the earliest people in the Ilala area as the 'small people' responsible for the rock paintings. In the 1800s, many people who became known as the Lala had migrated from the Luba region of the southern Congo. One of the earliest European travellers in the region was Silva Porto, a Portuguese slave dealer. He described a heavily populated region full of well-tended gardens and accomplished hunters. The population were animist in belief, and the role of ancestors, the afterlife and a maleficium dominated.[7] Since Livingstone first travelled through south-central Africa in the 1860s, the region from the Luapula River to Lake Mweru in the east was experiencing waves of violence, warlordism and predatory state formation, which became entwined with the ambitions of European powers.[8] The major local powers were the old kingdom of Kazembe, with its ruler, Kanyembo Ntemena, and a rival power base, ruled by Chief Msiri, to the south.

Mwenda Msiri Ngelengwa Shitambi, to give him his full name, was the son of a successful trader in copper from the east coast of Africa (present-day Tanzania). He invaded the area and established a powerful polity with the help of other Yeke, who became the new ruling aristocracy, building up power through force and slaves, his military force so effective because of his ability to purchase muskets. He ruled the new Yeke Kingdom (also called the Garanganze or Garenganze Kingdom) in south-east Katanga (in present-day DRC) from about 1856 to 1891. This copper-producing region, home to the Sanga, the Lemba, and other related groups, had been part of the western periphery of the Kingdom of Kazembe, whose ruler was forced to concede territory to him.

As Macola and Kalenga Ngoy have shown, these were complex polities, precariously wielding power across long distances, requiring hefty tribute or quotas in return for protection. With the 'wealth in people' rule for underpopulated regions in resource-challenged environments in full operation, subjects invariably survived through some form of elastic client–patron dependency, which could range from the giving of modest gifts to ivory to slavery.[9]

As we shall see, gun ownership and its impact on slave raiding and ivory hunting made scattered villagers and acephalous societies more vulnerable to Msiri's style of warlordism. Older patterns of tribute-giving (in the form of material goods or slaves, or both) by weaker, smaller units of people to stronger ones were extended and incorporated by Arab, Portuguese and mixed-race slave dealers, with trade routes moving people and materials to the east African coast but also down through present-day Angola. The demands, raids and even full-blown invasions by newcomers were facilitated by the new gun technologies that wealthy traders like Msiri could buy in bulk. Many African polities had no choice – where possible – but to incorporate the new modes of 'smash and grab' warfare into their patterns of governance in order to survive.[10] However, in the long term, Msiri's brutal pattern extraction, with this firepower advantage, would make him vulnerable to insurgency. In the face of attempts to dislodge him from power from the east, as Macola has shown, 'Msiri embarked on a systematic process of military modernization', with Msiri acting like a merchant prince of the Yeke warlord state, delighting in 'diabolical refinements of cruelty'. His reliance on imported gunpowder to sustain his Yeke war bands would prove his downfall, but in the meantime these broad patterns of gun-based plunder continued.[11]

Glave's dramatic 1894 depiction of the Chitambo region created an apocalyptic scenario of the forced migration or enslavement of the Ilala people to almost annihilation because of an 'uneven contest', since 'the Walala have but a few old flintlocks; the Awemba unlimited supplies of guns and ammunition ... [but] the Walala ... build good stockades of stout poles, with clay banking'.[12]

ii. Arab-Swahili Slave and Ivory Traders

Livingstone's final expeditions, in the late 1860s and early 1870s, and the return journey of his fellow explorers to the coast with his body, had been affected by local wars, slavery and the general destabilisation arising from the spread of firearms into the interior (see Map P.1). So-called warrior tribes, those centrally organised, with sufficient surplus to support armed wings, such as the Awemba, Barotse and Angoni, were engaging in slavery and capturing ivory, mostly to purchase (obsolete) European firearms, which traders from the coast were selling, in part to protect themselves from each other and from Arab-Swahili slave merchants. Smaller, weaker ethnic groups were forced to copy these tactics and raid each other. A favourite strategy was to incite ethnic groups against each other and then offer to sell them guns, cloth, beads, etc., in exchange for ivory or people. To defend themselves with stockades, for example, slave labour was needed, thus creating a vicious circle.

Livingstone and other first-generation missionaries overestimated and overstated the role of Arab-Swahili traders from the coast in the slave trade, ignoring wider factors such as the availability of European guns. Yet, despite the exaggeration of the problem and an anti-Islamic tendency within these missionary accounts, there is evidence that aggressive enslavement, especially of women and children, was spreading inland into the central African lakes region and hitting the Mweru-Luapula region harder in the 1880s. Arab-Swahili traders were taking advantage of a temporary weakening of British imperialism. The British navy had put pressure on the Sultan of Zanzibar to halt the selling of slaves in Arabia and south Asia in the 1870s and, around the time of Livingstone's death, fresh agreements were signed and a stronger consular presence established. The sultan's authority in eastern Africa, however, was declining inland, as German influence spread in what was to become, in 1885, their territory of Tanganyika. The British had been defeated in Sudan in 1885, so slave traders on the ground were able to set up powerful bases from which caravans could move around Lake Nyasa, encouraging groups like the Bemba (Wabemba) to prey on weaker polities, like the Ilala people and Chitambo. This set the Arab-Swahili colonisers on a collision course with European traders and with the more organised missionaries based around Lake Nyasa, close to the route of their caravans back to the coast.

iii. Missionaries

The area of central Africa through which Livingstone had passed during his final journey was not forgotten. Immediately after he died, a major gesture to honour him came in the form of a push by Scottish missionaries and entrepreneurs to extend 'Commerce and Christianity' in the Shire Valley around Lake Nyasa. Livingstone had been HM Consular Representative there, popularising a misguided vision of white colonisation to develop the region. Dr Robert Laws arrived in 1875, and more missionaries from the Church of Scotland arrived in 1876. Not far behind came the newly formed African Lakes Company, set up by two Scottish brothers, John and Frederick Moir, who had attended Livingstone's funeral. The vigilance of Scottish public opinion is often underestimated, but it was the so-called voice of Scotland, through church petitions and media coverage, that demanded British protection be extended to the Shire region.[13]

Under the terms of the General Act of the Berlin (or Congo) Conference of the 1884–5 Berlin Treaty, the principle of effective occupation was established for Africa whereby a European power could claim a protectorate if sufficient evidence existed to show authority on the ground.[14] This was the preference of the British government, which had the most informal presence on the continent and no appetite for footing the expense of formal rule. Initially, there was no government support other than a consulate, opened in the town of Blantyre, named after Livingstone's birthplace, in 1883. A commissioner for Nyasa District was appointed in 1891. Their thin white line, however, was threatened by Portuguese incursions, Yao slavers and Arab-Swahili slave traders penetrating from the north. The Moirs found their beads and cloth were less attractive to purchasers than guns and powder, and they struggled financially. In 1885, fighting broke out between mercenaries from the African Lakes Company and the main coalition of Arab slavers. As the violence escalated, volunteers were quickly found, including two young British soldiers on a hunting party, Captain F.D. Lugard and Alfred Sharpe. Lugard was slightly wounded in the fighting.[15]

Similarly, by the late 1880s, the area to the west and south of Livingstone's grave, and down to the Zambezi, was being eyed by the Portuguese, with their foothold in Mozambique, and incursions were being made into Nyasa District, but government support remained unforthcoming. Lord Salisbury, in 1890, had sanctioned British rule over Uganda, recognising German control of Tanganyika, and was content that Britain's anti-slavery tradition in Africa had been fulfilled. The final 'scramble' for central Africa could not fully begin, however, before the arrival of the final set of players.

iv.   European Imperialism, Concession Hunters & the Congo Free State

Before he died, Livingstone had been wandering about a swampy area in central Africa that would become part of Northern Rhodesia (Zambia) and the Congo Free State (DRC), but until the mid-1890s, the Anglo-Belgian border was in a state of flux, and the outcome was by no means certain. In the decade immediately after Livingstone's death, this inaccessible region was of little interest to the European powers, the governments of the day being uninterested in acquiring such territory due to the related costs. Only a few European explorers were interested in the wider regions, notably George Westbeech in Barotseland to the south, Dr Emil Holub in the Ila region and Victor Giraud, who, inspired by Livingstone, had made it to the Bangweulu Swamps.[16]

Nevertheless, Livingstone had been competing to find the headwaters of the Nile, believing it to be the Luapula. After Livingstone's funeral, Stanley resolved to return to Africa to finish the search in honour of Livingstone, focusing on tracing the course of the Congo River, an extraordinary feat which he accomplished in the late 1870s, proving that the Luapula was a tributary of the Congo.[17] Stanley's superhuman, controversial central African explorations came to the attention of King Leopold II of Belgium, who was intent on acquiring an empire to make him money, undeterred by rumours about Stanley's excessive use of force. Snubbed by the British government and unable to garner sufficient support from British manufacturing interests, Stanley eventually agreed to Leopold's offer of a modest salary as part of a harsh contract to return to central Africa.[18] With Livingstone's aims in mind and Leopold masquerading as a philanthropist, Stanley returned to the Congo to engage in further exploration, hewing Belgian military stations into shape en route.

Stanley's effective methods and association with Livingstone's memory and cause became vital components in Leopold's grand strategy to establish a bogus free-trade colony under the guise of anti-slavery. Leopold now had his sights on extending his reach deep into the Katanga region, which would inevitably bring his military forces into conflict with Msiri. Soon, the latest dynamic form of global capital – the concession companies – would take advantage of this warlordism pattern refashioned to cope with the insecure environment. The concession companies, under his rule, were given free rein to extract raw materials – first ivory and later rubber – in bulk. Their brutality has become legendary.[19]

By the late 1880s, concession companies, backed by investors drawn from across Europe,[20] were pressing forward across central Africa towards the areas that Livingstone had been exploring and where he had died, territory rumoured to be rich in minerals. Cecil Rhodes and his British South Africa Company (BSAC) were delayed by African resistance – an uprising in the south by the Matabele in 1893. He also embarrassed the British government with his failed Jameson Raid, his military expedition, in 1895, to bring down the government in the Transvaal, but this would not detain him for long. He celebrated his aims and methods by naming a fortified boma (administrative headquarters) on the border between Nyasaland and North-Eastern Rhodesia, after the leader of the raid. Fort Jameson was also known affectionately as Fort Jimmy.

During this period, European boundaries were either in a state of flux or non-existent. In 1894, the border between the Congo Free State and the British was finally agreed, and Britain assumed administrative responsibility for Nyasaland, which separated it from the rest of British Central Africa. This area would eventually become Northern Rhodesia. However, in the 1890s, Barotseland and North-Western and North-Eastern Rhodesia were still considered Rhodes's personal domain despite his reputation, local resistance and the flimsy line of military outposts. Nevertheless, the 'march of progress' proved unstoppable.

The Tree of Death and the Tragedy of Joseph Thomson

The first attempts to find Livingstone's grave and claim his legacy were instigated by profit-driven concession companies and young explorers for hire, but so challenging were the conditions that the first two attempts to find the tree by hardened men failed, resulting in multiple deaths. The long-term consequences for many central Africans were more dire.

By 1890, Rhodes was working with the African Lakes Company, paying them a subsidy to enforce 'law and order' to enable him to trade and pursue concessions. Conditions were deteriorating in the Nyasa region, and the British government assumed responsibility for law and order, appointing a commissioner for British Central Africa, Harry Johnston, in 1891. Johnston saw himself as liberal, whilst simultaneously advocating violent conquest. '[A] profound admirer of Stanley', according to his biographer, he was 'even more a disciple of Livingstone'.[21] He was an Africaphile, first visiting Tunis on a painting holiday aged twenty-one. Being five foot three inches tall, with a high voice, he perhaps sought beauty in young men since he had been denied it himself.[22] An ardent anti-slaver, his ideological beliefs never wavered: white settlement would bring the necessary civilisation; missionaries could spearhead it; and British colonisation would bring greater benefits to Africans than any other European style of rule.[23] This would shape the colonial history of Nyasaland, keeping Rhodes at arm's length.

While Johnston was somewhat appreciative of African life and culture, it did not prevent him being 'compelled by the logic of circumstances to shatter the power of the larger chiefdoms and to rely on force as his constant instrument'.[24] In 1890, the company had signed a lucrative concession agreement with the king of Barotseland, to the far south-west of the Ilala region and, in 1891, a large area of the north-west came under its administration. (Lewanika was the Lozi Litunga, or king, of Barotseland from 1878 to 1916, with a break in 1884–5). later paramount chief). Undermined by missionaries, who aided and abetted the company's offer, Lewanika, who was already under pressure due to the destabilising effects of the gun trade, prospectors and local aggressors, had little choice but to accept the forceful offer of company protection in exchange for material concessions

Rhodes was eyeing up the region of Katanga and engaged a young British explorer, Joseph Thomson, to make the dangerous journey from Nyasa deep into central Africa to meet with the Chief Msiri, whose Yeke kingdom was situated within the mineral-rich Katanga region. Born on St Valentine's Day 1858, Thomson was eighteen years old and embarking on his university training in Edinburgh when Livingstone's corpse had returned home. Scottish by birth and a geologist by training, Thomson was a darling of the elite metropolitan circle of explorers, active and 'armchair', following events through various learned society journals and the press. He was not always successful. However, he was a favourite of the RGS, an embodiment of the romance of youthful, intrepid, heroic exploration and a symbol of meritocratic manliness.

Thomson had many claims to fame and a suite of ardent admirers. In the employ of the RGS, he had travelled through Masailand to hold back German traders, failing to reach the summit of Kilimanjaro. He had lost his teeth and been impaled by a buffalo, and had returned weakened by disease. He published a detailed account of his travels and penned a romantic novel set in Africa.[25] (Rider Haggard based his most famous novel, *King Solomon's Mines*, on Thomson's exploits.) Thomson then upset German plans to expand into the Niger region, while employed by a British company. He had also spent a month travelling with a young J.M. Barrie, who was inspired to create the character of Peter Pan.[26]

Thomson's own best-sellers presented a romantic image of a self-styled gentleman explorer who spurned violence, honouring a Livingstonian 'gentleness with the natives'.[27] Thomson recounted his expedition through central Africa to the RGS at a packed meeting in November 1892. He flattered his audience, announcing how he had been 'in pursuance of the splendid enterprise which has marked its [the RGS's] short but brilliant history', since he had been offered the chance by the BSAC to explore British Central Africa and Lake Bangweulu. This was doubly attractive to him, he continued, being 'a blank space' on the map, and an opportunity to visit the 'sacred spot' where Livingstone had 'closed his great career, leaving his heart in the land where all his thoughts and aspirations centered'.[28] He proposed that the region be renamed Livingstonia.[29]

In reality, he was being paid by Cecil Rhodes to beat the Belgians to Katanga. When Thomson arrived in Nyasa District, he met Harry Johnston, who, in 1889, had just been made consul in Mozambique by Lord Salisbury.[30] Johnston had allegedly hatched a plan with Cecil Rhodes, after meeting him at a London dinner party, to make treaties with as many chiefs as they could in the area beyond Nyasaland (modern Zambia and Zimbabwe). In October 1889, the BSAC had received a Royal Charter of Incorporation, a mechanism by which the British government hedged its bets, allowing Rhodes to make money in return for administering south-central Africa. Rhodes's method, like the other concessionary companies, was to procure investment to pay for expeditions and military force that would offer chiefs 'protection' in return for exclusive access to virtually anything deemed potentially profitable for investors. Whilst trying to hold back the Portuguese along the Zambezi, Johnston came across Alfred Sharpe, a qualified solicitor and failed plantation owner (the plantation had been in Fiji), on an elephant hunt. Sharpe agreed to make a hazardous journey into the interior on behalf of Rhodes, to gain concessions for the new company. Portuguese forces and a German trader, Karl Wiese, forced him back to Nyasa.

In July 1890, Sharpe met Thomson by chance. Neither knew of the other's duplicate mission. They decided to take two different routes to reach Msiri's capital, Bunkeya. Thomson would take the western route, round the southern shore of Lake Bangweulu. The expedition did not

start well. He chose not to make treaties with the chiefs whose territory he wandered through. This was a tactical error since, closely following behind, was a party that included Wiese. Even before Thomson's
'ulendo had disappeared over the escarpment', their rivals were drawing
up treaties. Events went from bad to worse. Thomson was making for
Chitambo. Just as he reached the swamps, in September 1890, his party
was struck by smallpox. Word spread through the villages, and the group
was denied food or helpers. 'Every day began a new chapter in a story of
death and disease', Thomson recorded. They had no path, and their local
guide showed them only an 'irritating vacuity'. The caravan made for 'a
wretched spectacle', as 'disfigured men' either were left behind or staggered along at the back. Supplies had to be abandoned. The men went
for two days without food before reaching the new Chitambo village,
which was at some distance from the actual tree. Five men died there.

Unable to leave the camp (he was enforcing a strict quarantine),
Thomson sent his most 'intelligent and trusty headman' to find the
tree.[31] The actions of the headman (unnamed) horrified Thomson, not
because he brought back a handful of leaves, but because he had used
his knife to gouge out one of the letters carved into the trunk, and had
broken off a fragment of an old tin box. The leaves and part of the box
were sent back to England. Agnes, Livingstone's daughter, received the
letter 'D'. The African headman had not, in fact, found the tree, but had
instead ingeniously carved a substitute letter. So he began the tradition
of circulating leaves and bark as sacred relics of the Livingstone tree.[32]

Thomson knew that, with almost a third of his carriers gone, he had
no chance of making it to Katanga. He also fell ill. He 'pushed on' and
was able to form a couple of important treaties, including one with
Paramount Chief Mipisi, which would eventually yield Rhodes a large
piece of central Africa (which would become part of Northern Rhodesia)
at very little cost to himself. Now very ill, Thomson was forced to return
to Nyasa. He escaped the plague but became so 'broken down' that he
had to be carried on the return journey, then slowly nursed back to
health by missionaries.

Thomson's journalistic lectures and writings on central Africa, based
on his recent travels in Livingstone's Africa, endorsed a highly negative
view of the region. He was part of a growing number of spokesmen who
were portraying central Africa as bleak in outlook and needing urgent
backup. He depicted an interior where women and children lived in terror of slave dealers – who 'spread death and desolation over thousands
of miles' – including half-caste Portuguese dealers, who had a created
a 'pestiferous sphere'. He described the 'wretched inhabitants' caught
between the infamous blood feud between two powerful warrior chiefs,

Mpensi and Mwasi. Other negative stereotyping of Africa included the landscape itself: trees were often 'stunted and gnarled'; mud 'reeking' or 'repulsive'. In stark contrast, the settlements in Nyasaland and the Scottish missionaries were praised for only having 'moral weapons', being unaided by Maxim guns or the government. Likewise, the businessmen in the areas were lauded as the 'beau-ideal of commercial and philanthropic heroes'.[33] Typically, negative images of Islam and its followers were also circulated. Their beliefs were 'prejudices'; their reactions 'a frenzy'. This was perfect propaganda for commercial barons like Cecil Rhodes, who was keen to build a railway from the south to Katanga.

The RGS's discussion after Thomson's lecture unanimously concluded that 'this dark continent, this dark Africa, must see the light of civilization and humanity', and everyone displayed a typically optimistic Victorian sense of the possible: with a new journey time of three and half months, central Africa was now deemed less remote.[34] This view required a typically dismissive attitude towards the huge effort and loss of life associated with these journeys for African porters, cooks and guides.

Thomson's health never recovered from his failed attempt to find the grave. In 1892, he contracted pneumonia and tried to recuperate in warmer climes. He died in London in 1895, aged only thirty-seven. He was at least immortalised in writing by men who fell in love with him, and had an African gazelle and snail named after him.

'Livingstone's Son' and the Assassination of Chief Msiri

The competition to find Livingstone's grave accelerated the land grab. Thomson's goal had been to meet up with Alfred Sharpe by pushing westward, bringing him vital supplies of goods with which to sweeten the paramount chief, Msiri, whose territory covered much of the rich Katanga region to the south. Sharpe, however, became caught up in a long quarrel between those living on either side of the Luapula River. In the early 1880s, the Kingdom of Kazembe, to the east, endured violent Yeke invasions and heavy extraction, resulting in mass migration across the Luapula River to escape Msiri's rule. This was followed by a military stalemate. In 1885/6 its new leader, Kanyembo Ntemena, moved to increase his firepower, so posed more of threat to Msiri. However, it would be a rebellion of Sanga, rising up against Msiri's cruel rule, which would prove fatal through a combination of circumstances in 1891. Colonialist historian Kenneth Bradley, writing in 1958, took a simple view of his methods: he 'kept his throne by wholesale murder and protected his borders by making raids on the surrounding tribes'.[35] Kazembe had refused to give Sharpe a canoe, to prevent him crossing the river and reaching his rival, fearful that Msiri would gain advantages. Kazembe eventually allowed Sharpe to plant a British flag in exchange for the promise of military support. Carriers were provided as a result of the concession being agreed, on condition, in Kazembe's understanding, that they would take Sharpe home. Sharpe reneged and made it to Msiri's capital, Bunyeka. A hub of transcontinental trading, Bayeke saw slaves, ivory, salt, copper and iron sold to traders from places as far flung as Angola and Zanzibar. Msiri had been able to build up up a large standing army.

At the court of Msiri was the Reverend Frederick Stanley Arnot, known as 'the son of Livingstone'. Arnot had been born in Hamilton, Glasgow, in 1858, so Livingstone's family lived nearby, and Livingstone was his hero.[36] Arnot had learnt a trade with a view to becoming a missionary and had virtually followed in Livingstone's steps, arriving in the remote capital of Msiri's kingdom in 1886, the only white person to have been there for two years, after travelling up through southern Africa and the Kalahari, and becoming a confidant of Paramount Chief Lewanika of Barotseland. In return for permission to build a mission station and an orphanage, Arnot easily tolerated his patron's excesses. According to many pro-missionary accounts, Msiri's palace was marked out by skulls stuck on tall poles. He was 'the perfect savage'.[37]

Arnot had left the Church of Scotland for the Plymouth Brethren and took a more fundamentalist line against 'company' commerce being twinned with Christianity. Unlike Livingstone, he also actively promoted the role of women in missionary work.[38] Two additional Plymouth Brethren had been allowed to join Arnot. Arnot had sufficient influence over Msiri and his advisers to convince them to have nothing to do with prospectors or concession hunters.

Although Arnot had returned home due to ill health by the time Sharpe staggered into the capital, his line was adhered to. This was for good reason. As Macola has shown, the ways in which concessions were acquired were highly dubious at the best of times. Sharpe and others would insist that, through translators, they always explained to chiefs and their advisers that, in return for signing a peace settlement with the British crown (i.e. the company) and forbidding foreigners access to their economic assets, the company would assume responsibility for law and order: 'very ambitiously, the Company committed itself to assist ... in the establishment and propagation of the Christian religion, and the education and civilization of the native subjects'.[39] In this case, once the concession terms had been explained by the missionaries, Msiri had Sharpe deported under escort, back the way he came, to the north. So, in a bizarre twist of fate, Thomson and Sharpe had been indirectly blocked in their pursuit of the Katanga region by missionaries intent on living the Livingstone legacy.

However, a handful of Plymouth Brethren – his 'white slaves', as Msiri referred to them – could not save Msiri from the Belgian concession hunting mercenaries heading his way. By the early 1890s, Msiri's hold on power was slipping. Famine and the uprising that had resulted in a blockade weakened his power base, a situation he could not escape from as he lacked access to the precious commodity of gunpowder. In vain, he looked to Congo Free State forces to fight his enemies on his behalf.[40] Sharpe and Thomson's expeditions had come to the attention of King Leopold, who followed the RGS closely through the British press. Resolving to annex the region as quickly as possible, he sanctioned an armed Belgian unit to gain concessions by any means. Msiri refused and sought refuge away from his capital. He was hunted down like an animal according to sympathetic accounts. According to some, his fate was 'well-deserved'.[41] To the north-east of his capital, a Congo Free State military station was quickly built as a mark of effective occupation over the Katanga region and to keep the BSAC at bay.

Belgian imperialism in the region was on the ascendancy, reflected in the next attempt to reach Livingstone's grave. In 1892, a second Belgian Congo Expedition to Katanga was led by Captain Lucien Bia, who possessed all of the necessary credentials: the backing of the Katanga Company, a record for brutality and a large, twirly moustache. He could also boast of having been on a humanitarian mission, evoking the anti-slavery spirit. Visiting Scotland, Arnot had been given a brass memorial tablet for the tree from Agnes Livingstone (now Mrs Bruce), plus some cloth and various small items from the RGS, as a thank you to the chief for allowing the body to rest there and keeping the remains safe. But Arnot was too weak from ill health to make the journey into central Africa from eastern Angola, where he was resting, so he handed the symbolic gifts to the Belgians. The expedition was covered in the Belgian national press and its popular periodical, *Mouvement Geographiques*.[42]

Bia and his expedition relied on African porters and local intelligence to reach the new Chitambo village, arriving on 6 July 1892. They never reached the grave, although no clear explanation survives as to why. Some reports insist they could not find the site; others, that they refused an offer to be escorted there. Perhaps they were not seriously interested. Bia and his second-in-command, Lieutenant Franqui, stuck the plate on a tree in the village and left a note in French signed by Chitambo (the old chief's cousin): 'Lost far away in the midst of tall grass, it is only with more than hesitation, that the natives point out the place where is interred the heart of Livingstone'. They listed all of the gifts they presented, as required, which included three red fez hats, black parasols, a gun and a huge amount of cloth.[43] The locals watched in bemusement, unsure about the purpose of the brass plate. Bia, already weakened by bouts of malaria, caught a deadly fever in the swamps where Livingstone had become mortally ill. He died on 30 August 1892.

The Martyrdom of 'Stanley's Son'

British efforts to reclaim the site and the moral high ground followed hot on the Belgians' heels. Another young martyr would add to the sorrows and sentimentality around personal heroism and self-sacrifice which bound together a circle of English explorers and their many admirers.

Edward J. Glave was their pin-up boy by the early 1890s. He was a highly idealised, romantic figure even before his tragic death, in May 1895, aged thirty-three, after a long expedition through central Africa from Zanzibar to heroically expose 'the horrors of the cruel traffic in human lives carried on by Arab hunters'.[44] The aims of the expedition also included finding Livingstone's grave. Disguised as a white hunter, Glave travelled light, with twelve African men. He survived illness, the swamps, violent attacks, cannibals and famine – his journalistic accounts claim – before arriving at Matadi, the mouth of the Congo. Here, despite the dedicated nursing of a vicar, Lawson Forfeitt, and Clayton Pickersgill, the consul, he painfully died over three days, possibly in their arms.

It is worth dwelling on the emotions that his death aroused in other men since these might have been fairly widely shared. Because his letters sometimes had to travel over land for a thousand miles, the gap between the publication of his sensationalist account of finding Livingstone's grave and news of his death was very short, adding poignancy and tragedy. 'Glave's Journey to the Livingstone Tree: Glimpses of Life in Africa from the Journals of the late E J Glave' was published in the *Century Magazine*, after an extensive obituary, including a full-page photographic portrait.

Stanley could 'scarcely trust himself to write' when he heard of Glave's death. He was broken-hearted: 'I have at present no interest in the future whatsoever … I had more respect, admiration and love for him than for any other man I have ever met'. In a letter to Glave's brother-in-law, he recalled how Glave 'made you all go out of his cabin while he said goodbye to me alone'. Thinking of it now made him weep, Stanley confessed.[45] It remains intriguing as to why Glave wanted to be alone with him.

Glave had been given the name '*Mwana Tendele*' (meaning 'son of Stanley') by Africans at his station in the Congo, at Lukolela.[46] Glave had been extremely effective in running remote, fledgling control posts, volunteering for the most challenging. Considering Stanley's reputation for tough discipline, one might speculate that Glave, too, had a harsh, even sadistic attitude to discipline. Certainly, Stanley idolised him as a perfect version of himself. As Jeal writes: 'Ten years earlier, a disillusioned Stanley wrote revealingly to Harry Johnston, "It is about time I give up this search for the perfect man". In Glave, he believed he had found perfection'. Jeal interprets this as paternal love: Stanley was grieving for the man he had come to regard as a son, who had embraced the cause of Stanley's adopted father, Livingstone, dying in the attempt to find his grave.

The precise nature of the attachment between older and younger men that characterises colonial exploration and early rule will remain unresolved in the absence of records. Homosexual romantic love is a possibility, repressed or not, but so, too, is deep filial attachment in the absence of functional father–son family life. The heroics of expeditionary life created urgent needs: being obeyed and being seen to be obeyed was an important performative relationship for white men in the absence of any kind of absolute power during colonial expeditions, and young men and small boys followed orders more compliantly. Also, explorers became attached to the muscle-bound men who carried their lives and careers in their rough hands. Male physicality became all important. Less romantic interpretations abound. 'Given that a high proportion of these European adventurers had weird to near-manic personalities before they entered Africa', as Hopkins points, 'it is scarcely surprising that some of them were deranged when they left – if they did. Stanley himself was a few steps short of normality'.[47] Livingstone possibly helped send Sekewebu, his fellow explorer, mad and watched him as he committed suicide.[48]

Even if drugs, mental illness and alcohol played their part, death of a young man or boy – part of the expedition family –could generate intense feeling, which could also send men 'out of their minds'.[49] Many explorers and first-wave soldier-administrators experienced the loss of a servant boy whom they 'loved' as a son. These sorrows may well have been poured back into the imperial mission, increasing the vigour or callousness with which the mission was carried out.

Glave was mourned over the world as the perfect hero. One obituary, written by fellow explorer Robert Howard Russell, idolised the Livingstonian qualities in his life and death. Had he known he would die, Russell concluded, Glave would still have undertaken this mission to expose the evil Arab trade: so 'perished ... one of the simplest and bravest men of his time', with a 'fearless and transparent nature'. Russell also confidently wrote how this had won Glave the devotion and trust of not only his 'black followers' but also 'every native' with whom he came into contact.[50] Russell appeared to be mad with grief. Likewise, Richard Watson Gilder, a poet and the influential editor of *The Century*, was so moved that he penned a eulogy while on holiday in Venice. Drenched in romantic sentiment, it was, in part, criticism of an age cynical of 'noble rage' and 'great enterprise', a world at the end of the century 'withered and undone', but then came:

> Thy face of youth/Hero and martyr of humanity
> Dead yesterday on Afric's shore of doom!
> Ah, no: Faith, Courage fail not, while lives Truth,
> While Pity lives, while man for man can die,
> And deeds of glory light the dark world's gloom.[51]

The reality on the ground had been less romantic for all concerned. En route to the Livingstone tree, for 28 April 1894, he wrote in his diary: 'Marched from Karonga to Kaporo, four and half hours on a good trail, with four of five watercourses to cross; can manage without getting wet by straddling a native's neck'.[52] Glave's record of how he made his way through the swamps in search of the grave is classic Livingstone: a Victorian 'selfie'. Glave presented an image of himself as a man who was kind to his men, a man who resorted to only 'tactful jockeying', who was patient with the chief (and his 'repulsive' wives) and who recorded in fascinated detail the natural world he encountered. There is little acknowledgement of the contributions from his African companions. He is, according to his own record, the perfect gentleman explorer.

Adding credence to his views was the fact that he was successful where the Belgians had failed. Glave recorded reaching Livingstone's grave before the village. For 8 July, he wrote: 'This is a red-letter day in my career. I have visited the place where Dr Livingstone's heart is buried'. He found the thirty-foot tree – bearing a mass of foliage, unmolested and carrying the inscription – in a 'splendid state of preservation'. It was as if the very spirit of Livingstone was reflected in its glorious condition.

Glave was less enthusiastic in his diaries about the new village of Chitambo and the Belgian mission. Glave reached the new Chitambo village on 13 July and found the tree on which Captain Bia and Lieutenant Franqui had fixed the memorial tablet. He was disparaging about their failure to find the actual Livingstone tree The village they had visited had been abandoned two years previously, and the bronze plaque had disappeared. Glave constructed a detailed picture from the local chiefs and elders, adding that some of the older men remembered Livingstone and the cap he wore. Glave was informed that the new Chitambo village had been abandoned because of slave-raiding by a new wave of Bemba now coming from the north. The local chiefs insisted that they had been powerless to prevent the theft of the bronze tablet. They alleged that a party of slave-raiders had led a large caravan through the region eighteen months previously, under the control of two Swahili dealers, Kasaki and Karuma: 'These are coast men'.

Glave stressed in his polemical writings how the region was in a state of violent anarchy, with these traders trawling the region for slaves and then marching them in slave forks south to the Zambezi for export. The emotional impact of his news was huge. Readers would likely recoil in outrage. Arab slave dealers had apparently boasted how they had desecrated the white man's grave, and the brass plate from Livingstone's daughter had been melted down and turned into bullets.[53] Moreover, located somewhere between Livingstone's beloved river and the swamps that took his life stood their stockade, where locals were held captive prior to transit. In case any readers had missed the point, Glave concluded: 'This does not look as though slavery had had its death-blow; it should remind the world of its yet unfinished task'. This was potent anti-slavery propaganda, promoting British intervention in the region. Glave suggested a line of stations made up of fifty armed men, judging missionaries unable to prevent the spreading trade that was especially keen on young girls.

To add to his campaigning journalism, Glave included descriptions of how refugees from the slave raids were living, semi-starved, hidden in stockades or thick bush, and how murder and the slave chains fuelled by the new guns and ammunition had depopulated the region. Highly racist, negative representations of African men and African culture were also included: the bloated drunk who barged into his tent snacking on locusts; the unwillingness to keep huts clean; the aside that Africans generally did not grieve for their dead. Central Africa was once again depicted as the ultimate challenge for a bare-knuckled white adventurer who alone could rise above local superstition. What any young reader would surely remember is how Glave shot a three-and-a-half-foot puff adder, with a body that kept wriggling and found its way back down its hole. Glave's men asked him to move the body far away, believing that the snake would return to reclaim its head. Symbolic of the peace that white rule could bring, Livingstone's grave was represented as a pre-Lapsian paradise, with no snake; even the animals had been subdued by his spirit.

Glave carried a deadly secret to both graves which would not surface until the late 1890s. His journey to find Livingstone's grave and publicise his own remedy to stop the spread of Arab-inspired slavery had taken him through territory which was now under the jurisdiction of Leopold's expanded Congo Free State, which Glave had set up. Concession companies were using particularly brutal methods and a slave-based armed militia to force the locals to harvest rubber. Glave did not focus on these atrocities in his journalism (although he had not factored in dying). Only when Glave's diaries were published, in 1897, did they include the infamous accounts of African men being given a hundred lashes and Captain Rom's predilection for using native heads to adorn his flower beds. Stanley could not ignore his darling boy's words from the grave; he remonstrated with Leopold, but to no avail. Nevertheless, Glave's exposé had played a part in inspiring the mounting campaign against the Congo Free State, which another friend, Roger Casement, campaigner and homosexual, would make his passion. And Joseph Conrad's *Heart of Darkness* famously used his notes on Rom for the sadistic, deranged Kurtz.

Blood-Stained Missionaries and a Bit of a Cult

Glave's more modest legacy had been to create a rudimentary visitors' book at the grave. A large tree near the *mpundu* was chosen to start a tradition of carving initials on the trunk. The first European woman to reach the spot was a young twenty-something bride, who arrived there with her husband in 1897. Grace Tilsley had recently arrived in central Africa to work as a missionary. The Reverend Dan Crawford had been in central Africa since 1889, as a member of the Christian Missions in Many Lands, a Nonconformist organisation that also welcomed laymen. He had made for Arnot's Plymouth Brethren outpost at the court of Msiri. Crawford, aged twenty-six, then abandoned his view that 'a missionary married is a missionary marred'.

In April 1897, the first recorded Christian service was held at the tree, conducted by Crawford. His congregation consisted of his wife and the 'Ilala twinklers', as he called them, plus two mining prospectors. At the foot of the tree, Chief Chitambo presided as 'chairman Chief'. After playing 'Abide with Me' on his portable organ, Crawford read out Hebrews 11, then delivered a long sermon, in part to refute the disparaging remarks made by Harry Johnston about Livingstone's sincerity as a missionary. Chief Chitambo then produced the man who had apparently played the music at Livingstone's wake, who 'in quaintest Chaucerian Bantu' recited the ballad that he had composed at the time, which ended with 'Oh, the Lovely One is gone'. Then, those gathered sat around a fire, eating roast venison and trying to work out where the gold might be.

In typical British fashion, Crawford did not leave the area until he had built a low ornamental fence around the tree and recorded his disdain for the Belgians' failure. The 'Belgian proxies', as he called Bia's mission, had merely left 'an apologetic document' where they stuck up the tablet he disparagingly noted.[54] (Crawford had nursed the dying Bia.)

Crawford's account was circulated in Britain through the widely read British journal *Africa*. 'The Grave of Livingstone's Heart' contained his wistful image of 'a lonely deserted spot, with lions roaring the whole night long'. However, Crawford and his wife also enthusiastically reported the existence of the second grave – the old Chief Chitambo – unlike Glave. They also approved of the site and the double burial, finding it symbolic of their own idealised version of an ancient intimacy between white and black:

Old Chitambo, 'Ingeresa's' friend and 'Man Friday' of those past days, lies most appropriately on the off-side of the tree; so in death they are not divided. Livingstone wanted nothing more lovely and truly emblematic of his life than this! If it is true that a Blackman carried our Lord's cross a bit of the hard way to Golgotha, then here is an instance of a blackman helping to carry the Master's servant's cross.[55]

Crawford turned the account of their journey to Livingstone's grave into a book; illustrations came with captions such as 'A typical Arab fanatic'. Published in 1922, to coincide roughly with the fiftieth anniversary of Livingstone's death, it was written to fulfil a promise made to Silvester Horne, a fellow Scotsman and biographer of Livingstone, after they had attended the centenary celebration of Livingstone's birth at the Royal Albert Hall, London, in 1913. This was the only occasion when Crawford returned to Britain. Both, he confessed, were fanatics in their devotion to 'Saint David', and he quoted from the *Livingstone Cult* at the start of the book.

This narrative of reaching the grave would become an inspirational missionary text which passed down to the next generation another version of the Livingstone legacy. *Back to the Long Grass* (Crawford conceded he wrote the second half with his wife) was a personal account of retracing the route to Chitambo, interviewing Africans and Arabs who claimed to have met him. The book's subtitle, *My Link with Livingstone*, at one level signals his contribution to the great story of Livingstone's death, by holding the first Christian service at the grave.

Crawford is an important figure for understanding the reproduction of the Livingstone legacy in missionary Africa. For Protestants, and especially for Scottish missionaries, Livingstone offered refuge from the difficulties surrounding imperialism, allowing them to instead focus on a figure who embodied 'Christian dedication and compassion ... [and] Missions felt a special connection with Livingstone, for many reasons not least theological'.[56] Crucially, like Crawford, they were cocooned in a belief that they and Livingstone stood for a liberal racial attitude towards Africans. Crawford's writings were recommended to missionaries going to Africa who wanted to work 'in partnership' with Africans. His most widely read book was *Thinking Black*. Publishing it on the centenary of Livingstone's birth, in 1913, Crawford embarked on a publicity tour, in Britain, Australia and the United States, advertising himself as 'Livingstone's Successor'.[57] He marketed himself as the former 'private secretary' to one of central Africa's most despotic potentates. His role was merely that of confidant, he added quickly, but he boasted that he was able to lessen some of the chief's 'horrid cruelties' to his subjects.

Crawford's views on race would have been understood at the time as progressive and 'cool'. Crawford had translated the Bible into Bantu, a language, he explained, that was of infinite complexity, with thirty tenses. Nevertheless, *Thinking Black* and the liberal school were still based on fundamentally racist principles: to understand 'the African', one had to think in a different way; Africans were only redeemable as black versions of white people ('nude capitalists' or 'black suffragettes'). Moreover, Crawford spiced up his accounts with anecdotes of alleged sensational black cruelty, such as the five hundred brutalised wives of a particular chief.[58] Racist clichés abound: 'The average native is a clever rogue'. The limits of Crawford's progressiveness are revealed by his failure to see that the first Christian service around Livingstone's grave had already taken place when he was buried, and conducted by Africans.

Crawford's hold on the baton of the self-styled successor to Livingstone was strong. He was born in 1870 into a poor Scottish family in Greenock. His father died of tuberculosis, which Crawford also caught but survived. In Greenock, in 1888, he had met the Reverend Arnot. The Church of Scotland failed to meet his spiritual needs so, aged sixteen, he joined the Plymouth Brethren.[59] It was a burning desire to evangelise among the people whom Livingstone had written about during his last journey that took Crawford to central Africa, where the Brethren had a toehold. He, too, could not commit to a mainstream, sedentary life of converting Africans – he preferred exploring, hunting and shooting, and had a reputation for being difficult to work with and for being highly individualistic, with resolute opinions.

Like Livingstone, Crawford enjoyed a reputation for being sympathetic to Africans: he made an effort to learn the local languages and wanted to be buried in a native blanket. He also wrote about women; his wife likely encouraged him to devote attention to African women and their role in society. He praised their bravery. He mentioned the cooking of Halima, Livingstone's housemaid, and disparaged the sexist attitudes towards women in the home. Individualists like Crawford could be admired for being rebellious, anti-authority and coming from the honest-to-goodness working class. His writings were politically incorrect even for the time, veering into Victorian stand-up (a typical Crawfordism: there were three sexes: male, female and curates). He breezily described Chief Kazembe's drug addiction, and he caricatured with ease. Arabs disdained Africans, he confided, bonded to them by polygamy and slavery, a relationship that would last as long as Arabs could 'buy negroes as two-legged animals'.[60]

Crawford's fame through finding the grave enabled him to influence the next generation of 'maverick missionaries', who saw themselves as part of a tradition of respecting 'the African'. Herbert Pirouett, a lay preacher, always kept a copy of *Thinking Black* near to hand, in his posting to north-eastern Zambia in the early twentieth century. Crawford prided himself on the shared basic principle that the 'the African is a gentleman'.[61] James Joyce was so taken with *Back to the Long Grass* that he retraced Crawford's footsteps on a word-hunting expedition, borrowing from his texts and incorporating them into *Finnegan's Wake*.[62]

Another of Livingstone's legacies was enshrined in Crawford: a complacency about violence towards Africans. His book on finding Livingstone's grave included a shocking photograph of four white men with guns, in classic hunter pose, standing over their quarry: a pile of dead African men, their legs and arms flayed apart by the force of their killing. Crawford did not just witness the violence and brutality of European imperialist rule in south-central Africa; he was embroiled in it. Although Crawford had been one of the Plymouth Brethren who had deterred Msiri from negotiating with concession company men, as Arnot had insisted, Crawford had also stood by and watched Msiri's assassination on 20 December 1891, when the mercenaries of the Congo Free State came to town. The British born Canadian explorer/mercenary Captain William G Stairs, leading the expedition 'clashed with Msiri over his determination to force the CFS flag on the Yeke leader and refusal to furnish the latter with the gunpowder he craved'.[63] Bunkeya quickly distintegrated. The polity built on force and slavery fell apart. Slave women scattered, and the agricultural system of Bunkeya, a great irrigated area, collapsed. As the Yeke ruling elite (outsiders) had come to power as warriors and slavers, so they had little choice but to become mercenaries for the Congo Free State, and were instrumental in conquering Katanga for Leopold. As Robert Ross puts it, this was the 'bloody red line'.[64] Crawford simply moved west to start a new station, and then west again. He knew about the spread of violence from the growing numbers of refugees seeking sanctuary; his new nickname was 'Konga Vantu', the gatherer of people.

Crawford was content to focus his criticism on the Arab slave trade on the eastern side of the Luapula. He did lament that blood had been spilt and that the old days were gone forever as a result. Had he negotiated for the BSAC, in the Katanga region, it may have gone to the British. Belgian control north of the lake meant intense brutality. The Belgian state escaped public censure in its newspapers, which lacked a polyphonic range of interest groups strong enough to take on its monarchy and business elite. Nor did Crawford try to intervene when the BSAC spoiled for a fight so they could go to war against Chief Kazembe (though he had been provocatively allowing slavers to operate within his kingdom).[65]

Everyone had blood on their hands and walked in 'dead men's shoes', Crawford confessed at the end of *Long Grass*: 'Africa has an ugly way of levelling all European nationalities'. A British commercial agent acting for missions at one time in Angola, he confided, had enslaved, tortured and murdered thirty-two slaves, including children, in one go. Thumbscrews and drowning with slave chains were not uncommon. The British consul was sanguine about the case, Crawford insisted, because at the time, 'the murder of one or more slaves by white men is almost a daily occurrence'.[66]

Aged fifty-six, lying in bed, Crawford banged his hand against a shelf. He forgot to treat the small cut with iodine. The infection turned to gangrene, and he slowly died, aware of the mortal consequences of the spreading poison. He was buried in a wooden coffin.

The Company of Men and the Felling of the *Mpundu* Tree

In 1896, Glave had noted how the *mpundu* 'looks sturdy and healthy, and likely to last many years. I do not see how I can contribute to the future recognition of the place'. Moreover, he had confidently predicted that it would outlive any wooden cross he might have erected.[67] Yet three years later, BSAC's deputy administrator for British Central Africa, Robert Codrington, wrote a letter to the secretary of the RGS in 1899, beginning:

Dear Dr Keltie,

I have cut down the tree under which the heart of Dr Livingstone was buried and have the section bearing the inscription here.[68]

After chopping down the tree, his men hacked out the inscription. As the tree was still too heavy to carry, over three days they hollowed out the trunk. Then, they sewed it up in canvas and strung it on a pole. Codrington ordered his men to get rid of all the surrounding trees and bush to make a large clearing. Around this, they built a strong fence. Finally, they thrust a telegraph pole into the heart of the stump.[69] No mention was made of an African grave. A party would be sent back the following year to saw the remains into planks of wood. The Crawfords denounced his as 'official vandalism'. The locals revered such natural carvings, they pointed out, and referred to them as 'talking trees'. What had been lost, they fumed, was a 'genuine carved memorial in Africa by an African'.[70]

Codrington was convinced that the inscription had not been hacked out a day too soon.[71] Rumours had reached him that a syndicate of private speculators had been formed with the purpose of acquiring it. They had only delayed because they had assumed that the area was a giant swamp (a common misconception due to the conditions immortalised in Livingstone's last journal). On the day they reached the tree, the Crawfords had stumbled on two gold prospectors from the north and two from the south.[72] Publicity and interest was on the increase. In 1897, Hugo Genthe, a young, rich German-American professional traveller, managed to find the site, and his journal accounts were published in the embryonic official government newspaper for the emerging region.[73] A year later, he was killed by an elephant.[74]

Even if the tree had escaped the prospectors, Codrington insisted, so riven was the trunk with fungus and disease that it would have rotted through and the inscription been lost, within a few months. Now en route for London, it had its own physician. 'I am having it treated with naphaline and various other drugs', he reassured, 'and the opinion of our doctor here is that it is now quite free from rot or borers and is not suffering in the least from the delay in sending it home'.[75]

Codrington's all-too-eager personal triumph about finding the tree for his boss, Cecil Rhodes, was about as hollow as the trunk itself, in that it was achieved thanks to the lonely sojourns of the lesser-known hunter-explorer Poulett Weatherley, who had made his way to the site twice – once in 1896, in advance of the Crawfords, and a second time, in 1898, to map a route for Codrington, who had been told by Rhodes to find the grave.

In 1896, Weatherley's African men had cut a large path in front of the tree so that he could take some decent photographs of the fading inscription. This became an iconic image. However, it had entailed standing for a long time under a pile of blankets, which acted as a hood for the cumbersome mounted camera. In the 'suffocating heat', Weatherley had been left 'foaming with perspiration', uttering words, he admitted, that would 'not have born repetition'.[76]

Poulett Weatherley did not enjoy this; nor did he enjoy the company of men. He preferred animals – he could shoot them. His diary suggests he was another loner, unable to get along with others, convinced that both white and black had conspired against him. When he had written to Codrington asking for a job, Codrington had refused, saying that he was at loggerheads with everyone. 'Justify your claims', Weatherley wrote back, 'or stand convicted for a lie'.[77] To almost comedic levels, he constantly complained about Africa, about the 'insufferable heat', the 'vile cooking' and his 'utterly useless' headman. He held highly racist views of all the men who were making his expedition possible, to whom he often made his views known: 'They are lazy brutes, these Africans – too lazy to be cruel, they have no heart, no head, no affection, no sympathy, no gratitude – they are a compound of inordinate lust and indiscriminate appetite'.[78]

Yet the stereotype of the hardened hunter does not do justice to Weatherley either. On his second visit to the tree, in 1898, he had to be carried there in a hammock because of the heat. He often referred to himself in the third person and fretted about his appearance.[79] Livingstone's burial spot had no religious or spiritual significance for him. In fact, he hated it: 'No white man could stand six months in such a place', he wrote. 'The water in camp is undrinkable as far as I am concerned', he fumed, denied his morning cup of tea because 'I couldn't face purple'. He had no patience with missionaries and was baffled why they were in Africa. They would 'not get a single farthing out of me',[80] he assured himself, as he worked through his frustrations and loneliness with pencil and notebook, in the dark, sometimes after a drink.

Weatherley was also victim of the violence in the region, which he had experienced as a young boy. His father, Colonel Weatherley, originally from Newcastle, had fought in the Indian Mutiny. He had ended up in the Transvaal managing a mine and became caught up in the war against the Zulus in the privately funded Border Troop. Tragically, also on that front line were his three children. Colonel Weatherley's wife, Maria – once described as 'a flashy little woman who ... rode well, carried a revolver and used her whip on the natives' – had humiliated him by sensationally running off with another man.[81] This left the young Poulett and his two siblings in their father's custody. Shortly after the British defeat at the Battle of Isandhlwana (1879), Colonel Weatherley joined a foolhardy attempt to hold Hlobane Mountain. Hopelessly outnumbered by Zulu warriors understandably bent on revenge, many of the men were corralled and driven over a precipice to their death. Colonel Weatherley and his youngest son, Rupert, aged thirteen, were among the dead, who were slashed into pieces, their bodies so dismembered as to be unidentifiable.[82] The tragedy was covered extensively in the press in obituaries. *The Times* described Colonel Weatherley as 'a colonialist of distinction' who had fallen 'gallantly fighting to the last'. *The Graphic* also printed an image of his last moments, on horseback, outnumbered and pierced with spear wounds but 'cutting down Zulus with his right hand while grasping his son, a young lad, with the other'.[83]

Lieutenant Cecil Poulett Mountjoy Weatherley had been one of only seven members of the Border Horse Regiment to survive Hlobane. He was part of violent conflict in the Sudan and the Upper Nile, leaving the army as a captain. He would later become the first European to circumnavigate and survey Lake Bangweulu, which had killed Livingstone, at the age of thirty-six.[84] Poulett's diary alludes to a world where violence was a daily occurrence, personal and intimate. He repeatedly sketched captured human skulls placed on the top of wooden poles, marking the entrance to a slave dealer's compound. His diaries record the brutality of early colonial rule with an interesting twist, for 'that blackguard and coward Watson', out of jealousy and hatred of his friendship with the Wawemba, he claimed, had 'left no stone unturned to smash them'. (This was Blair Watson, a recently recruited tax collector employed by the BSAC, who, with the support of Codrington, went to war with any chief and tribe who refused to accept the new company's tax rules and fly the British flag.) They were brutally subdued.[85]

Weatherley was only relaxed when killing: 'I saw a doe reedbuck today and taking a standing shot – she being almost invisible in the long grass – killed her beautifully, with a bullet behind the shoulder'.[86] Executing the perfect death, in contrast to what befell his family, was perhaps a necessary act of daily consolation; after trauma, victims of the bloody colonialism and death of loved ones often turned perpetrator but, for some, it was not a choice; they were the wrong person, in the wrong place, at the wrong time. The macho, unfeeling, bloodthirsty white hunter, in this case, was a reluctant, hurt and dysfunctional exile.

Weatherley did manage to photograph the tree and found evidence of the fire built by Livingstone's men who had guarded the body, from three tiny anthills that had been burnt brick red by the flames. The *mulowo* tree in the fork of which Livingstone's body had been hung out to dry was still thriving, but the *mpundu* was 'fast becoming a mere shell after having kept guard so faithfully all these years'. This was a tragedy, for there was no more appropriate monument than 'the rugged tree standing over the spot ... inexpressibly solemn'.[87] Weatherley predicted that it would soon fall, either through fire or natural decay. Mycological experts later confirmed that this was likely: as the tree (*Parinari curatellifolia*) had been cut into so deeply by Livingstone's men, it was highly likely to have contracted a fungal infection.[88]

Damaged, misanthropic and violent men like Poulett were extremely useful to empire builders such as Robert Edward Codrington. Still only thirty years old, Codrington had been working for the BSAC for less than two years, hand-picked by Cecil Rhodes to relieve Captain Forbes, who had been too ill to continue in post. A year after his arrival, a Royal Order in Council from the British government had given the company formal administrative control over a vast area of British Central Africa. Although he had been born, in 1869, into a respectable Gloucestershire family with a history of loyal service in the British Royal Navy, Codrington chose instead to head for southern Africa in 1890. There, he quickly rose to the rank of sergeant in a colonial border police force in Bechuanaland (now Botswana). Next, he worked as a colonial tax collector in the emerging British Central Africa Protectorate. He was an immediate success and was remembered by European settlers as being 'a taciturn young man with an insatiable appetite for work and an extraordinary grasp of detail'.[89] Handsome Codrington liked to collect fine African artefacts and observe the natural world.

Codrington was remembered differently by Africans. He was known as '*Mara*', meaning 'it is settled' or 'no more discussion'. The use of violence to get things done was second nature but often came first. In the early 1890s, Codrington had been at the front line of the brutal white settler war against the Matabele further south, which had ended with the expulsion of Africans from their lands. In Nyasaland, Codrington broke the resistance of the Ngoni and Yao people.[90] Essentially, this was his job description while in Rhodes's employ. He employed young warriors from the Angoni tribe, who had recently been forced to submit to the company's authority, turning them into a brutal police force for the company, just as the Belgians had done in the Force Publique. Codrington justified these actions as normal and in pursuit of the Arab slave trade in the region. He would have believed that Africans were racially inferior and only understood violence.

Sir Alfred Sharpe, now in charge of Nyasaland, had been reminded to try to secure the tree's inscription by the RGS and Agnes Livingstone, who had read Weatherley's account. Both wanted to see it cut out and brought home. The only way to do this was via the BSAC. Codrington had been on one of his many administrative tours, mapping the area for the company with a prismatic compass and measuring heights using a boiling point thermometer. He claimed he took the initiative to make a detour to visit Old Chitambo in May 1899, now that its whereabouts were known. Aware that the RGS was anxious to get hold of the tree, he thought it 'a pity' if it did not end up at their London headquarters. He also knew that missionaries in London were anxious to borrow it, to kick-start a revival campaign. His boss was also very interested in the project. Codrington forwarded his map of the route from Fort Jameson (named in honour of Rhodes's failed attempt to topple the Boer Republic), the new capital, to the now ageing firebrand at his CapeTown office, requesting that it be shown to Rhodes as soon as it arrived.[91]

However, the company had been getting some bad press regarding its use of force. Codrington had already been publicly accused of employing 'dishonourable methods' in dealing with Africans by the Reverend Crawford.[92] At the time he was publicly organising the mission to save the tree, he was covertly planning a symbolic use of force to punish a chief for past offences and to show all others that 'the Company' was 'ready to make war if necessary'.[93] This was to 'make an example' of the last powerful African leader blocking BSAC control of the north-west (eastern Lunda). For several years, Kanyembo Ntemena, the then ruler of Kazembe, had been a thorn in the side of company tax collectors, and he was continuing to trade in slaves, selling neighbours to the Swahili traders. Violent incursions had taken place. Yet evidence suggests he was resigned to toeing the line. However, Sir Alfred Sharpe was planning a visit, and the recent subjugation of resistant groups of Wabemba had been successful. Codrington manipulated the facts, asking for a military force to 'bring him to reason' because Kazembe was being aggressive, allying himself with 'all the slavers and Coast men who are unreconciled to this Administration' and was linked to rebel groups on the Congo Free State side of the Luapula. Codrington got his way. Who would have doubted the motives and methods of the saviour of the tree? At the time, he publicised the enormity of his task and the pressure he had felt:

Personally I had great trouble and anxiety about it. If I had not made a good job of it, or ... I had got my boat swamped in the rivers, I should never have been forgiven. So I think I am quite right in getting the credit of its presentation to the Society.[94]

Codrington took great precautions against any possible disbelievers. He sent leaves from the tree so that Keltie could compare them with those already in the possession of the RGS. He forwarded a half-plate glass negative of the inscription, after taking a few prints for himself, including a copy of his map and journal.[95] He suggested to Keltie that it should be considered 'national property'. Agnes was never mentioned; she was bitterly disappointed that the tree did not reach Scotland.[96]

One might well recoil from Codrington's violence and deceitfulness, but the organisation and effort involved in the felling was impressive. At least twenty-five African men had to transport the section, which weighed two hundred pounds. The journey entailed the crossing of several large rivers. To do so, the men had to balance the section on a folding boat. Made in Oxford, the boat alone also weighed two hundred pounds and, to keep up with the main caravan, required twenty porters, working in relay teams, to carry it. There were no reports of casualties among the mixture of Yao and Angoni porters,[97] but, unable to solicit much help from the locals as they tramped through a terrain with a small and scattered population in stifling heat, these carriers stand out as nameless heroes, once again.

Codrington retired shortly afterwards, lucky to have risen so high, and to have survived. He was the perfect empire builder, both savage and civilised. He stressed the appropriateness of an iron pole from the African Transcontinental Telegraph Company staking out the heart of the tree: 'a symbol of European occupation, bringing with it the blessings of peace ... to the wretched peoples amongst whom Livingstone's last days were spent'.[98] When he finally arrived back in England, he was engaged to be married. He died of heart disease just before his wedding.

Conclusion

Imposing an imperial memorial in central Africa was a much longer and bloodier process than had occurred in Westminster Abbey. The race to find and then claim Livingstone's grave formed part of the European scramble for central Africa. The quest was largely taken up by a series of young male explorers, missionaries and soldiers. Details of their successes and failures were widely circulated among metropolitan audiences, through newspapers and journals. Contained within their accounts were highly negative, racist and sensationalist images of central Africa. Imperial propaganda about rule in Africa also benefited from their romanticised efforts and linked their pilgrimages to Livingstone's broader humanitarian mission: that of abolishing slavery. Some of these men died soon after, in their prime. Death, grief and loss created a particular emotional climate of heroic self-sacrifice around the establishment of colonial rule in central Africa: the nobility of men, loved and adored by many of their contemporaries; virtual fathers, sons and lovers, lost and mourned; remembered; and avenged.

These efforts to find the grave, locate the heart and then save the tree helped to cloak the violence of colonial rule under a humanitarian disguise. Anti-slavery was an ideal which many of the young explorers/journalists carried with them in the 1890s, continuing the impulses of Livingstone's imperial humanitarianism. However, the age of high moral imperialism was over. Livingstone's tree of death symbolises a central Africa superficially 'pacified' through violence and brutality. It was a cruel process. Slavers, concession companies, chiefs, mercenaries, administrators and missionaries of all nationalities played a part.

By 1900, the tree was gone and so was Chitambo's grave, his act of sentimentality denied, symbolising the erasing of African sensibility and humanity with the onset of colonial rule. The telegraph pole might have claimed the site, now a bald clearing of scorched red earth, but very little would dramatically change in the surrounding region. The fifty African porters who transported the tree trunk over hundreds of miles testify to the imaginative visions, perversity and waste of resources involved in imposing an imperial dream. But worse was yet to come.

NOTES

1 'I'm on the way to the promised land/I'm on the highway to hell', ACDC, 'Highway to Hell', 1979.

2 'Glave's Journey to the Livingstone Tree. Glimpses of Life in Africa from the journals of the late E J Glave', *Century Illustrated Monthly Magazine*, LII, New Series, XXX (May–October 1896), 765.

3 Conversation between Robert Codrington and Chief Chitambo, in Robert Codrington, 'A Journey from Fort Jameson to Old Chitambo and the Tanganyika Plateau', *Geographical Journal*, 15, 3 (1900): 228–9. For a history of this region, see A.D. Roberts, *A History of the Bemba: Political Growth and Change in North-Eastern Zambia before 1900* (Madison, WI: University of Wisconsin Press, 1973).

4 Hopkins, 'Explorers' Tales', 669–84.

5 Casada, 'Verney Lovett Cameron', 211–15.

6 Information emailed to author from Dr I.P.A. Manning.

7 M.A. Curie, *Livingstone's Hospital: The Story of Chitambo* (Bloomington, IN: Author House, 2011), 29.

8 G. Macola, *The Kingdom of the Kazembe: History and Politics in North-Eastern Zambia and Katanga to 1950* (New York: Palgrave, 2002), 167–97.

9 Macola, *The Kingdom of the Kazembe*, 167–97; Pierre Célestine Kalenga Ngoy, Bunkeya et ses chefs: Évolution sociale d'une ville précoloniale (1870–1992), unpublished PhD thesis, Leiden Institute for History, Faculty of Humanities, Leiden University, 2014.

10 Karen Jones, Giacomo Macola & David Welch (eds.), *A Cultural History of Firearms in the Age of Empire* (London: Routledge, 2013); Giacomo Macola, *The Gun in Central Africa: A History of Technology and Politics* (Athens, OH: Ohio University Press, 2016).

11 Macola, *The Gun in Central Africa*, 100, 102–103.

12 'Glave's Journey to the Livingstone Tree', 776.

13 A.J. Wills, *An Introduction to the History of Central Africa* (Oxford: Oxford University Press, 1964), 174.

14 Stig Förster, Wolfgang J. Mommsen & Ronald Edward Robinson, *Bismarck, Europe, and Africa: The Berlin Africa Conference, 1884–1885, and the Onset of Partition* (Oxford: Oxford University Press, 1989).

15 Wills, *An Introduction to the History of Central Africa*, 172.

16 Ibid., 161.

17 Jeal, *Stanley*, esp. chs 13–14.

18 Ibid., 233–57.

19 Adam Hochschild, *King Leopold's Ghost: A Story of Greed, Terror and Heroism in Colonial Africa* (London: Pan MacMillan), 199; for an alternative view, see Jean-Luc Vellut, 'An Archaeological Enquiry into Historical Discourses on Violence in the Congo Free State', unpublished conference paper presented at the conference 'Hard and Soft Power: Questions of Race, Intimacy and Violence and in the Comparative Colonial Toolkit' held at the University of Kent, 7–8 July 2014.

20 Ian Phimister, 'International Imperialism: The Violent Making of Southern Africa', unpublished keynote address at the conference 'Hard and Soft Power: Questions of Race, Intimacy and Violence and in the Comparative Colonial Toolkit' held at the University of Kent, 7–8 July 2014.

21 Wills, *An Introduction to the History of Central Africa*, 182.

22 R. Oliver, *Sir Harry Johnston and the Scramble for Africa* (London: Chatto & Windus, 1957), 18.

23 Johnston's career in Africa was relatively short because he lost his main backer when Lord Salisbury left office. In the employ of the Foreign Office (not the emerging Colonial Office) and determined to carve a distinct form of missionary colonisation in what would become Nyasaland, he would fall out with Cecil Rhodes, who had other ideas. Johnston was an evolutionary racist, believing that Africans were inferior but that, after hundreds of years (or if they could cross-breed with Indians), they would develop to the level of a European. Ibid.

24 Rev A.C. Ross, 'The African – 'Child or Man'. The Quarrel between the Blantyre Mission of the Church of Scotland and the British Central African Administration', in E. Stokes & R. Brown (eds.), *The Zambesian Past: Studies in Central African History* (Manchester: Manchester University Press, 1966), 332–51.

25 See Robert I. Rotberg, *Joseph Thomson and the Exploration of Africa* (London: Chatto & Windus, 1971).

26 Barrie's marriage was never consummated; his life was spent in deep emotional attachment to young men.

27 Joseph Thomson, *Through Masai Land: A Journey of Exploration among the Snowclad Volcanic Mountains and Strange Tribes of Eastern Equatorial Africa* (London: S. Low, Martson, Searle, & Rivington, 1885).

28 Joseph Thomson, 'To Lake Bagnweolo and the Unexplored Region of British Central Africa', *The Geographical Journal*, 1, 2 (February 1893): 97–118. Read to the RGS at meeting on 28 November 1892.

29 Thomson, 'To Lake Bagnweolo', 118.

30 See Oliver, *Sir Harry Johnston*.

31 Ibid., 108–9. Also retold in J. Desmond Clark, 'The David Livingstone Memorial at Chitambo's', *Northern Rhodesia Journal* (June 1950): 25–6.

32 Renema & van Zoelen, *You Took the Part*, 48–74.

33 Ibid., 101.

34 Ibid., 118.

35 K. Bradley. 'Salute to Adventurers', *Northern Rhodesia Journal*, 3, 6 (1958): 480.

36 Frederick Stanley Arnot, Dictionary of African Christian Bibliography, www. dacb.org/stories/demrepcongo/arnot_stanley.html. Accessed 5 July 2014; E. Baker, *The Life and Explorations of Frederick Stanley Arnot: The Authorised Biography of a Zealous Missionary, Intrepid Explorer, & Self-Denying Benefactor amongst the Natives of Africa* (London: Seeley, Service, 1921).

37 Mrs H. Gratton Guiness, *The New World of Central Africa: With a History of the First Christian Mission in the Congo* (London: Hodder Stoughton, 1890).

38 F.S. Arnot, 'Woman's Work for Woman and Our Mission Field', iv, Women's Foreign Missionary Societies of the Presbyterian Church (1889).

39 Macola, *The Kingdom of the Kazembe*, 169–70.

40 Macola, *The Gun in Central Africa*, 115.

41 Wills, *An Introduction to the History of Central Africa*, 181.

42 See Renema & van Zoelen, *You Took the Part*, 12–21, including a photo of Bia.

43 Ibid., 26–7.

44 K. Bradley. 'Salute to Adventurers', *Northern Rhodesia Journal*, 3, 6 (1958): 480.

45 Jeal, *Stanley*, 435.

46 R.H. Russell, 'Glave's Career', *Century Illustrated Monthly Magazine*, vol. lii, New Series, vol. xxx (May 1896–October 1896), 866.

47 Hopkins, 'Explorers' Tales'.

48 Jeal, *Livingstone*, 156.

49 Johannes Fabian, *Out of Our Minds: Reason and Madness in the Exploration of Central Africa* (Berkeley, CA: California University Press, 2000).

50 R.W. Gilder, 'Glave', *Century Illustrated Monthly Magazine*, vol. lii, New Series, vol. xxx (May 1896–October 1896), 868.

51 Ibid.

52 'Glave's Journey to the Livingstone Tree. Glimpses of Life in Africa from the Journals of the Late E J Glave', *Century Illustrated Monthly Magazine*, vol. lii, New Series, vol. xxx (May 1896–October 1896), 765.

53 Crawford, *Back to the Long Grass*. It was dedicated to the Nonconformist Scottish preacher Struthers of Greenock.

54 Crawford, *Back to the Long Grass*, 77.

55 D & G Crawford, 'The Grave of Livingstone's Heart', *Africa* (February 1898).

56 John Stuart, 'David Livingstone, British Protestant Missionaries, Memory and Empire', unpublished paper, 2012, 3.

57 'Livingstone's Successor', *Colonialist*, LV, 1349, October 1913, 2.

58 D. Crawford, *Thinking Black: 22 Years without a Break in the Long Grass of Central Africa* (London: London, Morgan & Scott, 1913).

59 Keir Howard, 'Daniel Crawford, 1870–1926', Dictionary of African Christian Biography, www.dacb.org/stories/demorepcongo/crawford_daniel. html; G. E. Tisley, *Dan Crawford: Missionary and Pioneer in Central Africa* (London, 1929).

60 Crawford, *Back to the Long Grass*, 340–1.

61 Interview with Dr Louise Pirouet, daughter of Herbert Pirouet, Cambridge, 4 September 2009. The phrase 'maverick missionaries' is hers. See also Mark

S. Sweetman, 'Dan Crawford, Thinking Black, and the Challenge of the Missionary Canon', *Journal of Ecclesiastical History*, 88 (2007): 705–25.

62 Robbert Jan Henkes, 'James Joyce in Africa: An Expedition to the Source of the Wake', *Genetic Joyce Studies*, 8 (2008), www.antwerpjamesjoycecenter. com/GJS8/JJ%20in%20Africa%2023May.jsp.

63 Macola, *The Gun in Central Africa*, 116.

64 Author correspondence with Professor Ross. I am grateful to Professor Ross and Dr Macola for their help in unravelling this history.

65 See Macola, *The Kingdom of the Kazembe*, esp. chapter 6.

66 Crawford, *Back to the Long Grass*, 340–1.

67 Glave, 'Journey', (1894). 778.

68 R. Codrington to J. Scott-Keltie, secretary RGS, 27 June 1899, 22 August 1899, RGS Archives, London.

69 Clark, 'The David Livingstone Memorial at Chitambo's', 30.

70 Crawford, *Back to the Long Grass*, 76.

71 Codrington, 'A Journey'.

72 D & G Crawford, diary entry for 1 August 1897, 'Africa', February 1898, quoted in 'The Livingstone Memorial'. An appeal by Sir Henry Morton Stanley, May 1899, RGS Archives.

73 Hugo Genthe, 'A Trip to Mpenzi's', *British Central Africa Gazette*, 1 August 1897.

74 'The Listener', *Northern Advance*, 21 June 1898.

75 R. Codrington to J. Scott-Keltie, 22 August 1899, RGS/IBS Archives, London.

76 Poulett Weatherley diaries, i, 9 November 1898, 42, PWE/1, RGS Archives, London.

77 Ibid., 2 April, 50(a), PWE/1, RGS/IBG Archives, London.

78 Ibid., 32.

79 Ibid., 14 November 1898, 48, PWE/1, RGS Archive, London.

80 Ibid., ii, 16 February 1899, PWE/2, RGS Archive, London.

81 See various submissions at www.1879zuluwar.com concerning Colonel and Rupert Weatherley.

82 William Watson Race, *The Epic Anglo Zulu War on Canvas* (Lancashire: Talisman Prints, 2007).

83 Obituaries in *The Times*, 5 May 1879, and *The Graphic*, 24 May 1879.

84 A fellow of the RGS, his achievements were published in its journal in two articles. He died in Bournemouth in 1932.

85 See generally Macola, *The Kingdom of the Kazembe* & Roberts, *A History of the Bemba*.

86 Weatherley diary, i, 51.

87 Extract from Poulett Weatherley's 1896 report quoted in 'The Livingstone Memorial'. An appeal by Sir Henry Morton Stanley, May 1899, RGS Archive; also diary entry for 14 November 1898, 48, PWE/1, RGS Archives, London.

88 G.D. Pearce, 'Livingstone and Fungi in Tropical Africa', *Bulletin of the British Mycological Society*, 19, 1 (1985): 46.

89 Kenneth Bradley, 'Adventurers Still', *Northern Rhodesian Journal*, 4, 1 (1959): 7.

90 Roger Summers and L.H. Gann, 'Robert Edward Codrington, 1869–1908', *Northern Rhodesian Journal*, 3, 6 (1956): 44–50.
91 R. Codrington to J.A. Stevens, Cape Town, 29 August 1899, BSAC A2/1/1, ZNA.
92 Macola, *The Kingdom of the Kazembe*, 194.
93 Ibid., 195.
94 R. Codrington to J. Scott-Keltie, 22 August 1899, RGS/IBS Archives, London.
95 R. Codrington to J. Scott-Keltie, 25 August 1899, BSAC A2/1/1, ZNA.
96 Correspondence with Henry Morton Stanley, quoted in Renema & van Zoelen, *You Took the Part*, 47.
97 Codrington, 'A Journey', 230.
98 Ibid.

4   The Graveyard of Ambition
Missionary Wars, Bachelor Colonialism & White Memorials, Chitambo, 1900–1913

> But I would walk five hundred miles,
> And I would walk five hundred more.
> The Proclaimers, 'I'm Gonna Be
> (500 miles)', 1988[1]

Livingstone's grave at Chitambo now lay within a young territory called North-Eastern Rhodesia. Its neighbours included Barotzi-North Western Rhodesia, and British Central Africa (which would be renamed the Nyasaland Protectorate in 1907). A new era needed symbols and a useable past, especially when colonial rule was more aspiration than reality. This chapter tells the story of the politics of the memorialisation of Livingstone's grave around Chitambo and its relationship with the initial consolidation of what tried to pass itself off as a colonial state in this marginal region. Remote, unusual and unforgiving, this was an area where mostly working-class men and women tried to make a new life.

Alongside, Livingstone's fans in Britain attempted to control the design of a 'fitting monument' in central Africa to his memory and to humanitarian imperialism. What eventually transpired was, like colonial rule itself, far more limited. There was no room in this sentimental memorialising for Livingstone's African followers or their work as humanitarians. A memory and vision of white pioneering and sacrifice were taking shape. Nevertheless, despite shared racisms, the politics of the grave were tricky. Local peculiarities, missionary factionalism and practical limitations trimmed aspirations in these remote regions. Hard-pressed administrators, aware of how little whites could do, tried to contain expectations and the potential disruption from the steady trickle of new arrivals, some more welcome than others. The expansion of the railway brought tourists and single women travelling alone.

Livingstone's burial site radiated huge emotional resonance, which rippled out from the region far beyond. The site attracted lone bachelors seeking solitude or a quiet place to die. Livingstone's family also helped

127

build up the emotional capital of the site by making very personal pilgrimages to the grave. This high-profile imperial family, with its dynastic humanitarian credentials, were a living link with Livingstone's high moral imperialism and a boon to metropolitan imperial propaganda. They were influential in shaping the conversation between Britain and Africa and in re-energising imperial humanitarianism for the next generation.

African Humanitarianism Denied

The history of the early memorialisation of Livingstone and his death needs to be read first against what was left out. Interest in the living memorials of Livingstone's death – the Africans who accompanied him – quickly evaporated. Much later, a handful of colonialists, often retired missionaries or government officials, occasionally attempted to piece together their lives in the letters section of publications such as the *Uganda Journal*. But efforts came too late to consult the living. Not until 1975 was there an in-depth reconstruction of the African contribution to British exploration. Donald Simpson's path-breaking history included Livingstone's 'dark companions'.[2] What has continually been overlooked is their own dedication to humanitarian work, anti-slavery and sentimentality.

As is well known, the RGS tried to honour the men (but not women) who accompanied Livingstone in life and death. They presented a Bronze Medal to Chuma, Susi and Wainwright, and had sixty Silver Medals made for the others as a mark of 'approbation of their fidelity and courage'.[3] They chose the engravers to the Queen. Nevertheless, copying Livingstone's image in high relief had been so tricky, the company made a loss of fifty guineas. Susi and Chuma received their medals accompanied by Waller at the RGS.[4] Jacob Wainwright, although still in Britain, did not accompany them, suggesting a continuing rift. The remaining medals were sent to the British consul in Zanzibar. Only twelve men were found. They attended a ceremony on 17 August 1875, conducted by Bishop Steere. Another five medals were sent on to Mombasa for the Reverend W.S. Price to distribute. The CMS had established a settlement there for freed slaves in 1875. It was named after Sir Bartle Frere, who had been sent by the Foreign Office to Zanzibar, after evidence went public – including Livingstone's – which claimed that the interior was in the grip of an epidemic of enslavement. Frere negotiated a treaty ban on the transport of human cargo with the sultan. Price transferred the Nassick School from Bombay. He employed many former pupils, likely including a number of Livingstone's followers. That left forty-two men with whom officials had lost contact already.

One of the African followers who chose to work in humanitarianism and anti-slavery in east Africa was Jacob Wainwright. He tried to hold down a job, first as a teacher of African Christians in Frere Town, employed by the Reverend Price.[5] Wainwright's visit to England 'seems to have unsettled him', wrote Harold Becker Thomas, who doggedly pursued the life stories of some of the men who had explored with Livingstone.[6] Wainwright had clearly become hostage to events when he agreed to accompany Livingstone's remains home, care of the CMS. The photograph of him on board the *Queen* (see Figure 1.1), accompanying the body after the coffin had been transferred from the *Malwa* so the remains could be taken ashore, shows a hauntingly sad expression. Wainwright had already lived through the trauma of enslavement, of dislocation, and of travelling with Livingstone, all over a relatively short time. After being freed, he had been packed off to India to enrol at the Nassick School (established in 1854, a hundred miles north-east of Bombay, by the CMS's Reverend William Salter Price; it meant a place of refuge). He had volunteered to find Livingstone with Stanley, and then agreed to serve the former on his last expedition. Jacob was part of the close-knit group of Christian-educated 'Nassicks', but he faced the glare of the world's media alone when he disembarked in England, travelling in the second mourning carriage to Westminster Abbey for the funeral.

Already in a state of high stress, Jacob was treated unsympathetically, with little concern shown for his former life. His clothes were ridiculed, and he was referred to in the press as a 'boy'. Waller had not wanted him sent to attend the funeral and had insulted him for being of a lower class than Susi and Chuma. Nevertheless, he had kept a diary for nine months after Livingstone died. His former headmaster told the press and RGS about its existence in 1874, and Jacob often read from it. Yet it was carelessly lost in London. Waller preferred to interview Susi and Chuma, sidelining Jacob despite his 'superior education'.[7] He was mocked and disliked by the residents of Newstead Abbey, Waller's residence, and also by several members of Livingstone's family. He was considered 'remarkably ugly; being almost an exaggerated Negro type'; Livingstone's younger daughter described how 'his brash manner made a very bad impression'.[8] Jacob had unsettled them by ditching the role of a servant for that of an equal. And why not, especially when he was giving talks to large audiences?

When back in east Africa, Wainwright threw himself into teaching, and William Price thought he was coping extremely well. 'Poor fellow', Price wrote, when weighing up how much Jacob's life had changed since his celebrity life in London.[9] But a few year later, Joseph Thomson came across him in Zanzibar, describing how he had 'fallen considerably' and was working as a doorman for a Zanzibari trader.[10] He seems to have turned to alcohol. According to Thomson, he had become so impudent and forward that the missionaries had sacked him. His habit of 'taunting his European masters with the fact they had never, like him ... [been] presented to Her Majesty' was found particularly annoying. Needs must, however. Missionaries now wanted to expand into eastern Africa, and Jacob was hired as a translator for a CMS mission in an area that would become Uganda. The Reverend Philip O'Flaherty believed he had saved him from 'the evil surroundings of Zanzibar into which unsympathizing masters and missionaries had thrown him'.[11]

There was no happy ending. Jacob worked as an interpreter at the court of King Mutesa and taught a class. Initially, O'Flaherty called him his personal servant, friend and 'a great comfort'. That was until he accepted 'a bribe', as O'Flaherty put it. He worked next for a 'strayed sheep' in the king's palace, in 1881, and O'Flaherty lost touch with him.[12] Jacob moved on again but returned to mission service, joining the LMS, this time as a translator of hymns and Bible passages. (The LMS had begun to move into the eastern Africa interior in 1876, when the Reverend Roger Price had set off for Ujiji.) A gifted linguist, emotionally complex and central to the success of so many explorers and missionaries, Jacob died in a tragic accident. In April 1892, he fell into a fire and overturned a pot of boiling water on himself, dying in agony of his burns.[13] A simple Borassus palm marked his grave until 1931, when American missionaries paid for a bronze tablet.

The surviving records of other men who were part of that epic journey myth whisper similar tales of abandonment mixed with achievement. Carus Farrar was one the five Nassicks who were paid eighty-seven dollars fifty by the British consul in Zanzibar, where they stayed after depositing Livingstone's remains. They alone were then sent to the CMS mission in Mombasa. Halima was paid only fifty dollars, despite it being known that she was Livingstone's cook, and even though she was also looking after another female member of the expedition, Ntaoeka.[14] Farrar recorded that he did not like the Reverend Sparshott's 'illtreatment [sic]', no doubt physical punishment, so he found work on a ship but was discharged at Aden. He paid for his own passage back to Bombay, where he dictated his account of the expedition to a CMS missionary. This account was published much later, in 1950, in the *Uganda Journal*, annotated by Harold Thomas.

Farrar, too, chose to work as a humanitarian. In Mombasa, he ran the CMS shop in Frere Town with another Nassick 'faithful', Chengwimbe, also known as Matthew Wellington (see Figure 4.1), who went on to run a settlement for freed slave boys at Shimba, south-west of Mombasa.[15] He

Figure 4.1 Matthew Wellington/Chengwimbe (1847–1935), the last survivor of the 'Nassicks', or 'Bombay Africans', who had joined the search party for Livingstone organised by Henry Morton Stanley. SOAS Archives. CWM/LMS/Home/Livingstone Pictures/Box1. File 8.

had also worked as Price's servant. Despite this impressive record, little detail of his life or death seems to have been commemorated. Matthew Wellington, as Simpson discovered, went on to work for the government of the Ugandan protectorate. He retired in 1911, and died in 1935, aged ninety. Astonishingly, the Treasury had refused to grant him a special pension of twenty rupees because of his service to Livingstone, as suggested by the Colonial Office.[16]

Much more is known about Susi and Chuma. They fared better. Chuma, the son of a Yao fisherman, born around 1850, had been sent into slavery twice before being rescued by Livingstone. This natural orator, popular, full of fun and 'an extravagant character ... with a soft side towards the female sex', found employment as a caravan leader on Joseph Thomson's expeditionary force to Masailand for ten dollars a month. Thomson was just twenty-one years old, so Chuma, although only a little older himself, proved indispensable. As Thomson wrote, 'He was ever at my elbow, with his ready tact and vast stores of information'. The RGS received a note praising him: 'Too often these poor fellows are allowed to sink out of sight simply because they have no one to speak for them'.[17] Yet this tended to be their fate. Thomson was unusual in the amount of space he devoted to describing Chuma, at the start of his book, wryly commenting how 'the vague expression of the Expedition ... "we" ... or the more egotistical "I" is very apt to swallow up a subordinate's individuality and valuable services'.[18] The success of an expedition lay in the 'native headman', he admitted and, among the 'Guild of Zanzibar Porters', none equalled Chuma as a caravan leader for white men. Thomson's praise no doubt led the RGS to award Chuma a silver sword and a second medal.

Chuma could speak twelve local languages, plus English, had an unrivalled eloquence during public speaking and so could motivate the men, enjoying a natural authority. Nevertheless, two major faults were pinned on him. First, a habit of lying (which Thomson believed was a vice that 'all half civilized negroes' possessed and was especially developed in east-central Africa). Second, vanity. This made him apparently extravagant and lavish in his expenditure. On his return to Zanzibar, Chuma discovered that his wife had died. Another expedition; another wife. He passed essential information back and forth between Zanzibar and Masailand, including key intelligence about the operations of the Swahili slaver traders, which he passed on to the British consul.[19] In 1882, Chuma died of tuberculosis in the UMCA hospital, leaving behind the sum of 309 rupees. In a touchingly sentimental gesture, in his will, he left ten dollars to the widow of Mabruki, from the sale of his sword, whom he had once travelled with; ten dollars to his freed slave servant; and the rest to Susi and a friend. Susi was with him when he died.[20]

Susi ought to have been widely memorialised for helping to lay the foundations of the Congo Free State and the UMCA, and for rivalling Livingstone in terms of his range of expeditionary achievements. At first, he found life difficult back in Zanzibar – 'Stinkibar'. He tried to work for a missionary, and then as a road builder. He had 'fallen into very bad drinking habits' and was 'in a state of destitution through his debaucharies'.[21] Thomson rejected him as a member of his expeditionary force in 1879. Stanley was less choosey, taking him to the Congo on his gruelling expedition of 1879–82. Stanley referred to him as 'the head chief of the foreign native employees'. One of his many key roles was to identify the site for the establishment of Leopoldville (now Kinshasa). Following Chuma's death and for the rest of his life, he worked for the UMCA in Zanzibar, and was vital for their ability to move around in the interior. He travelled widely with Bishop Smythies, who 'relied on him heavily'.[22] Susi acted as his envoy, peacemaker, translator and friend. Eventually, Susi agreed to be baptised; on 23 August 1886, he was – sentimentally – renamed 'David'. By the 1890s, he was terminally ill and paralysed. At some point, he sweetly gave Miss Barbara Smith, who worked there, a present of a dried flower and leaf that he had taken apparently from Livingstone's *mpundu* tree.[23] He died on 5 May 1891. An impressive funeral was organised, attended by the consul and conducted by the bishop, with two choirs and a procession. He left behind a young son.

Of the others, very little is known, and nothing of the women. When Stanley arrived in eastern Africa in September 1874, he searched out the men who had accompanied Livingstone on his last journey for work. He managed to sign up Mabruki, Uredi Manwa Seera and Ulimengo (who had also travelled with Speke earlier) and a further twenty-six men who had carried Livingstone's body to the coast, including 'the boy Majwara', who died of dysentery at an early stage. Only fourteen of the twenty-six returned to Zanzibar in November 1877, having survived one of the hardest, most epic of European explorations in Africa. Farajalla, who had supervised Livingstone's embalmment, died in battle; one went mad; Stanley handed one over to the locals after he was caught stealing; others died of illness or 'deserted'. To his credit, Stanley organised a ceremony at the US consulate in Zanzibar, so that they could finally receive their RGS Silver Medal, although the majority remained undistributed. He urged upon Kirk that the outstanding financial claims they were making for their work with Livingstone be settled in their favour. Uredi Manwa Sera had put in a disgruntled claim. Kirk pressed the Foreign Office and the RGS, who both responded favourably, but the sums were paltry. Livingstone's friends, including James Young, had sent money for the men after he died but, by the end of the nineteenth century, the British authorities in Zanzibar were aware that many of the men were living out their old age in poverty. A plan was proposed to provide them with the means to buy gardens in which to grow food, but nothing came of this apart from one small portion of land that was set aside for a few survivors.[24]

Few attempts were made to care for, let alone commemorate, the former child slaves. It was not until the late 1940s that the career of 'the boy Majwara' was written up in any biographical detail, even then only as a short article; and no further correspondence was generated until 1964. Livingstone did not write much about Majwara, other than he once had an insect in his eye. Majwara's job was to try to make Livingstone eat when he fell ill, and Livingstone apparently allowed this boy alone be at his side at the end. Majwara's subsequent neglect, considering his role in caring for Livingstone and then playing the drum in front of the corpse on the long journey to the coast, is a damning indictment of the imperial monomania about Livingstone and white heroics. Majwara's early life was as extraordinary as it was cruel. He was the son of a powerful warrior chief (Saza Chief of Buddu, or Pokino) in the Buganda region (Uganda), who was assassinated by the ruler, Mutesa, after falling out with him. The chief's successor sold Pokino's children into slavery. Majwara ended up in Unyanyembe, when Stanley stopped en route to the interior to find Livingstone. Stanley took pity on the young slave boy and bought him: he appears in his record as 'no.51 Majwara (boy) Uganda', one of three boys; or as 'a little boy'.[25] In contrast to Kalulu, Stanley did not furnish details about this boy's name or character. Despite his young age, Stanley used Majwara as his gun carrier. When Stanley assembled a force of men to return to Livingstone in 1873 to allow him to continue searching for the source of the Nile, he included Majwara within it.

Livingstone did at least record, in a letter, how he wished Majwara to be rewarded for his efforts. He received the same payment as the 'Faithfuls', footed by Captain Prideaux, the acting consul, after noticing their destitution. Majwara seems to have spent this quickly, necessitating his joining another expedition in order to survive. Still only a boy, he worked as a personal servant to Frank Pocock, one of the three white men with Stanley. He is hardly mentioned in Stanley's account apart from when he was presented to Mutesa (who had ordered his father's murder and his own enslavement). The king was so impressed by Majwara that he gave him a wife, whom Majwara called Tuma-leo. Majwara witnessed Pocock drowning towards the end of the journey, after which he carried Stanley's gun, another indication of his youth. As a 'tent boy' for the white men, he also served as a camp spy, reporting thefts of supplies.[26] Amazingly, he survived, receiving his medal at the end of 1887 with the other thirteen survivors.

Majwara ended his life in the company of fellow Livingstone veterans, who chose to work for expeditionary missionaries, trying to establish settlements in difficult territory, in dangerous, poorly paid work. He fleetingly appeared in a religious propaganda spat. In 1964, Father Faupel, writing about the history of the Roman Catholic expansion into eastern Africa, which had begun in 1878, suggested that Majwara had converted to Catholicism and was one of the martyrs burnt at Namugongo in June 1886, under the name Serunkuma, who was known to be a son of Pokino. That was declared to be false; it had been Majwara's brother.[27] Working as a cook for a CMS lay missionary in Zanzibar, he was reported in the *Church Missionary Intelligencer*, in 1879, as having decided to have nothing to do with the 'Mohammedan religion' because of their 'lies and deceits' and 'great cruelty of Arabs to slaves'.[28] Majwara was then apparently attending church and school regularly. Again, he followed a pattern of moving into missionary-humanitarian work. In the mid-1880s, he was working at the LMS mission station in Ujiji, set up by the Reverend Roger Price in 1876. Despite all that he had survived, Majwara drowned in Lake Tanganyika with six others when their boat capsized in October 1886.[29] He was only in his twenties; another one 'faithfully forgotten to the end'.

Whiteout: A New Memorial at Chitambo

In contrast, once the tree marking the burial place of Livingstone's heart was felled, the site became the focus of a huge effort in memorialisation. A source of emotional capital to help raise and then tie together a white-minority ruling class out of nothing was important to early state-building in the region. But imperialists and missionaries in Britain led the way with an eye to home audiences. In January 1899, Robert Codrington, the local administrator working for the BSAC, had offered the Free Church of Scotland in nearby Nyasaland a 'square plot of land around which the heart of Livingstone is buried', having first obtained the approval of his boss, Cecil Rhodes.[30] 'Poor old man, he would almost smile', wrote the new commissioner for British Central Africa, Sir Alfred Sharpe, in June 1899, referring to Livingstone and the irony of a company telegraph pole marking his 'death-grave'. Nyasaland residents then set up the Livingstone Memorial Committee and launched an appeal, raising a modest amount with the help of public donations in Scotland.

Livingstone had many other admirers, none more bullish when activated by sentimentality than Henry Morton Stanley. Stanley had been active behind the scenes since he learnt that the tree had been cut down. From his London home, and despite failing health, he showed that he remained faithful to his hero and imperial ideals to the end. After an appeal for help from the Nyasa Fund, he took over, making his own personal appeal in May 1899. The money raised so far, he explained, mounted 'to scarcely a twentieth part of that which is needed if a moderately durable memorial is to be erected'.[31] Stanley reprinted extracts from the sentimental accounts of the site written by Weatherley and the Crawfords, lamenting how Livingstone's last resting place was disappearing: a memorial was needed to mark the grave 'of the heart which for 32 years beat only for the benefit of the natives ... it is to Dr Livingstone that we owe the land now included under the name of British Central Africa'.[32] Stanley also used the opportunity to appeal more generally for investors in Africa, adding that, since 'the slave trade has been totally extinguished, order and administration have been established, the desire for industry has been implanted in the native mind'. Revealingly, he concluded, 'the age of experiment was over'; now, there was 'only profit for ourselves and posterity'.

Stanley commissioned the design of what he called a 'Monumental Obelisk' to withstand 'fire, flood, the influences of the weather, native depredations, etc'. A bronze cross made in London would crown a massive white obelisk:

48 feet long and 7 feet square ... it will rise to 38 feet ... over which a conical cap a minimum 2 feet high will be bolted to external flanges. The hollow within the column will be filled with cemented material ... sent in iron drums from this Country.

The cost came in at a massive £4,000. This did not include transport, since free passage had been solicited from the British government's Central African Administration, the African Lakes Corporation (on their steamers) and the BSAC. It did cover the estimated amounts of cloth and beads needed for distribution to ease its final journey and an estimated eight hundred and seventy porters. The RGS immediately put the brakes on these plans, dismissing them as grandiose and impractical. The bronze would be 'a temptation to the natives' or a natural target for charging elephants. Stanley had only managed to raise £800 and he was forced to accept a scaled-down version. He died in 1904, but his wife still donated the money he had raised to the RGS.

Nevertheless, once the large section of the felled tree trunk had arrived in London, the RGS announced details of the military operation to build a monument in its place. The RGS plan retained some of the largesse of the Stanley design: four hundred and fifty airtight cylinders weighing £50 each would be used to transport the materials; moulds of oak with a metal lining had been prepared for the blocks of the 'best cement'; and over three hundred of these would be used to create the twenty-foot-high monument designed by Alfred J. Brown. Poulett Weatherley judged it 'perfectly hideous'.

A large, white, phallic stone memorial was extremely welcome in an area where colonial rule was still being established. Fort Jameson, the nearest white settlement to the grave, had been built on the site of a former capital of Chief Mpenzi but was not even a year old (see Map 4.1). It was set to be the capital of the fledgling protectorate of North-Eastern Rhodesia, administered by the BSAC, and, in March 1899, had requested its first set of official stamps. In July, a postal service was established, and an order went out for uniforms and fatigues to kit out a new African police force.[33] But BSAC officials only felt sufficiently safe to relocate from Blantyre in 1900. A year later, the capital had twenty

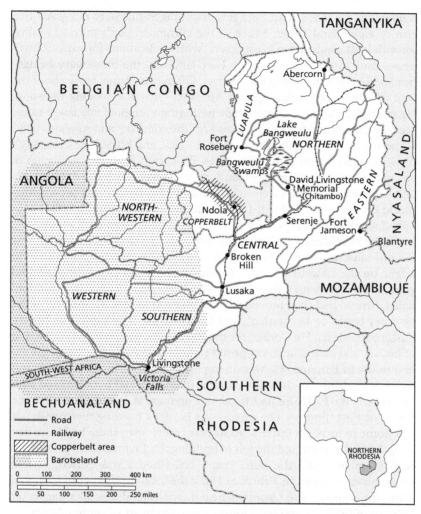

Map 4.1 Northern Rhodesia (Zambia), Protectorate of the United Kingdom, 1924–64, showing provinces

brick houses, and men were being sent out to establish new substations and to collect taxes from the African population.

Dreams of a gold rush and a white settler revolution never materialised in these bush towns. The region still remained relatively inaccessible without a railway, and there would be no significant mineral discoveries. The tsetse flies put off settler farmers. This left missionaries, traders and hunters, in the main, who were not discouraged but were not given free rein to annex land either. Much of the administration's time was taken up with land claims from prospectors, with applications for various businesses and with missionaries. In Fort Jameson, the missionary bridgehead had been a steamship up the river. Often complaints arose about the lack of official protection against Africans – 'natives' stealing firewood, for example, with no one seemingly bothering to uphold any law.[34] Local security threats and high death rates kept the company and missions close at the start. The clergy helped to tend the sick, and buried the company's men, providing them with tombstones. Protestant fiefdoms had begun to emerge in neighbouring Nyasaland, with enough money to build roads and organise a supply of electricity and water. But in this area, which would become part of North-Eastern Rhodesia, they would be more contained and had to compete for favours, soon turning on each other.

Unlike in aristocratic Kenya, the last eddy of Victorian migration was the no-nonsense, tough, working-class artisan, dreaming that this world might be the new El Dorado. Owen Stroud from Bournemouth had gone to Blantyre with a friend to establish a coffee plantation, but it had failed. Stroud had then moved to Fort Jameson to seek his fortune as the territory began to be 'settled', and he chose the new capital of North-Eastern Rhodesia. He worked for the BSAC, overseeing the construction of houses and shops, and was proud to have baked the first brick for the first house in Jameson. He was unemployed in 1899, as the jobs had run out, but Codrington, the administrator in charge, had been pleased with his work.[35] By 1902, he had become Foreman of Public Works for the BSAC at Fort 'Jimmy'. The capital was hardly a bustling metropolis – it was home to forty-six settlers (eight years previously, there had been just one). Stroud was offered the job of building the Livingstone Monument. In September 1902, the same year Cecil Rhodes was buried, Stroud began his expedition. In February 1903, the local newspaper in his home town, the *Bournemouth Guardian*, began serialising the builder-carpenter account of his 'long and hard journey into the heart of central Africa'.

'Mr Owen Stroud was sent up from Fort Jameson to erect the Livingstone Memorial, along with a few native artisans'.[36] Stroud was actually accompanied by seventy African carriers and artisans, all skilled men, for a task that was full of hazards and pressures. Poulett Weatherley had judged the region to be hospitable only for the shortest of stays: 'I do not think any white man could live there a couple of rainy seasons ... the stench from the vast marshes, when the water subsides, after the rains is poisonous to Europeans'.[37] The site itself had been desolate of human habitation. In 1891, an outbreak of rinderpest was described as having destroyed much of the wildlife apart from the puku (an antelope with a shaggy golden-yellow coat and short, thick horns). The villages were now rebuilding, and game was more plentiful at least, but the water was like brown sauce. Communication between Stroud and his men was difficult: they could only pronounce his name, 'Bwana Matrousa'. He was new to this kind of expedition. He learnt to start walking early and, if necessary, push on to the next boma to set up camp, even if it meant an eighteen-hour walk. He also availed himself of the option of being carried by hammock.

On arrival, Stroud was horrified to see a large, five-foot-wide stump no one had mentioned. With no shovels – they had only axes and hoes – Stroud's men had great difficulty in digging out and chopping up the stump. Stroud verified the pieces in a written declaration, which he took back with him on his return journey, first to Nyasa and then to Fort Jameson.[38] The African artisans had to do most of the construction work, making whitish-yellow bricks in a hastily built kiln on the spot. The end product was judged to be shorter and stouter but 'better proportioned than the original design'.[39] Stroud was given four telegraph poles and railway sleepers to construct railings around the monument, but one of them had to be stuck inside the neck to support the cross (see Figure 4.2).

Figure 4.2 The Livingstone Memorial built by Owen Stroud, Chitambo. Undated. SOAS Archives CWM/LMS/Home/Livingstone Pictures/Box 1. File 6.

He confessed later that a temporary wooden rail was used as the fourth railing after a visitor noticed only three iron poles.[40] Rather than using the two sets of bronze plates, one was set into the statue, with the lettering of the inscription individually soldered onto it. Stroud decided to plant some wattles and gum trees. He had used sixty-seven drums of cement during construction, which lasted from 16 August to 7 October. He was informed that the old chief's body had been buried on the other side, but this subject was never raised again. The tree stump was packed up to be carried back to Fort Jameson, and he dutifully returned the spare plates.

Bachelor Colonialism and the Diary of Owen Stroud

The diary Stroud kept during this period offers a rare insight into the world of a white working-class man in early colonial central Africa.[41] He was one of hundreds of low-skilled men heading into an interior in search of a better living. Often, no details survive documenting their inner lives. Stroud was writing for his home town, but not as a devotee of Livingstone. His account shows a man travelling under the constant threat of violence and ambush. One hunter warned Stroud to watch out for the Belgian police from the Congo, 'as they were now raiding in British territory, all cannibals, having just killed and eaten seven men from the Africa Lakes Corporation'. Stroud downplayed this threat: if they wished to eat him, 'they would have to fight hard', he wrote; but his gun never left his side. As one might expect, few details emerge about the African artisans and carriers who accompanied him; he showed no interest in their lives, emotions or views. Not one of his men is named, and although he chats to everyone, the identity of his interpreter remains a mystery.

Stroud's main interlocutors were chiefs or headmen, and he wrote much about them. He marvelled at wealthy chiefs such as Chief Karinga, who had two hundred huts, and gave him a sheep as a present. Others were pitied. Chief Kopa had been reduced to twenty followers and harshly described as 'the most miserable looking object of a nigger' Stroud had ever seen, being a dwarf of about sixty years of age. Stroud wrote more affectionately about the chiefs who lived in the vicinity of Chitambo. Like so many government officials who came after him throughout colonial Africa, he seems to have easily cultivated a soft spot for local chiefs, captivated by their charm and needing their help. The day after the party's arrival in Chitambo, twenty-two chiefs arrived bearing gifts, mostly fowl, offering their respects to the grave. Perhaps they were touched at seeing a young white man coming alone to honour the grave of his ancestor. Once the cross had been hoisted, Stroud repaid their hospitality with a feast to celebrate the completion of the monument. He bought local beer and flour, and shot mountains of game, giving them a great evening of eating and dancing. It was a lesson in the benefits of treating natives 'fairly', Stroud concluded. He liked the head chief so much, he left him his shirt and a pair of trousers.

The working relationship that Stroud had with his men echoes the nineteenth-century exploration caravans, with power and racial boundaries in a state of flux according to circumstance and need. The forced intimacy and isolation such a journey involved seem to have created an informal economy of affection, and Stroud's hard racism could soften when he felt sentimental. Stroud would always refer to 'my boys'. He tried always to bring home enough kill to enable his boys to eat well. He gave them a bonus after finishing the monument for having worked so hard. 'They deserved it', he proudly wrote. He wanted to take some back to Fort Jameson to train them as carpenters. The difficulty in hiring, he sympathetically explained to his English audience, was simply because 'they are so afraid around these parts'. True, Stroud was regularly carried in a hammock but, when danger arose, he insisted on sharing it, refusing to be carried across a crocodile-infested river, and instead stripping off to wade through, neck-deep, with the rest.

Stroud was a grafter, stopping off to do jobs for the new native commissioner, a man referred to only as Willis. He helped him track down tax evaders, which may have hardened his views, for Stroud's language with Willis changed. In Karinga and Kopa, he described 'lots of niggers' living in temporary grass huts to evade paying taxes. He recorded passing through 'two fine villages of niggers who were well made and rather nice looking for niggers'. Willis had been instructed to supply Stroud with eighty boys to help him reach Chitambo. The regime must have been strict, and Stroud implies he was handy with his fists. On the morning after their first night under canvas, Stroud awoke to discover that two 'artful' men had bolted. 'I should like to have caught them in the act', he wrote, because they 'would not have forgotten O[ld] Stroud for a long while'. When he later returned to the monument with Willis for a photo opportunity, one wonders what Stroud now felt the site represented. Stroud had not developed any new respect for Protestant missionaries. He baulked at their large salaries and dismissed their 'calling' as a career choice based on the high wages. In contrast, he praised the White Fathers for being men who went to central Africa to die and who put their congregations first. Only the UMCA came close, he added, wishing that people in England would give their money to help the poor at home rather than fund expensive missions.

Young missionary recruits probably had little in common with men like Stroud. A single man, he indulged his pleasures, smoking to relax and killing game. Much of his diary is peppered with accounts of the kinds of animals shot, the tracking of wounded ones and how the animals looked dead or dying. Readers would have been enthralled by his account of coming across a seventeen-foot python, a foot in girth. (No tale of African adventure and derring-do would leave out a struggle to kill a giant snake.) As Stroud could not afford the £25 big game licence, he could not kill any of the elephants he encountered, but his love of hunting was something he shared with the thin white line of lone bachelors he met along the way. These included four miners at a prospective gold mine, awaiting an expert opinion; Willis and his assistants, who wanted him to stay longer; Wright, the hunter-trader, who warned him about the cannibals; and Harvey, who owned a store and also begged him to stay longer.

Chitambo and Livingstone's completed memorial began to attract more bachelors. In 1904, the region's first tax collector, J.E. Hughes, was sent there to clear the ground around the memorial and plant baby cypress trees on the instruction of the native commissioner, Croad, who lived alone in Serenje, a new administrative post in the Ilala region. Travelling by night to escape the heat, the party had been stampeded by a rhinoceros. The box of seeds was dropped, with only a few seeds surviving, as each carrier fled for the trees. Hughes was content with planting just a few and was happy that Stroud's planting had failed as he judged there was no need for any more trees. 'Nothing could be more suitable', Hughes felt, than the forest around the monument, full of 'splendid indigenous evergreen trees', adding that there was 'a magnificent natural park waiting to be laid out'.[42] The locals had given him part of the root of the tree 'amongst which his heart was buried'. They told him Livingstone had not only died under this tree but that his embalmed body had been hung in its upper branches.[43] Hughes seems to have been captivated by the sentimentality of the encounter and place.

Hughes was born in 1876 and came from Derbyshire. He had arrived in Africa in 1901, inspired by his boyhood reading of James Fenimore Cooper's *Deerslayer*. He had only been able to stand seven years in company employment, handing in his resignation in 1908 to achieve 'full freedom as hunter and trader' once the suppression of the Arab ivory trade had allowed the wildlife to recover. He sought out the solitude of the Lake Bangweulu area, describing his home as a 'hermitage'. He was a loner, a boy-man who had never grown up; he had spent much of his adolescence in the company of a ferret. Typical of the single white male trophy-hunter-gatherer type, he made copious notes about his time living in the area between 1901 and 1919, which he published as a 376-page book containing jaw-dropping photos. Passionate about the African landscape, he provided forensic detail on its forests, rivers and inhabitants, affectionately dedicating the book to his friends, the 'big game of Africa'; yet, in most of the photos, the leopards or sable antelope are dead – shot or speared – and arranged in perfectly lifelike, classical poses. He apologised for a book 'without any plot, love interest or fiction', probably aware that it could not compete with accounts of central Africa containing sensational descriptions of cannibals, and photographs of them smiling, with bared, chiselled, pointed teeth for tearing out human flesh without having to resort to a knife.[44]

Living near Chitambo, Hughes also became obsessed with death. 'Our Natives' included details of their 'quaint' or 'queer little superstitions': the reincarnation of chiefs into man-eating lions and the idea that a stone placed in the fork of a tree could delay the setting of the sun. Every man belonged to a lodge (a *mwini*), such as the River Hog or Anthill Lodge, and would treat fellow lodge members, even if from another clan, as a brother, providing them with food and shelter. Hughes became more interested than most in burial customs and graves. He had come across graves with miniature huts used to mark the resting place of a chief. He had found graves in the Congo marked with sun-bleached crocodile skulls; elsewhere, small circles of antelope, hippopotamus skulls and Euphorbia denoted the grave of a skilled hunter. Nevertheless, his book was full of racial prejudice; he concluded, for example, that the life of a native was a 'fierce struggle for personal advantage, in which all the arts of subterfuge and mendacity are thoroughly and freely employed ... owing to lack of organisation'.[45] Women hardly register. One exception was in relation to the 'pernicious habit of smoking Bange' (a plant capable of causing a state of euphoria). He had seen native women in Fort Jameson 'with their breasts burnt off' because they had rolled over into the fire under its influence.

There was no reference to the local chief's burial site. The Chitambo memorial had become a white Livingstone memorial, the fruit tree replaced by barren foreign shrubs. The memorial failed to symbolise a relationship with Africans, with their fellowship and shared humanitarianism, and with what they did for Livingstone. The area, now abandoned by the locals and more desolate, seemed to have become a place consumed by death, rumoured to be full of tsetse flies. The records of the first administrators in the region hint at a place where the lost or fading chose to die. An unknown 'wanderer' died there some time in 1912; and R.M. Green, bachelor, built a hut nearby and passed away shortly afterwards.[46]

Company Men, Missionaries and the Livingstone Tree Relics

Late-company imperialism was morphing into early-state colonialism. Robert Codrington, another bachelor, played a huge role in this phase. Building up Fort Jimmy from 'nothing', he oversaw road building and encouraged some white settlement. He would later be lionised by white settlers for his achievements: life before colonial rule was referred to as 'B.C.' – Before Codrington.[47] Codrington was a king without a kingdom (which was, in fact, an area that seemed to attract more than its fair share of tsetse flies, missionary friction and maverick individuals), but he was made of stern stuff: a military-bureaucrat, with a schoolboy crush on Livingstone. Codrington had also experienced the challenges of moving around the area as Livingstone had on foot. He, too, had struggled against illness, as many of his colleagues had done, with less success. To those who shared his high esteem and affection for Livingstone, Codrington could behave in a very sentimental way, showing a softer side. Church and company in this area worked closely together.

Codrington had cut down the *mpundu* tree with a plan and purpose. He understood the feelings involved, reassuring the RGS that the cut section was being lovingly cared for and was in no danger while en route to London, recommending a generous coating of creosote and a glass display for this 'national property' when it arrived. However, he also arranged for the trunk to take an extensive tour of the region before it left, at a time when there were few roads and few certainties with regard to any kind of trip. Codrington had not been completely truthful to the RGS about the Livingstone tree: he had also made a number of large, sausage-shaped bricks out of the trunk for his personal use, to give away as gifts. Beneficiaries included 'generous subscribers' to a Livingstone memorial fund for a church.[48]

Codrington did this in part because he had developed a good working relationship with the LMS's local agent, the Reverend John May, who oversaw their now well-established station on the shores of Lake Tanganyika at Kawimbe, towards the far north-east of the new territory. In June 1899, May wrote to thank Codrington for his 'kindness and courtesy' in offering to send the tree section for the mission members to see.[49] They clearly regarded it as a feather in their cap that the LMS's early connection with Livingstone was being acknowledged. 'Every care would be taken of the tree', May assured Codrington; 'it will be placed under lock and key'. The section remained at this particular mission for twenty-four hours, allowing May enough time to gaze at the inscription 'with intense interest'. The next day, African carriers packed it up and took it away.

In January 1900, Codrington started to dispense the pieces of bark that had been chopped up, assisted by an officer working for the British Central Africa Company, based in Nyasa. Large quantities of bark and branch were authenticated with company seals and signed.[50] Numerous *mpundu* leaves were also preserved and sent out as gifts that found their way not just around southern Africa but all over the world. Many ended up in Scotland.[51] Tree and leaf relics became part of exhibitions and of presentation gifts to mission stations and churches in Britain, with one piece ending up in Canterbury Cathedral. Examples also exist of tree spatulas, or paper knives, and boxes: 'a small industry of creating domestic objects out of the wood' sprang up.[52] The Reverend May had written to Codrington delighted that the LMS mission at Kawimbe would soon be receiving pieces of the Livingstone tree to keep forever, signing off, 'I am, dear Mr Codrington, yours sincerely'.[53] May and his wife's young son had recently died of typhoid fever but, of course, May would betray no sign of emotion or self-pity in communicating the tragedy. The pieces of bark never arrived. They mysteriously disappeared en route. Three months later, May had to write again to Codrington, apologising for not thanking him, explaining the pieces of bark had gone missing and May was having the matter investigated.[54] It seems not to have been resolved.

Christian missionaries and company agents often worked closely together during the preliminary phase of formal imperialism during this era, both needing each other until they found their feet, before discovering that their differences and rivalries would push them apart.[55] Codrington and May were drawn together in friendship through a shared admiration of Livingstone and a lack of secure control over their environment. Church and company worked together to cast the rude net of administrative control over this part of central Africa. Missionaries were the 'lubricant' for the company machine, gathering local intelligence to help with taxation. The LMS conducted a census of its villages, with May reporting helpfully (and incredulously) that they all seemed 'to take very kindly' to the proposal that a tax be imposed on individual huts. Likewise, when the BSAC came under pressure in Britain over allegations of the ill treatment of Africans, May was happy to furnish Codrington with an account which he could forward to London to counter the bad press. 'We know of no forced labour in this district in the sense of it being unpaid', May wrote, usefully.[56] Native labour had been required by the recent boundary commissions, he confided, but when another request was made, this time by men who were laying down telegraph lines, fewer volunteers were forthcoming because it was the rainy season. 'Pressure was brought to bear on them', he admitted, quickly adding 'not of a harsh nature, as far as we know'.

Missionaries also repeatedly acted to diffuse imperial concerns over high levels of violence. Living not far from May, Chief Kera had been asked to supply forty men, further proof of the extent to which local labour constructed the building blocks of colonial rule. He offered eighteen and then 'assumed a defiant attitude by throwing up earthworks and arming his men'. Two of his villages had been burnt to the ground, food stores torched and precious cattle confiscated. But May added reassuringly that no crops had been targeted, plus the chief had been 'troublesome' for a while. May's attitude was that 'the native should give a certain amount of work in return for the protection offered him by the Administration'; in any case, that was also the deal for anyone living on his mission station land. There was a shared acceptance of violence as a just punishment. May ended with the Victorian equivalent of a legal disclaimer: 'We wish all dealings with the native could be of a peaceable and conciliatory nature'.

This was a brief golden age, during which the company and clerics worked easily together as long as missionaries knew their place. May continued to be the ideal junior partner, but tensions soon came to the surface. An LMS member of staff threatened the bonhomie when the Reverend Jones verbally abused two BSAC officials for their 'ignorance of native language and general incompetence', before refusing to surrender an African teacher who was wanted for tax evasion. Jones was instantly suspended.[57] In return for such loyalty, the mission seemed to ask very little – not that they had much bargaining power. The company needed them less and less once it had set up its holding operation. The LMS begged Codrington not to grant a licence to sell alcohol to a shopkeeper in the vicinity, but company policy was not to acquiesce to missionary morals. Meanwhile, back at their London headquarters, in 1902, Worldlaw Thompson, the LMS foreign secretary, had to reassure the company that it thoroughly opposed the acquiring of vast tracts of land because it might, down the line, raise 'serious questions of landlordship' among the local population.

The times were against Codrington and May's personalised cooperation and the mutual backscratching. The LMS was still benefiting from the tail end of the massive donations from Victorian industrial philanthropists, so had more cash available to undertake extension work 'among tribes not yet evangelised'.[58] However, the area was becoming more accessible, and other missionaries were keen to move in. Women philanthropists were also starting to take an interest. A Mrs Ida Cooke wrote to the BSAC from South Africa, asking where she could be sent to help to relieve the 'underdeveloped state and the dense darkness' of 'Central Africa' now that it was being opened up by 'railways and travellers'.[59] Codrington's nightmares were just beginning. By 1910, a magistrate was dealing with the land wars between the LMS and the White Fathers, fearing that, unless matters were sorted out, 'serious friction amongst the natives may result'. Codrington would soon discover that with a pristine white monument and the area opening up to more visitors, an unholy war would break out over the guardianship of Livingstone's heart.

Missionary Wars: Chitambo and the Livingstone Dynasty

Codrington's working life had in some ways become easier. There were fewer cases of the perennial problem of a 'very undesirable type of European who has come into these western lake areas of late', drawn in by rumours of gold and the prospect of buying cattle on the cheap to sell on further south. The most infamous case had been that of a German trader, Ziehl, who was in the employ of the North Charterland Expedition Company (a subsidiary of the BSAC), who had seriously injured a native man, amongst many other charges, and had launched an attack on an Angoni chief. He had also assembled an illegal mercenary native force, dressing them in uniforms that were exact replicas of the company's workforce, and arming them with Snider–Enfield rifles, so that they became 'the terror of the district'. Alfred Sharpe, commissioner and consul general of the British Central Africa Protectorate, and based in Zomba, called in the military, who arrested them. Whilst Codrington had jailed the armed Africans in Fort Jameson and fined Ziehl £5 pending his trial for more serious offences, now including murder, Sharpe considered Codrington's response lenient and pressured him to curb this lawlessness. The subsidiary company blamed 'native treachery' and, if ignored, intended to arm the Africans in self-defence. Codrington took a firmer line after this. Ziehl served two years in prison with hard labour for raiding native villages and stealing cattle, although he seems to have escaped the murder charge. The BSAC was not in a position to bear grudges and later re-employed him, granting him a permit, worth £1,000, to buy cattle.

Codrington had also learnt how to keep the Foreign Office onside in cases of rumoured brutality against Africans. In the case of the fiesty M'Pensi, the company had asked for and obtained military assistance from the British Central African Administration. However, this involved 'much harsh treatment of the natives', which now made cooperation very difficult, and had damaged trade. BSAC officials were rumoured to have confiscated twelve thousand head of cattle for their personal gain.

Luckily for the BSAC, they remained in the clear as far as the Foreign Office was concerned. Lord Salisbury had given his approval to the punitive expedition because a request had gone out saying that Europeans were in imminent danger. They had been rescued, order restored and the chief removed, with Lieutenant Colonel Manning, now playing it by the book, keeping his superiors informed. Three thousand of the confiscated cattle were returned and, despite concerns about the use of excessive force, the Foreign Office dropped the matter, feeling that 'fair play' had been resumed.

This remote area of bush was still not so attractive, and prospective settlers realised they could do very little there. Nevertheless, Alfred Sharpe found a lot to complain about, including miscegenation. In 1903, he wrote a long letter to Codrington after his tour. The letter was full of gripes, but top of his list was an encounter in a village near the town of Choma. A small, half-caste girl 'was brought up for me to see' by a local man. It had been a pitiful sight and had upset him.[60] The little girl was described as 'miserably thin'; her mother had died, and she had been ill for a long time, suffering terribly. The local gossip was that the girl had been fathered by a white man known as 'Chipal pata', the company official, Warrington. 'No one of course with reason can say much as to the custom of white men having a country wife', Sharpe wrote, but it was 'abominable for any white man to make no provision for his child'. Sharpe passed the messy problem to Codrington; Chipal pata had been told Codrington would be in touch.

Fort Jameson's white community was slowly adding flesh to its scrawny bones. In 1902, 'a small but growing community of Europeans at Fort Jameson and the various missionary bodies are anxious to set up a church'.[61] The nearest was a Dutch Reformed Church ten miles away. Codrington had received letters from the LMS and the Free Church of Scotland asking if they could set up substations. He refused since it was 'the wish of European residents of there to have someone from the Church of England', a clear reflection of their background. In sympathy, Codrington opted for the Society for the Propagation of the Gospel in Foreign Parts (SPG). A budget of £150 per annum had already been set aside, and it was hoped that the SPG would foot the rest. They obliged. In November 1905, they decided that the Reverend Bell would take up the appointment, transferring from the society's Bombay diocese.[62] No church had yet been built, and an appeal was made to top up the company's grant. Things went well. The chaplain and his wife arrived, and a modest church was quickly constructed. However, with only two pupils remaining by 1908, the chaplain's annual income from the company was reduced by half.

Yet sentimentally, Codrington did not deviate from his original plans for Chitambo to honour Livingstone. After interviewing Dr Prentice from the Free Church of Scotland, Codrington formally offered the mission, in August 1904, a chance to establish a substation there. This offer came despite the great pressure from the UMCA, which had always wanted to push westwards and acquire more land. The offer stood until 30 September 1905. After that time, the offer would be made elsewhere. It was very much Codrington's personal preference; he added that, as an incentive, and in order that medical work be taken up within the mission (which was what he always had in mind), he would recommend to the Livingstone Memorial Committee that they give them a grant of £100 from their surplus funds.[63] The committee eagerly accepted the offer, although they needed an extension until the end of 1905.

Nevertheless, the Reverend Dr Robert Laws cheerfully reported back to Codrington that two of their missionaries, the Reverend McAlpine and John Riddle Henderson, were to visit Old Chitambo, taking with them 'tried native teachers whom they are to leave in the district, and thus begin work'.[64] Fundraising in Scotland was bound to prove fruitful, Laws assured him, since it would 'reach and touch the hearts of many'. Sensing that they might be on a roll, he then listed all the new mission substations that they had planned. Codrington put the brakes on, warning that it was not part of the deal that any substations be opened where only Africans would be in charge.

Fundraising in Scotland was going ahead full steam. Indirectly, Codrington had helped to raise money for churches that would go against his impulses and prioritise African teachers of the gospel. In 1906, an auction was held in Glasgow of Livingstone tree relics – 'Memento Blocks', as they were advertised in the press. These had been apparently donated to the Livingstonia Committee. The large bricks, cut in Africa, cost 10s 6d; smaller paperweights with a silver heart in the middle, presumably made in Scotland, 5s 6d.[65] The proceeds were to be divided between two church building projects: 'a Livingstone Memorial Church in Fort Jameson and Chitambo extension of the Livingstone Mission'.

A chasm was opening up between white views on the capabilities and role of African Christians. Yet these pioneering African Bible extension workers were the beginning of a mass movement of indigenous Christian conversion that would dramatically shape the social and cultural landscape of this part of Africa. For some missionaries, in the Livingstone tradition, souls trumped race, and they were relaxed about Africans doing their work; they were few in number, and there were few white settlers around to protest. Always mindful of their manners, the African Christian teachers and humanitarians began to spread out, teaching reading and writing in English, schooled in the tradition that they owed their salvation to the pioneering inclusiveness of Livingstone and missionaries like him; and also to 'Scotland's love to Africa', as the Reverend Morrison had put it to his African congregation when they had gathered around the grave.[66] Careful, conservative and keen to learn the scriptures, they loyally carried forwards a sentimentalised, idealised version of Livingstone's love of Africans and good race relations.

Although the company remained sympathetic to the effort and investment that had gone into the Livingstonia Mission at Blantyre under the auspices of its founding father, the Reverend Dr Robert Laws, Codrington nevertheless restricted further expansion, a policy which Wallace, his successor appointed in 1908, firmly upheld. Laws had tirelessly tried to negotiate the extension of his 'kingdom' and improve the terms by which missionaries were obliged to abide, in accordance with the rules set down by the company. He even badgered them to ask the directors to grant them an extra 105 square miles, deemed necessary as a natural buffer zone to protect what they had built up.[67] The 39 square miles that they had were more than ample for their work, they were informed during a number of long exchanges.[68]

Tempers frayed when, to ensure a Scottish victory, Livingstone's family were brought into the dispute. In 1905, a rumour started that the company was going to give the land around Livingstone's grave to the White Fathers, who had established a presence not far away and were seeking to expand. A telegram swiftly arrived on Codrington's desk at Fort Jameson. Livingstone's daughter, Mrs Agnes Bruce, insisted that arrangements be made for custody of the remains by Protestants in order that the objections and wishes of the family be respected. Codrington's reply barely contains his irritation, since both the LMS and the Free Church, he pointed out, had been repeatedly reassured since 1899 that Chitambo was reserved for a mission in memory of Livingstone.

Two years after this scare, the Free Church of Scotland feared that they were about to lose Chitambo again, claiming they were the victims of 'Anglican aggression', according to the sympathetic headline above a long letter to the *Glasgow Herald* published in December 1907. Mission rage was in the air in response to an apparently 'unbrotherly' act committed against the Presbyterians.[69] The UMCA had gathered at Great St Mary's Church of Cambridge University to mark fifty years of their work. At this event, an appeal was launched, backed by a number of high-profile Anglican bishops, to raise money for a third diocese in North-Eastern Rhodesia and the construction of a mission station on the sacred site of Livingstone's burial place. This planned Anglican diocese trespassed on the established area of activity of the Scottish missionaries, came the terse response: it contained 'the spot where Livingstone had died'; and they already had two men working, including Livingstone's own nephew, having raised £1,000 in donations for their work.

In a personal letter to Codrington, from Dumbarton, Lord Overton continued: had they not worked hard? Would Ngoniland have been annexed in 1904 'without the firing of a single shot'? Had they not laid the preparatory ground? Had they not accepted the generous boundary of the White Fathers around Chitambo? Codrington's reply was unsympathetic. Those who made the decisions nowadays, he wrote, were in London and did not mind rival missions in the same field; and when it came to bringing the Church of England into closer contact with 'her peoples', he had always been 'naturally a strong supporter'.[70]

Nevertheless, Chitambo and Scotland clung together, weathering the storm under the new Anglican skies. Together, they produced what would be described by one visitor as 'the real memorial to David Livingstone', thanks in part to the sentimental bond with the region felt by Livingstone's descendants and the Free Church of Scotland. In 1894, Livingstone's nephew, the son of Mary's brother, Malcolm Moffat, had joined the mission in Livingstonia, Nyasa. In 1906, he was ordained as a minister alongside a local man, David Kaunda, who would go on to have a son baptised Kenneth (destined to be Zambia's first president). Following in his uncle's footsteps, Malcolm fell out with many of the missionaries there and was deemed more suitable for outreach work. He arrived in Chitambo to survey the site in 1907 with his wife, Marie. The area had a reputation for quietness and solitude, which did not suit the other missionary man sent there with him, a qualified medic from Aberdeen, Dr Alexander Brown. Brown left in 1912, but not before they had set up a mission station and hospital with three beds, treating two thousand five hundred people according to their records. In 1914, there were also fourteen mission schools in the region.[71]

Key additions to the team were Fileman Kamanga and Ester Nyankalu, who had walked three hundred miles there from Nyasa and had helped to build and run the station. In 1913, Hubert and Ruth Wilson arrived. They were, respectively, a doctor and a nurse but, more importantly, they were the grandchildren of David and Mary Livingstone and had been appointed in the centenary year of Livingstone's birth by the Livingstonia Committee of the Free Church of Scotland. Meanwhile, Chitambo continued to be sentimentalised by the locals as a symbolic site and also as a place of death. They told and retold the story of how Livingstone had died there and of how 'Chief Chitambo Mukulu' was also buried there; the hospital, they saw as a place where Africans went to die.

Pilgrimage Tourism

By 1910, the region had a façade of white settlement, and the first tourists were finding their way to Chitambo to visit the monument. A cottage had been built near the memorial and huts for African porters, although the latter had fallen into ruin. The visitors' book was stolen, so it is difficult to establish how many travellers to the region did make a pilgrimage there. Visitors were mainly military men on hunting expeditions, aristocrats, professional writers or single women on goodwill imperial missions to visit infant white communities. Fort Jameson was alerted in March 1908 to the possible arrival of a Captain Thornton, who was contemplating a shooting trip to North-Eastern Rhodesia; then to the arrival of Major Whitla, London Naval and Military Club, who, in addition to introductions, wanted easy credit.

The first solo female traveller arrived in January 1909, when the authoress Charlotte Mansfield's arrival was forewarned. Later the same year, Hélène, Duchess of Aosta, sister to the Queen of Portugal and cousin to the King of Italy, announced her intention to visit. She planned a trip through the area, 'shooting wherever possible' and travelling with only three other companions. Having journeyed through Africa previously, she was determined to travel incognito and ignored warnings about a local outbreak of sleeping sickness.[72] She made a modest request for two hundred carriers and five mules. The local administration was appalled. It was unsafe to travel without a 'whiteman in charge', cabled back a furious official called Wallace from the field, so 'request one'. African attacks on white women in Southern Rhodesia were now periodically reported in the settler press. Headlines were typically sensationalist and alarmist, such as the attacks on 'Salisbury ladies' in 1902, headlined as 'The Pampered Rhodesian Native: A Spreading Evil'.[73]

Another lone female traveller planning on touring the area was Miss King Church, honorary secretary of the Victoria League. Concerned largely with educational and social matters, with branches throughout the empire, the organisation was affiliated to the Guild of Loyal Women in South Africa and its Graves Commission. The Rhodes Trust had written a letter on her behalf, introducing her to promote ties between the white Dominions, as 'a most gifted and charming lady'. Impressively, she was travelling alone through southern and central Africa for a year, 'occasionally' wanting to talk to someone. It was a sign that this part of Africa was now being brought into the orbit of the genteel female imperial welfare networks, including those set up in South Africa.

Naturally, the largest group of pilgrims to the area were missionaries and Christians, including members of the Livingstone dynasty. They bulked up the numbers of a steady trickle of pilgrimage tourism. Some turned their visit into a published account for audiences back home. The Reverend James Morrison of the United Free Church of Scotland, in his book *On the Trial of the Pioneer*, a history of Scottish missionaries, ended with an emotional account of his visit to Chitambo, interspersed with the 'facts' of Livingstone's last journey.[74] This was a promotional text for the church, targeting a juvenile audience. In his preface, he wrote how 'the history of missions throbs with romance on every page', which 'the general reader would do well to realise'. He certainly did his best to convey this. Chitambo was now 'the most sacred plot in Africa', which had been committed 'to our care', he wrote, and where lies 'the mighty heart that loved Africa so well' – 'that great loving heart that had throbbed and bled for the sorrow of Africa's children'.[75] Around it was 'a land of grown up children ... pathetically eager for instruction'. The reality was less romantic: after emerging from the swamps, Morrison was led to the clearing, along a broad road. Alas, he had no time to savour the scene:

for the moment I stepped into the square with head uncovered, I was furiously set upon by swarms of tsetse flies ... for rash and fury, I had encountered nothing like [this] ... In vain we thrashed about us with leafy branches. They swarmed on us like bees and we were compelled to beat a hasty retreat to the cottage and slam the door.[76]

Media coverage kept the Livingstone grave alive, so to speak. In 1915, Livingstone's only surviving child, Anna Mary Livingstone Wilson (born in Kuruman in 1858), visited the monument, and the encounter received global press attention. In the account she wrote up for publication, she made no reference to the First World War. Widowed in 1910, she had travelled for a month up from Cape Town to make the visit. Her son was still at the mission station, marking out the boundaries and clearing the ground. Controversially for the colonial administration, he was accompanied by African teachers, who were holding services in the nearby villages, 'practically untouched ground'.[77] Written by a woman, this is one of the first expedition accounts to give precise details about clothing. White dresses and muslin blouses were the uniform of the practical female camper. In subsequent talks, Anna Mary spoke about shopping and African women's clothes, having purchased antelope skins from them, which they wore, customised with tattoos.[78] She was also travelling with her daughter, Ruth, a trained nurse, and both her children had made the pilgrimage a year before. Anna Mary was constantly bitten by tsetse flies.

A highly sentimentalised account was written up for the *Missionary Record* under the heading 'Family Gathering at Livingstone's Grave'.[79]

The writer imagined a dying Livingstone, with glazed eyes, sundered from his wife's death, unable to take comfort from the knowledge that his final resting place would be visited by those who 'love them'. Yet 'the spot has become one of the earth's sacred places'. Even Chisira, the 'toothless old blacksmith', and the boys, who usually just played *chisolo*, (a local board game played with rows of holes and three stones) had apparently been so affected by the pious gathering that they 'loosened their tongues and opened up their hearts'.

Aided no doubt by the local efforts to solve the fly problem, Anna Mary approved of the monument and its surroundings, as illustrated by her account published in *Cornhill Magazine* in 1916. It was 'wonderfully impressive'; being in the 'heart of the African bush' gave it 'a feeling of something holy, a sense of something vast'. She sentimentally imagined that it was what Livingstone would have chosen: one of 'Nature's own sanctuaries, sun-bathed and fair'. It was a personal and emotional account; Anna Mary found it impossible to put her feelings into words, going over her version of her father's death as she walked around, more conscious than ever of the enormity of his followers' achievement. This was a compliment which stood in contrast to her negative views of 'the childish, irresponsible, underdeveloped nature of the African native'. Carried to the site in a machila (like a stretcher), Anna Mary had no doubt that, if attacked by a lion, their men would 'be up the nearest tree without further thought for us' because, although the men carried spears, she confided, 'one never knows what the native will do'.[80]

Chiefs and elders who had been alive at the time of her father's death came to pay their respects to Anna Mary, bringing gifts of *wunga* (a sort of biscuit) and chickens. They wore European coats over their loincloths. Chitono insisted that Livingstone had died in his mother's hut, where he took her. Anna Mary did not believe this version. She believed the tree had been struck by lightning. She was told that their old chief was also buried there. The lack of any memorialisation for him, or for the men who carried Livingstone to the site, was not raised by anyone.

Conclusion

This chapter has been a story of absences, as well as of the uses of remembering during early colonial rule. It illustrates the gap which quickly opened up between the metropolitan version of imperial capabilities and power, and the reality on the ground in remote, inaccessible parts of the African empire. The transformative capacity of colonialism, for both black and white, was severely limited in regions such as Ilala, where very little had changed apart from the imposition of a harsh racial divide, symbolised by the use of the term 'nigger'. The absence of memorialisation for Livingstone's men, either for their exploration with him or for their humanitarian achievements in their own right, finds a parallel in the disinterest in marking the grave of the African chief buried alongside Livingstone. Yet the tree, its trunk and leaves were invested with huge sentimental significance.

Death fed an ideology of sentimental imperialism. Even as men attempted to live the imperial vision, illness, pain and an early grave were common. Heroism, sacrifice and death fuelled an emotional memory of white settler pioneering. Death also lay at the heart of the early colonial rule for the indigenous population. The suppression of opposition was recent; the new capital of the region, Fort Jameson, had been established only a year after the Angoni had been repressed. The violence involved did lead to questions being raised in the Foreign Office. But the foundational violence in British Central Africa was viewed at the time in relation to the understanding that the other European powers were more brutal. The revelations during the first decade of the 1900s of the Belgian Congo were covered by the press and served to reinforce British imperialism's sense of its liberal qualities. Regional newspapers like the new *Central African Times* carried items on the continuing slavery in Portuguese territory. 'Inhuman barbarities' was the headline announcing the capture of twelve slave dhows in 1902. Twelve slave dealers were killed in the liberation of over seven hundred slaves, 'all in chains'.[81] Reports were published about 'German cruelty to natives' and about the discussions in Germany about moving towards freeing slaves in East Africa, Togo and the Cameroons.[82]

This chapter also supports the premise that colonial rule on the ground is unique and particular to a region and cannot be shoehorned into generalisations about white settlerdom. The partial extension of a thin film of rule in and around Chitambo was both typical of the remote, inaccessible regions in colonial Africa and also shaped by local circumstances and individuals, including a Scottish/British competitiveness.

The Livingstone grave at Chitambo was memorialised as the beating heart of liberal imperialism thanks to visitors, newspaper coverage and missionary printing presses. But Chitambo also became a monument to white pioneering. It created possibilities for missionary expansion and, in turn, problems for the administration, as the Scottish missionary frontier came up against Anglican ambition. For the lone bachelor, it was a place of contemplation, sadness and death; for others, more concerned with the reality and practical demands of survival, it had no sentimental significance. The steady trickle of hunters, traders and skilled artisans were each others' pioneering heroes.

The first missionaries in the area had first tried to work closely with the BSAC but quickly had to find alternatives. In 1913, the Free Church's nearby mission station had installed its own printing press and was translating scripture into the vernacular. By the start of the First World War, the area was starting to attract more visitors. The war brought a telegraph system and the extension of a main road built by a Mobile Column (gang workers who slept in tents). Yet personalities and relationships remained disproportionately important. The fates of the tree, its bricks, the monument and the mission station were all profoundly affected by Robert Codrington's sentimentality towards Livingstone. Codrington survived the dangers of ill health in the field, unlike many of his contemporaries. After eleven years of faithful service, he decided to leave while he was still able, with his health and a knighthood, packing up for England in 1908.[83]

Yet in other parts of southern Africa, white settlers were now self-strengthening. The opening of the new parliament of the Union of South Africa in 1910, ending a century of Anglo-Boer conflict, was attended by British royalty. The Prince and Princess of Wales also accepted an invitation from the company to visit Southern Rhodesia and Northern Rhodesia (now amalgamated from North-Western and North-Eastern Rhodesia).[84] They did not care to visit Chitambo and stand above Livingstone's old heart. Instead, they made for Victoria Falls. They were met by Lord and Lady Winchester and eighty men from the Northern Rhodesia Constabulary in a new town, making its debut on the Anglo-global stage. It was called Livingstone.

NOTES

1 A Scottish pop-folk duo who are brothers. The song was reissued in 2007 for a campaign to raise money for Comic Relief, a UK charity event for children in Africa.

2 See Simpson, *Dark Companions* for detailed reconstructions of the working lives of many of the 'followers' and others.

3 Pridmore & Simpson, '"Faithful to the End"', 192–6. This includes a useful compendium of sixty followers.

4 See Helly, *Livingstone's Legacy*; Pettitt, *Dr. Livingstone, I Presume?*, 124–78.

5 *Church Missionary Intelligencer*, April 1876, quoted in H.B. Thomas, OBE, 'The Death of Dr Livingstone. Carus Farrar's Narrative', *Uganda Journal*, 14, 2 (September 1950): 127.

6 Thomas had been a CMS missionary, a Uganda colonial official and a historian. See 'H B Thomas, OBE: In Memorium', *The Uganda Journal*, 36 (1972): 1–2. He edited the text for publication written by Carus Farrar.

7 Simpson, *Dark Companions*, 101.

8 Pettitt, *Dr. Livingstone, I Presume?*, 152–3; Simpson, *Dark Companions*, 101.

9 Price quoted in Simpson, *Dark Companions*, 137.

10 J. Thompson, *To the Central African Lakes and Back: The Narrative of the Royal Geographical Society's Central African Expedition, 1878–80* (London: Sampson, Low, Marston, Searle & Rivington, 1881), i, 34.

11 H.B. Thomas, OBE, 'Jacob Wainwright in Uganda', Notes, *Uganda Journal* 15, 2 (September 1951): 204–5.

12 Ibid.

13 Simpson, *Dark Companions*, 142.

14 'Carus Farrar's narrative', *Uganda Journal*, 125, fn 1.

15 Ibid., 127.

16 Simpson, *Dark Companions*, 189. Rather late in life, the Reverend W.J. Rampley, a missionary. edited and helped publish his reminiscences, *Matthew Wellington: Sole Surviving Link with Dr Livingstone* (London: SPCK, 1930).

17 Simpson, *Dark Companions*, 153.

18 Joseph Thomson, *To the Central African Lakes and Back, The Narrative of the Royal Geographical Society's East Central African Expedition, 1878–80* (London: Sampson Low, Marston, Searle, & Rivington, 1881), ii, 31–2.

19 Ibid., 135.

20 Ibid., 161.

21 Ibid., 33–4.

22 H. Thomas, 'Note', 'Carus Farrar's Narrative', *Uganda Journal*, 127: 115–28.

23 Renema & van Zoelen, *You Took the Part*, 69.

24 Simpson, *Dark Companions*, 188–9.

25 Stanley, *How I Found Livingstone*, 238.

26 Jeal, *Stanley*, 516, fn 45.

27 H.B. Thomas, 'Note: Livingstone's Muganda Servant – A Postcript', *Uganda Journal*, 28, 1 (1964): 99–100.

28 Ibid.

29 Simpson, *Dark Companions*, 142.

30 David Kerr Cross, Honorary Treasurer, Livingstone Memorial Committee to Codrington, 31/01/1899, BSCA A2/1/1, ZNA.

31 'The Livingstone Memorial. At Chitambo's, British Central Africa. H.M. Stanley', May 1899, RGS/IBG Archive, London.

32 'The Livingstone Memorial. At Chitambo's, British Central Africa', May 1899, RGS Archives.

33 See various correspondence for 1900 held in BSAC1 A2/1/1.

34 Dr Laws to R Codrington, 12 January 1901, BSAC1 A3/10/07, ZNA.

35 R Codrington to Owen Stroud, BSAC A2/1/1.

36 J.E. Hughes, *Eighteen Years on Lake Bangweulu*. With an introduction by Major H.C. Maydon (London: The Field, The Field House, 1933), 192. Desmond Clark uses virtually the same phrase in Desmond Clark, 'David Livingstone Memorial at Chitambo's', *Northern Rhodesia Journal* 1:1 (1950): 24–33.

37 Poulett Weatherley, Diary 2, 16 February 1899, PWE/2 RGS Archives, London.

38 For a discussion of the bark's mysterious movements, see below.

39 Clark, 'The David Livingstone Memorial at Chitambo's', 31.

40 Hughes, *Eighteen Years on Lake Bangweulu*, 192.

41 All references from Stroud are taken from his diary, reproduced in three long instalments in the *Bournemouth Guardian* on 21 February, 28 February and 8 August 1903.

42 Hughes, *Eighteen Years on Lake Bangweulu*, 192.

43 Ibid., 193.

44 See, for example, Campbell, *Wanderings in Central Africa*, with its frontispiece photo of 'cannibal woman of position' and especially pages 158–9.

45 Hughes, *Eighteen Years on Lake Bangweulu*, 71–3.

46 Information gratefully received from I.P.A. Manning, a district officer in Bangweulu in the 1970s. See his forthcoming book.

47 Bradley, 'Adventurers Still', 7.

48 C.R. Rennie, district commissioner, Fort Jameson, to chief secretary, Livingstone, 2 April 1928, RC/1021, ZNA.

49 The Reverend John May, secretary, Tanganyika Committee, to Robert Codrington, deputy administrator, NE Rhodesia, 12 June 1899, BSAC1 A3/10/10, ZNA.

50 For an impressive selection of photographs of bark and leaves tracked down, see Renema & van Zoelen, You Took the Part?, 48–69.

51 I am grateful to Professor John MacKenzie for sharing this information with me.

52 Renema & van Zoelen, *You Took the Part?*, 65.

53 May to Codrington, 21 January 1901, BSAC1 A3/10/10, ZNA.

54 May to Codrington, 28 March 1901, BSAC1 A3/10/10, ZNA.

55 For two of the best accounts of this complex set of relations, see Richard Price, *Making Empire: Colonial Encounters and the Creation of Imperial Rule in Nineteenth-Century Africa* (Cambridge: Cambridge University Press, 2009) and Andrew Porter, *Religion Versus Empire?: British Protestant Missionaries and Overseas Expansion, 1700–1914* (Manchester: Manchester University Press, 2004).

56 May to Codrington, 23 June 1899, BSAC A3/10/10, ZNA.

57 May to Codrington, 25 May 1899, BSAC A3/10/10, ZNA.

58 May mentioned a bequest of £250,000 from a loyal backer, Arthington, in Leeds: May to Codrington, 28 March 1901, BSAC A3/10/10, ZNA.

59 Mrs Ida Cooke to secretary, BSAC, 2 August 1900, A3/10/2, ZNA.

60 Residency, Zomba, 9 March 1903, BSAC1 A3/8/2, ZNA.

61 R Codrington to secretary, 6 January 1902, BSAC 1 A3/10/08, ZNA.

62 H.H. Montgomery, SPG to secretary, BSAC, 11 February 1905, BSAC A3/10/08, ZNA.

63 R. Codrington to Dr Prentice, 2 August 1904, BSAC A3/10/7, ZNA.

64 Laws to Codrington, 28 April 1905, BSAC A3/10/7, ZNA.

65 Renema & van Zoelen, *You Took the Part*, 63–4.

66 The Reverend Morrison, quoted in Curie, *Livingstone's Hospital*, 69.

67 See various correspondence over a number of years, but especially the final plea from Laws, 16 November 1910, BSAC1 A3/10/7.

68 Secretary, North Eastern Rhodesia, to The Secretary, Livingstonia Mission, United Free Church Offices, London, 17 March 1911, BSAC1 A3/10/7.

69 'Presbyterian Missions in Central Africa', *Glasgow Herald*, 19 December 1907, BSAC1 A3/10/07, ZNA.

70 Lord Overton, Dumbarton to Codrington, 31 December 1907; and his draft reply, 5 February 1908. Ibid.

71 Curie, *Livingstone's Hospital*, 36–63.

72 See various correspondence, BSAC A1/4/11, ZNA.

73 *Central Africa Times*, Blantyre, 19 April 1902, ZNA.

74 J.H. Morrison, *On the Trail of the Pioneers: A History of a Sketch of the Missions of the United Free Church of Scotland* (London: Hodder & Stoughton, undated).

75 Ibid., 174–5.

76 Curie, *Livingstone's Hospital*, quoting Morrison's description, 66–9.

77 Ibid., 72–9.

78 *Mount Ida Chronicle*, Volume XLV, 3 March 1916. 'Livingstone's Grave: African Pilgrimage of his Daughter'.

79 Quoted in Curie, *Livingstone's Hospital*, 80–2.

80 'Livingstone's Monument. Letter from Mrs Wilson Livingstone, Chitambo, 2 Aug 1915', *Cornhill Magazine*, 40 (1916), 383–9, RCS Collection, Cambridge University Library.

81 *Central African Times*, Blantyre, 19 April 1902.

82 Ibid., 19 January 1902.

83 B.L. Hunt, 'Kalomo-Livingstone in 1907', *Northern Rhodesian Journal*, 4, 1 (1959): 17.

84 Prince of Wales to Abercrom, 24 April 1910, BSAC A1/4/11, ZNA.

5 White Settlers, Frontier Chic & Colonial Racism
How Livingstone's Three Cs Fell Apart

It's a marvellous night for a moon dance.
Van Morrison, 1970

In 1905, a tiny new settlement in central Africa was named Livingstone in memory of the man who had discovered the nearby Victoria Falls. It quickly punched above its weight, becoming the capital of Northern Rhodesia in 1911, when North-Western and North-Eastern Rhodesia were amalgamated. The 290,587 square miles of territory were romantically described by the colonial historian Lewis Gann as 'a land of limitless horizons, and nothing moves the stranger more than the sheer immensity of the veld'.[1] Southerners always considered it remote and backward. The distance from Lusaka to Cape Town was measured as the same as London to Kiev. It was not just its shape that was awkward. The BSAC administered the region until 1924, when the Colonial Office took over the protectorate (see Map 5.1). However, the company retained mineral rights and the freehold of vast tracts of land.[2] Despite nestling close to one of the greatest natural wonders of the world, Livingstone the town lost its status as the territory's capital in 1936.

This chapter explores the colonial history of this unusual frontier settler town in relation to the memorialisation of Livingstone. White settlers were often rather unsentimental about high-Victorian liberal humanitarianism. Indeed, this chapter marks its death. Nevertheless, 'white settler pioneer man' and the general achievements of life 'on the frontier' were routinely celebrated through Livingstone the person. Sacrifice, struggle and disappointment made bravery, stoicism and toughness important emotional qualities to revere, celebrated at memorialisations, especially through a vibrant, outspoken local press. European domination was precarious but defiant to the end, which came quickly. There was little sign of conceding any ground to nationalists by the 1960s 'wind of change' era; a perfect illustration of how

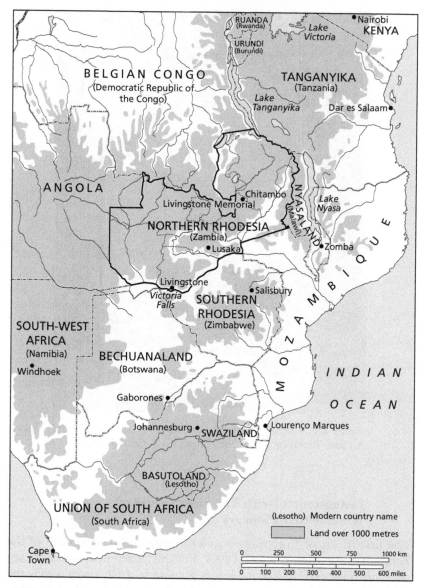

Map 5.1 Northern Rhodesia and surrounding territories, *c.* 1955

disconnected imperial worlds-within-worlds became. As the end of British colonial rule approached, emotions ran high. Disappointment, anger and racism poured into each other, like the waters at the Boiling Point of the Victoria Falls (see Figure 5.1).

Figure 5.1 A family admiring the Victoria Falls, March 1961. Hulton Archive. Photo by S.T. Darko/Three Lions/Getty Images.

Livingstone's Drift: The Slow Spread of White Settler Pioneers

The first trickle of Europeans began to settle in the area north of the Zambezi River from the late 1890s onwards. They believed that they were not just making history but beginning it. In January 1905, the BSAC drew up an agreement with the Paramount Chief of Barotse. He had granted, as 'a free gift ... all the land within my territory situated within a radius of fifteen miles of the north bank of the Zambesi River at the Victoria Falls'.[3] There was no mention of the Leya people who had inhabited the adjacent land for generations.[4] He also agreed to sell, for £100 each, 'blocks of land not greater than 8 miles square for the development of townships, 'on condition that all native rights shall be observed or the holders of such rights compensated'. Initially, the BSAC had contemplated 'locking up' the North, keeping it free from white settlement, but to avoid being burdened with extra costs, it then promoted settlement, attempting to limit the arrival of 'speculators, wastrels, amateurs and low Dutch'.[5] The first settlers were ex-Army and police force; retired administrators, railway workers and post office workers; traders; and the obligatory odd English aristocrat. The single largest group were Afrikaners escaping the Boer War.[6]

African boatmen had identified the best spot and method to cross the river above the Falls at this point in its 1,700-mile journey to the Indian Ocean. Sekute's, or Sekuti Drift, as it was known, was the narrowest part of the river, between the Falls and the nearby rapids, but was still between six hundred and seven hundred yards wide. In 1898, when it became a designated company post, the company installed a barge there. The barge was paddled by Barotsi men; the mules had to swim behind.[7] It took 'pioneers' with all their possessions, including cattle, up to a fortnight to cross it.

Cecil Rhodes had forced the railway line up through from the south, and it reached Victoria Falls in 1904. When the magnificent iron bridge across the gorge was finished in 1905, it was a woman, the daughter of the railway contractor, who drove the first ever steam engine across it.[8] The distance from the top of the bridge's highest span to the ground below was equal to that of the height of the dome of St Paul's Cathedral.[9] According to Rhodes's instructions, it was to be close enough to the Falls that passengers could feel the spray on their faces. The gorge could now be traversed in minutes.[10] The human cost had been high: along parts of the railway line, it was rumoured that Paulings, the contractors, had dug one grave for every sleeper laid.[11]

Death and disease always took their toll, instilling a strong sense of struggle, sacrifice and pride in stubbornness within white settler identity. The initial settlement, in effect a tiny port town made up of wooden trading posts and shacks, had a high death rate due to the fly-infested river marsh, crocodiles and lions. A graveyard was built before any church. It was 'a society of coarse men', living in mud huts and tents, in transit, who enjoyed drinking and gambling.[12] Africans helped with the building of more permanent dwellings and shops, plus the school run by the Reverend Coisson, the first missionary, from the Paris mission. He kept apart from other Europeans. Although he evangelised among Africans and set up classes for African boys, his racial views were hardly enlightened: 'How dull these people are', he wrote, complaining about chiefs being drunk at his service and talking all the way through. 'These people are disgusting because of their dirtiness; they tire you because of their stupidity but nevertheless one is attracted to them'.[13]

Ominously, the first doctor there soon died of blackwater fever in 1903, as did the first pharmacist. Initially, the settlers performed their own funerals, as someone died every month or so. One settler would be chosen as the undertaker, and a coffin would be bashed out of whisky cases and dragged by ox cart to the cemetery. All the residents would turn out in everyday attire, the men in rolled-up shirt sleeves.[14] Nevertheless, in 1904, a census was carried out and tax collected. It identified sixty-eight Europeans: forty-five men, seventeen women and six children.[15] It was especially tough for the first women living at the Old Drift, also known as Livingstone Drift. Major Hood, visiting in 1902, pitied the missionary's wife who had had four children in four years and intermittent fever. Hood was horrified that it had taken another woman two months to get there, with African porters mischievously insisting on crossing at river points where she had to wade through neck-deep, 'naked natives holding onto her'. Hood was appalled that she had to do her own washing. He longed to be able to offer the women a change of underwear, a spare blouse or skirt, 'not to speak of stockings'.[16]

Yet, despite the high death rates, no one wanted to move away from the settlement. Once it became clear that the railway would attract more residents and tourists, BSAC Administrator Robert Croyndon planned a new town around the newly built government buildings, away from the malaria-infested swamps, to 'preserve the features of the Falls'.[17] A number of rowdy meetings were held between the residents and the company during May 1905. At an open meeting on 19 May, one of the earliest written references appears to a future town called Livingstone. Many 'Old Drifters' furiously objected to the idea of moving to the sandy ground, far from the Falls, believing that their tourism-based businesses would never take off: 'Do you think people [will] enjoy a six mile walk or drive through heavy sand?', one store holder demanded; was 'the country so beautiful that a township would mar the beauty?'[18]

A furious debate raged between the two sides: the sentimentalists and the utilitarians. The 'Old Drifters' tried their best, insisting that 'this is an age of the survival of the fittest, and sentiment must give way to practicality'.[19] Neither side invoked an argument that included the Leya.[20] The settlers did not get their way. Croyndon was adamant that he was not going to 'handicap for ever the commercial and sentimental prospects' of the area just because a handful of businesses were forced to relocate, believing that sentiment and commerce could 'run together'. The prospects were good. In 1906, the railway reached Broken Hill (Kabwe); in 1909, the Katanga mining region. White settlement had followed the

railway belt at the Lusaka's, the mining camps, and at the new administrative substations, such as Ndola. As the only rail depot between
Bulawayo and Katanga, Livingstone would be the gateway to the mining region of the north. In 1907, the commercial stalemate was ended
when the BSAC decided that Livingstone would become the administrative capital of North-Western Province. Following the amalgamation of
North-Western Province and North-Eastern Province in 1911, it became
the capital of the whole region. The BSAC bought the comparatively ele-
gant North Western Hotel for its headquarters, thanks to Codrington's
efforts.[21]

A further divide quickly opened up between company officials and
other employees. The railway guards and ticket collectors, who often
worked night shifts, were itinerants and kept apart from the main social
group of the town unless they were hospitalised, as happened regularly, due to their high levels of exposure to malaria.[22] They had been
offered Christian ministry first by the railway mission – 'the travelling
church' – that spread up with them from South Africa. As workers settled
in Livingstone, more regular services and a burial site for railway workers
and other semi-skilled working-class whites became necessary. Thus the
first Presbyterian congregation in Northern Rhodesia was established, in
1926. The David Livingstone Memorial Presbyterian Church was built
on the road to the Falls near the railway yards rather than on the more
exclusive, residential hill.[23] This would be the only Presbyterian church
of Southern Africa in the region until 1956. Nevertheless, in the bars and
poker rooms, such as those in Deadrock (Livingstone Drift), there were
'no class distinctions, no etiquette and no jacket'.[24]

Settler memories of the early days were of a time of death, feeding their
sense of entitlement to a monopoly of heroic pioneering and starving
them of sentimentality. Murray-Hughes was hospitalised in Livingstone
in 1910 with veld sores on his legs. His bedside companion slowly died
of sleeping sickness. He felt hugely emotional recalling the sound of the
town of Livingstone in the early morning. A Scottish bandmaster had
been teaching the African Barotse Native Police band the last post. He
described them as 'raw savages'.[25] It was also the individualism and simplicity that was the stuff of nostalgia: a time of rule bending; and a financial world where there was no jargon such as 'inflation' or 'the welfare
state', when the local bank manager's currency included elephant tusks,
gold watches and firearms.

Early life was a mixture of deprivation and glamour, a sort of pioneer
chic. Electricity was rationed, and the lights went off at midnight, wink-
ing ten minutes before as a warning. The town was never 'one of the
country's beauty spots', as one colonial official's wife put it.[26] The streets

were 'brooding', 'weary' and 'sombre', with bungalows darkened with heavy mosquito nets, giving a 'battered weary appearance'. Occasional lemon and orange trees, bougainvillaea, pawpaw and frangipani relieved the drabness. An open-air cinema was set up in 1916, but it lacked a screen. People brought their own deckchairs and, in the rainy season, wore raincoats. The first European regatta was held up river in June 1905.[27] Shooting clubs, including separate ones for ladies, were among the earliest and most popular white pastimes.[28] During the First World War, settlers banded together to make up a private mini-army, as most possessed guns. One of the earliest gatherings of visitors was a General Missionary Conference for Northern Rhodesia, held in 1914, significant for the way in which it gave expression for the first time to 'an incipient Christian "public opinion" in the territory'.[29]

Visitors usually regarded a stay in the town as 'part of the adventure into darkest Africa' because of its 'deficiencies'. A mixture of imperial frontier, the Wild West and elemental Africa, it was on the tourist trail because of the Falls and became a venue for conferences. Accidents, suicides and deaths were the less glamorous side of whites living in sight of the spray. The heat and altitude, combined with millions of flying ants and the 'burning approach of the rains', meant that October was known locally as the suicide month for it could send people mad. One family had regular nightmares about a Sunday picnic to Livingstone Island, above the Falls, to see the tree where Livingstone had carved his initials. A woman in the party dropped a kettle into the water, bent over to retrieve it and toppled in. Another member of the party slipped in while trying to save her. He clung to a rock, and the woman was only just plucked to safety before she was swallowed by the waters as they rushed over the four-hundred-foot abyss. Many had stories of swimmers attacked by crocodiles, such as the young boy who suddenly disappeared in a swirl of water. His leg bitten off at the thigh, he died in hospital a few hours later.[30]

Class prejudice ran deep. The poorest of the poor whites were 'bywoners', the Afrikaner labourers employed on Afrikaner farms, who lived in mud huts. Anti-Semitism was rife among company officials, partly because they believed that the Jewish traders would sell anything to Africans. The Susman brothers were two young Jewish entrepreneurs, originally from Lithuania. Elie Susman obtained a licence to trade from the BSAC in 1901 and crossed the Zambezi to buy cattle (trek oxen and animals for beef).[31] The brothers had established close links with the Lozi and were on good terms with the ruling elite of Barotseland. Most of the whites in Livingstone regarded this as a dangerous betrayal of white solidarity and were particularly offended by the brothers' engaging in 'hearty handshakes' with Africans.[32]

Crucially, a local newspaper helped to project and knit together a white culture based on shared pioneering, regular outrage and racial superiority. Frank Leopold Moore, an English chemist, had been among the last to leave the Old Drift. He set up a weekly newspaper, the *Livingstone Mail*, in 1906, and devoted much of his energy to popularising his own views through the editorials.[33] His wife researched and wrote the 'Notes and memos'. The paper defined and reflected the strong, unsentimental local views: a dislike of missionaries, the BSAC, Colonial Office interference and local government. For some, Moore 'was a white supremacist, but his paper was relatively free of colonial racism'.[34] Others called him 'the old beast', who worked tirelessly to 'remove the spectre of potential black influence', even floating arguments for union with South Africa.[35] Livingstone had become the territory's unofficial capital of white racism.

Racial Segregation and the First Protestant Churches

Racial segregation had been informally imposed immediately. With the emphasis on hotels catering for white tourists from the south – with over a hundred arriving in 1906 – the 'colour bar' was ruthlessly and cruelly sustained, ironically in the town that bore Livingstone's name, justified publicly on the grounds of avoiding damaging the economy. Yet African labour was the backbone of much of the town's growth. Africans lived confined to an area called Maramba Township, as best they could. They were only officially recognised by the government as having a right to live in towns as late as 1946;[36] yet only white pioneers were venerated and memorialised for having put up with the difficult living conditions.

Harold Williams arrived in 1914, aged eleven. He remembered when the town only had sandy roads and a network of tracks running over them. 'People moved around in trolleys ... which were pushed by Africans'.[37] This practice no doubt established an informal economy of racial subordination that was reinforced by the 'bucket system' of sanitation. Outside toilets backed onto the lanes, for bucket collection in the early morning by Africans – bucket boys – a system that continued into the 1940s.[38] There was little acknowledgement of the black pioneers, humiliated in the workplace having to earn money. Africans, Indians and 'coloureds'[39] felt the psychological pain of 'social discrimination' on a daily basis, barred from shops, hotels and other public places, many living in shacks at the bottom of large garden plots and working as cleaners or gardeners. As one resident put it, 'All households had a boy whose sole object was to carry water and collect wood'.[40] Many were tasked with futile enterprises such as growing English vegetables and flowers. Young black children were called *piccanini* (a racist American slang term for black children of African descent which came out of the antebellum American south, when race-based slavery was legal).

Written colonial sources under-record racism. Bullying, belittling, unfair demands and a sense of entitlement, as well as everyday physical punishment, cruelty and violence, were of course naturally sidestepped. Attempts to establish white settler communities and the good life in poorer areas were fraught with economic insecurity, frustration and anger, which could find an outlet in domestic violence. But white accounts project the pioneers' idealised image of restraint and patience. Intimate letters from an early visitor to the area – Major Hood, a white officer surveying the region for mining prospects – that were sent home to his wife, nicely illustrate how things worked in practice. Always beginning, 'Darling Own Little Wife', the major professed, 'I am going to tell you everything'. He confessed to 'trying so hard to exercise control over my temper: if I can learn to control it with the natives I think I shall have succeeded in some way'.[41] The significant point is that Hood believed that he showed restraint and fairness yet regularly used force. He insisted that it was important to keep a 'firm hand'.

White settlers, of all nationalities, always believed that they knew the Africans best and better than each other. 'If only the Belgians were not so naïve about their "native soldiers"', Hood wrote, instead believing their innocent protestations that they were not pillaging villages over their borders. 'The native', he pronounced, 'is a natural liar', and believes that everyone else is one too. 'I am always particularly strict with my servants ... a lesson to raw chiefs and porters'.

Hood, like others, could reassure himself that he remained civilised and was not heartless, because he engaged in selective displays of love and sentimentality, describing for example his inscribed locket, which meant that he could 'wear you [my little Girl] all round my neck – all the time' – but not in the bath, he reassured his wife.[42] Similarly, white settlers were no doubt comfortable with their casual racism in daily life because of their negative assumptions about Africans, especially the men. Commonplace views they held about Africans included that the men never showed emotions, that wife-beating was still a major pastime, and that an end to tribal warfare had resulted in mindless beer drinking. Moreover, after coming into contact with civilisation, 'the native regrettably loses his manners'. Witchcraft was still judged to be very popular and, likewise, 'there is still a relentless cruelty': one would never see a deformed native for example, and African women who breastfed were 'primitive'.[43] Stories were retold of African men attacking white women. One cautionary tale concerned two lone female tourists enjoying the rainforests opposite Victoria Falls. Suddenly, an 'African sprang out of the thick undergrowth', attacking one of them. In the struggle, they edged towards the precipice. One of the women slipped into the white-out, falling hundreds of feet. What little remained of her body was found days later downriver.[44]

Ironic for a town bearing Livingstone's name, its first Protestant church, initially to be called St David's, was for whites only. (The Paris mission had established a presence at the Old Drift, the Anglican Church Railway mission supplied a minister from 1904 and the Bishop of Chichester made a visit to carry out confirmations.)[45] In 1907, the Anglican mission put pressure on the administration to establish a Protestant church. A local committee was set up to raise funds through holding various activities, such as dances and boat races, as well as selling Codrington's Livingstone tree relics. Bishop Hine and three missionaries laid its foundation stone in 1910, in thick bush. The white community built and paid for the church, insisting that it was for Europeans only. The bishop rejected this racist distinction and threatened to leave. A compromise was reached: in principle, the church would be open to all races; in practice, the bishop's African staff would worship elsewhere.

At the back of the church, which became St Andrew's (the first missionary, according to the Bible), a 'black chapel' was built for Africans to worship in.[46] Settlers offered to pay for a church for Africans at Maramba. African Christianity may have been more vibrant and popular. When Miss Mackintosh, a Presbyterian, visited in 1920, she found only a dozen people in the congregation of St Andrew's, out of a possible five hundred, and matins was barely attended.[47] Far more popular was the flourishing amateur dramatics present in the town from its origins. Men and women performed on stage as early as 1906, when the Court House hosted a 'Grand Evening Concert' in aid of the Livingstone Church Building Fund.[48] The much-admired Miss Antoinette Sterling, a governess, sang 'Dreams of Home', composed in memory of the explorer, which was advertised with his portrait, and dedicated to Stanley.[49]

The Anglican community and upper echelons of Livingstone's white society organised and hosted the town's first major event, a celebration in 1913 to mark the centenary of Livingstone's birth. It consisted of a public tea followed by speeches in the Barotse Centre (the town hall): Africans were not allowed in the church itself. The *Livingstone Post* recorded that nearly everyone in the town attended. It then turned into a sporting event for children and, in the evening, the Livingstone Club hosted an evening of dancing and recitals.

Sir John Wallace, the local administrator and joint organiser spoke, followed by Bishop Hine from Mpanza and then the missionary Reverend Louis Jalla. The first two speeches focused on Livingstone's life and explorations, with a particular emphasis on the connection of 'that pioneer' with Northern Rhodesia and the town itself. Over fifty Africans were present. Jalla seems to have been the only speaker to address 'the respect in which Livingstone was held by the natives, and to the trust they reposed in white men in consequence'.[50] The use of the term 'native' here, before a mixed audience, is instructive of attitudes. The lack of any significant commentary about Livingstone's humanitarian aims and aspirations for African Christianity is striking. The event was a way to project and celebrate the exclusivity of a moral community of whiteness, a community who defined themselves against sentimentality or emotionality towards people and instead invested it in the landscape. In this exclusive moral community, it was the pioneering Livingstone who was remembered.

The Statue of Livingstone and the Lost Memorials

The history of this white memorialisation of Livingstone reflects the broader pattern of settler disappointment and failure. The First World War had hit the tourist town badly. Having guns, the settlers had formed a private mini-army; others had joined up. By the 1920s, efforts were being made to lure business back. Livingstone was still a good-time small town, with the romance and danger of the Falls, its lunar rainbows and a champagne-based cure for blackwater fever.[51] Hotels hosted a 'bust', or lock-in. The governor's statement at the Imperial Press Conference in Livingstone trumpeted the Falls 'as the greatest scenic attraction in the world', advertised the three high-quality hotels in the town and outlined plans for infrastructural development. Major Sir Hubert Young encouraged his audience to return, waving a brochure entitled 'Hints on Seeing the Falls'.[52] In 1925, the Prince of Wales visited. He enjoyed his evening of dancing so much that he insisted the clocks be turned back for an extra hour so they could continue. The Livingstone Boat Club entered its 'most flourishing period during the 20s', and the boathouse committee raised enough money to buy new boats.[53] Membership rose to 175, but then a young man drowned in the swimming enclosure. Membership fell to forty by 1938, and the Second World War all but finished it off.

Yet, settlers further south often fared far better, as reflected in the first major initiative to memorialise Dr Livingstone. The Federated Caledonian Society of South Africa decided to raise £15,000 for a bronze statue to honour Livingstone. This was William Lowe's idea in

1920, and he established a Livingstone Memorial Committee. The Caledonians wanted the government to grant them a site by Victoria Falls. They were repeatedly refused. The government unanimously agreed that the most appropriate site would be Chitambo,[54] in line with the policy of protecting the Falls from any kind of man-made development. The South African Scots insisted that it had to be near the Falls. Lowe died in 1933, a year before a massive bronze statue was eventually unveiled, organised and paid for by Caledonian societies in the Union of South Africa and the Rhodesias,[55] but it was erected in Southern Rhodesia, its government there having fewer reservations and a more powerful settler lobby.

At the time, the imposing statue of a rugged Livingstone, looking purposeful, was described – generously – as a 'veritable triumph of inspired realism'. It was designed to reflect the strength of character and resolve of the pioneer, the 'Missionary-Explorer-Liberator', who 'pushed the jungle shadows back to light a continent' and whose 'soul goes marching on'.[56] The ceremony, held on 5 August 1934, consisted of eighteen separate parts. The participants included the acting governor and his wife, Livingstone's nephew Hubert Moffat and the Bulawayo Caledonian Society Pipers. The Reverend James Gray delivered the address. He had had a long career as a Presbyterian minister, pioneering new churches for settlers in South Africa and Southern Rhodesia. He had also been chaplain to the Scots Fusiliers in the Second Anglo-Boer War (1899–1902). His address was conservative and racist in tone. Most of it was taken up with a long, sympathetic history of Livingstone's heroic life, including the conversion of Stanley to Christianity after meeting him. Part of a deep concern for the heathen in the Christian world, Livingstone and others came to Africa to bring 'Christian light and civilization. Africa was the dark continent ... vast masses of human beings were there living in a state of mental and spiritual barbarism'.[57]

The colonial reality was hardly a light touch for Africans. The 1908 Masters and Servants Ordinance adopted a typically harsh, militaristic approach to African employment law, with heavy punishments. The use of force to discipline was not unusual. Gann argues that the arrival of cars and lorries in the 1920s reduced some of the harsh burden placed on African men but increased the distance between the races.[58] By the 1930s, the 'tiny frontier ruling class', which was increasingly made up of miners and railway workers, were 'racist, fascist-leaning', and the Colonial Office's 1922 Paramountcy of Native Interest directive had provoked 'fevered outrage' among the small and scattered white population.[59] In 1911, there were 1,497 settlers compared to an estimated 826,000 Africans. These figures crept up to 10,000 in 1935, with the

African population at 1.4 million (in 1946 there were 22,000 settlers to 1.6 million Africans).

True to their pioneering identity, the amalgamation with Southern Rhodesia was robustly rejected, but, unfortunately for the town of Livingstone, Lusaka, further south, became the new administrative capital in 1935. The blow was somewhat mitigated by having a new museum. The administration was always keen to have 'traditional handicrafts ... and native made objects' – which were rapidly being 'replaced by cheap imported goods' – preserved for posterity. In 1934, a growing collection was given its first home in the old Magistrate's Court in Livingstone, called the David Livingstone Memorial Museum.[60] In 1937, another government initiative helped the town's finances and reputation: the establishment of the Rhodes-Livingstone Institute to research the impact of European rule on Africa. It incorporated the museum, which gradually expanded its David Livingstone collection and exhibition to cater for white tourists.[61]

Nevertheless, setback followed setback in the town's bid to relaunch as the Henley-on-Thames of central Africa. In 1936, a series of Afrikaner claims were made that Livingstone had not discovered the Falls. The chair of South Africa's Historic Monuments Commission, F.S. Malan, had publicised claims that Carolus, or Karl, Tirchardt, a Voortrecker, had got there first.[62] South African historian and editor of the diaries of Louis Tirchardt (Carolus's father), Dr Gustav Peller, also backed him in the press. Carolus had apparently crossed the continent in the late 1830s and seen the Falls, carving his initials on a baobab tree, a story he told his friends much later, which they confirmed. Immediately, Servaas Le Roux, director of the Rhodesian Historical Collection at the Empire Exhibition in Southern Rhodesia, rubbished these claims. This was not first-hand evidence, he argued, insisting that he had long researched the journeys of the old Boer hunters, linked to the Western Transvaal and further north, such as Jan Viijoen, Martinus Swartz and Petrus Jacob. Le Roux explained that the source of the confusion was that, in the Boer accounts, 'the great cataract' referred to was the Kebrasa Rapids.[63] Another South African historian dismissed Le Roux, because his own research had confirmed Livingstone was the first. This was a bitter dispute, reflecting the anti-British feeling within Afrikaner nationalism.

More serious for the town was the fate of the 1940 Livingstone Centenary Celebrations, to mark the centenary of Livingstone's arrival in Africa. Planned from 1938, it was the largest ever event in the town, and the governor had suggested a Livingstone Fortnight, to include a pageant about the discovery of the Falls, the unveiling of a joint

Livingstone-Rhodes Memorial, golfing tournaments, a regatta and a special issue of postage stamps. The aim was to attract visitors from the south but also from Europe and America.[64] A committee was set up and, after much correspondence, a formula for a series of joint celebrations with Southern Rhodesia, to coincide with her half-centenary (1890–1940) was decided. So meticulous were the plans that the events in Livingstone were designed to coincide with a lunar rainbow over the Falls. Even the finances were worked out with Salisbury, after tortuous discussions.

On 3 September 1939, Britain and France declared war on Germany. All plans were suspended. In May 1940, Southern Rhodesia made known that it would run a scaled-down version of the event. Also still keen was James MacNair, chair of the Scottish National Memorial to David Livingstone, and author of a recent book on Livingstone. Both were curtly informed that no celebrations would be held in Northern Rhodesia.[65]

The 1955 Anniversary of Livingstone's Sighting of Victoria Falls

After the trauma of the Second World War subsided, white settler Africa enjoyed a period of prosperity. In the 1950s, as the Copperbelt entered a boom period, the number of Europeans increased from 37,221 in 1951 to 64,800 in 1956 (the number of Africans rose from 1.7 million to 2.1 million). By the 1950s, the average income was a respectable £1,000 per annum. Northern Rhodesia was becoming more of a permanent place of residence, no longer 'a land without grandparents', although three-quarters of the white population in 1951 had still only lived there for five years or less.[66] Nevertheless, English was not the first language for 25 per cent of the settlers.

Livingstone was not progressing apace, however, even with a new international airport. The town made an unsuccessful bid in 1952 to become the 'Federal Capital of Greater Rhodesia'.[67] It was also a year of embarrassment: at the Closer Association Conference, the host (Britain) received complaints from local whites because African delegates were put up in a hostel used by white civil servants.[68] However, 1955 marked the half-centenary of the birth of the town and the centenary of David Livingstone reaching Victoria Falls, so the town council planned a year of celebrations from a hard-nosed business point of view. Central African Airways was advertising long weekend trips to Victoria Falls flying from the Copperbelt for £27 8s.[69] The *Livingstone Mail* headlined 'WE MUST ALL HELP', since 'much of Livingstone's prosperity depends upon events such as these and conferences'.[70]

However, the local council faced huge obstacles and was forced to accept a scaled-down version of their vision. They never managed to obtain a grant from the central administration. Meanwhile the Rhodes-Livingstone Museum, in contrast, had secured £11,400 from the Northern Rhodesian government to fund their own centenary exhibition. The federal government had been more supportive. The event was used by the governor general and Sir Arthur Benson as propaganda for the continued racial partnership.[71] A letter was read out from Senior Chief Chitanda of Broken Hill, who recalled 'that very interesting occasion ... which I would call a non-colour bar gathering in Victoria Hall', where 'we had the chance of talking to the Europeans, some of whom did not know the Africans'. The chief went on to pronounce that 'if such practice continues I am quite sure that the whole question of partnership will be resolved'.

African participation would be severely limited. The council's committee had wanted to invite the Paramount Chief of the Barotse and the Royal Barge, but the colonial government refused to pay for 'a vast entourage of indabas, paddlers, drums'.[72] A more modest suggestion was to have each district commissioner stationed alongside the river ask the headmen and chiefs to put forward local men – paddlers – who would bring their own 'dugouts' for mokoro racing;[73] but no transport could be offered. African participation was mostly as girl guides. The Centenary Pictorial Supplement, available in November, projected a success story.[74] It was a white world of fun, sport and relaxation.

Finally, after a summer of sport and festivals, on 16 November 1955, Livingstone's statue on the Southern Rhodesia side of the Falls was the site for a day of public commemoration. It was also a public holiday for the territory. The ceremonies were flanked by music provided by military bands. No one was allowed into the specially built enclosure without a ticket, where schoolchildren of all races were to stand,[75] but the problem for the Colonial Administration was this: it was now too risky to invite any adult Africans. In October 1955, the secretariat in Lusaka wrote to all provincial commissioners asking them to invite their chiefs but warning that the committee was unprepared to cover the cost of a large retinue and that it was 'at least possible that the African Congress might imply that chiefs are being invited to approve of the Federation'.

It was only two years since Britain's Conservative government had gone ahead with the Central African Federation (the partial administrative amalgamation of the Rhodesias and Nyasaland, which went against African opinion, which instinctively judged that any form of union would bolster racial rule). Both services were religious in tone, and it was the 'earnest wish' of the municipality that the day should be 'a memorable one for all races'.[76] The irony was that, for the commemorations to be projected as a multiracial success, ordinary African people had to be kept away.

Livingstone's Christianity & the Problem of African Nationalism

So surreal were the racial politics in 1955 that two different memorials had to take place. One emphasised the 'Christian Livingstone', which carried political significance in terms of African nationalism, and the other the 'pioneer Livingstone'. The first event was more personal to Livingstone, and designed by the LMS. The hymns were Nonconformist. Halfway through, Livingstone's grandson, Dr Hubert Wilson, unveiled a commemorative tablet from Chitambo. He was followed by a long address from the chair of the LMS, the Reverend Cecil Northcotte. A hymn symbolic of racial inclusiveness – 'All People That on Earth Do Dwell' – was followed by a prayer, read by the African LMS missionary preacher Aaron Mwenya.

In contrast, the second ceremony marked a rededication to continuing the 'high Christian aims and ideals'. It was a mix of senior politicians, officials and Anglicans. It began with the national anthem and included hymns, prayers and an address from the archbishop of Central Africa. The lesson was read by the prime minister of Southern Rhodesia, Garfield Todd; the unveiling of a plaque of rededication was carried out by the governor general of the federation, Lord Llewellin.

Thousands attended, according to the *Livingstone Mail*, with hundreds driving up by car from Lusaka.[77] Local criticism was only levelled at the guest list.[78] The *Livingstone Mail* was less enthusiastic in its coverage of the Northcotte address. The newspaper focused on what the day meant for the residents of the town, especially those who remembered it as just 'a northern outpost'. Livingstone, for them, was the remarkable geographer and pioneer whose 'great faith in God carried him through terrible hardships' and who had 'refused the request of Queen Victoria to return to England'.[79] The organiser, Councillor Baldwin, intertwined the good work 'began by our predecessors, headed by Dr Livingstone' with that of the 'farsighted people who laid the foundation for the Federation of the Rhodesias and Nyasaland'.

The *Central African Post* took up the theme, with a very affectionate portrait of Livingstone and his legacy. He was the ultimate white pioneer-hero, 'one of the first men who ever set foot in this country, possibly the toughest of the lot ... He must have had an inside like a steam boiler. For months on end he lived on native food. He could drink water ... putrid with rhino's urine and buffalo's dung ... He must have been yellower than a Chinaman ... !'[80] But the paper was keen to make a political point, launching Livingstone as the 'patron saint of the Federation'. Central Africa was his land geographically and spiritually but, the paper believed, he had become lost 'in these turgid times in a changing Africa'. The paper invited its readers to imagine what Livingstone would have thought of central Africa if he were still alive. The issues of the day were defined as African economic and industrial revolution, racial tensions, the Colonial Office's welfare policy and African nationalism. Most challenging was the tangle of 'economic and racial antagonism that had had to be faced daily'. The editor singled out an 'incomplete Christianity' that seemed to lack vigour and initiative in dealing with them. Livingstone was invoked as a good Christian, the patron saint of progressive race relations, code for speaking to African nationalists.

Such entwining of a liberal Christian legacy and racial partnership around arch pioneer Livingstone was reinforced by the newspaper's unusual decision to reproduce Northcotte's address. Northcotte had spoken of 'the mighty potential for good which lies in the partnership of the races'; Livingstone's legacy was the hope for 'a Christian civilisation in the heart of Africa', and his 'character of a gentleman', which was defined as being 'honourable in his dealings with both Europeans and Africans'. Northcotte called for a return to Christianity to solve the vast problems facing modern Africa. Lacking 'initiative and vigour', he implored central Africans to turn again to Livingstone's 'energy and dedication' for inspiration, to his 'spirit of goodwill, of patience, and unselfishness and determination to answer the questions which Africa raises'. Today is 'everybody's Africa', he concluded.

In contrast, the federal government's aim was to use a generic Christianity to promote racial partnership and to encourage Africans to accept the status quo. This meant not listening to African nationalists. Instead, a necessarily vague call to 'love the Lord thy God and thy neighbour as thyself' was made. There were now African 'neighbours' crammed into urban compounds, squeezed into servants' quarters at the bottom of their English rose gardens or, as in Livingstone's Anglican church, worshipping round the back. An African Christian political discourse was theologically liberational, racially inclusive and anti-federation.

In any case, many white settlers did not experience the day as Christians, of either the liberal variety or the much more racially conservative. The *Northern News* ran a short piece entitled 'How Ndola celebrated the day'.[81] Many drove to the river, swam, sailed or went fishing. Others worked; it was 'just another day'. The item ended with the observation, 'Many people did not know why they were having a holiday. "Something to do with Livingstone", they said'.[82] A man from Lusaka who had spent three years planning to go by canoe and sleep on the riverbank along the route Livingstone had taken, had his request to the Federal Film Service for a cameraman to accompany him rejected on the grounds that it would have little news value.

By mid-November, Livingstone town was again in a slump.[83] The removal of more government departments from the town and the recent boom in building, encouraging businesses to open up without enough long-term trade to sustain them, were blamed. As a tourist destination, however, the town faced basic infrastructural obstacles: it lacked a proper main road, its shops were outdated, it had no good cinema screen and none of its restaurants served food after 9 p.m. – although many visitors often excused the obvious shortcomings on the grounds that they were 'modern pioneers'.[84] Relying on tourism was not enough, others fretted. More seriously, even the pioneers were beginning to leave. Skilled artisans who had arrived from Britain many years ago were moving out in larger numbers. These were 'people and their families', the *Livingstone Mail* lamented, who 'always maintained the high standard of living *we are entitled to* [my emphasis] in this country'.

Tension, Rivalry and Repression

The late 1950s were 'troubled times' in Northern Rhodesia, as one colonial official put it diplomatically. Political demands, civil disobedience, fear and retribution resulted in escalating violence. The African anti-colonial and anti-federation movements were becoming more organised and bold, organising meetings and rallies as best they could with their limited resources. Few Africans could read and write because of the woeful provision of education and, in the absence of a lingua franca, nationalistic politics had been held back.[85] However, the imposition in 1953 of the Central African Federation by Britain's Conservative government had given African politics more urgency and emotion, as fears of further racial discrimination and loss of land circulated. The federation in effect decolonised more power to British south-central Africa's white minority.[86] Harry Nkumbula, president of the African National Congress (ANC), had symbolically burnt a copy of the British White Paper on federation and called for two days of national prayer. The administration's view was that a 'firm hand was needed' and that they had to 'stop the rot' but, by the late 1950s, they faced mass protests and boycotts of officially controlled goods such as sugar, when the rumour circulated that the government had poisoned them. Bridges were burnt, and open armed conflicts broke out. In the north-east for example, a breakaway Christian sect, under the leadership of Alice Lenshina, took against the government and nationalist parties. Supporters insisted on the right to govern themselves and claimed to be taking a stand against the widespread practice of witchcraft in the region. Members of her Lumpa Church refused to pay taxes, kidnapping two of the local chief's police officers. The armed unit the provincial commissioner deployed to break up the group were attacked with cudgels, axes and outdated pistols. His district commissioner was peppered with arrows, and vehicles were set alight.[87] A full-blown war resulted in over seven hundred fatalities, the banning of the movement and the indefinite detention of its leaders. Many supporters temporarily vanished across the border into the Congo.[88]

Rivalry between the two main African national parties, the ANC and the newly formed United National Independence Party (UNIP), was also escalating.[89] According to an eyewitness, 'the bitterness between them 'was, on occasion, more intense than that displayed by them for their colonial masters'. Disagreements over tactics and goals had resulted in mass disaffection from the ANC, which resulted first in a new, radical Zambia ANC (ZANC), but ZANC was quickly banned (following a convenient rumour of a nationalist plot to kill whites in Nyasaland), and so UNIP was born. From 1960, UNIP was led by Kenneth Kaunda, ex-secretary general of the ANC. Nkumbula and Kaunda were fighting for domination as the nationalist surge across Britain's territories sped up the official timetables for independence. Yet, in late 1959, senior officials at the Colonial Office still believed 'our pace is not being forced; we are discharging our responsibilities in an orderly manner, not abrogating them prematurely'.[90]

Many senior party activists were arrested and jailed. Ten days before Harold Macmillan's historic 'Wind of Change' tour of Africa, in 1960, which included three days in Northern Rhodesia, Kaunda was still in prison for sedition, serving nine months as the president of ZANC. The colonial administration was out of touch. Kaunda and senior figures were now running UNIP, riding a wave of popularity. The eleventh-hour intervention of the mining magnate Ronald Prain, who saw the surge and a future possibility of cheaper, black skilled labour, ensured that Kaunda met Macmillan and his senior advisers.[91] Kaunda informed them that the federal 'partnership' was hollow at a time when 'the whole country was divided between black and white, politically, socially and economically' and 'power resided with a minority'.[92] 'Come to my house and see how I have to live', he invited Macmillan. They were not 'wild men', but men who believed in 'the rights of all men'.

Macmillan's short tour increased African repression and ratcheted up racial tension. The amateur attempt to blow up the Savoy Hotel in Nodal, where Macmillan lunched, was an opportunity for the chief secretary to drum up support for a Public Security Bill to strengthen the existing emergency ordinances of which Kaunda and others had fallen foul.[93] This included banning printed material considered prejudicial to public security, prohibiting meetings, restricting the movement of individuals and, in certain circumstances, the governor had the power to detain without trial. The number of police was also increased. When the Queen Mother was mobbed in Lusaka on a subsequent visit, the Conservatives were quick to use it as an opportunity to raise predictable concerns about law and order. 'Were there enough police?' the Conservative MP, Briggs Davison, asked Iain Macleod. Fifty new senior officers and forty-nine junior officers was the reply.

The Wind of Racism Is Blowing through This Town

Harold Macmillan read the lesson in the Anglican church in Livingstone on the last day of his tour of Northern Rhodesia.[94] For many present, the irony of his high Anglican gesture was unmissable. Some of the British press corps realised that the Africans in the congregation had only been allowed in to hear him as a one-off special treat.[95] They had been shocked also to learn hotels had dropped their 'colour bar' just for his visit. Sydney Jacobson of the *Daily Mirror* called for Macmillan to be made aware of 'window dressing'.[96] The media both documented and contributed to a growing, comforting perception in Britain that her self-styled liberalism on race was being undermined by white settlers for whom there was little sentimental attachment.

The white community largely viewed the nationalist call for independence as a fanciful wish of the 'illiterate masses'. Publicly, they insisted that white Northern Rhodesians 'would not care if a black or white man represents them in parliament … once the standards of education and civilization of the African are the same as the European'.[97] They blamed the British government for failing to educate African women as the drivers of 'civilization', warning that legislation to enforce social integration would be 'as evil and inhuman as segregation laws'. Like South Africa's prime minister, their hero, they too blamed 'English conservatives' prepared to take seriously 'a few thousand Africans' because 'British nationalism' had become 'weak and effete'.[98]

In return, African nationalists derided the South Africans. In December 1959, the president general of UNIP contacted the Conservative Overseas

Bureau. Chona wrote disdainfully that it was a great pity that he was going to visit 'damned (according to Africans) South Africa where systematic exploitation and humiliation of the natives is going on (while Britain refuses even to condemn this)'.[99] African trade unions submitted a number of memoranda to Macmillan which emphasised racial injustice.[100] They wanted universal suffrage, equal pay and an end to the 'lopsided development' of Northern Rhodesia. They defined racial rule for him: a minority enjoyed exceptional wealth, political power and prestige; privileges related to health and education meant that they possessed 'more than average energy and social skills, by which to influence events'; and that half of African schoolchildren in towns had no access to basic education was a universal hurt.[101] Racism was a powerful source of emotional capital on which the nationalists could draw. In the transport and mining industries in particular, the typical African experience was of the European who 'treats himself as an employer when he is an employee just as the African is'.

For Africans living in Livingstone in the late 1950s, the experience of the colour bar was overwhelming. Livingstone's earliest African political organisations – the welfare institutions of the interwar period – had often been forced to seek redress from 'outrageous cases of racial discrimination'.[102] William Chipango, working in the late 1950s as a young railway employee, and an active trade unionist, recalled the humiliation of the colour bar in the everyday, having to go to hatches at the backs of shops to be handed merchandise. Wamu Lewamba and Wakumeto Sililo, young boys whose parents made a living fishing on the Zambezi River just above the town, would dread going into town to sell in the market because of the fear this generated in case they met and did something wrong in the eyes of a white person.[103] Many Africans were terrified of Europeans. If a European wanted to take an African to the cinema, he had to telephone the district commissioner in Livingstone to request permission, then, if granted permission, warn the cinema. He would be given a seat in a special box, separate from the white audience, while his African companions had to endure further embarrassment from the film certification announcement: 'Not suitable for children under twelve or Africans'. The *Northern News* tried to put a positive spin on race relations, post-Macmillan, apprehensive that public sentiment and ignorance in Britain would decide their fate. Europeans were learning, the paper insisted, 'to replace arrogance with tolerance', and Africans, to their credit, had advanced towards civilisation at a rate once thought impossible.[104]

Race relations in the late 1950s were worsening. In 1959, the ANC launched a 'partnership campaign'. 'Beat the colour bar' targeted hotels, cinemas, churches and hospitals to try to change attitudes.[105] According to the African trade unions, there was 'much less contact now ... between the two major races'.[106] Competition for skilled and industry-based jobs, and fear of servants becoming 'uppity', generated greater distancing. Africans felt that racial discrimination in the workplace had increased, with a knock-on impact on social relations in general. Colour bar practices had become more pronounced in all public places. Any Europeans prepared to take a risk and go against this hardening of attitudes, they noticed, faced 'a social cost' that was now 'sufficiently heavy as to dissuade Europeans from taking the risk'.

Livingstone produced a high tide of colonial racism, largely because of its white-orientated tourist economy. Hotels and restaurants serving food and alcohol were unwilling to cater for black customers. In March 1960, the African Minister for Education – one of a handful of Africans brought into the executive in 1958 – was forced to ask his white driver to go into a bar to buy him a beer, as he was not allowed to do so. Sitting in the government car outside, a white man shouted at him: 'Why don't you park like Europeans ... you bloody kaffirs ... you think you are bwanas because you drive in beautiful cars'.[107]

Recreational space became a battleground, as Africans tested their rights under new race relations legislation. This had come into being in September 1960 and included district race relations committees, answering to a central committee at the secretariat, to investigate cases where the laws were being ignored. The new laws outlawed barring entry to hotels and restaurants, unless they served spirits, which of course most did. African nationalist politicians were unimpressed. The legislation had been rushed through, they pointed out on the eve of the Monkton Commission, a British government inquiry into how the federation was working. Officially, the aim was to end racial discrimination in hotels but, in reality, UNIP told the governor, the administration was uninterested.[108]

Pressure was also coming from London in 1960. The Labour Party began to use race to undermine Macmillan's 'Wind of change' triumph, irritated by the Tory propaganda victory surrounding the prime minister's apparent reaffirmation of Britain's liberal reputation on colonial rule and race. A few MPs asked awkward questions that exposed how ridiculous and impractical the colour bar was. Turning the spotlight on the gap between the rhetoric and reality, picked up by journalists on the tour, fell first to the Labour Party's Barbara Castle.[109] She tabled a parliamentary question about cases of African civil servants in Northern Rhodesia being refused hotel accommodation in Salisbury on grounds of their colour. Her colleague, George Thompson, MP, then asked Iain Macleod about the racial restrictions on cinema entry in Northern Rhodesia.

There were none, came the reply; proprietors did exercise control to varying degrees, but legislation was being considered to make refusing entry illegal. Macleod offered reassurances that night passes were apparently no longer required, and the identity card requirements were also being examined. Northern Rhodesian officials were irritated by this kind of pressure and interference from the Colonial Office and Lusaka. They saw themselves duty-bound to preserve the status quo, fearing a breakdown in race relations and violence if whites were pushed too hard.

Internal pressures on race were also increasing. The town of Livingstone was regularly in the spotlight regarding 'colour discrimination in public places'. A prominent Indian businessman in the town found himself unable to book accommodation through a local travel agency.[110] A senior UNIP official wrote to the governor about the case of the Reverend John Bright, 'a negro Bishop' of an African church, who had been refused admission to a hotel. No support had come from the district commissioner either: 'We the African people feel humiliated'.[111] Moreover, another hotelier attacked the administration for 'leading the way on racial discrimination'. The new African ministers for African Education and African Agriculture were booked into hotels, but white officials stayed separately in official residences. The gripe was that this showed that the government was discriminating on race alone, whereas the business community was 'forced to in order to avoid financial disaster'; and if anyone complained it would lead to a white boycott.[112]

The colonial government avoided dramatic changes (so as not to 'cause friction between races' and impede constitutional advance) by instead introducing a complex set of regulations. These were also absurd. In 1959, the sale of alcohol or spirits to Africans had been allowed, except in bars where spirits were sold (i.e. European ones). The 1960 Race Relations Ordinance then allowed Africans to purchase alcohol in airports or railway lounges and made racial discrimination in hotels, other than in bars or lounges that served spirits, illegal. Clubs were excluded, which meant that some theatres got around the legislation, claiming to be a form of club. No legislation was added to prevent discrimination in shops, on the extraordinary grounds that such discrimination no longer existed. Officials also reassured themselves that the best hotels did not practice discrimination, but even the administration confessed that it was not on 'good ground' when it faced questions in the legislative council in 1962.[113] The rules also meant that, if a black person could prove he was from outside the country, then legally he could be served spirits in a bar.

Meanwhile, hoteliers in Livingstone found ways around the legislation, clearing their verandas of chairs, installing dummy bars with empty bottles of spirits in their lounges and forcing Africans to pay for lunch in advance.[114] Many carried on regardless. A number of investigations had to be made by the Central Race Relations Committee into hotels, mostly in Livingstone, following complaints and rumours about discrimination. Between September and November 1960, a number of hotels were tested. The resulting report was upbeat, as the findings had been better than expected. Diehards still existed who would fight to the last ditch but, generally, 'the average man is really quite a reasonable chap', keeping an eye on the future. The main problem was deemed to be African prostitutes, now a great nuisance everywhere.[115] Another survey, in early 1961, again reported that things were settling down, the main problem now being apparently African men using garden areas as urinals. An article in the *Northern News* reflected the so-called progressive white view that the colour bar could not disappear overnight but that a great deal of progress was being made.[116]

However, the submissions to the Central Race Relations Committee and its continual investigations into hotels reveal just how ugly race relations had become. When a complaint was made about a café owner refusing to allow Africans to sit down, the response in defence was typical: nothing was known about the new rules, and only the dirty ones were refused; anyone who was reasonably dressed and not smelling would in future be let in.[117] Africans complained about not wanting to enter premises where they would be called 'a bloody monkey'. Again, Livingstone seems to have been the worst place for discrimination in public. In 1961, the provincial commissioner suggested that the secretariat should be 'acquainted with the peculiar situations which arise in Livingstone'.[118] In 1964, so many 'unfortunate incidents' had come to the attention of the prime minister regarding alleged racial incidents in the town and inflammatory speeches by the police and certain Europeans that, in July, discussions took place about the possibility of a formal commission of inquiry.[119] Independence might well look like a blessing.

Independence

This deterioration on the ground was a manifestation of the frustration and anger felt by many white Northern Rhodesians at Britain's capitulation to African nationalism, combined with the particular circumstances in Livingstone. By the time of his 1960 tour, Macmillan had decided that Africa must be decolonised sooner rather than later. His Secretary of State for the Colonies, Iain Macleod, moved faster than he would have liked, setting in motion a process that delivered a rushed transfer of power in less than five years. Elections were held in Northern Rhodesia in 1962, but only after a sustained campaign of violence. UNIP and the

ANC won two-thirds of the votes; the federation was dead, colonial rule nearly over.[120] In December 1963, the head of police met with the secretariat to discuss urgently plans for the handover and independence ceremony. The colonial cabinet decided in August to give the Kaundas a set of silver for the president's table, and suggested an elephant's foot for the footstool to accompany his chair. Instructions were given that all colonial notepaper containing official letterheads had to strike through the phrase 'Her Majesty's Service' and replace it with 'On Government Service'.[121]

A month or so before Independence Day, on 24 October 1964, the physical replacement of colonial signs started and 'NRG' was removed from all government vehicles. All European names were dropped: Broken Hill become Kabwe, for example; Fort Jameson, Chipata. Yet, despite the cruel racial history of Livingstone, the name survived. It was the personal wish of Zambia's first president that it should not be changed after independence. The debates over whether to drop his name from the museum reflect the broader attitudes. Parliament agreed that the name 'Rhodes' would have to go, 'the great exploiter and arch-apostle of imperialism', but attitudes to Livingstone were more sentimental and fluid. William Chipanga, now the town's first African mayor, argued that the name was associated with the colonial past and should go, but an alternative position put forward by others on the Livingstone Museum committee was that Livingstone was also 'associated with the betterment of humanity ... he deplored the slave trade and slavery in Africa which he witnessed'.[122] When the argument of pragmatism was added – tourist revenue from an association with the discoverer of Victoria Falls – it was decided to retain the name. In the judgement of Dr Friday Mufuzi, this is a mark of 'Zambian resourcefulness'.

Conclusion

The town named in honour of David Livingstone, the arch icon of humanitarian imperialism, ironically became one of the most racist places in the territory. Many townspeople saw its commercial future as a nostalgic pioneer fantasy destination for white tourists from Southern Rhodesia and South Africa. It existed in an almost parallel universe from indigenous peoples. Victoria Falls drew whites together with its splendour and glamour, but many struggled to survive in the shadow of disease, accidents and death, and the failed pioneer economy of constant money worries.

Livingstone remained insular, distinct and separate during the comparatively short period of formal colonial rule. The town's remoteness repeatedly thwarted local aspirations to become the Henley-on-Thames of central Africa and thus a lucrative whites-only holiday destination. During the era of the 'great pioneer' struggle, British commemorations of Livingstone had envisioned a 'new Africa', following the apparent transformation in colonial Africa inspired by the death of the great explorer-liberator.[123] The imperial vision was a world without struggling white settlers. But the dream never materialised, and the contrasting good fortunes of wealthier whites further south, from the new mining towns, intensified frustrations. Yet the settler colonial vision stubbornly persisted even on the margins: an Africa without Africans.

When white racism and black nationalism competed head on, political parties looked to beg, steal and borrow from the Livingstone 'humanitarian' to score points. By the 1950s, two versions of Livingstone now stood side by side – the pioneer and the missionary – in local memorialisations. David Livingstone's legacy could no longer be the white moral righteousness of the pioneer settler. Now evoked by nationalism's sympathisers was a healing, liberal Christianity and racial partnership. Livingstone was being used to stall the end of empire by many Europeans – and by many Africans to justify its ending. White commerce and 'civilisation' had remained hostile to Africans throughout the period of colonial rule in frontier towns like Livingstone. In the late 1950s, settler emotions ran high and were expressed in part through a hardening of racism in Livingstone in the run-up to independence. Hotels, bars and restaurants were the front line of aggressive and violent confrontations. The town was once again an out-of-control frontier, as local police forces ran out of manpower and resources to enforce the petty rules of the colour bar.

Yet the first generation of African leaders chose to keep the name, which had managed to stand for something more than settler racism – for a young, Christian and forgiving generation. Also, a new generation of white pioneers had arrived by the 1970s, many feeling it was their mission to help dismantle the deeply entrenched racial divisions.[124] Multiracial congregations now fill the church pews, and the name has not been changed to this day. But it is claimed, among some of its African residents, there remains a deep-seated fear of white people and their unpredictable, emotional reactions towards them.[125]

NOTES

1 L.H. Gann, *A History of Northern Rhodesia, Early Days to 1953* (London: Chatto & Windus, 1964), ix.
2 Ibid., 49–99.
3 'Copy of signed agreement with Lewanika, Ngambela, F V Worthington Ford, Aitkens, Lealui, 8 February 1905; and Statement on land purchase', July 1904, BSAC, BS2/78, ZNA.

4   See Chapter Seven.

5   H. Birchenough, 'Report' for the BSAC, 1912, quoted in Gann, *A History of Northern Rhodesia*, 130.

6   Ibid., 131–43.

7   'Letter no 5, from Major Hood to Mrs Hood', 22 May 1902', 1. Livingstone Museum Archive.

8   Editorial note from Mr Trayner [*sic*] 'The Railway reaches the Falls Bridge', *Northern Rhodesia Journal*, 6 (1965): 260.

9   Gann, *A History of Northern Rhodesia*, 126.

10 Ibid., 139.

11 R. Murray-Hughes, 'Livingstone, 1910–11', *Northern Rhodesian Journal*, 4, 3 (1957): 359.

12 Gann, *A History of Northern Rhodesia*, 140.

13 Letter from the Reverend Coisson quoted in Duncan Watt, 'A History of Livingstone Town', unpublished thesis, undated, copy held in Livingstone Museum Archive, G5 2/1, 10.

14 Ibid., 16–17.

15 'Livingstone District Notebook', KSC/4/1/, 6, ZNA.

16 'Letter No. 5, Major Hood, 22 May1902 to Mrs Hood', 1. Livingstone Museum Archive.

17 'Letter about preservation of features' from W.H. Milton, BSAC, October 1903, A1/2/3, ZNA.

18 'Report of a meeting held at Livingstone, May 19th, 1905', Rhodes House, Bodleian Library of Commonwealth and African Studies, Oxford University, 1–2.

19 Ibid., 3.

20 For the Leya story, see Chapter Seven.

21 Kristin Ese, *An Historical Guide to Livingstone Town* (Harare: CBC Publishing, 1996), 22–3; Watt, 'A History of Livingstone Town', 88.

22 Murray-Hughes, 'Livingstone, 1910–11', 359.

23 Author interview with the Reverend Dr David Mkandawire, Pastor, David Livingstone Memorial Church, Livingstone, 21 June 2005. As the church's brief history on line describes it's origins, 'Our name honors the legacy of missionary pioneer Dr David Livingstone, who first brought the Gospel here in 1854. David Livingstone loved Zambia. He died in Zambia, and as he requested, his heart is buried in Zambia'.

24 Early settler quoted in Watt, 'A History of Livingstone Town', 14.

25 Murray-Hughes, 'Livingstone, 1910–11', 356.

26 C. Fitzhenry, 'African Dust', undated, Mss Afr.s.16, Special Collections & Western Mss, Rhodes House, Bodleian Library of Commonwealth and African Studies, Oxford University, 70–1.

27 'The Zambezi Regatta, 1953: Rhodes Centenary Celebrations', brochure, 1/-, 3, published by the *Livingstone Mail*, Livingstone Museum Archive, Livingstone.

28 S.R. Denny, 'Notes on Target Rifle Shooting in Northern Rhodesia, 1905–1935', *Northern Rhodesian Journal*, 4, 2 (1957): 112–20.

29 Gann, *A History of Northern Rhodesia*, 116.

30 Fitzhenry, 'African Dust', 75–7, 78–9.
31 Hugh Macmillan, *An African Trading Empire: The Story of Susman Brothers & Wulfsohn, 1901–2005* (London: I.B. Tauris, 2005), 18–19, 49.
32 Ibid., 60–1.
33 Ivor Graham, 'Newspapers in Northern Rhodesia', *Northern Rhodesia Journal*, 5, 5 (1964): 421.
34 Macmillan, *An African Trading Empire*, 44.
35 Robert I. Rotberg, *Black Heart: Gore-Browne and the Politics of Multiracial Zambia* (Berkeley, CA: University of California Press, 1977), 214, fn 6, and 174.
36 Gann, *A History of Northern Rhodesia*, 368.
37 'N.R. Pioneer's farewell message: "Leadership needed to command the respect of Africans"', *Northern News*, 15 November 1955.
38 Watt, 'A History of Livingstone Town', 75.
39 This term referred to people of mixed-race parentage. It was a term that had developed in Britain's Cape Colony (1795–1910). It referred to people from African (Khoisan and Bantu), European and Asian (Austronesian and South Asian) ethnic backgrounds.
40 Fitzhenry, 'African Dust', 71.
41 Letter no. 4 17/02/03, 3. 'Extracts of letters from Major G B Hook to Mrs Hook, 1902–03', G4/2, Livingstone Museum Archive, Zambia.
42 Ibid., 5 July 1902, 4.
43 Fitzhenry, 'African Dust', 61–7.
44 Ibid., 77–8.
45 J. Roden, *Northward from Cape Town: The Anglican Church Railway Mission in Southern Africa, 1885–1980* (York: Sacram, 1999).
46 Author interview with the Reverend Jackson Katete, Pastor, St Andrew's Church, 22 June 2006.
47 'History of the Church', St Andrew's Church Livingstone, Information Leaflet, 2.
48 'Programme of Grand Evening Concert, 16 April 1906, H1/3/7, Livingstone Museum Archive. Men and women sang solos, duets and played the violin and performed Scottish airs in the first half. After the interval came a play. See also Gann, *A History of Northern Rhodesia*, 140.
49 Advertisement, 'Dreams of Home', H1/3/7, Livingstone Museum.
50 Quoted from the *Livingstone Mail*, F. Mufuzi, 'The Livingstone Museum and the Memorialisation of David Livingstone in Colonial and Post-Colonial Zambia, 1934–2005', in S. Worden (ed.), *David Livingstone: Man, Myth and Legacy* (Edinburgh: National Museums of Scotland, 2012), 134.
51 Macmillan, *An African Trading Empire*, 148–9 and 27.
52 'Spend Your Next Vacation at Livingstone', undated; 'Hints on Seeing the Falls', undated, H12/3, History Collection, Livingstone Museum Archive.
53 'The Zambezi Regatta 1953', ibid., 4.
54 See various correspondence between the secretariat and members of the Caledonian Society, RC/1021, ZNA. For background, see J.M. MacKenzie, with N.R. Dalziel, *The Scots in South Africa: Ethnicity, identity, Gender and Race, 1772–1914* (Johannesburg: Johannesburg Wits University Press, 2007).

55 'David Livingstone Memorial Statue. Programme for the Unveiling Ceremony at the Victoria Falls on Sunday 5th Aug, 1934', H/7/2, Livingstone Museum Archive.

56 'Foreward', ibid.

57 'The Address by Rev James Gray, LL D, Unveiling Ceremony', ibid.

58 Gann, *A History of Northern Rhodesia*, 171.

59 Rotberg, *Black Heart*, 170–1.

60 'The Rhodes-Livingstone Museum, 1934–1951, Report for 1950', 4–7. Priced: Two Shillings, Rhodes Livingstone Museum Archive.

61 See Mufuzi, 'The Livingstone Museum', 131–7.

62 See numerous newspaper articles, including from *Bulowayo Chronicle*, the *Cape Argus* and the *Johannesburg Star*, for 1936 held in the Livingstone Museum Archive.

63 'The Great Rapids of the Zambesi', *Cape Argus*, 21 November 1936.

64 'Minute by His Excellency', 19 March 1938, SEC1/1973, ZNA.

65 Chief secretary, Lusaka, to organising secretary, Salisbury, 22 July 1940; James McNair to governor, 5 May 1940 and note of reply, SEC1/1793, vol. xi, 138, ZNA.

66 See Gann, *A History of Northern Rhodesia*, esp. 443.

67 Various correspondence, Roy Welensky Papers, Rhodes House, Bodleian Library, Oxford; MSS Welensky 1726.

68 Rotberg, *Black Heart*, 295.

69 For a detailed account, see Joanna E. Lewis, 'Rivers of White: David Livingstone and the 1955 Commemorations in the Lost "Henley-on-Thames of Central Africa"', in J.B. Gewald, Marja Hinfelaar & Giacomo Macola (eds.), *Living the End of Empire: Politics and Society in Late Colonial Zambia* (Leiden: Brill, 2011), 161–206.

70 Ibid., 180.

71 Extract from a regional newspaper, Livingstone Museum Archive.

72 The Secretary of the CCC to the Resident Commissioner, Mongu, Barotseland, 11 January 1955, ibid.

73 Letter to district commissioners (Mongu, Sengana, Shesheke, Livingstone) from secretary of CCC, 13 January 1955, ibid.

74 *Livingstone Mail*, centenary pictorial supplement, November 1955, ZNA.

75 *Central African Post*, 17 November 1955, ibid.

76 Draft invitation to provincial commissioners, 1 October 1955, SP1/11/32, ZNA.

77 *Northern News*, 15 November 1955.

78 'THE UNINVITED GUEST', editorial, *Livingstone Mail*, 18 November 1955.

79 'FEDERATION PAYS TRIBUTE TO A GREAT MAN', *Livingstone Mail*, 18 November 1955; 'Editorial', *Livingstone Mail*, 16 November 1955.

80 'Legacy of Livingstone', *Central African Post*, 9 November 1955.

81 *Northern News*, 17 November 1955.

82 *Central Africa Post*, 15 November 1955.

83 Ibid., 11 November 1955.

84 *Livingstone Mail*, editorial, 'We must all help', 8 July 1955, ibid.

85 A. Roberts, *A History of Africa* (London: Heinemann, 1976), 196–8.

86 Andrew Cohen, *The Politics and Economics of Decolonization in Africa: The Failed Experiment of the Central African Federation* (London: I.B. Tauris, 2017).

87 Dennis Frost, 'Memoirs', 90, Mss.Afr.s.2196, Rhodes House Collection, Bodleian Library, Oxford University.

88 D.F. Gordon, 'Rebellion or Massacre: The UNIP-Lumpa Conflict Revisited', in J.-B. Gewald, Marja Hinfelaar & Giacomo Macola (eds.), *One Zambia, Many Histories: Towards a History of Post-Colonial Zambia* (Leiden: Brill, 2008), 45–76.

89 See generally G. Macola, *Liberal Nationalism in Central Africa: A Biography of Harry Mwanga Nkumbula* (New York: Palgrave, Macmillan, 2010), and M. Larmer, *Rethinking African Politics: A History of Opposition in Zambia* (Surrey: Ashgate, 2011), 21–53.

90 Miss Brimblecombe, on behalf of Sir Hilton Poynton, CRO, Colonial Office to D.R.J. Stephen, Cabinet Office, 22 December 1959, CAB 21/3157, BNA.

91 'Notes of a meeting', 21 January 1960. Eight Africans were present. PREM11/3065(1), BNA.

92 Ibid., 4.

93 'Mr Macmillan not to see Dr. Banda', *Times*, 25 January 1960.

94 J.E. Lewis, '"White Man in a Wood Pile": Race and the Limits of Macmillan's Great "Wind of Change" in Africa', in S. Stockwell & L.J. Butler (eds.), *The Wind of Change: Harold Macmillan & British Decolonization* (Basingstoke: Palgrave, 2013), 70–95.

95 Author interview with Father Jackson Katete, St Andrew's Church, Livingstone, Zambia, 20 June 2009.

96 'A Memo to Macmillan: They are Hiding the Colour Bar from you says the Man from the Mirror', *Daily Mirror*, 27 January 1960, BLN.

97 *Central African Post*, 22 January 1960, ZNA.

98 Peregrine Worsthorne, *Tricks of Memory: An Autobiography* (London: Weidenfeld & Nicholson, 1993), 196.

99 M.M. Chona to R.D. Milne, UNIP, 6/7/3, UNIP Archives, Lusaka.

100 Petitions held in NR11/84, ZNA.

101 Roberts, *A History of Africa*, 218.

102 Ibid., 197.

103 Author interview, Lusaka, Zambia, 16 June 2009.

104 *Northern News*, 21 January 1960, NR11/84, ZNA.

105 Confidential note, 25 May 1959, ibid.

106 Quoted in Lewis, '"White Man in a Wood Pile"', 84–8.

107 G. Musumbulwa to Ag Chief Secretary, 8 March 1960, CO/3/1/1, ZNA.

108 Ag Sec of UNIP to Ag Governor, 1 February 1962, CO/6/1/8, ZNA.

109 See Ann Perkins, *Red Queen: The Authorised Biography of Barbara Castle* (London: Pan Books, 2004), reported in the *Telegraph*, 21 January 1960.

110 Secretary to District Race Relations Committee Livingstone, to secretary, Central Race Advisory Committee, 27 February 1962, CO3/1/1 Race Relations, ZNA.

111 Acting national secretary, UNIP, to acting governor, Lusaka, 1 January 1961, CO16/1/8 1960-64, ZNA.

112 Proprietor of Westwood Hotel, Abercon, to Race Relations Committee, undated, ibid.
113 Note for under-secretary, Lusaka, 1 September 1962, ibid.
114 'Report on Livingstone Hotels', ibid.
115 Report on Race Relations at hotels – 1 September to 17 November 1960. See also NR Police HQ Circular, 9 January 1961. Ibid.
116 *Northern News*, 18 September 1962, ZNA.
117 Special meeting of the Kitwe District Race Relations Committee, 6 March 1962, ibid.
118 PC to CS Lusaka, 16 January 1961, ibid.
119 PM to DC Livingstone, 11 July 1964, CO/3/1/1, ZNA.
120 D.C. Mulford, *The Northern Rhodesia General Election 1962* (Nairobi: Oxford University Press, 1964).
121 Various correspondence, NR11/84 and CO2/1/3, ZNA.
122 Mufuzi, 'The Livingstone Museum', 141–2.
123 See discussion in Chapter Seven.
124 Author interview with Mrs Margaret Whitehead, widow of the Reverend Whitehead of St Andrew's Church, who did much to promote interracial socialising and tackle racism; Livingstone, 9 July 2009.
125 Author interview with a long-standing resident of Livingstone since the 1970s, Livingstone, 22 April 2013.

6   'The Hearts of Good Men'

1973, the One-Party State & the Struggle against
Apartheid

We were told about him by my great-uncle Shingoma, who met him
in person twice near Mazabuka. He was a tall, strong man. He had a
British wife called Mary, and we were told by my grandfather that she
was the daughter of another British man in Africa, who was less popular
than Livingstone. The villagers in Shingoma's area would congregate
to welcome the white man. He would arrive with his African companions and would at times partake of the African hosts' food and drink.
According to Shingoma, Dr Livingstone would use sign language to
communicate with people. He would point to heaven to indicate 'God'.
He would encourage people to love each other by shaking their hands
with a smile. One of his most difficult tasks was to teach the villages
about the hydro or rain cycle. He would point at a body of water, make
gestures of steam rising, then point to the clouds, then gesture rain. The
villages would await his arrival with eagerness. He twice promised to
return after he had witnessed the Falls, and twice did so. The third time,
it didn't work. The great man had died of malaria.

Reminiscences of retired Tonga UNIP intelligence officer,
Southern Province, 2005

This chapter looks at how the Livingstone legend lived on after the end
of colonial rule in this part of Africa. It offers a case study in the continuity of imperial and post-imperial regimes through an exploration of
the usefulness of the memory of Livingstone to a newly independent
Zambia. In 1973, Livingstone was feted and worshipped with the same
emotion and sentimentality as he had been in 1874, with the same discourse of the heart. Symbolic of the continuity between the moral rhetoric and political practice of the colonial and postcolonial state, the place
chosen to revive and display a Christian liberal moral community was the
Chitambo graveside, unchanged since 1902. Bizarrely, Livingstone, the
gatekeeper of colonialism, received the greatest national ceremony in life
or death from an independent African government. British officials seem
to have been excluded from all events.

By the time of the hundredth anniversary of the death of David
Livingstone, in 1973, Zambia had been independent for nearly a decade.

Figure 6.1 Dr Kenneth Kaunda, the prime minister of newly independent Zambia, inspecting the new Zambian (Northern Rhodesian) police at their training barracks near Lusaka, 16 March 1964. Photo by Central Press/Getty Images.

But the world was not a postcolonial one for its people. 1973 was a crisis point for two reasons related to this reality. First, Kenneth Kaunda's UNIP had been in power since it won the first elections to accompany British decolonisation and its triumphant, peaceful acceptance of power on 24 October 1964 (see Figure 6.1). But unity after independence was elusive. The new African government found it impossible to produce policies which offered a populist and radical alternative to colonial rule. Growing political opposition triggered a set of responses which had all the hallmarks of the colonial state. All of the political parties, including its biggest rival, the ANC, had been banned in 1972. Under a new constitution, adopted in 1973, by and large only UNIP candidates now stood for election in December to a 'unicameral' National Assembly. Only the president of UNIP was allowed to run for the presidency of the whole country. Thus the 1973 centenary offered a political opportunity at a crucial time for Kaunda and a 'besieged political elite'[1] to restore moral legitimacy after imposing the unpopular one-party state.

Second, tensions with Zambia's neighbours, under white-minority rule, were coming to a head. Symbolically, the year was also the tenth anniversary of the end of white-minority rule in British colonial Africa, for in 1963, the unpopular imperial federation (Northern and Southern Rhodesia, plus Nyasaland) had been dissolved as part of the 'wind of change' realignment of British decolonisation, which now accepted a fast-track route to majority African rule. Zambia and Malawi had walked away from the wreckage, free at least. But Southern Rhodesia had declared independence from Britain in 1965, heralding the beginning of Ian Smith's rule of Rhodesia. Here, as in Angola, Mozambique, Namibia and South Africa, African nationalists were brutally suppressed. With the Cold War raging, southern Africa's racist regimes were not about to cave in, and cloaked their racism in their denunciation of Communism. Commemorating Livingstone's death in 1973 offered intimidated African politicians an opportunity to launch an emotional critique of apartheid.

The Problem of Opposition for the Nationalist Party

'TOURISTS JET IN', read the Zambian *Daily Mail*'s headline for 27 April. It was accompanied by a photograph of a group of formidable, middle-aged Scottish ladies dressed in smart skirt suits and dresses, and wearing Sunday hats. They were members of the Royal Scottish Geographical Society. The group of nineteen were the first on the Livingstone Centenary Safari Tour of Zambia. Lasting seventeen days, it had been organised jointly by the Zambian National Tourism Bureau and British Caledonian Airways. Lusaka's twin city, Los Angeles, was also organising a similar visit. British diplomats were conspicuous by their absence.

However, behind the flowers and smiles lurked a regional and national political crisis. Kaunda had been re-elected as Zambia's president, unopposed, in December 1973, and would be re-elected in 1978 and 1983, and again in 1988. The presidential cult and UNIP's appropriation of the liberation struggle were in full swing, and yet another anniversary came to the aid of the party in 1973. Kaunda's forty-ninth birthday fell on 28 April 1973. The *Zambia Daily Nation* ran with an editorial bearing the affectionate headline 'HAPPY BIRTHDAY KK'.[2] Kaunda, assisted by his 'faithful lieutenants' and the people, had delivered independence from the 'yoke of colonial rule'. The 'birth pangs of a new nation' were described as the enemies of a young nation's freedom.

Other newly independent African states were busy going down the same route, shortly after independence delivered to them the colonial bureaucratic apparatus virtually intact. Keeping it so was their aim.[3] The colonial state, barely altered as a bureaucratic framework under the rapid transfer of power, had used monopolism, top-down intervention, centralism, intolerance of opposition, and force, so the blueprint was close at hand. Likewise, the 'former colonial masters' and their superpower friends in the Cold War were unprepared to step in and spoil the party. Yet this was a rickety façade of power and control. In the face of domestic opposition and regional instability and threat, the very move to a one-party state was not simple to impose.

Fear and insecurity mixed uneasily with a sense of political entitlement and chauvinism. Many African nationalist parties like UNIP came to believe that they alone had been central in delivering freedom. Many members had had to endure hardship, and leaders had endured imprisonment, violence and exile. A key source of the insecurity felt by the post-independence first-generation politicians came from the inherent difficulty in holding together the support that they had garnered during the anti-colonial struggle. In the context of rival political parties, the winning party at independence had supporters hastily pulled together out of shaky coalitions, benefiting from anti-colonial feeling and a shared Christian identity. But those affinities and partnerships had to operate across regional, class and ethnic divides deepened by colonial rule. Meanwhile, once in power, the winning party's supporters' expectations were difficult to manage, since millions wanted a better deal, and fast, once colonial rule ended.

Internal opposition was bubbling away from the start of Kaunda's rule. Livingstone town was a key battleground. It was home to the first African Zambian to be detained by the newly independent state. William Chipango had been a leading trade unionist, representing railway employees during the 1950s; he was also an ANC supporter and a passionate anti-colonialist. After independence, Chipango became the first black mayor of Livingstone. From the outset, he railed against the early signs of UNIP authoritarianism and creeping interventionism in local government. He would get his complaints published in the local press. One such complaint was his allegation that only customers with a UNIP card were being served at one of Livingstone's main pharmacies.[4] According to his account, he immediately embarked on a vigorous programme of housebuilding to compensate for the colonial deficit. This meant the council had to purchase large amounts of building materials, which they could get most cheaply and efficiently from Rhodesia (formerly Southern Rhodesia). However, after Southern Rhodesia's Unilateral Declaration of Independence (UDI) in 1965, Kaunda wanted the Livingstone mayor to break off contact and forget about the contracts. Chipango refused, wanting to get on with the housebuilding. After his re-election, he was arrested and detained and, as we have seen, was accused of being involved in the plot with Rhodesia to bring down the government.[5] Chipango's arrest began a period of twenty-one years of persecution, detention, imprisonment and torture.[6] He was part of a steady trickle of political opponents subjected to state brutality.

In the late 1960s, UNIP brought in new legislation that enabled the party's central committee to appoint mayors. Chipango was part of a growing problem of popular mayors who opposed the government. Opposition groups were more effectively stifled from the start of the 1970s. The declaration of the one-party state meant that critics could be imprisoned for treason, beginning a period which for Chipango contained 'memories too painful to want to go over often'. Nevertheless, a new United Progressive Party (UPP) had been formed in 1971, largely out of divisions within UNIP and the independently minded, cattle-owning communities of Southern Province,[7] which area was a thorn in the side of the party throughout 1973. Its new minister described the year for the province as 'difficult'. Speaking at the opening session of the Third National Assembly in the Second Republic, William R. Mwandela listed a serious drought, food shortages, the closing of the border by Smith in February, landmines and a bomb that had gone off in a cabinet minister's office, which was rumoured to be linked with the unrest in Southern Province. But he remained upbeat: the new 'One Party Participatory Democracy' would bring 'stability', he reassured his audience.[8]

It would also bring repression and restrictions on freedom of speech. There had been a huge drive to register UNIP branches, as all ANC offices had been 'dissolved'. Control over the media was announced. A new mast in Livingstone brought television to the province for the first time. To deal with the effects of this on freedom of speech, and in particular with accusations that the elections were chaotic, the government took action. At his first meeting with all district governors in Southern Province, held in Livingstone at the beginning of 1974, Mwandela told them that his office had to be consulted 'before any political statement was made to the press particularly on the delicate issues like elections ... you will undoubtedly agree with me as friends ... too much of this rather unfortunate habit of rushing to the press at the least opportunity'.

Escalating Tensions from the 'Silent Pool' of White Racism

Connected to UNIP's drive towards stable, absolute control was the regional context of continuing white-minority racial rule.[9] As a new territory in a southern Africa dominated by apartheid South Africa, Zambia's political elite still had to be concerned about securing the country from any kind of invasion, and with displaying competence and authority as a non-aligned nation on a predominantly white and racially prejudiced international diplomatic stage.[10] In Zambia's case, its domestic authoritarian drive also has to be understood in the context of the day-to-day impact of a still very colonial-looking world rammed up against its borders.

Ian Smith's white-minority-ruled Rhodesia was a hostile neighbour across the Zambezi River, just at the other end of Victoria Falls. Likewise, banned and operating in exile, the ANC in South Africa were stepping up their anti-apartheid campaign, and liberation movements in Mozambique on its border, and Angola further afield, were engaged in bloody insurrection against Portuguese settlers, the colonial state and the national army. Although independence was around the corner in Lusophone Africa, Rhodesia kept going for another five years, and apartheid for another sixteen, for a while each helping the other, Rhodesia moving goods in and out via South Africa and Portugal, despite the UN embargoes. Zambian officials genuinely feared an invasion. In March 1972, an alleged plot by the Rhodesian security forces to invade the country was uncovered.[11] Backed by South African soldiers 'posing as mercenaries', the plan was to invade and take over key towns and cities. The Zambezi border was declared a restricted zone in September 1972. A full-blown border crisis unfolded from the beginning of 1973, along with a Rhodesian blockade.

On the eve of Livingstone's centenary commemoration, the sense of imminent threat was strong. In late April, a white Rhodesian civilian on the Zambezi was shot, his death blamed on Zambian security forces. In an upbeat counter-propaganda attack, the Zambian government claimed that it had evidence that he had been shot by mistake by the South African police, secretly operating on the Rhodesian side of the border, and that 'all the racists knew it'. African schools had been shut across the border, the foreign minister, Elijah Madenda, claimed. These schools had been ordered to produce pamphlets in the local vernacular to undermine the 'freedom fighters', but many African teachers, he assured his audience, had altered key passages, for example by changing the phrase 'Whosoever supports or shelters the guerillas will be punished severely' to 'Whosoever supports ... will be awarded a lot of money'.[12]

Nevertheless, the regular pattern of Smith blaming Zambia for the so-called terrorist attacks by providing bases posed an unnerving, ever-present threat. Speaking that same day, Ian Smith issued one of his many warnings that 'security could not be assured when a mere imaginary line on a map was the border' and that 'anybody who believes that simply because we clean up a certain area and pushed terrorists across the border the danger is over, is indulging in wishful thinking'. Ominously for Zambia, he signalled that the bases across the border would eventually be 'completely cleaned out' in order to remove the 'guerrilla menace'.[13] The Victoria Falls area was tense, a virtual war zone.

Allegations were then made by Rhodesia that Zambian soldiers had shot at a group of white swimmers heading towards the Zambian side of the river, near the Victoria Falls power station. Reports filtered through that two Canadian women tourists had been killed and an American man badly wounded. The government tried to contain this potential global public relations disaster, claiming it was inconceivable that genuine tourists would not have been warned about the tense situation. And any soldier would be naturally fearful that their 'waterproof gear' might conceal explosives.[14] It insisted these were allegations only.

However, the deaths of these swimmers in the Silent Pool on the Zambian side of the gorge, shot by Zambian forces, were soon confirmed. The government next claimed that the girls had been lured to the area to provoke such an incident in order to 'rob Zambia of international sympathy'.[15] On the offensive, the government called on the UN to punish countries that were evading sanctions against Rhodesia, under the headline 'World must unite to beat Smith'. Additionally, Britain's 'protective policy' was listed as one of the key pillars of the rebel regime.[16] The British government and its press were attacked in an editorial for their indifference to racial rule in Rhodesia and political internment without trial. Instead, they hid behind the argument of not wanting to be racist, unless a white man was caught up in its evil laws.

Not surprisingly, the town of Livingstone would not be the focus of any major commemoration of the centenary of Livingstone's death in 1973, and no record survives of any official celebration. It was 'jarring', one reviewer wrote in the Zambian *Daily Mail*, that his statue was in 'rebel' Rhodesia. Likewise, it was an irritant that the white explorer was still credited with having discovered the Falls, when he had merely drawn the world's attention to them.[17]

However, the town was also ignored for more local, personal and long-standing domestic reasons: Kaunda and UNIP had long struggled to impose themselves on Livingstone and Southern Province in particular, the heartland of his political rivals, which included Tonga patriots, the ANC and Harry Nkumbula loyalists, and powerful, assertive chiefs such as Chief Mukuni of the Leya people, who were building up a strong political following around the Victoria Falls region. After independence, the rivalry and enmities continued, despite the ANC's decline under the dissolute Nkumbula.[18] In the ANC strongholds, junior government employees deflected any anger and resentment from either side by carrying both

ANC and UNIP party cards.[19] Despite their internal problems and the new system for selecting MPs to favour UNIP, ANC supporters still did well at the 1968 elections.

Meanwhile, Kaunda had been busy constructing a moral case for single-party rule by UNIP. He tried to combine his strongly held Christian principles with models of state intervention based on socialism. His humanist philosophy drew on Gandhi, symbolised by a white handkerchief he carried to suggest a commitment to non-violence. From Kaunda and the UNIP leadership's perspective, they were dealing with obstinate, bourgeois traitors – which was how they viewed men like Chipango – some of whom were prepared to work with Smith's 'rebel' regime. In their view, these traitors had to be contained for the good of the country and the party's forward-looking developmentalism. Kaunda could also draw on a reputation as a moderate and a loyal ally of Britain, the Commonwealth and the West. He had, for example, earlier tried to prevent Tanzania's Julius Nyerere from rushing ahead with Chinese funding for the Tan-Zam railway. He worked hard to maintain that reputation and enjoyed some affection and support from members of the former British colonial administration. A sympathetic biography by Richard Hall, *The High Price of Principles: Kaunda and the White South*, targeted that audience – a move to head off criticism of the 'etatist' ruling party and its growing authoritarianism.[20]

Kaunda's solid international support and reputation contrasted with his domestic situation, however. In an election year, Kaunda needed to sell his political philosophy of 'humanism' and the common sense of the second national development plan. He had launched his 'man-centered society' in a pamphlet in 1967, inspired by Julius Nyerere's Arusha Declaration. In this pamphlet, a mishmash of socialist, African and Christian doctrines, Kaunda – romantically – looked back to the pre-industrial, precolonial idyll of traditional village life, underpinned by communal values.[21]

He built on this and, in 1973, Longman published his *Letters To My Children*, with a supportive forward by the Reverend Dr Colin Morris from the Church of Scotland. It was pitched as coming from the heart, written as an apology to his family. Nevertheless, the self-styled father of the nation was also on the defensive, accused of being a pacifist who was signing detention orders. Here, he set out his version of Christianity for the modern African man, a Christian humanism. His parents' Christianity had seemed over-simplistic to him – missionaries had 'made the cult of misery a way of life'. However, he also saw how the gospel released a power in Christian men and women: 'There was power in my mother's prayers ... and when those Lubwa Christians sang the old chorus – there was power, power, power in the blood of the Lamb – it meant something'.[22] He declared a positive view of Islam, too, believing that it gave men a belief in themselves.

Dr Sholto Cross, contemporary reviewer of the unusual book, admired the author's shrewdness and range of skills as a politician running through the text. The heartfelt high Christian principles, and his confessional sentimentality within, raised the stature of Kaunda's presidency. Cross, an academic with experience of working in Zambia, judged diplomatically that 'it might be argued' that the book revealed a manipulative figure 'whose Machiavellian skill is to project an image of passionate yet humble sincerity which belies the ruthless party boss within'.[23]

Nevertheless, there were authentic roots that pulled Kaunda genuinely towards a spiritually inspired critique of materialism and wealth creation. He was born on 28 April 1924 to parents who were poor migrants to Northern Rhodesia. First-generation Christian converts from Nyasaland (Malawi), they enrolled their son in Lubwa Missionary School in northeastern Zambia. After attending Munali Secondary School, Kaunda became a schoolteacher there, and then its headmaster (1944–7). In the 1950s, he was drawn into the fermenting anti-colonial Christian nationalist movement.[24] A missionary education had bequeathed a not wholly negative view of white rule: 'I was a thorn in the flesh of the missionaries who taught me at school and the District Commissioners', he reminisced. 'I was often given a thrashing for daring to challenge the authority of the white man', but he added that he never doubted their good intentions, then or now, despite their 'unconscious racial bias'.[25] Kaunda, like millions of young Africans, was exposed to vernacular missionary texts and school history textbooks which glorified Livingstone as the man who had brought Christianity to Zambia.[26] Writing his book drew Kaunda towards seeing the value of a big Livingstone commemoration, and the Church of Scotland would unwittingly give further moral and discursive support to the one-party state.

Kaunda's 1973 Graveside Appeal to the 'Hearts of Men'

The tense atmosphere of 1973 would deliver David Livingstone the largest national commemoration in a postcolonial state, as its political rulers sought to recreate a single moral community and tap into the power of Christian community. At the national level, a number of events were planned for 1 May, taken as the day of Livingstone's death (also a special day in the International Socialism calendar). 'A century to the day', at Chipundu, the small village that had grown up near the monument, 'President Kaunda and his entourage, representatives of various

Christian movements, members of the Livingstone family and pilgrims from outside Zambia' would, according to the Zambian *Daily Mail*, travel to where Livingstone's heart was buried, 'not only to remember a dead man but to be at the place where a freedom fighter died'.[27] There were three speakers: Kaunda, Mr Livingstone Armstrong (a great-nephew of Livingstone) and, representing the Christian Church in Zambia, the Reverend Jackson Mwape.

The celebrations had been scheduled to last four days but they were cut to one day 'for health reasons'.[28] No mention was made of any involvement by Chief Chitambo, although he did participate.[29] Treated as distinguished guests were the forty British visitors. These included Kate Armstrong, Livingstone's granddaughter, who was over eighty years old; two of Livingstone's great-granddaughters; and, impressively, the two daughters of Owen Stroud, who had built the obelisk. Also forming part of the visiting entourage were students who were being sponsored, because of their interest in medicine, nutrition agriculture and education, plus representatives of the Bible Society of Wales and the Welsh Secretary to the British and Foreign Bible Society, billed as the link to Stanley. A thousand people walked to the clearing.

It was not the only national event. On 29 April 1973, an interdenominational rally was held in the Dag Hammarskjöld Stadium at Ndola.[30] Five hundred Christians gathered to listen to Vice President Mainza Chona. The Zambian *Daily Mail* accompanied its front-page coverage with Chona's photo and the headline, 'Fight today's slave traders, world urged: LIVINGSTONE'S WORK MUST GO ON, SAYS CHONA', with a special feature on Livingstone inside.[31] The names of Livingstone's relatives were listed. A film company in Zambia also marked the occasion with 'In His Steps'. Multimedia Zambia had produced a film about 'a modern Zambia which is the best dream of David Livingstone'. The Bible Society of Zambia produced a leaflet entitled 'Men Free'. The Zambia Cultural Services Dance Troupe gave a special performance. The BBC worked with Zambia Information Services to cover events at Chitambo. Zambians were also aware that a service was being held at Westminster Abbey.

A few newspapers in Britain covered the event. *The Guardian* carried a photograph of Kaunda unveiling a new plaque which had been added to the obelisk, unchanged since 1902. *The Times* detailed events at Chitambo and quoted the Reverend Jackson Mwape, president of the United Church of Zambia, who led the contingent of clergy. It made for comforting reading in Britain, no doubt, that Mwape was insisting that, without Livingstone, 'all Africans would have gone overseas as slaves like the Negroes in America'.[32]

Although attention has focused on Kaunda's famous – and overly generous – declaration that Livingstone was Africa's first freedom fighter or its first nationalist (which especially delighted Scottish Livingstone fans), the extensive activity and rhetoric which accompanied the 1973 centenary is richer and more complex. The Livingstone story was retold to an audience who were perhaps less interested. The roles of Susi and Chuma were given more prominence in order to Africanise the imperial tale, but that aspect was not the major focus of the memorialisation. Significant contributors to the attempt to mobilise a politics of affection included senior church figures like Mwapa, who was extensively quoted in the national press. For example, the Reverend Kingsley Mwenda, secretary of the Christian Council of Zambia, gave a long interview in the Zambian *Daily Mail* on 30 April 1973. It may also be the case, considering the material and tone, that senior church figures also had a hand in Kaunda's big speech at Chitambo, and in other long editorials in the national press.

Kaunda and the ruling political regime used the 1973 centenary of Livingstone's death to make political capital from an emotional appeal to their Christian support base. Not only did Kaunda begin his highly publicised address to a man dedicated to alleviating human misery (because 'he was a man of God. An exemplary Christian … .in the glow of love which Christianity inspired in him') but he also ended his Chitambo address in the style of a sermon, using classic Christian theology, and calling on all Zambians to 'love the Lord thy God with all thy heart'.[33] Press coverage reported his call for an end to the neglect of reading the Bible. Livingstone, he pointed out, believed that the teachings of the Bible were the only basis for the 'rights and privileges of modern civilization'. Such a literal view would have delighted conservative and evangelical groups in particular. Kaunda had UNIP officials prepare a list of all of the Christian churches registered with the Zambian Christian Council, Christian-based organisations such as the Boy Scouts, and all 'sects', such as the Blackman's First Church.

Second, the centenary provided a much-needed opportunity to give legitimacy to Kaunda's personal political crusade around the notion of humanism. Many references linked it to Livingstone's belief and practices. He would be remembered as 'a great humanist', being one of the very few white people to treat Africans as human beings. The *Daily Mail*'s editorial ended with the point that behind Livingstone's greatness was 'his great humanity'.[34] The Reverend Mwape played his part, stressing that 'Zambia has always been a country which seems to be on the right side of thinking about man, as our philosophy of humanism explains. What Livingstone did was to mankind as a whole'.

Despite the obvious political instrumentalism behind such rhetoric, Kaunda did have a personal and sentimental link to Livingstone and the liberal face of the British Empire. His father, David, had been one of the first teachers to be trained at Mwenzo, Nyasaland, set up by the Scottish Livingstonia Mission.[35] Here, people were encouraged to think of themselves as Africans and take up church leadership roles. No subject was off limits, including a sustained critique of European racism. They were taught that the Bible insisted that all human beings were the same. David Kaunda set up a school in Chinsali, in Northern Rhodesia, and was central in establishing an embryonic political party, the Mwenzo Welfare Association. His son was schooled in a deep sensitivity to racism and an awareness of the power of public opinion.

In his speech, Kaunda used Livingstone to thread together Christian belief, selfless public service and humanism. He moved to conclude that 'those of us who believe in Christianity like Livingstone, those of us who are working to reconstruct this country on the basis of the philosophy of humanism', had a similarly great challenge and needed to put aside greed and selfishness – perhaps a reference to his 'capitalist' political opponents at home. In case his political message was unclear, next to his photo on 2 May, a front-page article hammered it home: 'The challenge to carry on Livingstone's work', and Kaunda was insistent that Zambians were 'under an obligation to pick up where Livingstone left off' and to reconstruct the nation on the basis of 'the philosophy of humanism'.[36]

Nevertheless, the use of the memory of colonial rule and Livingstone in 1973 also reveals just how nervous the Zambian political elite were when criticising white Rhodesia and apartheid South Africa. Dealings with such bully-boy states had to be done with great trepidation and delicacy. Both were now gingerly attacked through the politics of memorialising Livingstone. Choosing as the theme for the commemoration the crusade against slavery, past and present, enabled the Zambian regime to achieve this. Livingstone was lionised for his campaign but, as the many speeches stressed, slavery took many forms and was alive and well. In one of the few direct references to apartheid, the *Daily Mail*'s editorial railed against South Africa, where slavery still existed 'in dehumanising form. The same applies to Rhodesia where man's inhumanity to man is seen daily in its most sickening form'. It also contained one of the few direct references to the evils of colonialism and racism.

Vice President Chona was able to use the occasion to criticise modern forms of slavery as the 'evil practice of apartheid', insisting that the international community 'should shudder' at the dehumanisation taking place. He also added in witchcraft and bridal dowries. Livingstone was held up in noble contrast as a non-racist. According to Kaunda, he had been capable of making a 'dispassionate appraisal' of the qualities of the African people, unlike the majority of his time. Indeed, he was credited with calling people 'Zambesians'.[37] The Reverend Mwende blessed Livingstone for having endangered his own life 'for the sake of people of a different colour and upbringing. He took on the duty and never looked back'.[38]

With this powerful myth of interracial intimacy and connection down the Livingstone generations restated, a very emotional and sentimental politics of affection was being mobilised. Livingstone was described as one of the very few whites 'who saw beauty in the soul of the black man', and the *Daily Mail*'s editorial repeatedly used the word 'love'. Livingstone became so intimate with Africans – eating with them, healing them – that 'he got to understand and love them'.

And the African people of those times paid back with love. They looked upon him as a companion. And when he died, they showed their love for him by taking his body to his own people even at the risk of their lives.

Similarly, Kaunda spoke of being at the place where the great man had been tended by Africans who had grown to love him, of how Livingstone had generated 'an irresistible response in the hearts of good men of all races and creeds' and of how he had had a 'great capacity to love'. Kaunda contrasted Livingstone favourably with the selfishness and aggression of Rhodes, pronouncing that 'force conquers but it is love which prevails'.[39]

In some ways, Kaunda's rhetoric in particular could be dismissed as a reproduction of the colonial myth of Livingstone and the colonial view of the African view of Livingstone – a passive internalisation of imperial propaganda. The discourse of loving hearts sounds the same as in 1874. Looking back at his working life as a district officer in Northern Rhodesia, Dennis Frost wondered in his memoirs why the memory of Livingstone was 'preserved so vividly', why 'Mandala – the one with the spectacles' was not forgotten (Livingstone wore a hat). His enquiries led him to conclude that Livingstone was remembered not just because he was associated with the missionaries who had set up the first schools and hospitals but also because of his reputation for 'gentleness, patience and persistence against all odds', which was unique in the local experience, where 'ruthless and cruelty' were the norm.[40]

There were always personal stories of a meeting and sighting, as the opening quote illustrates. Frost's own particular story was that he had once met an old woman who said that she remembered the time when Livingstone had passed through her village. As a small child, she and her mother had been captured by Arab slavers, and she eventually became the junior wife of her captor. It was possible, Frost concluded, but judged it unlikely. Whatever the reality, as the quote which began this chapter illustrates, many people believed that Livingstone and their ancestors were connected.

Returning to the Heart: The Chitambo Grave after 100 Years

Chitambo had provided the solemn, moving backdrop to the emotional 1973 commemoration of the moment Livingstone had passed away. The location was the spot where Livingstone had died, a site that was presented as virtually unchanged since. The white obelisk, built by Owen Stroud and his men in 1902, still rose out of the bare earthen square cleared by Robert Codrington's labourers in 1899. It had evolved, if that is the correct term, as a place that would be kept separate from the local community and not cater for tourists. The only threats to its aloof status as the most 'historical and solemn monument' in central Africa occurred during the colonial period. The first came from Lieutenant Colonel Sir Stewart Gore Browne, owner of a large estate in Northern Province. And the second came from Amon Kunda, a poor ex-fisherman from Mpika with a history of mental illness.

Born in London in 1883, Gore Browne was part of a distinguished upper-class British imperial family. His grandfather had been governor of New Zealand and Tasmania. Gore Browne went into a rifle brigade after education at Harrow. He worked in Natal and was employed by the Anglo-Belgian Boundary Commission in 1911 when he first visited Northern Rhodesia. In between, he drove racing cars. A heroic survivor of the Western Front, he decided to settle in Northern Rhodesia to recover from the First World War and to fulfil a boyhood ambition of owning and running a large estate and country house.[41] After hearing in 1914 that the BSAC was selling tracts of land cheaply, he visited the area, home to the Bemba. His vision and their labour made it possible. So the estate of Shiwa Ngandu came into being, from the Great North Road. It was an English mansion in a remote part of central Africa. He had a reputation for fairness towards Africans, enjoying a close relationship with his driver, with whom he went on long holidays. Nevertheless, his nickname among his workers was 'Bemba' (for 'rhinoceros', as he had a furious temper). In 1938, he took up political office in the colony's legislative council as the Representative of African Interests, a post he held until 1951, when he began to support the first generation of African nationalist politicians.

Since Chitambo was not that far from his estate, Gore Browne made at least two visits to the monument, once in 1939, and again in 1940.

Newly in his official post, he took it upon himself to conduct a one-man crusade to make the site reflect his particular sentimental view of Livingstone and his paternalist brand of the liberal project of empire in Africa. Gore Browne had been at Chitambo, helping to build a rural dispensary, in 1939. But he had long nourished plans for the site, plans which he had already discussed with the governor.[42] He had strong feelings on a number of points. Most seriously, the monument, in his view, was dilapidated and in need of repair; it was clear that it was beyond the mission station to maintain the upkeep of such an important site. He pointed out that the date of Livingstone's death on the bronze plaque was incorrect. He wanted a perimeter fence to be built around the site. Finally, he wanted the 'hideous' rest house demolished and a new one built to accommodate visitors at the turn-off on the main road, although he did not want it developed for tourists.

Gore Browne 'returned to the attack', as the secretariat put it, in 1941. He fuelled the controversy over the actual date of Livingstone's death, suggesting an additional memorial, rather than just a correction, was needed to mark the centenary of Livingstone's voyage to Africa. The most appropriate form for this, he argued, would be 'the development of welfare work for Africans near the place where his heart was buried'. Gore Browne suggested that a hospital, school and agricultural station be built[43]. He also called for the abolition of the status of game reserve around the site because of the effect of this on the densely populated area. People, not animals, should come first. He claimed that the site still remained in a dilapidated state; a claim which the provincial administration hotly refuted.

This extensive shopping list of changes became the subject of lengthy discussions, interrupted by the war and then reconsidered in 1947. The Livingstonia Mission of the Church of Scotland wanted the arrangements to remain but was overruled by the administration.[44] The local administrator took over its running, setting aside £20 for repairs, but kept costs down by refusing to build new lavatories. Many of Gore Browne's suggestions about providing better services for the local population were rejected. The nearby dispensary would be extended rather than a hospital built. However, a new school was built in 1950, two miles from the site. The status of game reserve was dropped.

Perhaps the first influential white official to spend any length of time at the site, Gore Browne had at least spoken to the local inhabitants. Two further issues had surfaced. The first was the way in which local people were regularly beaten up when passing through the nearby Belgian Congo. This was described as a long history of atrocity, with echoes of the King Leopold era. Few statements survive. One that does was written by

Kesamu Subili, who claimed to have been assaulted repeatedly by Chief Mongo in Lukubi village in the Congo. The Congolese were demanding £1 for the return of his bike, which they also damaged.[45] A second problem was the local chief. Gore Browne asked: 'Should not something be done for the present Chitambo?' He had been deposed because he was absent in the Congo, but for no other reason. As the nephew of Old Chitambo, his restoration would be a 'gracious gesture' and 'a cause of great satisfaction to the old man', who could build a village nearby.[46] This also took place.

Ironically, Gore Browne's African welfare memorial was blocked by local missionaries. As discussions and arguments dragged on throughout the 1940s, the view of the Livingstone dynasty in the area, the Moffats, crystallised into an opposing camp, with supporters in the administration. The area was not overpopulated, they insisted. But the most powerful argument they made was that the rugged loneliness of the site reflected Livingstone's life as a lone spirit, as his family life showed. They also argued the number of tourists visiting was negligible (perhaps about half a dozen per year), due to the extreme remoteness of the place. If better lavatories were built, moreover, as Gore Browne had wished, these would only be used by hunting parties from the Copperbelt, who were already a thorn in the district commissioner's flesh. And finally, they pointed out that the area was in a tsetse zone and considered insalubrious, and the surrounding land extremely flat and boring, so any change was pointless.[47]

Just before the matter was to be finally debated by the executive council, in October 1948, out of the blue came an unprecedented act of vandalism against the treasured monument. The four pillars around it were smashed, the top of the obelisk broken off at a length of three feet and seven trees cut down. The gravekeeper reported that the attack had taken place on the night of 14 October 1948. Suspicion first fell on the previous gravekeeper, who had been sacked the previous year. He had continued to pester the new district commissioner, wanting to be reinstated or given a pension.[48]

The disgraced gravekeeper was saved from being charged when a twenty-year-old man, Aron Kunda, confessed. He refused to make a formal statement but admitted to having bought a chisel and four-pound hammer, borrowed a bicycle and headed for the monument to smash it up. Afterwards, he drank for two days.[49] He was judged as having had 'no motive whatsoever'. The provincial commissioner was furious, regarding this case as another scandalous example of 'criminal half-wits returned to their villages'. He himself had been stalked by an African, he claimed, who had threatened to burn his house down. This man was in his view, like Kunda, mentally unbalanced but regrettably not considered bad enough for the asylum.[50]

Aron Kunda's life story, as it is known up to 1948, is a sad one. His diagnosed depression had possibly been triggered by the death of his mother. He had then moved around, taking up various trades, and had done well but, in his words, he had been bewitched by people jealous of his success. He recovered after receiving medicine from the witchdoctor and again worked itinerantly, before his 'heart went wrong'. He was then in and out of hospital and became violent, smashing windows, fighting with other patients and going to prison. His sister agreed to take him in, but he had another turn, and she became frightened, so her husband took him back home. This is when he decided to break up the Livingstone Memorial.

The monument's desecration prompted a final round of official discussions. This time public opinion was involved, since the vandalism had attracted press coverage. Several local officials thought that it would be a good time to consider a new memorial, as the current design was not particularly good. But the Moffat position prevailed. When the chief secretary reviewed the case again in June 1948, especially the suggestions made by Sir Stewart (knighted in 1945), he concluded that the memorial's present isolation 'should not be interfered with'. It was judged to be a fitting symbol of 'a man whose whole life's achievements were the results of an environment of personal loneliness, isolation from his fellow countrymen, and submerging of self in the surroundings of primitive Africa'.[51] This view prevailed, and the Ancient Monuments Commission decided that no further action would be taken.[52] The monument was restored to what it was previously, except that chains were hung from the pillars and cars blocked from driving down the avenue. It was thus kept as a memorial less to celebrate imperial triumph and achievement, more to acknowledge loss and the experience of isolation and sadness.

The site has remained largely unchanged other than the white monument being encased in black granite in 2014, giving it a slightly sinister feel. It stands in the square clearing, approached by a short avenue of trees, set behind an iron gate and fence. Between two hundred and three hundred visitors every year, mostly white, turn off the Great North Road between Serenje and the Makuku Bridge, which crosses over the Chambeshi River that merges into the extraordinary Bangweulu Swamps, so vast that the earth's curvature can be observed from the single road. Tourists turn off at the sign pointing to Chief Chitambo's Palace and Courthouse, where they can request an audience with the hospitable chief if he is not presiding over local court cases or accusations of witchcraft. They then travel about five miles down a narrow track to Chikundu village. The resident curator from the National Museum shows visitors the plaque marking where Livingstone died, explaining that the tree to the right of the monument is an offshoot of the original *mpundu*. Two young women from the village, in baking heat, sweep the site clear of leaves every day.

It remains a solemn, strange, empty place, but it is not always quiet. Locals tell of strange lights coming from the monument at night. Livingstone's ancestors, it is rumoured, often visit the grave, coming up from the river. Locals also say the site is regularly used by wizards and witches during the hours of darkness. The grave is a favourite spot for their ceremonies and rituals because of its apparently patent magical powers.

Conclusion

Livingstone and the 1973 commemoration had an important political and propaganda role in the early history of Zambia's one-party state at a time of mounting tension within and without. The commemoration offered an opportunity to rebuild lost moral capital, to rally and unify UNIP's Christian support base and to criticise white-minority rule. Critically, Kaunda was forced to rebrand UNIP and disguise the broken political community. It was not just a strategy for strengthening the hold on power by providing the perfect opportunity for the president to publicise his Christian humanism as a legitimate, moral and African alternative to democracy and a multi-party system. Kaunda and his ministers also gingerly launched a strong attack against apartheid South Africa and its aggressive white neighbours, a reminder of the vulnerability felt by anti-apartheid 'front line' states like Zambia. It was this ongoing struggle that led to Livingstone being generously labelled by the regime during this period 'Africa's first freedom fighter'.

As the quote at the beginning of this chapter shows, a sentimental affection for Livingstone pervaded what might be loosely termed the first generation of nationalist Christian Conservatives' view of Livingstone's type of colonial rule. This affection was based on an understanding, or myth, passed on by missionaries, African pastors and juvenile Christian literature, that Livingstone had been generous to Africans, had given them things they had not had – such as Christianity and scientific learning – and had been far kinder than other white men who came afterwards. The former UNIP intelligence officer from Southern Province had a family story about Livingstone and a personal connection.[53] He believed that Livingstone had sat down with his ancestors and given them a rational or modern theory of how the world worked. Kaunda's 1973 ceremony drew on this kind of gratitude and respect, and helped it to survive longer. An important part of the popular memory of Livingstone was that he was not racist but, rather, capable of engaging in everyday intimacies with them: he sat on the ground with them; he ate the same food.

The crisis of 1973 was weathered, and the one-party state was not overthrown, either by white racists or by internal opposition. Kenneth Kaunda only had to accept defeat, finally, in 1991, after twenty-seven years in power (equivalent to the years that Nelson Mandela had been imprisoned). Kaunda had been encouraged to stand down by Julius Nyerere, who had done likewise in Tanzania, in the mid-1980s, but he yielded to public pressure to reinstate multiparty politics. Having retired gracefully, he then tried to make a political comeback, and the constitution was changed to prevent his re-election. He was once detained on a charge of treason, and escaped an attempted assassination. When he announced that his son, Wezi Kaunda, had been murdered, in what he believed to be a political assassination, he publicly wept. He lost another son to HIV/AIDS in 1986 and was the first African leader to go public about the problem and extent of the disease. When I asked Kaunda why Zambians were so fond of Livingstone he paused, looked up with tears in his eyes, and replied, 'Because he was one of us'.[54]

NOTES

1 G. Macola, '"It Means As If We Are Excluded from the Good Freedom": Thwarted Expectations of Independence in the Luapula Province of Zambia, 1964–6', *Journal of African History*, 47 (2006): 43–56, 56.

2 *Daily Nation*, 28 April 1973, ZNA.

3 John Lonsdale, 'Have Tropical Africa's Nationalisms Continued Imperialism's World Revolution by Other Means?' *Nations and Nationalism*, 21, 4 (October 2015): 609–29.

4 Letter dated 4 December 1965, SP1/14/9, ZNA.

5 See discussion below.

6 Author interview, Livingstone, 3 July 2009.

7 On the UPP as an opposition movement, see Larmer, *Rethinking African Politics*, 62–89, and more generally for a political history of Zambia.

8 'Speech by Minister for Southern Province', undated, SP1/14/9, ZNA. Mandala was one of many in government schooled in the colonial tradition. He had published on local government after independence. For an analysis of colonial governance and its interplay with Africa, see David M. Gordon, *Nachituti's Gift: Economy, Society, and Environment in Central Africa* (Madison, WI: University of Wisconsin Press, 2006).

9 Roberts, *A History of Zambia*, 237–45.

10 For a general background, see Andrew DeRoche, 'Non-alignment on the Racial Frontier: Zambia and the USA, 1964–1968', in Sue Onslow (ed.), *Cold War in Southern Africa: White Power, Black Liberation* (London: Routledge, 2009), 130–55.

11 *Daily Mail*, 21 May 1973.
12 'Smith's allies shot Rhodesian – he blamed us', *Daily Nation*, 27 April 1973.
13 'Smith threatens guerilla bases across border', *Daily Nation*, 28 April 1973.
14 'Rhodesia is to blame', *Daily Mail*, 10 May 1973, ZNA.
15 *Daily Mail*, 21 May 1973, ZNA.
16 *Daily Mail*, 22 May 1973, ZNA.
17 'Kazembe's book will sell Zambia to tourists', *Daily Mail*, 2 May 1973, ZNA.
18 Macola, *Liberal Nationalism in Central Africa*.
19 Interview with a community development officer after independence, quoted in Frost, 'Memoirs', 88.
20 Richard Hall, *The High Price of Principles: Kaunda and the White South* (London: Penguin, 1973). See also David G. Coe & Cyril Greenhill, *Kaunda's Gaoler: Memoirs of a District Officer in Northern Rhodesia and Zambia* (London: Radcliffe Press, 2003).
21 Roberts, *A History of Zambia*, 246–7.
22 Kenneth Kaunda, *Letter to My Children* (London: Longman, 1973), 18.
23 Sholto Cross, 'Politics and Criticism in Zambia: A review article', *Journal of Southern African Studies*, 1, 1 (1974): 109–15, 113.
24 The long-standing conflicts within Christian nationalism and humanism as part of this process have been explored by David Gordon in 'Kwacha! Christianity and the Nationalist Imagination in the 1950s', paper presented at the 'Zambia in the 1950s' conference, Leiden University, Netherlands, 25–27 September 2008; and 'Conflicting Visions of Christian Liberation in Post-Colonial Zambia, paper presented at the African Studies Association conference, Washington, D.C., 17–20 November 2011.
25 Kaunda, *Letter to My Children*, 93.
26 Interviews and discussions in Livingstone during the 2013 celebrations suggest that this is still a dominant, albeit fading, view.
27 'Tourists jet in', *Zambian Daily Mail*, 27 April 1973, ZNA.
28 Fred Mule, 'Dr Livingstone remembered', *Zambian Daily Mail*, 30 April 1973.
29 Interview with Chief Chitambo IV, Palace of the Chief, Chitambo, 2 September 2014.
30 *Guardian*, 4 May 1973.
31 *Zambian Daily Mail*, 30 April 1973, ZNA.
32 'Zambia pays tribute to Dr Livingstone on centenary of death', *Times*, 1 May 1973.
33 'An Address by His Excellency the President, Dr Kenneth Kaunda to commemorate the centenary of Dr David Livingstone on 1st May 1973', 1 & 8, ZNA.
34 'Editorial', *Zambian Daily Mail*, 30 April 1973.
35 Roberts, *A History of Zambia*, 196–7.
36 Zambian *Daily Mail*, 2 May 1973.
37 Kaunda address, 5.
38 Fred Mule, 'Dr Livingstone Remembered', *Daily Mail*, 30 April 1973.
39 Kaunda address', 3, 5.
40 Frost, 'Memoirs', 79.

41 Rotberg, *Black Heart*; Christina Lamb, *The Africa House: The True Story of an English Gentleman and His African Dream* (London: HarperCollins, 2005).

42 Note on the Livingstone Memorial and the neighbourhood, Lt Col S Gore Browne, July 1939, SEC1/1717 (1), ZNA.

43 Lt Col S Gore Browne to chief secretary, Lusaka, 18 October 1941. Ibid.

44 Secretary, Church of Scotland, to chief secretary, Lusaka, 13 August 1939, SEC1/1717, ZNA.

45 Statement Signed, 5 July 1939. Ibid.

46 Note on the Livingstone Memorial and the neighbourhood. Lt Col S Gore Browne. July 1939. SEC1/1717 (1). ZNA.

47 Note from S.G. Philips, 17 June 1948. Ibid.

48 C.J.W. Flemming, DC, Serenje to PC, Central Province, Broken Hill, 19 October 1948. Ibid.

49 'Case history of Amon Kunda' sent to Chief Secretary by PC, Central Province, 18 November 1948. Ibid.

50 Covering letter, ibid.

51 Draft of Note on the David Livingstone Memorial at Chitambo, Chief Secretary, June 1948. Ibid.

52 Minute IV, Ancient Monuments Committee Meeting, Ibid.

53 Anonymous respondent to author questionnaire, Lusaka, July 2009.

54 Author interview, Cambridge, 22 August 2005.

7   'Chains of Remembrance'

Livingstone, Sentimental Imperialism and Britain's Africa Conversation, 1913–2013

Finally, we return to the subject of an emotion culture in Britain – a history of a sentimental imperialism sustained by multiple forms of Livingstone memorialisation and studies – from the time of colonial rule, up to the present day. This chapter examines how the Victorian legend of Livingstone lived on in metropolitan discourse through public commemorations and popular biographies. It exposes the incestuous relationship between sentimental feelings towards Livingstone, arguments for empire and imperial propaganda throughout the twentieth century. 1913 was the centenary of Livingstone's birth; 1973, the centenary of his death; and 2013, the bicentenary. At each major milestone, commemorative events, popular biographies and what might loosely be termed Livingstone studies marked a particular anniversary.

They matter because between 1913 and 1973, attitudes towards empire were often softened by feelings of sentimentality, generated and framed by commemorations, books, talks and newspaper coverage focused on Livingstone. An emotional conversation about Livingstone kept the belief alive that the British Empire in Africa was fundamentally humanitarian, built on good race relations and non-violent. Livingstone consistently pumped the beating heart of British liberal imperialism (see Figure 7.1).

Those responsible for this continuity of belief throughout most of the twentieth century were the Livingstone 'experts', mostly men, writing in tribute to a masculine hero, whom they admired, often believing him to be symbolic of a 'lost' ideal of manliness or the past (see Figure 7.2). For some, he offered a nostalgic sojourn into their childhood world and was a personal reminder of their fathers and grandfathers. Their feelings of admiration were more often personal rather than the product of an agenda to deliberately promote empire or mask its excesses. Nevertheless, the 'horrors' of the slave trade Livingstone depicted in his texts and in images, plus his sacrifice (and that of those who came after him), made them emotional about British motives in Africa (see Figure 7.3). The Arab slave trade, the violence depicted against women and children, and

Figure 7.1 'Livingstone: His Message'. All British Picture Company Ltd. Series Four. Undated. Popperfoto / Editorial #: 477862617. Photo by Popperfoto/Getty Images.

so on opened up a natural space to praise the humanitarian motives and ideals of the British Empire in Africa. Many of the Livingstone sentimentalists, whose influence over the voice of imperial liberalism was profound, were Scottish. Often evangelicals or academics, or both, they naturally found in Livingstone's stance, determination and poor background a proud son who epitomised a Scottish self-understanding of being kinder to 'natives', and who was much nicer than the English. Nevertheless, no one could stop Livingstone falling from grace in 1973.

Figure 7.2 American illustration of Henry Morton Stanley greeting Doctor Livingstone. Caption reads: 'Doctor Livingstone, I presume? Said Stanley'. Hulton Archive. Photo by Culture Club/Getty Images.

Livingstone Centenary Celebrations: Imperial Achievements and the 'New Africa' on the Eve of the First World War

The first major British commemoration of Livingstone since his death in 1873 fell forty years later in 1913, the year before the outbreak of the First World War. As one would expect, the growing tensions emanating from Germany and continental Europe gave events a strongly propagandist

Figure 7.3 Depiction of male, female and child captives driven into slavery by Arab slave traders, c.1875. The men are fastened together with slave forks. From *The Life and Explorations of David Livingstone*, c.1875. Hulton Archive. Photo by Ann Ronan Pictures/Print Collector/ Getty Images.

flavour. However, the preoccupations of British central Africa's pioneer settlers in their memorialisations in Livingstone town, as we saw in Chapter Five, were not shared. White settler predicaments were not the medium through which Britain engaged with or understood Africa at this moment.

Rather, it was through a conversation about British liberal progress and her great developmental role in Africa.

An important element was Livingstone's daughter, Anna Mary, who would visit the Chitambo grave in 1915. She featured prominently in the 1913 commemorations, routinely covered in the press, giving events an extra emotional and personal feel. She unveiled a bronze statue of Livingstone on 15 March 1913, at the Livingstone Memorial Church, Blantyre, Scotland, symbolic of the growing importance of Livingstone in the Scottish pantheon of great public figures.[1] The *Daily Telegraph*, one of a number of national newspapers covering the event as a major news story, acknowledged that events in Blantyre were the most important celebrations up and down the country.

The commemoration was a welcome opportunity to air some long-standing domestic tensions. Silvester Horne, a prominent, charismatic Congregationalist and Liberal MP, delivered one of his legendary speeches at the Albert Hall, before an audience of Nonconformist men. They had gathered for a special Livingstone event, under the auspices of the National Brotherhood Federation. Born in England and educated at Mansfield College, Oxford, and at Glasgow University, Horne used the occasion to lambast English universities for letting poverty bar the admission of brilliant students, urging them to 'follow Scotland's lead in that respect'. It reflected, he concluded, 'the invincible snobbishness of the English people'.[2] Nevertheless, many national newspapers took the opportunity to rally readers behind a figure who was the British or English hero of liberal imperialism. They did so through detailed biographical sketches that formed a major part of their coverage. Most, like *The Times*, commented on Livingstone's innate kindliness, honesty and 'instinct for dealing with savages ... not uncommon in men of British stock'. It ended with a reference to his African name, 'Ingeressa', or 'the Englishman', pronouncing without hesitation how well it was 'that the memory of such a life should be bound up with the name of his country'.[3]

Scottish commemorations were different. They enjoyed a particular intimacy and family feel, with many of Livingstone's relations in attendance. In Glasgow, at the 'People's Palace', the event was marked with an exhibition of relics, many donated to the city by Livingstone's children. These included 'native objects' – bows, arrows, spears, swords, beads etc. – but also more emotive items, such as 'an article of pathetic interest': the bowl from which Livingstone ate his last meal.[4] Likewise, the central event was an exhibition held at the Royal Scottish Museum, Edinburgh, which featured Livingstone's maps, clothing, scientific instruments, two bibles, a pencil and, 'most pathetic of all, [are] his little notebooks which he carried to the end'.[5] The effect of this level of connection with his descendants resulted in some extraordinarily emotional speeches, illustrated by the verdict of the United Free Church's retired moderator, in Blantyre, that Livingstone was 'the prince of all explorers. Not only did he explore the heart of Africa, but he also explored the heart of the African'.[6] It was a world and a century away from white settler memorialisations.

'All Scotland is stirred over the centenary of David Livingstone' was how one Scottish journalist described it for an English audience. Livingstone was their ideal missionary, he continued. Other great missionaries, 'she has in plenty', but

that dour, silent man of indomitable will, simple, brave and self-sacrificing, has captured her affection and aroused her imagination. Today was 'Livingstone Sunday' and from most of the pulpits in all the cities and great town, the villages and rural parishes, and in their Sunday schools, the subject of the sermon and the school lesson was 'Livingstone, his work and his ideal.[7]

Scottish events took on a real celebratory and party feel. In Greenock, a mass gathering of schoolchildren, boy scouts, schoolteachers and distinguished speakers heard shipping magnate Arthur Cairn describe Livingstone as 'a great missionary, a great explorer; and a great Scotsman. (Applause)'. In Aberdeen, 'a meeting for lads' took place, designed for the Boys Brigade, Boy Scouts and any other male apprentices and lads. The address was given by the Reverend Donald Fraser; other speakers at the various events were also renowned Livingstone specialists, who similarly would go on to write popular biographies, such as M'Lean Watt and James Buchanan.[8]

Scottish events were also practical in design as well as nationalistic. One agenda was humanitarian, raising money for the Livingstone Memorial Fund to fund medical work in central Africa and to train medical missionaries in Scotland. The number of different churches working together was unprecedented. A 'united missionary meeting' was held in the evening in Glasgow, with representatives from Scottish and English missions – including the LMS – the judiciary, the university senate and the Royal Faculty of Physicians and Surgeons. Messages from Booker Washington and King Khama of Bechuanaland were read out, indicative of the international polyphony of this African humanitarian imperialism.[9] Another practical purpose was to counter media criticism of missionary work. A favourite device was to stress Livingstone's hardships and tragic death using the trope of suffering: 'in order to penetrate through darkest Africa ... to bring the light of Christianity and civilization to the natives. (Applause)'.[10] Here, also, was an opportunity to deny claims Livingstone was a mere traveller. This accusation was refuted, with a repeated stress that it was not fame, greed or power that had drawn Livingstone back to 'the dark continent' but his call from a higher command 'to suppress finally slavery or to die in the attempt'.[11]

People in Scotland were less interested in events in England, which was just as well, for there was much taking place that would have angered them. In some ways, official arrangements took a similar turn as they had done when Livingstone's corpse had returned in 1874. 'Cold shoulder from the Foreign Office', was how Wales's premier newspaper, the *Western Mail*, described the main official commemoration for the anniversary, an event held at the Royal Albert Hall with an address by the Archbishop of Canterbury. Asquith, the prime minister, had sent apologies in a note in which he commented that Livingstone's memory would never perish. This was judged by some to be more annoying than a compliment. According to Sir Harry Johnston, an old colonial hand from central Africa's early days and an arch imperialist, the government had failed to publish many of the letters that Livingstone had sent to them during his fifteen years in their service; this 'cold shoulder' reflected the decreased interest in the opening up of Africa'.[12] This was taken up by the *Daily Mail*, which headlined with Sir Harry's accusation: 'state neglect of a hero'.[13] His 'corrective acid' centred on the government and press's continual neglect and devaluation of missionaries. The lack of recognition of such a hero made Sir Harry feel ashamed to possess a knighthood. He added Charles Booth and Dr Barnado to the list of humanitarians who had been neglected by the honours system.[14]

Sir Harry, part of a London-based elite with influence, was one of the dominant voices heard throughout the 1913 commemorations, now that Henry Morton Stanley was deceased. He would give talks to the main geographical societies up and down the country: In Manchester, he was introduced as 'a worthy successor to Livingstone'. He offered a personal (and very British) link of his own to try to compete with Scotland's intimacy with Livingstone: he claimed to have been carried, when in the Congo with Stanley, by the same 'stalwart native' who had carried Livingstone.

The task of an imperial mission being passed down to the next generation, and everyone being part of the same imperial parentage, if not family, were at the fore of these high Anglican-Livingstone memorialisations. Sir Harry stressed that his own work in central Africa, as well as that of Cecil Rhodes, aided by the 'large mindedness' of Lord Salisbury, all stemmed from Livingstone's journals. He also praised Manchester and its industry for 'opening out' Africa with a policy of 'peaceful development of the world' (perhaps a reflection of the storm clouds gathering over Europe).[15] Lord Curzon (arguably India's greatest and most patrician viceroy) and Henry Morton Stanley's widow, Lady Dorothy, were among guests at the RGS's event. Lord Curzon described Livingstone and the 'grandeur' of his work, in the language of the times, as 'an inspiration to our race'. Born without social advantages, with few prospects and with no powerful backers, Livingstone had nevertheless 'hewed his way through the world' because of a combination of 'boldness … fertility … courage … noble endurance in suffering … self-sacrifice to the death'.[16]

Injecting increased emotion and sentimentality into the conversation was Lady Dorothy's very personal contribution: she had found a draft of a lost letter from Stanley to Livingstone on the day after Stanley had torn himself away. It showed a young man full of 'true emotion', so affectionate and lonely that 'the idea of service uniting him to Livingstone' was sincere, she insisted. Its romantic tenderness may have been why Stanley had chosen to withhold it, for in metaphysical sonnet form, he wrote: 'Though I am not present to you bodily, you must think of me daily … Though you are not before me visibly, I shall think of you constantly … in this way the chain of remembrance will not be severed'.[17] The words must have been delivered with heavy emotion considering her own bereavement. The headline 'Stanley's affection for Livingstone: Pangs of Parting' put it mildly. By now, Stanley's Welsh origins were common knowledge. The *Western Mail* drew its readers in with a reminder that David Livingstone had been found by a Welshman, that Stanley's characteristics were more Celtic than Teutonic and that Wales's own Griffith John had found similar success in China, working as a missionary and translator.[18]

A universal empire of sentiment was unfolding, it seems, for according to the press, 'people of all classes, from the highest to the lowest' were uniting to pay homage, all over the world, on an imposing scale. London events included a multi-denominational choir singing the Livingstone Cantata at the Albert Hall; a prayer service at the grave in Westminster Abbey in the forenoon; on the Saturday, 'a demonstration by a National Brotherhood', a Nonconformist federation, where it was announced that, in the past week, 2,500 meetings of men and women had taken place to draw inspiration; and, on 26 March, at St Paul's Cathedral, the lord mayor attended a service with the Bishop of Winchester and representatives from the City.[19] Nationwide, churches and halls held celebrations, or demonstrations as they were called; the LMS's Livingstone Memorial Fund was also popularised; *The Times* advertised an appeal by the Sudan United Mission in London to address the alarming situation that there were 'at least 50 pagan tribes' without a missionary. The Archbishop of Canterbury endorsed the appeal as a 'sacred obligation', hoping that the centenary 'may be widely used as an occasion of stimulating a public sense of our responsibility' in this regard, especially in central Africa.[20] Lord and Lady Gladstone were leading celebrations in Cape Town; Cambridge was hosting a special event; and the US president had sent a cable of congratulation.

As in Scotland, there were strange effusions from men, overcome with emotion as they recalled reading about Livingstone's bravery and sacrifice when they were boys, perhaps tinged with nostalgia for fathers and grandfathers long passed. The Archbishop of Canterbury described how Livingstone made 'the very fibre of the nation tingle with his quiet heroism', for he possessed 'illimitable energy ... unrivalled, dogged perseverance' and he had 'a devouring love for his fellow men'.[21] Silvester Horne also got carried away at the Albert Hall. Livingstone, he argued, apparently 'threw the spell of his personality wherever he went'; 'the aroma ... the fragrance of his influence' were still felt by Africans today; they were 'wild in their philosophy' but 'in his fidelity he was sublime'.[22] The audience lapped it up.

The Reverend Dan Crawford, one of the first white men to journey to the grave, was in the audience at the Albert Hall when he experienced a life-changing epiphany.[23] Crawford was also contributing to the many commemorative pieces contained in church publications and missionary journals. *The Christian* included a lecture from Crawford in January 1913, which contained a highly personal reflection, stressing the depth of affection Africans felt for Livingstone. He drew on evidence from his visit to Chitambo. Missionaries were often mocked for being of the 'soft type', he claimed. Livingstone was a Mr Softy but 'armed to the teeth with the tones of command'. He was remembered as 'Mr He-hath no toes', 'Mr He Sleeps on the waves' and 'Mr Dew Dryer'. Arabs remembered him for his hearty laugh.[24] The reminiscences of a sailor who had shared a sea voyage with Livingstone also circulated. He recalled a man 'so much beloved' by 'the natives', with wonderful eyes, 'keen with a twinkle of humour ... his soul shone through'. It was less what he said than how he said it: 'It was his apparent mastery of 'native tongues' that had won him such respect. Livingstone was also portrayed as the grieving widower: his wife's death had 'left him a broken man'.[25]

A big worry for the generation that had established colonial rule in Africa was that there was now a generation 'that did not know him'. So, many newspapers published short biographies. The most detailed, sentimental and illustrated of these was the *Daily Telegraph*'s souvenir page of 19 March 1913. This sketched out Livingstone's work in 'darkest Africa', his noble career, his meeting with Stanley, his great personality and his life lived without fear. It also lingered on the 'Last Scene of All', when

Susi had come into the hut and 'touched Livingstone's cheek with his dusky finger'. Readers were invited to imagine what thoughts had gone through his mind.[26] The tender, kind, macho Livingstone was framing Britain's conversation about its imperial mission in Africa.

It was a vision with little space for African contributions. There was barely mention of the role of Livingstone's African followers in his achievements. *The Times* did, however, discuss how his followers had honoured him in death by carrying his body, but this was negatively interpreted: the response of the African natives, 'usually so changeable and inconsequent in their moods', was merely a testimony to Livingstone's influence.[27] Repeatedly, it was his character that was stressed or his capacity for endurance – 'an example of the purest Celtic type', according to the Duke of Argyll in a published article.

Likewise, the emotionalism of Livingstone's death and burial was repeated. The powerful effect of Livingstone's funeral was recalled by many newspapers. It led to the 'sorrowing admiration of an entire people', according to Curzon. Moreover, the 'outburst of sorrow' once his death became known, and after his 'solemn burial in Westminster Abbey', was credited with sparking a national effort to 'carry out the last wish of his heart, the abolition of the slave trade'.[28] Patriotism was in the air: Livingstone was a man 'for whom the world cannot be too thankful ... It is the centenary of a great pioneer, a great gentleman, and a great man'.[29] It was inevitable that the focus of this popular coverage remained on character and national achievement in the nervous atmosphere of 1913. Yet for some, it was the moral resolve of the world's conscience that was wavering, as evidenced by the Congo atrocities and continuing Portuguese slavery: was 'England devoid of her ancient credit and tradition?', asked the Tartan-phile Silvester Horne. Liberals stressed a man who stood for 'peace, goodwill and brotherhood between races and man', as 'Europe lay under the shadow of Armageddon'.[30]

However, the commemoration was ultimately a conversation about Britain's positive imperial role in Africa. Again and again, coverage ended in a very positive (and unrealistic) declaration of belief in the transformatory power of British colonial rule. Lord Curzon had insisted that 'Africa had changed since Livingstone's day beyond all human recognition', with settled territories and demarcated frontiers replacing 'lawlessness and inter-tribal warfare'.[31] Not just a European interest, he continued, it was now nearly a possession. A long editorial in *The Times* on 13 March was pure propaganda, announcing confidently that 'a new Africa had arisen ... thanks in great measure to his [Livingstone's] own wonderful achievements'. Typically, he had struggled through 'pathless wastes', but there were now 'thriving settlements'. He had walked through 'the dark

places of Africa' and won the cooperation of 'the savage tribes'. In exposing the horrors of the slave trade and stirring up the public conscience,
Livingstone had laid the 'foundations of the new Africa'.

Yet few concerned themselves in any precise way with this 'new Africa'.
One exception was a long piece in the *Glasgow Herald*, on 'Nyasaland:
Then and Now'. White exploration and missionary pioneering were the
'then'; the 'now' was a tour of the new towns, Zomba and Livingstone,
with their churches, nearby estates and bustling markets. Contemporary
Africans did appear, either on macadam roads – with 'shy looks and
naked bodies', coming from the distant interior – or as self-confident
mine workers with pockets full of money, wearing dull European suits.
Not surprisingly, the Reverend Donald Fraser's account ended optimis-
tically: 'A community of a million souls has entered into a new era of
settled peace and constant progress'.[32] It was only Lord Balfour who
turned to Africa and considered the reality of white settlement for race
relations. In one of the many speeches at the three-hour Albert Hall
commemoration, he informed the audience that it was all very well to
honour pioneering exploration, but contact between black and white
peoples 'raised many problems'. Without elaborating, he called on governments and missionaries to work harder and more closely together in
regard to 'the problems of white and black'.[33] His words clearly fell on
deaf ears.

The Twentieth-Century Genre of Victorian Inspirational Biography

The First World War intervened in the normal running of empire, suck-
ing up more African manpower and materials, before yielding to a par-
simonious peace dividend for colonies, which in turn folded into the
Great Depression. But continuity in the form of an imperial sentimentality about the liberal humanitarian mission in Africa was maintained
throughout, in large part due to an emotion culture around Livingstone.
Carrying on the late Victorian and early Edwardian conversations about
Britain and its project of empire were not just Livingstone commemorations but the genre of 'inspirational biography'. This remains an
important area within the large, amorphous field of Livingstone studies. Inspirational biography was the most important factor in delaying
serious consideration of the mythic aspects and propagandising effect of
writing on Livingstone, which in turn was a brake on critically assessing
Britain's record in Africa and its use of force in the colonies.

Livingstone boasts one of the numerous diverse collections of biographical works over time, geographies and types of author. The most significant

are religious-inspired, Scottish nationalistic publications, or the male professor oeuvre, subgenres that often overlap. They reflect well the polyphony of interest groups about empire more generally, and the way in which highly personal and emotional views of Livingstone fed into a positive view of empire more generally. Until the decline in Sunday school and church attendance in Britain from the 1960s, most British men and women would have been exposed, within a Christian teaching framework, to an inspirational biography written for children. Livingstone's and empire's popular endorsement required less sustained input from the press as a consequence.

One of the early popular publications in this field, was C.T. Bedford's *Livingstone of Africa: Heroic Missionary, Intrepid Explorer and **the Black Man's Friend*** (my emphasis). Published first in 1925, it is replete with upper-class idioms of the day (from 'rascals' to 'queer little collections' to 'wretched') and provides more details about Livingstone's pets than his followers. It ran to fifty-nine pages and multiple editions, and contained maps and illustrations, emphasising adventure, exoticism and bravery. Bedford did not hold back from terrifying young readers with horror stories about cannibals and the slave trade, describing one area as 'a valley of dry bones', with dead slaves at every turn, skeletons tied to trees, women stabbed to death along the path and children lying abandoned in chains.[34]

Livingstone was but one figure, of course. The book was part of a series, Seeley's Missionary Lives for Children, and there were many others like it. The Missionary Library for Boys and Girls had a Livingstone book in its collection alongside other titles, including *Barbrooke Grubb, Pathfinder* (often described as the Livingstone of South America) and *Missionary Heroines of the Cross*. Performing the same function were the adult versions, in series such as Remarkable Missionary Books. An author of numerous books in this genre was the Right Reverend Donald Fraser, a Scottish missionary. Alongside his *Winning a Primitive People* was *Africa Idylls: People and Places in Nyasaland*, advertised with an enticing quote from a review in *The Scotsman*: 'This book is the black man in flesh and blood interpreted by a man of vision and of an understanding heart'. But, unlike his fellow 'remarkables', Livingstone's biographies went far beyond the juvenile missionary and missionary hero literature.

Scottish evangelicalism and liberal thought found expression through genre. The most influential and most copied inspirational work, penned as an act of memorialisation, was that by arch biographer the Reverend Professor William Garden Blaikie. He set the standard for male emotional disinhibition towards Livingstone and stands as a towering example of the power of such an authorial voice available to Livingstone, being Nonconformist-evangelical, Scottish and respected as a theological scholar, publishing many books.[35] Blaikie was a socialist and committed to social reform for the poor, one of his titles being *Better Working Days for Working People*. He was a philanthropist and temperance campaigner. His approach to writing about Livingstone was highly sentimental, emotional and intimate, partly because he had known Livingstone, had been bred in the same tradition of the Free Church of Scotland and was a Scottish patriot (he also wrote for the influential Famous Scots series), but also because he had a strong evangelical bent (he had hosted Dwight L. Moody, the American evangelical and pancultural revivalist, in Scotland). He also had experience of newspaper journalism. He wrote in his 'Personal History' of Livingstone that when death, 'with all its touching circumstances, became known', an 'electric spark seemed to fly, quickening hearts on every side ... the statesman felt it ... the merchant ... the explorer'.[36]

Many subsequent inspirational biographies repeated this 'thrill' in relation to attitudes towards the slave trade, often quoting Blaikie, directly or indirectly. In *Livingstone the Pioneer* (typically given as a Sunday school award for biblical knowledge), Starritt explained, in a chapter on 'HIS IMMORTALITY', that because a final appeal on behalf of the victims of slavery came, in Blaikie's words, 'not from the living voice but from his tomb, it should gather from *a thousand touching associations* [my emphasis] a thrilling power that would rouse the world and finally root out the accursed thing'.[37] Quoting from Blaikie, it was as if a 'parliament of philanthropy' had met, Starritt stressed. The religious biography was an evangelical text, with the dual purpose of shoring up Christian commitment among ordinary working people and encouraging overseas missionary humanitarianism.

The Scottish inspirational biographies often contained a powerful but quiet celebration of Scottish achievement, alongside advancing liberal thought on race and colonialism. James MacNair's *Livingstone the Liberator* (1940) was one of the last tartan bursts of classic hero worship.[38] It contained a long, detailed chapter – 'Boy and Student' – on Livingstone's upbringing, which stressed how he considered himself a Highlander. This inheritance was listed positively, of course: he had inherited an impulsive generosity, imagination and fire and 'an instinctive understanding of African tribal ways'. From his lowland ancestors, he had inherited 'determination, hatred of oppression, a self-reliant practical temper, and a sense of humour'. It was his lowly, humble origins which were presented in effect as the spring of his superior morality and of his lifelong adherence to staying in his place: 'my own order, the godly poor'.

By the 1940s, any such biography wanting to keep within the tradition of liberalism would now have to address what Africa was, both then and now. MacNair illustrates well how Victorian thinking still dominated views on Africa: Africa had no history until outsiders arrived – either Arabs penetrating or European thrusting into the continent. Likewise, racial categorising was still highly derogatory and narrowing, with Livingstone credited with a lifelong attachment to the Bantu, who were 'of higher type that the Hottentot, a people when chance of development is given them, of considerable mental powers' but still 'a child race, naturally superstitious and capable at times of acts of great cruelty'. Naturally, Arab slavery and Boer aggression were criticised, contrasting with the young Livingstone, whose 'sympathies were entirely with the African'; he was a man who 'never feared to speak his mind'. One of the most measured yet sympathetic biographical studies to date is generally agreed to be Reverend Andrew Ross's *David Livingstone: Mission and Empire*.[39] Making a plea for balance, Ross, a Scotsman and scholar, used his lifetime of study of Livingstone's writings, particularly his letters, to create an empathetic picture of his tragic life. Livingstone's private dreams and inner feelings are contrasted with the reality created by the greed and cruelty of others and an empire for which he was not responsible. Here, the key dynamic was the romanticised notion of passion – the passion of faith and theological certainty.

Livingstone biographies, written and published over the century, were often very similar, some of the lighter ones borrowing from the more hefty tomes. Similar arguments were repeated, and the genre was a key diffuser of conservative attitudes to empire. The Livingstone inspirational biography was also the domain of the retired professor. A significant number turned a lifelong passion into serious books or biographies, often in retirement. That was not the excuse for Professor Sir Reginald Coupland, Beit Professor of Commonwealth History, All Souls College, Oxford. His 1945 publication, *Livingstone's Last Journey*, was not just the product of a boyhood fascination. He had been knighted for services to the British Empire as an adviser on Palestine in the 1930s and on the constitutional crisis in India during the Second World War. In 1923, he had written a biography of William Wilberforce and was one of the first British historians to take the British Anti-Slavery Movement seriously, ensuring that its archives were deposited in Oxford – at Rhodes House, interestingly. Coupland took a Whiggish approach. Anti-slavery had been the cornerstone of the British Empire, justifying that empire and proving Britain's moral leadership in world history. Writing about Livingstone was an extension of his own career in the empire and a chance to take his views to a wider audience.

However, patient acceptance of a positive imperialistic view was beginning to run out. G.B. Masefield, in the *Uganda Journal*, reviewed the book in 1947. A former agricultural officer, educated at Winchester College and at Balliol College, Oxford, Masefield fell into the liberal tradition of colonial officials. The book had irritated him. Pleased on the one hand that in the 'age of debunking', Livingstone emerged still 'as the greatest Briton who ever worked in Africa', Masefield criticised Coupland for neglecting to include details about the people and culture Livingstone had mixed with, and for failing to use oral evidence, since there were those alive who remembered figures such as Livingstone and Stanley.[40]

Coupland died suddenly before a rival appeared. Frank Debenham, OBE, Emeritus Professor of Geography, Cambridge University, had used the latest print technologies in 1955 to produce a biography framed by the death, illustrated throughout with maps, copies of drawings done by Livingstone or facsimiles of photographs. The tragic romance of this Christian love story, *The Way to Ilala: David Livingstone's Pilgrimage*, was published to coincide with the centenary anniversary of Livingstone's siting and naming of the Victoria Falls in Zambia in 1955. Debenham also wrote a long introduction to the Rhodes-Livingstone Museum's Centenary Exhibition guide.[41]

Although Debenham's tone was sober and unsensationalist, it was certainly imitative of the genre of manly geographical adventure, as his chapter 'Swamps of Destiny' evidences. But by this time, no serious biographer could sidestep the mounting criticism of Livingstone – his desertion of his family, his mental derangement, his guilty conscience and his self-inflicted martyrdom. Debenham delicately tackled the issue of why Livingstone could travel for years with slave dealers. Comparing him with 'a queer character' whom he once met in the Kalahari, who was a shy, eccentric recluse, Debenham had two solutions when tacking Livingstone's shortcomings, the first of which was to blame Africa: Livingstone's behaviour had been a consequence of 'his African experience, working upon a mind which was inclined to mysticism'. The second solution was not to dwell on them. Since the whole biography was framed as *Pilgrim's Progress* meets *Heart of Darkness*, with extracts from Bunyan beginning every chapter, and a death tinged with failure and disappointment, ultimately Livingstone survives as a sympathetic figure, on a doomed but spiritual mission.

In 1957 came the publication of a biography written by a medical doctor and academic, Michael Gelfand, funded by the BSAC.[42] Gelfand cleverly stressed the medical side of Livingstone's explorations, including his willingness to treat Africans and use local medical knowledge, plants and mixtures: Livingstone the pioneer of alternative remedies was born, the friend to Africans recycled. White-minority rule in southern Africa desperately needed to align itself with soft, paternal-racial rule. New angles were also supplemented with new sources presented by academics, through huge amounts of edited letters, journals, expedition notes and correspondence. From the 1940s through into the 1950s, Professor J.P.R. Wallis published edited collections concerning the contributions of men on the Zambezi expedition and the Moffat missionary dynasty, all of which involved Livingstone.[43]

The London School of Economics and Political Science (LSE) was also part of the continual replenishing of Livingstone studies. The distinguished anthropologist Professor Isaac Schapera collected, edited and introduced huge amounts of Livingstone material from 1959 to 1974. This refreshed the databank and made available for a new generation primary sources outside the official archives. According to Andrew Roberts, Schapera 'led the way in rescuing Livingstone studies from hero-worship and hagiography'.[44] For example, Schapera edited and introduced *Livingstone's Missionary Correspondence, 1841–1856* (1961), a collection of letters that Livingstone had written to the directors of the LMS while living and working in southern Africa. Schapera himself was an expert on the anthropology of the region. Yet the book's subtitle was pure Victorian: *Dawn of Mercy on a Dark Land.*

Nevertheless, Schapera undertook a forensic analysis of the 'voluminous correspondent, who needed neither encouragement nor exhortation to write', he archly commented, exposing his recurring tendentiousness.[45] He also pinpointed two character flaws in Livingstone, namely his meanness (towards his colleague Edwards) and his propensity to 'recall events differently from the way in which they occurred' – for example, his decision to go off travelling into the Kalahari had been made before he found the lack of converts frustrating. As Schapera concluded, the generally accepted narrative of Livingstone the missionary was 'more pious than accurate. He was too great a man to need being treated in such a way'.[46] Schapera called for 'future biographers to re-examine aspects of his character and history'.

The End of the Love Affair: Britain and the 1973 Commemorations

That re-examination finally came around the centenary of Livingstone's death, which fell roughly a decade after Britain lost her empire in Africa. It was a time when newly independent colonies were embracing one-party state authoritarianism, and when Rhodesia and South Africa were using all-out violence to maintain white supremacy. Yet there was little political fallout or national recrimination.

In Scotland, Livingstone commemorations were less problematic, for two reasons. First, memorialisation had been cultivated through the image of a great Scotsman, who at least behaved better than the English in Africa. Second, imperial mission had been tied tightly to the involvement of the Church of Scotland, which had divested into grass-roots development and aid to Malawi. These helped insure the 'special relationship' with Livingstone against the disinterest and more destructive mood taking hold in England. Scottish church services were to be televised in Scotland. The Christian Council of World Mission, in collaboration with the Church of Scotland, was producing a memorial wallet containing photographs and facsimiles of letters written by Livingstone.

Further south, events were more muted. Since 1913, Livingstone commemorations had been very slowly diminishing in number and scale. In the 1920s, it was left to the missionary organisations to mark the fiftieth anniversary of Livingstone's death. Many, in line with the mood behind the League of Nations and the growing social and welfare activities of professional charities, stressed Livingstone as a man of peace in the commemorative pamphlets.[47] The 1930s were fairly quiet unless there was the anniversary of the death of someone who knew him, a recollection of someone who knew him, or the discovery of a new letter. The *Christian World*, for example, reported the death of Matthew Wellington, in June 1935, as the loss of 'The Last Link with Livingstone'. In 1938, *Chambers Christian Journal* republished the recollections of his daughter, Agnes.[48] One exception was in 1953, when a new statue to Livingstone was unveiled at the RGS headquarters in Kensington. Guest of honour was Rt Hon Oliver Lyttleton, Secretary of State for the Colonies in the new Churchill government. He looked back to his forbears, quoting Lord Curzon's view of Livingstone as having opened the door of Africa to the outside world.[49] With the Mau Mau being brutally suppressed at the time, in full knowledge of the British authorities in London, there was no lingering over liberal paternalism or humanitarian sentiment.

Unsurprisingly, given that Britain had handed over colonial power in the 1960s, when the time came in 1973 to mark the hundredth anniversary of Livingstone's death, national events were more scaled down. The RGS put on an exhibition, and a supplement to Livingstone was published in the *Methodist Recorder*, but generally, national newspapers devoted few column inches to his life and commemorative events. Only a few covered details of the three major ceremonies, in Blantyre, Chitambo and Westminster Abbey. Likewise, the two major national commemorative initiatives hardly registered. Both took place in Scotland. One was a

£250,000 appeal by the Livingstone National Memorial Trust to extend the Blantyre Museum, which incorporated the tenement block that housed Livingstone's birthplace. A recreational complex was planned, to include a jetty, boathouse and ski slope, that would be an addition to the African pavilion, where artefacts and Livingstone memorabilia were kept. It seems that the anniversary was being used to improve the leisure facilities for local people, a somewhat tenuous link with Livingstone.[50]

A second, instrumental approach can be identified in the attempt to link Livingstone's liberal humanitarianism with official overseas development. Strathclyde University was to open a David Livingstone Institute of Overseas Development Studies with an annual lecture (Livingstone studied at Anderson's College, which Strathclyde had absorbed). Professor Robert Gardiner, executive secretary of the United Nations Economic Commission for Africa, connected Livingstone with modern development, claiming 'Livingstone foresaw the idea of helping developing countries and tried to help Africans with technology and agriculture'. The aid department of the Colonial Office had been changed to Overseas Development after African independence. Livingstone offered a still needed opportunity to stress the humanitarian tradition of British intervention in Africa, bypassing colonial rule. Gardiner called for more appropriate technology and agricultural systems, more Africanisation and a closing of the growing gap between African economies and the provision of infrastructure. Worthy it certainly was; exciting it was not.

Professor Gardiner also spoke at the main national commemorative event, in May 1973 at Westminster Abbey. According to Dennis Baker, reporting for *The Guardian*, 'the imperial past' was all but banished, as representatives from the British high commissions were present; only some of the missionaries, most over forty, with grey hair, 'had a patrician flavour'.[51] Baker drew a distinction between explorers who were slave traders and fortune hunters, motivated by 'ruthless greed', and Livingstone, the missionary, scientist and humanitarian. Aside from the subtle defence of British liberal colonialism, Gardiner's only political statement was a vague call to end the violence being waged in parts of Africa. Thus there was no mention of apartheid South Africa, white-minority rule or racism.

Although writing for a left-wing newspaper, Baker was still enabling his readership to subscribe to the rose-tinted, chocolate-box view of Britain's imperial record. He expressed a generation's relief and discreet pride that Livingstone was not subjected to the 'unfashionable taint of colonialism'. As a retired senior colonial official put it, after his experience of trying to find work around this time, popular attitudes were such that any mention of being a colonial administrator 'conjured up images of Blimp-like figures who thrashed the natives' whilst arousing 'the collective conscience of ordinary people who had become accustomed to being ashamed of their previous colonial heritage'.[52]

The 1973 centenary of Livingstone's death did not resonate with a national mood or shape a new cultural politics as in 1874. Yet it was not absent either. A remarkably upbeat and quirky coverage of the anniversary in the *Daily Mail* took the form of a seventeen-part daily cartoon strip series about Livingstone's life. Over three weeks, Gary Keane and Neville Randall wrote and illustrated a daily 'FOCUS ON LIVINGSTONE'. The story of Livingstone's life was outlined in some detail, with sketches from well-known illustrations, and included Mary, a line of Africans in chains, maps and an image of Susi. Fast-moving and factual, probably aimed at a younger readership, it followed a typical Victorian narrative of heroism and lacked precision; for example, Livingstone apparently 'died alone in a grass hut, in an unknown, unadministered area of Africa – The modern state of Malawi'; the drawing of him wearing a white nightshirt at the side of a bed for 1 May, 4 a.m., ran with: 'CHUMAN [sic] and SUSI entered the hut. Livingstone was kneeling by his bed as though in prayers. His cheeks were cold. "Great Master was dead"'.[53] Yet not even the *Daily Mail* stuck faithfully to the orthodox superhuman Victorian heroic view. The Livingstone story was now more complex in the telling, although not problematised as a figure through which to conduct any post-imperial 'reckoning'.

Livingstone 'Found Out'

The big media story of the 1973 centenary were the biographies now exposing Livingstone's flawed character. 'Chilly, crusty and domineering' and convinced that he was right about everything were just some of the 'Not what we presumed' headline details in a review of a book on missionaries by Geoffrey Morehouse.[54] Readers were told how Livingstone had 'boasted' that he never followed another man's orders; how he had deluded himself into believing he was following God's orders, when in reality he was simply pursuing his own wish to explore; and how he had harboured petty hatred towards other men. However, beyond that, readers were not forced to consider anything negative about either colonial or white-minority rule other than Livingstone's 'unpleasant foibles'. Moreover, a review of the same book in the *Daily Mirror* found that the image of Livingstone as told by the spinster Sunday school teacher of childhood was more or less intact. Livingstone's only sin was that he had preferred exploration to missionary work. It was even understandable that he had packed off his 'tiresome wife and four children' so that they would not cramp his style.[55]

The 1973 commemorations came to be dominated by 'Livingstone Revealed'. 'Found Out!' and 'Feet of clay' were the headlines which were being fed by a number of new biographies or special collections on Livingstone. There was an almost palpable rejoicing and rush to acknowledge Livingstone's flaws – an act of fairly circumscribed contrition, perhaps a using Livingstone as a fall guy for postcolonial guilt. Richard Hall, in *The Observer*, focused on Tim Jeal's 'dazzling' biography, which would cause 'a gnashing of teeth' in rectories up and down the land.[56] Jeal's book, as already discussed, was an iconoclastic exposé of the 'myth' of Livingstone. Many critics jumped on Jeal's reporting of Livingstone's poor treatment of his wife and family and, as Hall put it, his 'less than Christian' attitude towards his fellow white explorer-travellers. Cantankerous and intolerant, 'he almost broke the heart of artist Thomas Baines', accusing him of stealing, charges which were proved groundless. Hall did include Professor George Shepperson's centenary verdict that stressed a man who 'loved Africa' and 'loved Africans', getting on much better with them. For all of Livingstone's liberalism, Hall concluded that he had backed the intervention of Britain's superior civilisation, white settlement and British businessmen in Africa, believing the latter to be the most 'upright and benevolent in the world'.[57] Yet the review ultimately exonerated British colonial liberalism, agreeing that the 'slightly dotty' Livingstone had campaigned against the slave trade and the Devil, and remained in the Victorian consciousness.

For many at the liberal centre of the political spectrum, Livingstone was now the tragic hero, his soul tormented by a continent that had not become Christian and his reputation as a great explorer now in doubt. Livingstone's tragedy was the tragedy of empire: good intentions, much sacrifice, then a few wrong turns. In this conversation, at this time, the sentimentalising of the tragic hero out of his depth was still possible, while dispensing with any self-congratulation about the imperial past. Yet there was no serious probing of the implications of that intervention or of colonial rule in general. By pinning on Livingstone the mistakes of a misjudged past, Britain could well feel satisfied it was dealing critically with that past. Thus Jeal and others in 1973 were making crucial interventions at that time that had the effect of helping postcolonial Britain deal as painlessly as possible with its colonial past in Africa by allowing readers to position themselves as critical of Livingstone the reality but not the ideals. The anniversary did not lead to further discussion of Africa's economic or political situation in the seventies.

However, the left-wing *Daily Mirror* was more brutal: 'Saint' or 'a prize bungler?' Their coverage only stretched to announcing a BBC documentary made to mark the anniversary – 'Livingstone Lost and Found' – which used new evidence. Livingstone's single convert had lapsed, the paper chirped, and his second expedition had been a complete disaster.[58] It was a theme that others followed. The *Geographical Magazine* published a long piece on 'Livingstone the obstinate explorer', advertised as a reappraisal of the legend to commemorate his death. Again, his character flaws and failures were the story – difficult to get along with, failing to find the source of the Nile, refusing to follow basic geographical common sense – but these were mitigated with sentimentality, wrapped up in a tragic love story: 'He chose to stay and die in the Africa he loved'.[59] *The Times*, too, following the same trend, published a long extract from Timothy Severin's *The African Adventure*. The focus of the extract was Livingstone, as the giant of the six Victorian explorers Severin covered. Again, it was an exposé of Livingstone's flaws, also including the way he disobeyed his missionary society and showed himself incapable of commanding a large expeditionary force. Yet he seemed to have a magnetism and hold over a number of powerful men, from financial backers at home to slave dealers and chiefs. The extract ended on the sensational parts of the story that were intact: the powerful effect of the 'macabre splendour' of the African embalmment and the burying of the 'desiccated remains' in a funeral service 'that bordered on the imperial'.[60]

Livingstone-bashing looked set to continue. Victoria Brittain, left-wing journalist and campaigner against white-minority rule in southern Africa, reviewed a biography of Livingstone by Judith Listowel, *The Other Livingstone*, in 1974. Brittain seems to have found the author as equally interesting as, if not more so than, the book. Listowel was a pioneer feminist in some ways, who had studied at the LSE in the 1920s against her Hungarian family's wishes. She had attacked Nazism and taken on the powerful pro-German London elite after learning about the concentration camps. Versed in five languages, she was only able to return to her native Hungary after the 1957 uprising. Likewise, Listowel herself found the spark which ignited her research also more interesting – the Hungarian explorer, László Magyar, who had travelled around central Africa, learnt eight local languages and married an African princess. He had travelled around the Congo basin nearly thirty years before Stanley and the Portuguese but only published in Hungarian, so little was known about him in Europe. In her book, Listowel argued that Magyar had idolised Livingstone and travelled five hundred miles to meet him, but 'Livingstone, jealous of another white man being in his territory refused to meet him' and pretended never to have heard of him when asked.[61]

Livingstone was 'his own hero', according to Roy Lewis's review for *The Observer*. Lady Listowel had visited Mozambique and found evidence that the Portuguese Candilo Cardosa had discovered Lake Nyasa first, even giving Livingstone a map which he had plagiarised.[62] His 'feet of clay', as Victoria Brittain put it, were laid open by Listowel in a damning portrait of a man whose reputation rested on so many others. Cotton Oswald, Listowel's 'lost British hero', enabled Livingstone to rise to stardom. He had organised and paid for their Kalahari expedition, but Livingstone barely mentioned his crucial role as a hunter and interlocutor on the trip. Meanwhile, Oswald, who was so modest and generous, when he realised that Livingstone's new fame rested on his version of Lake Ngami, simply burnt his diaries to remove the evidence. Listowel's verdict was that Livingstone was 'a terrible liar, who stole other people's reputations and ... drove his wife to drink, his children to sickness, and in one case to death'. The interview was also a chance for both women to express dismay at British politics, with perhaps the continued support of apartheid in mind, Listowel lamenting a lack of 'pride and spirit'.[63]

As already discussed, Jeal's biography was the most influential and damning with regard to exposing the myth of the 'great' man, 'great' explorer, 'great' evangelist and 'great' humanitarian and his shady dealings with his servants, slaves and family, categories that were not always distinguishable in his mind. Hot on Jeal's heels came another revisionist biography, from a doctor who had joined the Colonial Medical Service in 1938 and worked in central and southern Africa. Oliver Ransford's *David Livingstone: The Dark Interior* ticked lots of boxes, with its psychological profiling of Livingstone as a manic depressive, prone to insanity and delusions, partly a consequence of being Scottish-Celtic, stressed and celibate.[64] Although not universally applauded due to a lack of evidence, nevertheless, it reintroduced contemporary verdicts which backed up Jeal's insistence that Livingstone was a nightmare to his family, close friends and most of his associates. Emotions began to run high.

The clash of opinion between Africans and Anglo-Americans went public. Professor William R. Ochieng's objections to commemorate Livingstone and his character assassination (discussed in the Introduction) prompted strong rebuffs from the African linguist Professor Lyndon Harries, from Wisconsin, and the historian Dr Roy Bridges (of the University of Aberdeen). Both men defended Livingstone in print against these 'bold assertions'. They pointed out that Livingstone had come from a poor background, had been committed to spreading the gospel and had not been carried around by Africans in a hammock. Ochieng, however, stood his ground. Livingstone's 'legend' and the 'lie' had so moulded attitudes in Europe that Livingstone might be a 'great man' to Anglo-Americans but, as an African, he would resist 'attempts to force down my throat ... [the] human greatness of this nineteenth century British imperialist, hippy and spy'.

A younger generation of mainly male scholars enthusiastically contributed to the 1973 commemorative events through new research. This was a defining era in British imperial and African studies. Academics who had watched the end of empire with relief were now enjoying demolishing the establishment's view – that Africa had no history – through their teaching and research at both British and African universities. Livingstone would not be spared but was still considered worthy of study, in part because of the lack of rigorous scholarship on such a huge figure. Many were destined to become the first generation of African and imperial professors in British universities. These included the future SOAS Professor of central African History, Andrew Roberts, who argued in Edinburgh that Livingstone's records could be used as sources for those engaged in the pressing task of researching African history.[65]

Maintaining the study and reputation of Livingstone was increasingly becoming the duty of a distinctly Scottish network involving the University of Edinburgh and the National Library of Scotland. Professor George Shepperson, of the University of Edinburgh, represents this tradition of Livingstone studies, as does the Reverend Dr Andrew Ross, who used evidence from the time to argue that Livingstone was able to view Africans, if not their cultural practices, beliefs and morality, as equal, citing remarks from figures such as William Monk, editor of David Livingstone's Cambridge lectures, who saw in Livingstone's work in Africa evidence of 'the unity of the human race'.[66] Another major intervention in the 1970s was that of Donald Simpson, who began to redress the neglect of the study of African contributions to exploration, holding the influential position of Curator of the Royal Commonwealth Society Collection.[67] This U-turn in the view of the balance between European and African contributions to exploration was to be extended by Johannes Fabian's *Out of Their Minds*, which also drew attention to the mind-altering illnesses and hallucinogenic states that many explorers worked through. Finally, Dorothy Helly's seminal 1987 study of Victorian myth-making, (discussed in the Introduction), exposed the activities of Horace Waller. The fall of Livingstone was complete, and imperial historians tended to flee the scene.

Livingstone's Partial Resurrection

After the shock of the 1970s, it would be the dynamic field of British and American Victorian studies, and the 'cultural turn' in general, that combined to breathe new life into the study of Livingstone after his biographical roasting. Slowly, Livingstone studies become a little more respectable again. His relevance to understanding empire as cultural history, to Scottish studies and empire and to the white settler experience, but most of all to African history, especially precolonial, saved him.[68]

The game changer was a pioneering exhibition, held first at London's National Portrait Gallery and thereafter at the Scottish National Portrait Gallery, Edinburgh, which was accompanied by a beautifully illustrated book, *David Livingstone and the Victorian Encounter with Africa*.[69] The book's advisory editor was the pioneer historian of empire and popular culture John MacKenzie, who from the late 1980s had kept the academic spotlight on the importance of Livingstone (and Scotsmen and women), which was part of his broader argument and seminal work on the extensive reach and influence of empire within British metropolitan culture, identity and self-understanding.[70]

At the conference, Dr Andrew D. Roberts recounted how his research into precolonial central African history had relied on Livingstone's detailed writings to help reconstruct the history of the middle and upper Zambezi. Livingstone had exaggerated his role in explorations, Roberts pointed out, and enthusiastically used firearms, plus his representations of central Africa were flawed. Nevertheless, in his talk (which to date has never been published) Roberts also put forward a number of arguments that went against the revisionist grain. 'Again and again', he insisted, reading his work, 'one is struck by an extraordinary degree of cultural relativism'; he was unimpressed by pseudo-scientific racism and saw commonality between black and white – both being '"a strange mixture of good and evil"'.[71]

Nevertheless, the book reflected the field and future trends. Tim Jeal's biographical account illustrates that this flawed Livingstone had become the orthodox view. Jeal's opening gambit was that it was now harder to understand Livingstone's 'exceptional fame' when 'he had failed in all he most hoped to achieve', converting only one African (who later lapsed); had sent missionaries to their death; and had mistaken the upper Congo River for the source of the Nile. Nevertheless, Jeal's detailed outline of a controversial, packed and self-destructive life ended on a positive: an inherent optimism, born of stubbornness, inflexibility and obsession, led Livingstone to failure and greatness. Angus Calder wrote about Livingstone, self-help and Scotland. The geographer Felix Driver stressed the neglect of the presence of African explorers more generally and the need to delve more deeply into the 'culture of exploration' in Victorian Britain. He stressed the power of the 'martyred explorer' in popular culture at the time, as well as the role of unconditional support of powerful pressure groups for explorers like Livingstone, arguing for the 'authority of science over religion', although it was a 'wide network of interests that sustained Livingstone both in his life and after his death', which he later suggested needed more investigation.[72] Tim Barringer highlighted the corresponding amount of visual imagery that Livingstone and his companions circulated in Britain.

MacKenzie had the final word, making a compelling case in 'David Livingstone and the Worldly After-Life: Imperialism and Nationalism in Africa' for the big-impact thesis of Livingstone after his death – from the memorials to the heroic myth, Livingstone missions and the Scramble for Africa. He stressed 'the Victorian capacity to create and manipulate major myths', with Livingstone 'the subject of the most powerful instrumental myth of the age'.[73] MacKenzie's talk was full of delightful vignettes, such as how Samuel Smiles's *Self Help* – the Victorian DIY manual for life – had sported a photograph of Livingstone as the frontispiece after he died; how the Reverend Horace Waller creepily had sent a strand of Livingstone's hair to inspire General Gordon's Christian mission in Sudan in 1874; and how the RGS's survey of the geographical partition of Africa in 1893 had pronounced that 'the death of David Livingstone had turned the "scramble" for the continent into a kind of holy crusade'.[74]

Significantly, MacKenzie also hinted at a uniquely powerful emotional appeal 'across class and nation ... to an otherwise class conscious age'. As Jeal explained, Livingstone's fame rested not on what he had done but on 'what he had come to represent. In the eyes of the public he owned all the virtues they most wished to possess: bravery, philanthropic zeal and selflessness'. Although the tension persisted between Jeal and MacKenzie over the former's demolition of Livingstone's reputation, which would run and run, both agreed that he could not be charged with all crimes of colonialism. MacKenzie rallied against his tarnished reputation, suggesting instead a complex man, liberal for his times, who had disliked the harsh racism of explorers like Richard Burton and who had criticised the brutality of Governor Eyre's response to the uprising in Jamaica; he showed kindness and paternal feelings towards the Kololo; his rhetoric was of freedom for Africans, albeit freedom from enslavement and spiritual degradation; and he was held in affection by many African nationalist leaders (John Chilembwe, the first freedom fighter against colonialism, born in today's Malawi, owned a copy of a Livingstone biography). The Scottish tradition of defending Livingstone's afterlife reputation was alive and kicking.

Nevertheless, historians were generally slower to catch on, and the field was extended and enriched by English literary scholars. They began by revisiting writing by and on Livingstone, and looked for the meanings embedded in texts and images featuring him, illuminating the colonial period and contributing to the cultures of racism, domination and devaluation. In comparison, few of the new imperial historians were initially interested in Livingstone. In 2001, I presented my first paper on Livingstone, at a conference, Locating the Victorians, on a panel about death.[75] It was a lonely place. Colleagues asked why? Had not enough been written about a nasty, brutish and short colonialist-racist-patriarch? Was there not a danger of becoming an apologist for empire by studying a figure who had given it a giant moral fig leaf, if not several? Why contribute to the already oversubscribed 'big man' school of history by focusing on the macho explorer? The only good thing about him was that he was dead.

Yet English literary studies were forging ahead in their textual analysis of Victorian culture. In 2007, a Victorian literature specialist, Clare Pettitt, produced a short study of popular print journalism, books and films, focusing on the encounter between Livingstone and Stanley in 'darkest Africa' as a case study of the connections between exploration, journalism and missionary imperialism.[76] She highlighted the large amount of journalism, books and later film covering this encounter, and linked this to the revolution in print technologies of the time, as well as to political issues such as the changes in the Anglo-American relationship in the 1870s. Adrian Wizniki, an American literary studies expert, has returned scholars to the issue of Victorian knowledge production. Wizniki further exposed Livingstone's misrepresentation of Africa, from his basic cartography to his staged account of the Nyangwe Massacre in 1870, which was used by the anti-abolition movement to pressure the government into opposing the Zanzibar slave trade.[77] It was an exciting moment in Livingstone studies when a US company digitally rescued the draft of Livingstone's original version of the events, which was shown to Wizniki by an eagle-eyed curator at the Livingstone Museum, Blantyre. Wizniki interpreted the significance of the edits as showing the incremental process of Livingstone's subsequent airbrushing, arguing that he had found evidence that Livingstone had not only hushed up the murders committed by his own slaves but had also passively recorded the massacre rather than intervening to help to stop the killing. It also spawned an extensive website offering a wide range of sources for teaching and research. Livingstone studies had joined the digital age.

Thanks to the digitisation of nineteenth-century newspapers, coverage of large periods can be achieved quickly, as testified to by Oliver Cook's analysis of the popular responses to Livingstone's books, which demonstrated the emotional loyalty to Livingstone among the press.[78] Meanwhile, one of the first doctoral theses on Livingstone in a generation was completed in 2011 by Justin Livingstone (no relation), from the Department of Literary Studies, the University of Edinburgh, on the breadth and richness of Livingstone's textual legacies. This became a book in the influential Manchester Studies in Imperialism series.[79]

The participation of African scholars such as Dr Friday Mufuzi and Dr William Kaulso, and of women, in a global conversation within Livingstone studies is a recent phenomenon. Dorothy Helly was the first woman to break through the male domination of Livingstone studies, but her contribution is often neglected. A heated debate about the veracity of Stanley's infamous phrase 'Dr Livingstone I presume' was played out in the media between Tim Jeal and Clare Pettitt. A pioneer in establishing the importance of women missionaries and dynasties using Mary Livingstone as an example was Janet Parsons.[80] Zambian scholars have led the field lately in acknowledging the irony around Livingstone's mission and writings.[81]

Taking up Mary's cause was journalist and author Julie Davidson. *In Search of Mrs Livingstone* (2013) is a revisionist account of Mary Livingstone's role in her husband's success. 'Silent partner; forgotten wife' summarises an argument that stresses the benefits that Livingstone obtained from the respect that the Moffat family name commanded when he began his journeys, as well as the importance of her loyalty; self-sacrifice and wide-ranging competency to his early successes.[82] As Davidson pointed out, the single, unflattering photo of her that was often used, which made her look like a man, sentenced her to obscurity and derision. David Petruisic and Brian Murray have made exciting interventions in the field of Livingstone studies from the perspective of the histories of masculinity and Anglo-Saxon, Victorian and African tropes, each debated and idealised through Livingstone.[83]

In Zambia in 2013, Brian Stanley convincingly argued that Livingstone could only have been a Scotsman, a beneficiary both of the development of medical training for men from poorer backgrounds and of deeper Scottish Enlightenment thought.[84] In the field of the history of science, a far more nuanced account of the ill-fated Zambezi expedition was provided by Lawrence Dristas, who, following Driver's call, contextualised the aims, challenges and achievements in relation to the broader dynamics and the many individuals caught up in the drama.[85] Likewise, the role of the technological changes on which Livingstone hitched a ride has been studied in depth in relation to the vast photographic legacy that Livingstone and his entourages left behind. Thus James Ryan and Jack T. Thompson, in their separate studies – on exploration and missions, respectively – include sections on the impact of Livingstone's very carefully constructed photographic images, using evidence of his instructions to the camera operator, such as 'I want only young ones'.[86]

One of the unique features of Livingstone studies, which has remained a constant, is its entwinement with commemoration. Apart from the case of 1973, this pattern tends to produce assessments that veer towards the conservative and sympathetic,[87] since the events enshrine an element of remembrance, stimulate sentimentality and attract diehard fans. The comparatively new field of memorialisation studies has naturally brought Livingstone into its fold.[88] In 2012, one of the most creative books on memorialisation imaginable was written by two artists, who examined the Livingstone trees and relics.[89]

In 2013, an international conference was held in Zambia to commemorate the bicentenary of Livingstone's birth. The conference was designed to bring British, US and African academics together for the first time to discuss Livingstone's life and legacy, and colonial rule.[90] At the opening ceremony, in Livingstone, with an official delegation from the government and House of Chiefs, the Zambian national anthem was sung with pride and feeling, its echoes of the South African anthem and the struggle for freedom sending shivers down the audience's spine. Later, many wept as a local Anglican priest and humanitarian described the cruelties of contemporary child slavery in Livingstone, including teenagers diagnosed with emphysema due to breaking stones. Another speaker, when speaking of his expedition on foot, retracing Livingstone's journey in Malawi, also broke down, recalling the generous welcome he had received en route from some of the poorest communities in Africa. There were also at least two very heated exchanges over how a conference on Livingstone was another form of propaganda aimed at minimising the racism and violence of empire. They nearly resulted in a physical confrontation. Emotions ran high over the two days.

Numerous conferences and publications, usually with a strong emphasis on memory and legacy studies, appeared in 2013. A special edition published by the Scottish Geographical Society, with a strong Scottish presence and edited by Justin Livingstone, themed textual analysis and remembrance, calling for Livingstone studies to be recognised as a serious field.[91] *David Livingstone: Man, Myth and Legacy* likewise heralded an exquisite exhibition at the National Museum of Scotland, by curator, Dr Sarah Worden.[92] The Archival Unit and History Department at the School of Oriental and African Studies organised an extensive collection of Livingstone ephemera and missionary archives to explore the nature of this evidence, under the heading 'David Livingstone: The Life and Afterlife', with an accompanying booklet.[93] The Centre for the Study of Journalism and History at the University of Sheffield organised a one-day international symposium on Livingstone and also published a special edition on his legacy for African journalism.[94]

The events, too numerous to list in full, included a seminar organised by the Minister of the Nonconformist Church in London, where Livingstone had worshipped; a lecture entitled 'Hope as Missional Impulse: Beyond the Legacy of David Livingstone', by Dr Michael Jagessar, moderator of the United Reform Church, with a response from Professor Brian Stanley (who gave a paper in Livingstone, Zambia), organised by the Council for World Mission;[95] a wealth of international events organised and coordinated by the Scottish Livingstone 200 Committee and the government of Malawi, including 'A Wreathlaying Ceremony to Commemorate the Bicentenary of the Birth of Dr David Livingstone, 1813–1873', complete with Boy Scouts brought down from Blantyre to act as stewards;[96] a number of interviews and debates organised by BBC Radio; and a documentary with the National Geographic Channel produced by Sky Vision.[97]

2013 also saw the publication of a revised edition of Tim Jeal's acclaimed 1973 biography, forty years on. In his new preface, Jeal admitted to only having to make substantial changes to the chapter on 'Livingstone and the British Empire' to 'give clearer insight into the extent of Livingstone's posthumous influence on Africa's subsequent colonial history', conceding ground to only one historian, Dorothy Helly, on the extent of the fiddling of the last diaries.[98] The Livingstone scandals covered in the media – Livingstone's secret African love child and his involvement in the Nyangwe Massacre – were dismissed due to a lack of any real evidence. Another giant in the field, John Mackenzie, also made new contributions, pleading for a return to the man and his writings, to rescue him from analyses that concentrated on imperial networks, followers and mythmakers. Attacking Jeal for missing out the Scottish and evangelical dimension to Livingstone's life, he also lambasted Pettitt for claiming that, had Stanley failed to find Livingstone and generated such international publicity, Livingstone would not be remembered at all.[99] Acknowledging the importance of newspapers as sources, he argued that their new availability online would yield fresh insights, for example, into how his reputation remained largely intact throughout his life, undented by the failures of the Zambezi expedition. MacKenzie also called for a fuller acknowledgement of the circumstances of Livingstone's death and funeral at Westminster Abbey.

Conclusion

Professor Lynda Colley summarised the British Empire as being 'a complex and persistent beast. And it has claws'. It also had a soft underbelly: a history of emotion. Sentimental feeling has been a feature of Britain's conversation with itself about empire. In relation to British colonial Africa this was regularly expressed through commemorative events, popular writing and press coverage about Livingstone. In particular, male academics (often retired), evangelical Christians, and Scotsmen found the chance to make a contribution to the genre of inspirational biography rather irresistible.

Memorialising David Livingstone and reliving the 'touching circumstances' of his death helped sustain the rose-tinted view of empire by framing Britain's involvement in Africa through romantic image of humanitarian endeavour, superior race relations and Christian values. An over-arching 'emotion culture' unique to Britain held sway across much of the twentieth century, buttressed by Livingstone's posthumous presence. Generations in Britain and Africa from the late Victorian era to the 1960s had their views of what Britain was doing in Africa softened by an emotional narrative of innocence, sacrifice, masculine duty and national pride. It was set to continual play. It began with childhood exposure to Christian juvenile texts and was reinforced with adult heroic biography. The sad ending was always the same, and this sentimental imperialism did much to stave off Britain's appetite for a serious critique of colonial rule in Africa until relatively recently. It helps explain why, for so long and for so many, the British Empire was understood as a liberating, peaceful, humanitarian project; one that was far less racist and harsh than any other empire in Africa.

NOTES

1 *Daily Telegraph*, 17 March 1913.
2 *Manchester Guardian*, 24 March 1913.
3 *Times*, 19 March 1913.
4 *Glasgow Herald*, 11 March 1913.
5 *Manchester Guardian*, 17 March 1913.
6 *Daily Telegraph*, 17 March 1913.
7 *Manchester Guardian*, 17 March 1913.
8 *Aberdeen Journal*, 8 March 1913.
9 *Glasgow Herald*, 12 March 1913.
10 The Reverend M'Lean Watt, Greenock, quoted in the *Glasgow Herald*, 13 March 1913.
11 Ibid.
12 *Western Mail*, 20 March 1913.
13 *Daily Mail*, 20 March 1913.
14 *Manchester Guardian*, 20 March 1913.
15 *Manchester Guardian*, 31 March 1913.
16 *Manchester Guardian*, 18 March 1913.
17 *Western Mail*, 19 March 1913.

18 Ibid., 19 March 1913.
19 *Daily Mail*, 28 February 1913, and *Observer*, 2 March 1913.
20 *Times*, 18 March 1913.
21 Ibid., 20 March 1913.
22 *Manchester Guardian*, 24 March 1913.
23 As discussed in Chapter Six.
24 '*The Christian*', 23 January 1913, extract in Box 3, Jacket A, Folder 1, Livingstone Collection, SOAS Archive.
25 19 March, *Daily Telegraph*, 'Reminisces of Mr Work on Gorgon'. Ibid.
26 *Daily Telegraph*, 19 March 1913.
27 *Times*, 19 March 1913.
28 Ibid.
29 *Times*, 19 March 1913.
30 *Manchester Guardian*, 24 March 1913.
31 *Manchester Guardian*, 18 March 1913.
32 *Glasgow Herald*, 15 March 1913.
33 *Manchester Guardian*, 20 March 1913.
34 Bedford, *Livingstone of Africa*, 51.
35 *Dictionary of National Biography* (1901 supplement), 'William Garden Blaikie (1920–1899)'.
36 W. Elmslie, *Among the Wilds of the Ngoni* (Edinburgh: Oliphant Anderson & Ferrier, 1899), foreword.
37 Starritt, *Livingstone the Pioneer*.
38 MacNair, *Livingstone the Liberator*.
39 Andrew C. Ross, *David Livingstone: Mission and Empire* (London: Hambledon, 2002).
40 G.B. Masefield, 'Review of Livingstone's Last Journey', *Uganda Journal*, II, 2 (1947): 129.
41 Frank Debenham, *The Way to Ilala: David Livingstone's Pilgrimage* (London: Longman, 1955); 'One Hundred Years Ago: The Discovery of the Victorian Falls', by Frank Debenham, OBE, in *The Life and Work of David Livingstone: A Brief Guide to the Livingstone Collections in the Livingstone Museum* (Bulawayo: Mardon Printers Ltd, 1955), 13–20.
42 M. Gelfand, *Livingstone the Doctor* (Oxford: Basil Blackwell, 1957).
43 For example, Wallis, *The Zambezi Expedition*.
44 Roberts, 'David Livingstone: The Man and His Work', 2.
45 I. Schapera, (ed.), *Livingstone's Missionary Correspondence, 1841–1856* (London: Chatto & Windus, 1961), xii.
46 Roberts, 'David Livingstone: The Man and His Work', 2.
47 'Why Remember This Man?', pamphlet, DL/5/4 RGS.
48 See various newspaper clippings in CWM Africa – Odds Livingstone Box A, SOAS Archives.
49 F. Driver, 'David Livingstone and the Culture of Exploration in Mid-Victorian Britain', in John MacKenzie (ed.), *David Livingstone and the Victorian Encounter with Africa* (London: National Portrait Gallery, 1996), 135.
50 *Guardian*, 27 January 1973.
51 *Times*, 17 April 1973.

52 Frost, 'Memoirs', 185.
53 Gary Keane & Neville Randall, 'FOCUS ON FACT – Doctor Livingstone (16)', *Daily Mail*, 11 May 1973.
54 'Not what we presumed!', *Daily Mail*, 5 April 1973.
55 'Exploring Livingstone', *Daily Mirror*, 5 April 1973.
56 Richard Hall, 'Livingstone revealed', *Observer*, 6 May 1973.
57 Ibid.
58 'Explorer under scrutiny', *Daily Mirror*, 23 April 1973.
59 'Livingstone the obstinate explorer', advertised in *The Times* and the *Daily Mail*, 2 May 1973.
60 Timothy Severin, 'The African Adventure', *Times*, 5 May 1973.
61 Victoria Brittain, 'How a hero's feet of clay were uncovered, reluctantly', *Times*, 11 October 1974.
62 Roy Lewis, 'Found Out!', *Times*, 26 September 1974.
63 Brittain, 'How a hero's feet of clay were uncovered, reluctantly'.
64 Oliver Ransford, *David Livingstone: The Dark Interior* (London: Palgrave Macmillan, 1978).
65 A. Roberts, 'Livingstone's Value to the History of African Societies', paper presented at the 'David Livingstone and Africa' conference, Centre for African Studies, University of Edinburgh, Edinburgh, 4–5 May 1973, 49–67.
66 Andrew Ross, 'David Livingstone: The Man Behind the Mask', in J. de Gruchy (ed.), *The London Missionary Society in Southern Africa, 1799–1999: Historical Essays in Celebration of the Bicentenary of the LMS in Southern Africa* (Athens, OH: Ohio University Press, 2000), 37–54.
67 Simpson, *Dark Companions*.
68 One example of hundreds would be I.S. MacLaren, 'Exploration/Travel Literature and the Evolution of the Author', *International Journal of Canadian Studies*, 5 (Spring 1992): 39–68.
69 MacKenzie (ed.), *David Livingstone and the Victorian Encounter with Africa*.
70 John M. MacKenzie, 'The Imperial Pioneer and Hunter and the British Masculine Stereotype in Late Victorian and Edwardian Times', in J.A. Mangan & James Walvin (eds.), *Manliness and Morality: Middle-Class Masculinity in Britain and America, 1800–1990* (Manchester: Manchester University Press, 1987).
71 Roberts, 'David Livingstone: The Man and His Work', 18.
72 Driver, 'David Livingstone and the Culture of Exploration'; Driver, *Geography Militant*, 72–3.
73 'David Livingstone and the Worldly After-Life: Imperialism and Nationalism in Africa', in *David Livingstone* (1990), 206.
74 Ibid., 208.
75 Joanna Lewis, '"Laying to Rest a Victorian Myth": The Funeral of David Livingstone', panel on Death at the 'Locating the Victorians' conference, University College, London, 10–12 September 2000.
76 Pettitt, *Dr. Livingstone, I Presume?*.
77 A.S. Wisniki, 'Livingstone's 1871 Field Diary: A Multispectral Critical Edition' http://livingstone.library.ucla.edu/1871diary/
78 Cook, 'The immortalisation of David Livingstone'.

79 Justin D. Livingstone, *Livingstone's 'Lives': A Metabiography of a Victorian Icon* (Manchester: Manchester University Press, 2014).

80 Janet Wagner Parsons, *The Livingstones at Kolobeng 1847–1852* (Gabarone: Botswana Society and Pula Press, 1997).

81 Walima T. Kalusa, 'Elders, Young Men, and David Livingstone's "Civilizing Mission": Revisting the Disintegration of the Kololo Kingdom, 1851–1864', *International Journal of African Historical Studies*, 42, 1 (2009) 55–80; Friday Mufuzi, 'The Livingstone Museum and its contribution to Zambian History: 1934–2006 PhD Thesis (Lusaka: University of Zambia, 2012) and 'The Livingstone Museum and its memorialisation of David Livingstone in Zambian colonial and post-colonial history, 1934–2006' in Sarah Worden (ed.) *David Livingstone: Man, Myth and Legacy* (Edinburgh: National Museums of Scotland, 2012) 131–53; and Sjored Ripma, *David Livingstone and the myth of African Poverty and Disease* (Leiden: Brill, 2015).

82 Julie Davidson, *Looking for Mrs Livingstone* (Edinburgh: St Andrew's Press, 2012).

83 B.H. Murray, 'H M Stanley, David Livingstone and the Staging of "Anglo-Saxon" Manliness', *Scottish Geographical Journal*, 129, 3–4 (September–December 2013): 150–64.

84 B. Stanley, 'The Missionary and the Rainmaker: Livingstone and the Scottish Enlightenment', paper given to the 'Imperial Obsession' conference, Livingstone, Zambia, 18–20 April 2013.

85 L. Dristas, *Zambesi: David Livingstone and Expeditionary Science in Africa* (London: I.B. Tauris, 2010).

86 J.R. Ryan, *Picturing Empire: Photography and the Visualization of the British Empire* (Chicago, IL: Chicago University Press, 1998); T.J. Thompson, *Light on Darkness: Missionary Photography of Africa in the Nineteenth and Early Twentieth Centuries* (Grand Rapids, MI: Eerdmans, 2012).

87 For example, the Imperial Obsessions conference, held in Livingstone, Zambia, began with two addresses (by a government minister and by the head of the House of Chiefs), the singing of the Zambian national anthem and a prayer by the outgoing director of the museum; local church leaders were among the audience. Everyone was careful to avoid offending the views of others, the Zambian participants being reluctant to offend the visitors, in line with their ethos of hospitality and welcome.

88 See A.E. Coombes, *Reinventing Africa: Museums, Material Culture and Popular Imagination* (New Haven, CT: Yale University Press, 1994), and, on Livingstone and Zambia, see the many articles published by the pioneer of Livingstone and public history in Zambia, Dr Friday Mufuzi, keeper of the Livingstone Collection, Livingstone Museum, Zambia.

89 Renema & van Zoelen, *You Took the Part*.

90 http://blogs.lse.ac.uk/africaatlse/2013/04/23/african-nationalist-or-imperial-agent-david-livingstone-analysed/. Accessed 1 June 2014.

91 J. Livingstone (ed.), 'Special Issue: Livingstone Studies: Bicentenary Essays', *Scottish Geographical Journal*, 129, 3–4 (2013): 137–291.

92 S. Worden (ed.), *David Livingstone*.

93 *The Life and Afterlife of David Livingstone*, SOAS, London, 2013.

94 M. Conboy, J. Lugo-Ocando & S. Eldridge (eds.), 'Two Hundred Years after Livingstone: His Legacy for African Journalism', Special Issue, *Ecquid Novi: Journal of African Journalism Studies*, 35, 1 (2014).

95 www.cwmission.org/cwm-council-guest-lecture-hope-as-missional-impulse-beyond-the-legacy-of-david-livingstone. Accessed 15 June 2014.

96 Order of Service, Westminster Abbey, 19 March 2013, 6.30 p.m. The president of Malawi, H.E. Joyce Banda, laid a wreath. www.westminster-abbey.org/worship/special-services/past-special-services/2013/march/livingstone-bicentenary-wreathlaying. Accessed 15 June 2014.

97 www.pbs.org/wnet/secrets/episodes/the-lost-diary-of-dr-livingstone-about-this-episode/1103/. Accessed 15 June 2014.

98 Jeal, *Livingstone*, xi–xviii.

99 J.M. MacKenzie, 'David Livingstone – Prophet or Patron Saint of Imperialism in Africa: Myths and Misconceptions', *Scottish Geographical Journal*, 129, 3–4 (2013): 277–91.

Conclusion

'When last I died (and dear, I die As often as from thee I go ...)'
The Legacy, John Donne

'To Her Majesty' ...
Queen of the white people who love the black man.
Daily News, 15 February 1858, RGS Farewell Dinner to Livingstone[1]

The British Empire in Africa had a unique emotional life. Sentimentality helped sustain interest and support for the empire in the metropole. It strengthened the resolve of early colonial rule, gave unity and strength to white settlers, and drew in Africans as well. It could be manipulated by very different political regimes, from colonial to metropolitan to postcolonial. An emotion culture around the death and memorialisation of Livingstone made a powerful contribution to the ideological power of the British Empire, its polyphonic properties and the very Victorian project of an empire in Africa. Romanticised views of white heroism, sacrifice and humanitarianism blended together to produce an emotional force field and high-moral imperialism, drawing subsequent generations to follow in the footsteps of dead men. This great Victorian myth machine contributed to the history of the moral-emotional life of the nation, the history of the private self, the history of masculinity and to the Scramble for Africa. The popular presentation of Livingstone's death and the role of 'his' freed slaves was a highly sentimentalised fiction. The emotional response it generated bequeathed a sentimental view of 'the heart' of the British Empire and thus shaped the popular understandings of the liberal empire throughout most of the twentieth century and limited appetites for a critique of its violent methods. But it was African responses that made this initially possible. The apparent devotion to the death by Livingstone's African followers bequeathed a powerful and useful myth about Britain's superior race relations in Africa: that these relations were innately tolerant and even tender.

The Power of Death

This book has shown in more detail how Livingstone's unusual death impacted on British imperial propaganda and the history of her engagement with Africa. It began with a prologue about the memories of a heroic but upsetting death, an intimate experience of that death and a view of a touching African response to it. The presence of death, it has been argued in the first two chapters, helped create the high-water mark of Victorian moral imperialism in Africa, an important filament in the emotional history of empire. Livingstone's death, according to contemporaries, created the 'cult of Livingstone' and a 'thrill' in the 'hearts of men', and caused 'a thrill to run through the whole of Christendom ... that would rouse the world'.[2] William Blaikie, in his influential Victorian biography, dwelt on 'its touching circumstances' that 'did more for Africa than he could have done had he completed his task'. He described the effect being as if the Christian world had met and passed a resolution; the statesman, merchant, explorer and missionary felt it. Waves of missionaries soon left Britain for central Africa. Livingstone's 'death in harness'[3] effortlessly transformed him into the poster boy for Britain's liberal empire project in Africa.

The affecting appeal of Livingstone to the sentiments was grounded in his everyman persona: a life of achievement and failure, his humble beginnings and the sense that people knew him through his diaries. He straddled the Scottish Enlightenment, evangelical Christianity, the movement that embraced scientific rationality. He took these to Africa in the mid-nineteenth century. He stood on the threshold of the rise of the working man as an equal to other classes of men. Unlike most other British explorers, he was a working-class maverick missionary-explorer without an independent income. Responding to Livingstone's heroism and tragedy in the late nineteenth century offered one way in which men and women could display feeling, compassion and humanity.[4]

Livingstone became central to the 'performance heroism' of the late nineteenth century, when the 'agents of state, civil society and commerce' hijacked the press and popular culture.[5] Moreover, the tragic death scene remained a staple of inspirational biographies throughout the twentieth century. Many popular accounts still remain faithful to Waller's vision. In 2012, Christian Focus Publications, based in Scotland, reprinted its children's book *David Livingstone: Who is the Bravest?* It closes with 'as he knelt down in his little hut by the Zambezi River. It was time to pray to God. And it was then that God took David home to heaven just as he had promised'.[6] Adventure tourists in Victoria Falls are not immune either: 'As Richard Gammon concluded his talk about Dr. Livingstone, our river boat was nearing its dock on the Zambezi River. His final words about Chuma and Susi transporting the body had brought tears to Gammon's eyes. At least, I think they did. Hard to tell because I was looking at him through my own tears'.[7]

Today, Christian evangelical sermons also still use Livingstone's death to illustrate the power of faith lingering in the painful demise of a man who had apparently been one of 'the biggest swaggering atheists on the planet': with a 'shoulder ripped apart', 'completely blind in one eye', his 'body began to shrivel'; he was 'roasted', and he died 'wracked with pain ... on his knees praying'.[8] His death resonated strongly with first-wave explorers, settlers and missionaries, grappling with mortal diseases and high death rates. Livingstone's death had an even greater impact on African audiences. A white man had died for them, they were told, from malaria – a local battle that many lost – so that they could be 'saved'. Stripped of its Victorian airbrushing, Livingstone's death can, even today, move to tears the most sceptical audiences, as I found in Africa 2013.[9]

Livingstone's Funeral, High Imperialism and the Cult of the Heart

The early chapters of this book explored how news of Livingstone's death and his funeral became a fixed moment in 'the fluctuating situations' of moral evaluation, as Hume termed this aspect of the philosophical lived experience.[10] In 1874, 'internal and external sentiment' merged, with moral argument, domestic politics and popular sentiment combining to force a political response to Africa. When the press covered news of insults to his family and the scandal of a government that was unprepared to pay for his funeral, this tapped into and unleashed the hurt and anger of the everyday experience of many: Livingstone was not being treated as he deserved, particularly by the ruling elite. This helped to rally supporters and diminish dissenters.

A 'cult of the heart' and the concept of the inner emotional life have been shown to be useful in understanding the role of sentimental feeling in sustaining an imperial culture of emotion. The age of transition to full adult male suffrage in the last half of the nineteenth century had a role in attitudes to a humanitarian policy towards Africa. The private self sought recognition of its intrinsic value and properties in the public sphere whilst at the same time maintaining the right to exist freely: 'allowing the self the room within which to govern itself'.[11] Ordinary men and women wanted recognition as being worthy of dignified treatment by society in order to alleviate working lives full of 'sorrow', 'suffering' and 'struggle'; speaking 'from the fullness of the heart' as opposed to 'counterfeit humanity'.[12]

Livingstone embodied wisdom through simplicity and humility, as well as ordinary human fellowship without airs and graces, and honesty. In a 'discourse about the condition of humanity', and the concept that 'the heart was the centre of humanity'.[13]

The cult of the heart, therefore, was a strategy that attempted to resolve what Rancière calls 'the proletarian situation', namely 'the assertion of the humanity this situation denies'. God and religion were the solution, but it was a religion born of the heart of true, honest working men – warm, reliable, neither venal nor an expression of high Anglican coldness and formality. In this view, 'God is realized in the heart', and the cult of the heart was a means of asserting a 'religion of humanity' – the collective force needed to defeat a world full of evil, suffering and sorrow.[14] Livingstone embodied the application of contemporary 'technologies' designed to develop the 'freed self'. His dramatic death led to a rededication and display of these, but even more in death: character, religious duty, 'the romance of improvement', self-help and an acceptance of the rationale of science and the rule of law.[15] And it was through the realm of the family – the device through which the self-made man and woman made a bid for recognition and respect in the wider social milieu – that the correct levels and types of emotions were expressed (typically, kindness, fairness and tenderness).

Livingstone's death in the mid to late Victorian era unleashed a tussle over 'the heart of the nation', over whose heart it was and how that heart should behave. By the late 1870s, William Gladstone referred to the 'great human heart of this country' which beat outside parliament and which it was dangerous to ignore.[16] Whereas Joyce emphasises the role of the press coverage of the massacres by Turkish Muslims of Bulgarian Christians in 1876, in the final act of the politics of the British heart, this book stresses the revival of anti-slavery, Livingstone and Africa as a defining moment.

The death and funeral of Livingstone were not simply a moment of collective mourning; they were an important moment of national self-understanding, whereby Livingstone became the heart of the nation through the celebration of shared sorrows and his sacrifice to the anti-slavery cause. It was part of the process of imperial self-fashioning, in that we have the creation of a powerful fiction through the understood narratives that his life represented to millions of men. The romance of British imperial power in Africa was being made through a highly masculinised display of the 'hidden hearts of men'. It offered a device through which the inherent violence, inequality and unfairness of the encounter were filtered through a romantic, sentimentalised ideal. Tears of guilt over slavery, materialism, self-obsession and a lack of Christian feeling could, in turn, lead to a new assertiveness not just in politics but also within the social order itself.

Anti-Slavery and Imperial Humanitarianism

Livingstone's death poured sentimental feeling into the empire project in Africa through the issue of anti-slavery. A large amount of 'moral capital' oozed from Livingstone's death and funeral,[17] which enhanced Britain's self-image as the giver of 'the gift of freedom'.[18] The lobbying of Livingstone's supporters in the press and beyond was focused on Livingstone as the liberator, symbolised by his 'pathetic death' in Africa, the bravery of his 'followers' and the touching presence of freed slave Jacob Wainwright at Livingstone's funeral. Never directly interviewed nor given a history of his own, Wainwright was, in many ways, as disembodied as Livingstone's corpse. We never get to know him from his own feelings. He was understood as the mould of a contemporary embodiment of the black man on the abolition seal, freed slave supplicant or the black anti-slave activist, Olaudah Equiano adopted by William Wilberforce: a freed slave mannequin.

Blaikie prophesised that, due to Livingstone's death, 'AFRICA SHALL LIVE'.[19] Thus, initially, an emotional view of Livingstone, the Christian 'liberator', was at the fore of a manipulated imperial memory, helping to steady Britain's view of its mission in Africa, as a liberal one, for the entire duration of the empire.

This research has underscored the tight relationship between the press, the abolition movement and the evolution of a 'moral policy' on Africa which pushed British intervention in Africa. As Huzzey has argued, 'Convincing public arguments could unleash terrifying outcries against negligent statesmen'. Frederick Holmwood, political agent in Zanzibar (and interviewer of Susi and Chuma mentioned in the prologue), observed in 1879 how 'the period of cheap journalism' conveyed to politicians 'the unmistakable expression of the nation's wishes' for the suppression of the slave trade.[20] Obituaries praised Livingstone's mission to open Africa 'to the light of religion and civilization, and extirpating the slave trade, which is the main hindrance to that beneficent consummation'.[21]

Livingstone's death marked a crucial moment in the history of the abolition movement, playing an important role in Barnett's history of 'humanitarian imperialism'. It parallels the 'gesture politics' of the white act of manumission, in order to provide 'moral visibility' and show 'a public declaration of the generosity and abstract goodness' on the part of the giver.[22] This book has underscored how influential networks of anti-slavery sentimentality were at home. A new imperial humanitarianism worked effectively to direct Britain's Scramble for Africa.[23] Victorian concerns about ending suffering or a 'humanitarian "impulse" intersected with debates around anti-slavery, colonial administration and the protection of indigenous peoples'.[24]

Memorialisation, Colonial Rule & an Imperial Culture of Sentiment

This book has used Livingstone to tease out another dimension to British colonial rule and independent Africa through paying attention to sentimental feeling on the ground. Moving next to Africa, Chapters Three to Five narrate colonial futility. They charted the doomed nature and end of high imperial sentiment, tracking the pilgrims to Chitambo to find his grave, and the politics of early colonial rule in the area and the history of white settlement in Livingstone.

Subsequent official acts of imperial memorialisation of Livingstone would never again match the high emotionalism of 1874, mediated by the different and unique political, social and cultural configurations of each age. But individual responses and official ceremonies could take forward the emotional life of empire. This book has built on the work of Sybren Renema and Timmy van Zoelen, who traced a history of commemoration centred on the Livingstone trees – particularly the tree under which he was buried – examining their actual sites of commemoration in Africa and the allegedly authentic pieces of 'sacred' Livingstone trees, from bark to leaf, which were circulated and kept in museums and missionary archives. Their research showed the continuity in the attitudes towards 'relics', which remain largely unchanged from the Victorian era; the ways in which memorialisations can be profoundly eccentric and impossible to control by external forces: 'while we are capable of rendering an object understandable by linking it to a story, we cannot control our emotions and thoughts on encountering it'.[25] Also, they unleashed the potential 'romance' of memorialisation. Livingstone met his wife under a tree in Africa; he said his final goodbye to her by spending Christmas next to her grave under a baobab in 1862.

This book highlights the role of romantic memorialisation in early colonial rule and in the consolidation of white settler society in central Africa. A series of personal pilgrimages to Livingstone's grave in the 1890s reveals an emotional history to the establishment of colonial rule. The impulse to memorialise Livingstone in central Africa produced a group of willing martyrs in the 1890s, as Chapter Three revealed. Those who perished in so doing inspired strong feelings. The grave at Chitambo was cherished as a symbol of the loneliness and sorrows of men. From Owen Stroud to Robert Codrington, these bachelor empire-builders lived a solitary, peripatetic existence. As they became hardened by circumstances, illness and disappointment, sentimentality wore thin towards Africans but persisted towards each other, distracting from acts of physical and emotional cruelty towards 'the native'.

Missionaries fought to stake a claim to the Chitambo grave and build up empires within empires. Livingstone's descendants became part of this struggle. The Livingstone memorial, as Chapter Four showed, became part of the white settler understandings of themselves, caught in the contradictions and cruelties of colonialism. Livingstone memorialisations were the points at which heroism and emotion could be given a public outlet and the pioneer settler celebrated.

Pioneer settlers in the town which bore Livingstone's name also tried to commemorate his life in ways that enhanced their own image, as Chapter Five illustrated.What was left out and who were left out is equally insightful in the politics of commemoration, with little attention being paid either to Livingstone's more liberal reputation or to his African followers, but the white racist colonialists could not erase Africans from the Livingstone narrative forever. In the messy colonial struggle to maintain white rule in the 1950s, what Livingstone stood for was drawn into the struggle against nationalism. The 1955 memorialisation in Livingstone required two ceremonies, for two different moral communities. By the 1950s, African congregations would find the theology of the gospel a rallying cry against the immorality of colonial rule and the corruption of race relations. Had not their ancestors carried Livingstone's body back to the coast?

Finally, the last three chapters argued Livingstone went through partial resurrection – the trail of sentimental feeling never went totally cold. Livingstone's reputation did not fall beyond redemption after the end of colonial rule in Africa. Missionary and Scottish missionary literature for Africans always made much of that gesture, and this would find its way into Livingstone's largest national commemoration – by a postcolonial state, as Chapter Six argued. In 1901, a publication in the inspirational biography genre that had found its way to central Africa (again, a popular Sunday school prize), forming part of a Famous Scots series, devoted a whole chapter to 'TheTribute of the Africans'.[26] James MacNair's pocket-sized, New Testament-style *Livingstone the Liberator*, published in 1940 to mark the centenary of his departure from Britain for Africa, found its way to the continent but made no mention of the war in its preface. It seems to have been written outside real time, with itsVictoriana descriptions of Livingstone's lifelong commitment to creating 'a storm of moral indignation' that would 'sweep the EvilThing into Hell'. Such literature no doubt inspired African readers who pondered the epilogue – 'Like Master, Like Followers: He is truly great who makes others great' – to carve out their path of liberation from the moral injustice of racial rule.[27]

Commemoration and memorialisation have been effective mechanisms for pursuing political advantage, and this book has shown how Livingstone has always been used by others to great effect, even in the post-independence era. Under pressure from apartheid South Africa, in 1973, Livingstone came to the rescue of the ruling party's dubious moral basis for changing the constitution and Kaunda's dwindling support. The British government had no place at the memorial ceremony at the graveside in Chitambo, where the president once again used the language of the heart, emotion and feeling to mobilise a constituency of support.

Sentimentality has been shown to be genuine and to be manipulated by political regimes. This book illustrates the difficulty in separating its dual characteristics. Western sentimentality belongs to the history of 'the cultivation and practice of our moral-emotional faculties'. It is an 'appeal to tender feelings'; as Kant described it, it is a 'melting compassion'. For Solomon, it produces sympathetic feelings and a capacity for engagement far beyond the self or one's immediate environment. What this suggests is the existence of a nebulous but nevertheless present and powerful force field: an 'emotional economy'. Thus we can judge sentimentality as the expression of human empathy, pity, fondness, compassion; it has an innocence and a spontaneity that make it intrinsically genuine; it is linked to the development of human emotion and the ability to shed tears. However, sentimentality can be a substitute for real action, a barrier to politicisation or rational critiques of the source of the perceived wrong. According to this negative view, it is fake emotion, built on superficial feeling; it is inappropriate responses; it is cheap and melodramatic, a display of emotion that is more artifice and self-indulgence.

This book is built on the view that a deep study of historical circumstances, and the responses and views of individuals, allows for a better understanding of sentimentality as a manifestation of its negative or positive properties, or a mixture of the two. Real or fake, what is useful to the historian is the agency of an emotional economy; the outcomes of a politics of affect and affection and whether a 'vast dumb tenderness' can actually change politics.

The Press, Inspirational Biography & Britain's Conversation about Africa

The book has highlighted the usefulness of print journalism in understanding the history of the British Empire. Newspapers were used throughout. As official records become increasingly discredited, careful analysis of press reporting and newspaper history are assuming greater importance. Simon Potter has argued that from the late nineteenth century, 'extensive coverage and commentary in a national and regional press' is a vast, untapped resource; similarly, John MacKenzie has stressed that a more extensive analysis of the press coverage of Livingstone would shed light on his role in the empire.[28]

Newspapers have exposed more fully the role of Livingstone and his memorialisation in Britain's conversation with itself about Africa, its imperial mission and notions of humanity. Livingstone's death and the response of his African followers brought about a peculiar type of sentimentality to the future imperial project in Africa, which the press did much to shape, and individual journalists who had initially met Livingstone, to subsequent ones who read about him. Empire liberalism became infused with an emotional energy, intimate motif and a very British humanitarianism with regard to its encounter with Africa. The Victorian model of the explorer-journalist laid down a prototype for the British press's Africa Correspondent across much of the twentieth century.

However, newspaper coverage was often led by public opinion created through other means. Inspirational biography and commemorative events, as Chapter Seven showed, gave Livingstone's life-after-death strength and durability within imperial propaganda. This 'structure of feeling' is a key reason why criticism about imperial violence, exploitation and abuse was always muted. Livingstone bequeathed a sentimentalised view of British imperial power in Africa and the good white man in Africa. Livingstone biographies usually contained a summary of the goodness and ideals of colonial rule for each particular generation. One biography, published in the mayhem of 1940, concluded by asking what of the future for 'Imperialism' in the 'uncertain world that lies ahead?' The only type that deserved to continue, MacNair insisted, was Livingstone's: 'an imperialism that is prepared to accept responsibility for undeveloped races ... in a spirit of unselfishness that steadily keeps their interests in view'.[29]

Publications on Livingstone were the mother's milk of Christian Sunday schools and missionary teaching. Starritt's *Livingstone the Pioneer* was published by the Religious Tract Society, one of their Beacon Biographies, and a popular Sunday school prize. Livingstone shared the spotlight with John Bunyan, Garibaldi, Joan of Arc and James Chalmers of New Guinea, one 'of those immortal dead who live again/In minds made better by their presence, live/In pulses stirred to generosity'.[30] It was a celebration of boyhood innocence that claimed to be universal in its relevance, 'for it is in truth, the story of every boy's dream, the story of every boy's heart, before the world has touched with little prudences and discreet ambitions of commercialized civilization'.

Livingstone biographies were, until fairly recently, regularly gifted down the generations. In 2013, on the occasion of the bicentenary of Livingstone's birth, Michael Barrett, Professor of Biochemical Parasitology at the University of Glasgow, recalled how Dr Richard Le Page, a life fellow of Gonville and Caius College, Cambridge, who first taught him about tropical diseases, 'once kindly gave me a first edition of Livingstone's MissionaryTravels'. Le Page had grown up in Northern Rhodesia (Zambia). 'Livingstone was a huge figure there, an inspiration', he recalled. Professor Barrett noted for posterity how his family and friends fought against the tsetse fly; how they 'extended the electricity network out into the bush and built hospitals and schools'.[31] The sentiment expressed here and elsewhere was that Livingstone was long dead but that good men in Africa live on.

African Sentimentality and Humanitarianism

Livingstone's dying in 'the heart of Africa' and his body being carried back by his African followers created an unusual narrative of a very intimate moment and set of personal encounters. The actions of African men and women told a story which allowed for an emotional connection with the more abstract arguments for intervention in Africa. This book has underscored Africans' role in the giving of the ultimate propaganda gift to the project an empire in Africa. It has also revealed the role of African humanitarianism in colonial rule and beyond by setting out the lives of Livingstone's followers in more detail, adding to the growing field of research on black mission humanitarians. [32]

Thus, this story has highlighted the powerful role Africans had in the construction of the liberal myth of British rule in Africa. Abolitionists and missionaries now had fresh evidence of the potential of freed slaves in Africa because the selfless act and courage shown by Livingstone's men in carrying his body for nearly eight months to the coast. It was interpreted as clear proof of the potential for civilisation even in the 'darkest' regions of the continent. Such an act of love by his followers, it was believed, stemmed from Livingstone's kindness, generosity and non-violence towards Africans; not for nothing had his men chosen to bury his heart in 'his own dear Africa'. The decision of African men and women to carry Livingstone's body back to the coast gaveVictorians the first black heroes of Africa whom they could not ignore, as well as the opportunity to pause for a moment of national mourning and reckoning. However, the role of African women had been dropped, and soon even his male followers were also forgotten.

African Christian congregations in British colonial Africa were the group most exposed to the sentimental myth of the Livingstone–black man encounter. Livingstone had shown loyalty to certain chiefs, and was even famed for having supplied arms to them against the Boers and for having praised the manliness of their honour and bravery in fighting for their freedom.[33] He had shown sympathy towards certain tribes. He was understood to be no great critic of African men who enslaved their own people. He wanted African men to know the gospel. In the hours leading up to his death, he wanted his favourite African boy by his side. He had apparently wanted to die in Africa; his heart was buried there; and so kind and generous was he to his men that they risked their lives to return his body. He had 'allowed' them to be brave.

This book has underscored the sentimental feeling of Africans, who have held on to a generous and tender image of Livingstone from his death in 1873 onwards. During racial rule, an image of Livingstone, the friend of Africans, who ate with them and died because he wanted to stop slavery, inspired millions of mission-educated African Christians. Kaunda's revival of the discourse of the heart, during the African 1973 celebrations to mark Livingstone's death, illustrates this great affection for a man believed to have treated Africans as having hearts and souls.

Most people in Zambia believed, and many still do, that Livingstone brought Christianity to the region, even though today, as Bishop David of Lusaka's Anglican Cathedral of the Holy Cross admitted, for the younger generation, 'the strength and power of his image is slipping away'. His younger assistant agreed.[34] In 2013, even Livingstone's town councillors were unaware that Livingstone was associated with anti-slavery, but they still had a sense that he had helped to bring Christianity to the region and was important for tourism.[35] This reflects the fading importance of the colonial period in general; so much has happened since independence; and oral family histories were always rooted in precolonial narratives. Livingstone performs a lesser role in and around Victoria Falls, being more of a secular saint for tourism.

Today, it is often the poor in central Africa who remember Livingstone most, in the same way that their predecessors did, and with the most generosity and sentimentality, partly because of the teaching from ministers who have a particular calling to work in the most deprived communities. Squashed into pews on Sundays, relying on the church for a range of support from the cradle to the grave, the humanitarianism of many African pastors supports a variety of educational and welfare activities.

In 2002, the Reverend Christopher Mkandawire took up his post as the new minister for the David Livingstone Memorial Presbyterian Church, which still stands in Livingstone on the road to Victoria Falls. He was conscious of the legacy that he had to uphold when taking on this role. He looked to the 'courageousness' of Livingstone, as he interprets it: 'doing something quite scary, coming to an area that no other white person in England would think of going at the time; where there was still cannibalism in some parts; his vision to open up the interior'.[36] He also looked to the first railway missionaries, often Presbyterians, trying to save workers building the line, who then decided to establish this church for them. 'The principle had been the same', he continued: 'giving people access'. So in 2004, he set up a youth centre next door. The church now has a nursery and junior school and is heavily involved in supporting HIV/AIDS sufferers. 'Sympathy', he added wryly, 'was no substitute for action'.

Pastor Michael Zulu arrived in 2005 to run the new youth centre and specialises in teaching music. 'Livingstone was praying as he died and he died on his knees', he informed me, and, 'he spoke on this land. He made us mission-minded and we stand on that prayer'.[37] Bishop David still mentions Livingstone in sermons from time to time, mostly as an example of sacrifice and the passion he had for the gospel. However, 'The passion that he had for the African people remains a big thing for us', he concluded, and 'if not for him we would be Roman Catholic'.

Of course, popular memories of Livingstone and colonial rule are now more varied. A cross-section of people of all ages and occupations were asked in Lusaka what they knew of Livingstone. Responses included: 'He was a good man with African interests at heart'; 'He died of Malaria'; 'He married Moffat's daughter'; 'He brought the word of God to us'; 'He taught us to wear clothes and how to use guns'; 'He was like other white men and sent by their queen like everyone else'; 'I don't even know him'; 'He's the one who highlighted the evils of the slave trade'; 'He befriended the Africans who became his close friends'; 'His heart is buried in Africa'; 'I never saw him'; and 'His companions carried his body back because they loved him'. Some agreed: 'He was better than white men during the colonial period and today'. A few argued: 'We should not commemorate Livingstone because the only person whose death is to be commemorated, as brought out in the Bible, is Jesus'.[38]

When asked 'what would he think or do if he were here today?' responses included: 'He'd feel bad'; 'He'd be sad, as this is not a Bible-based society and has deviated from the word of God'; 'He'd be very happy'; 'He'd be sad'; 'He'd apply sanctions to the Government for mismanagement: we are suffering'; 'He'd preach abstinence'; 'He'd start an NGO'; 'He'd be shocked at the number of bogus Christians'; 'Like other white men, he'd emphasise the use of condoms'; 'He'd be shaking his head in disbelief at our leaders. They simply replaced the white man but continued colonising us'; 'He'd find us a cure for AIDS'; and last, but by no means least, a truly brilliant comment: 'He would hand out condoms with one hand and take money with the other'.

NOTES

1 Extract from a toast on the occasion of Livingstone's imminent departure to Southern Africa, the new title credited to him after his recent explorations amongst the tribes of that region. Quoted from Cook, 'The immortalisation of David Livingstone', 16–17.
2 Blaikie, *The Personal Life of David Livingstone*, 317.
3 *Daily Telegraph*, editorial, 27 January 1874, 6.
4 For a discussion of the display of the correct formula of acceptable manly behaviour, see Murphy, 'H M Stanley', 150–63.
5 M. Jones, B. Sebe, J. Strachan, Bertrand Taithe & Peter Yeandle, 'Decolonising Imperial Heroes: Britain and France', *Journal of Imperial and Commonwealth History*, 45, 2 (2014): 788.
6 Catherine Mackenzie, *David Livingstone: Who is the Bravest?* (Tain, Scotland: Christian Focus, 2012).
7 http://gullible-gulliblestravels.blogspot.co.uk/2014/05/the-africa-journals-ch-42-dr.html. Accessed 26 May 2015.
8 Raul Zacharias, www.youtube.com/watch?v=3pn7V2kfvKE
9 For example, some of my audience cried at the beginning of my presentation on his death, at the conference 'Imperial Obsessions: David Livingstone, Imperial and African History Reconsidered', Livingstone, Zambia, 19 April 2013 (hopefully not because they had heard me speak before).
10 Quoted in Rothschild, *The Inner Life of Empires*, 4.
11 Patrick Joyce, *Democratic Subjects: The Self and the Social in Nineteenth-Century England* (Cambridge, UK: Cambridge University Press, 1994), 15.
12 Ibid., 59.
13 Ibid., 60–1.
14 Ibid., 41–8.
15 Ibid., 104–23.
16 Ibid., 205.
17 Christopher Brown, *Moral Capital: Foundations of British Abolitionism* (Chapel Hill, NC: University of North Carolina Press, 2006).
18 Marcus Wood, *The Horrible Gift of Freedom: Atlantic Slavery and the Representation of Emancipation* (Athens, GA: University of Georgia Press, 2010).
19 Ibid., 388, 325.
20 Huzzey, *Freedom Burning*, 174.
21 Ibid., 152.
22 Wood, *The Horrible Gift of Freedom*, 43.
23 Gjersø, 'Continuity of Moral Policy; Gjersø, 'The Scramble for East Africa'.
24 Rob Skinner & Alan Lester, 'Humanitarianism and Empire: New Research Agendas', *Journal of Imperial and Commonwealth History*, 40, 5 (2012): 729–47, 729.
25 Renema & van Zoelen, *You Took the Part*.
26 MacLachlan, *David Livingstone*, 132–7.
27 MacNair, *Livingstone the Liberator*, 356.
28 J.M. MacKenzie, 'David Livingstone – Prophet or Patron Saint of Imperialism in Africa: Myths and Misconceptions', *Scottish Geographical Journal*, 129, 3–4

(2013): 277–91. In literary studies, see Pettitt, *Dr. Livingstone, I Presume?* and Justin Livingstone, *Livingstone's 'Lives': A Metabiography of a Victorian Icon* (Manchester: Manchester University Press, 2014).

29 MacNair, *Livingstone the Liberator*, 363–4.

30 Starritt, *Livingstone the Pioneer*, 160.

31 www.newstatesman.com/sci-tech/sci-tech/2013/02/what-david-livingstones-legacy-200-years-after-his-birth

32 B. Everill, 'Bridgeheads of Empire? Liberated African Missionaries in West Africa', *Journal of Imperial and Commonwealth History*, 40, 5 (2012): 789–805.

33 See C. Petrusic, 'Violence as Masculinity: David Livingstone's Radical Racial Politics in the Cape Colony and the Transvaal, 1845–1852', *International History Review*, 26, 1 (2004): 20–55.

34 Author interview with Bishop David and the Reverend Robert Sihubava, Lusaka, 8 July 2009.

35 Author interview, 30 July 2009; Livingstone town hall, Discussion after talk given by Professor John MacKenzie, 22 April 2013.

36 Author interview, 22 July 2009, Livingstone.

37 Ibid. His mission is education and he strives to create a family community at the youth centre, particularly for the many children who have lost a close family member.

38 A sample of the answers received in response to fifty questionnaires distributed at Manda Hill, Lusaka, June 2009. I am grateful for the help of Besa Mwaba with this, especially in completing questionnaires on behalf of those respondents who were unable to write.

Epilogue
The Testimony of Pastor Manduli

> You the British have abandoned us. We were once together but
> now ... We have the ties of the colonial period but now you forget our
> connection and forget the past.

I am Pastor Manduli, general secretary of the Christian Church of Central
Africa, Kabwata District, Lusaka. My parishioners struggle and suffer.
They look to God and each other to keep going. Many have to get by on
one meal a day, asking themselves: 'Do I take transport to get to work
today, or do I use the money to eat and walk for a couple of hours?' People
often lose their focus on Christianity once they get a good income ... I
have received a grant from the Norwegians to raise people's awareness
about basic rights within the constitution and to encourage people to vote.

I am a descendant of the first Christian church in Central Africa.
My grandfather, Mwense, was baptised into a mission that is affiliated
to David Livingstone's own LMS, a sect called the Church Mission of
Many Lands. The family came from Luapula District and, one day, set
out on foot for Stewart Gore Browne's estate in Chinsali in order to
translate the Bible into their own language of Bemba. It took them four
days to get there and they stayed for a month. Later my father was part
of a breakaway church because you could be taught to evangelise but you
were allowed to wear trousers. You still had to call them 'the Bwanas'.

From the Central Africa Students Bible Church emerged our Central
Africa Christian Church. Many were staunch supporters of the nationalist movement, and it was one of the few churches to stand up and offer
prayers when invited to do so at UNIP rallies, when many people were
too fearful, aware of the 'dos and don'ts' of the colonial masters. The
people at that time had an incredible faith. They really believed that God
would save them, that he would liberate them. At that point, physical liberation was paramount. There were areas, for example, that were second
class, which you could visit, but areas in the centre of town were first
class, and you needed a pass. In shops, the Africans had to go to a special
pigeonhole to buy their goods and not pass inside.

260

After independence, my father became a successful businessman, at one time importing bubblegum from Kenya. He invested massively in a hotel but lost most of his money in a scam regarding the proceeds when he sold it to the government. He became bishop of the Church, and from him I learnt bookkeeping. I carry this book with me to enter the full details of any meeting and new acquaintance.

I heard about Livingstone from the evangelicals. The story I heard again and again was that 'if you compare the way in which he behaved to how other white people behaved, then truly this person has come from God'. Look, his followers took his body back so it could be buried at his home. That was the love for the man. He was truly one of us.

My dad was there at the time of colonial rule. He felt the way of the missions. David Livingstone was practical. What he ate, his followers would eat. I have relatives in the north whose ancestors used to be with Livingstone. That history has passed onto me. People still hear about him today in school, in church and in the places where he was. He was a godsend. We were used to whites who were rough. He was from a different sphere. He taught us there were also nice white people.

In my sermons, I bring in Livingstone on the theme of enduring suffering and sacrifice to make him relevant to the everyday lives of the people. Just to bring the word of God, he gave up a comfortable life to live in Africa in its raw state. It baffles me, though, to this day, what sort of communication he used. He must have used sign language to teach the people. And how did he survive the conditions and malaria?

There is a little cave near where he died, where there are remains of Stone Age Man and the area is full of tsetse flies. But I want it understood by European people that he did NOT discover the Falls. You must put that. Africans had known about them for a long time. But I feel very strongly on this other point: I would gladly say he was a saint.

Index